YOTSUBA&!

13

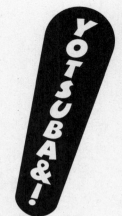

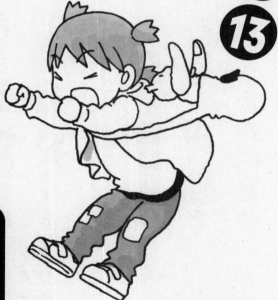

KIYOHIKO AZUMA

CONTENTS

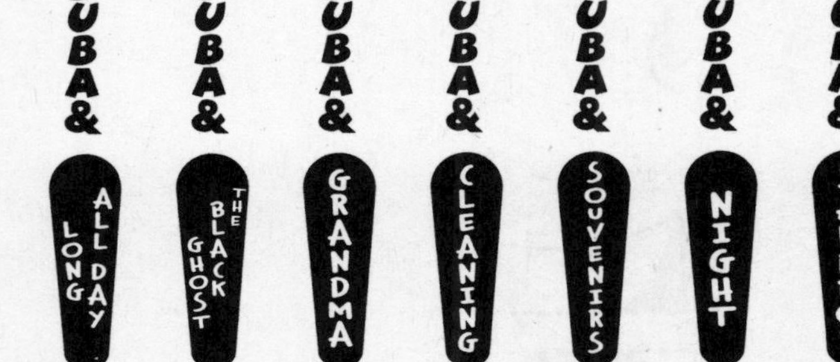

YOTSUBA&!
KIYOHIKO AZUMA

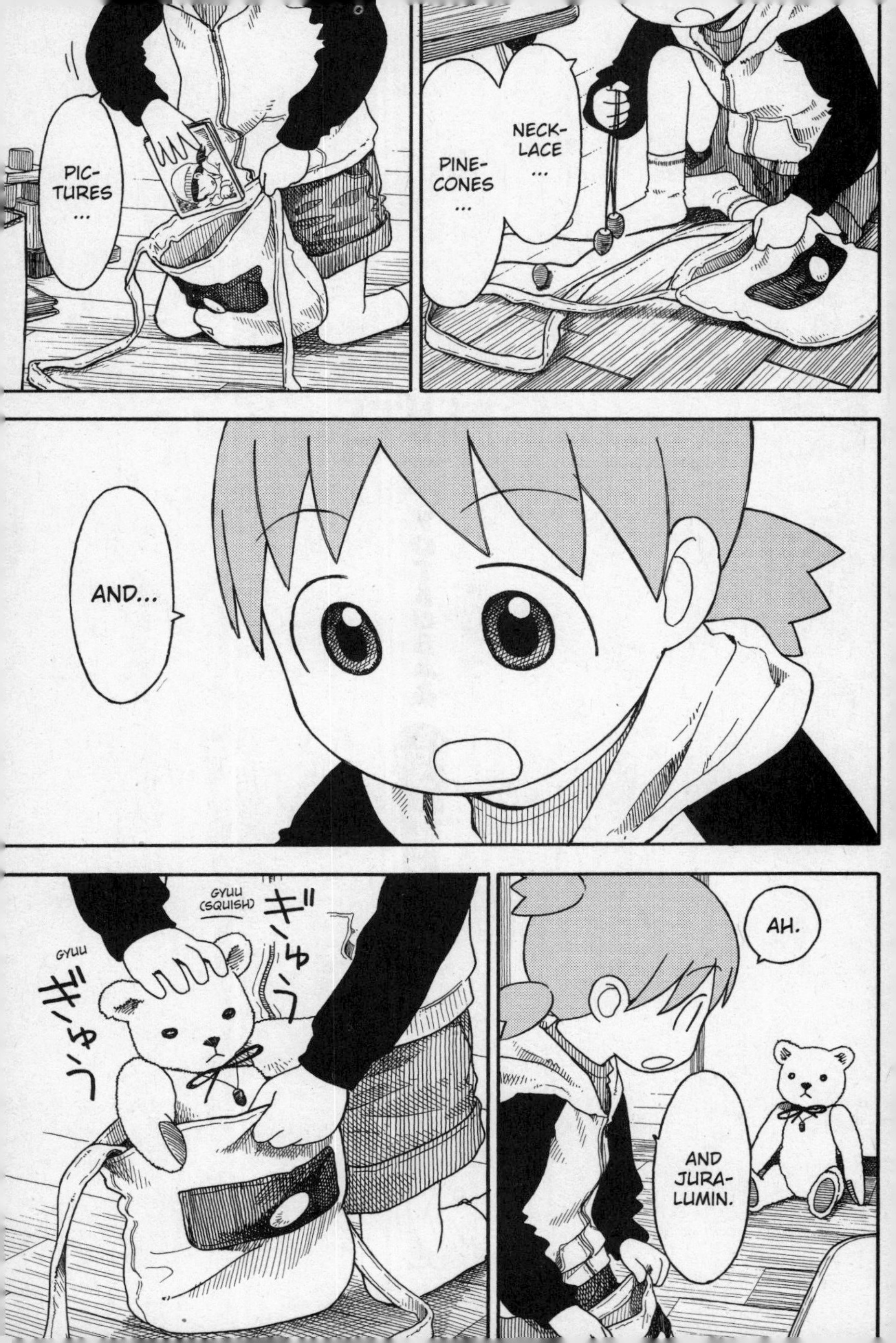
NECKLACE...
PINECONES...
PICTURES...
AND...
AH.
AND JURALUMIN.
GYUU (SQUISH)
ぎゅう
GYUU
ぎゅう

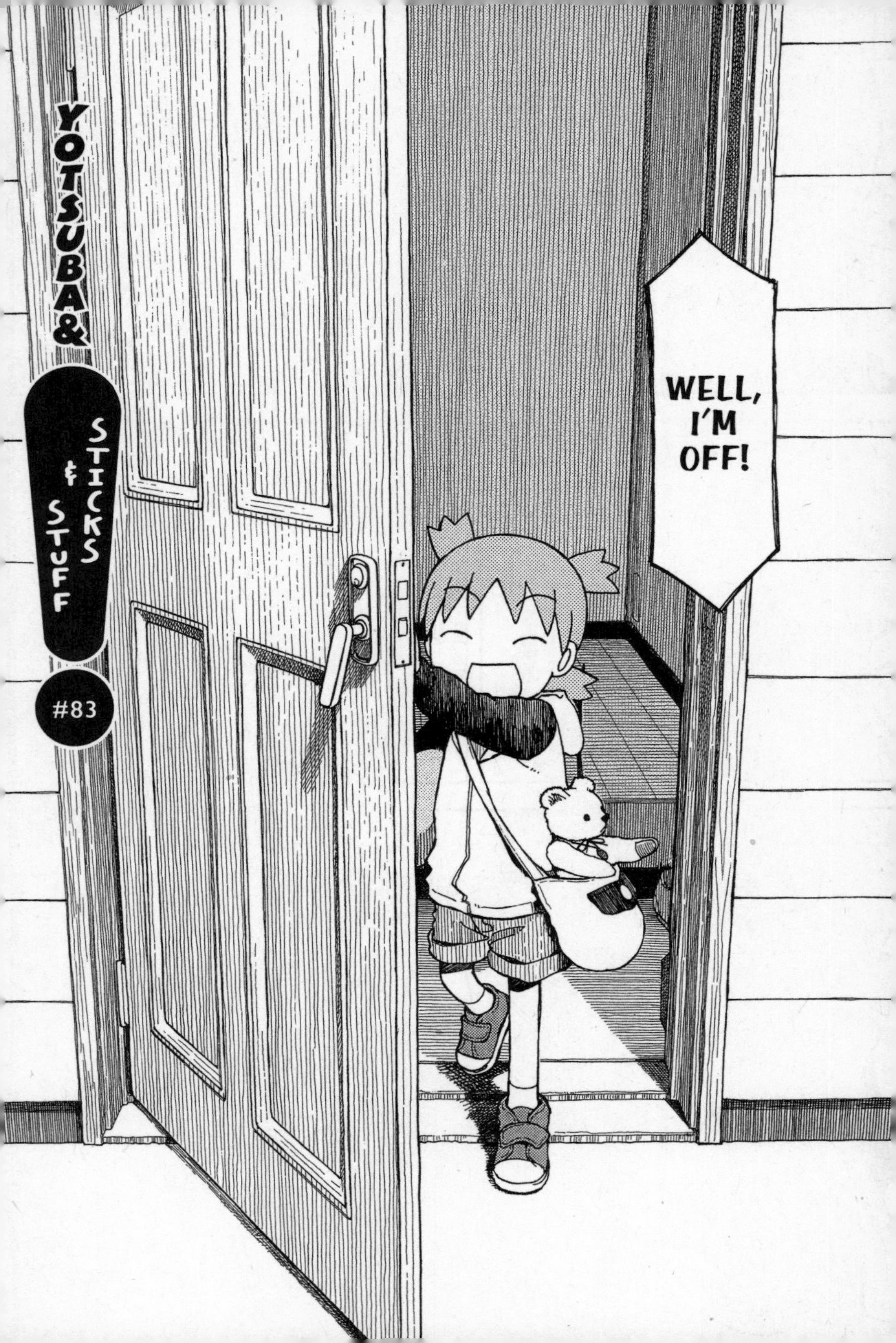
YOTSUBA&
STICKS & STUFF
#83
WELL, I'M OFF!

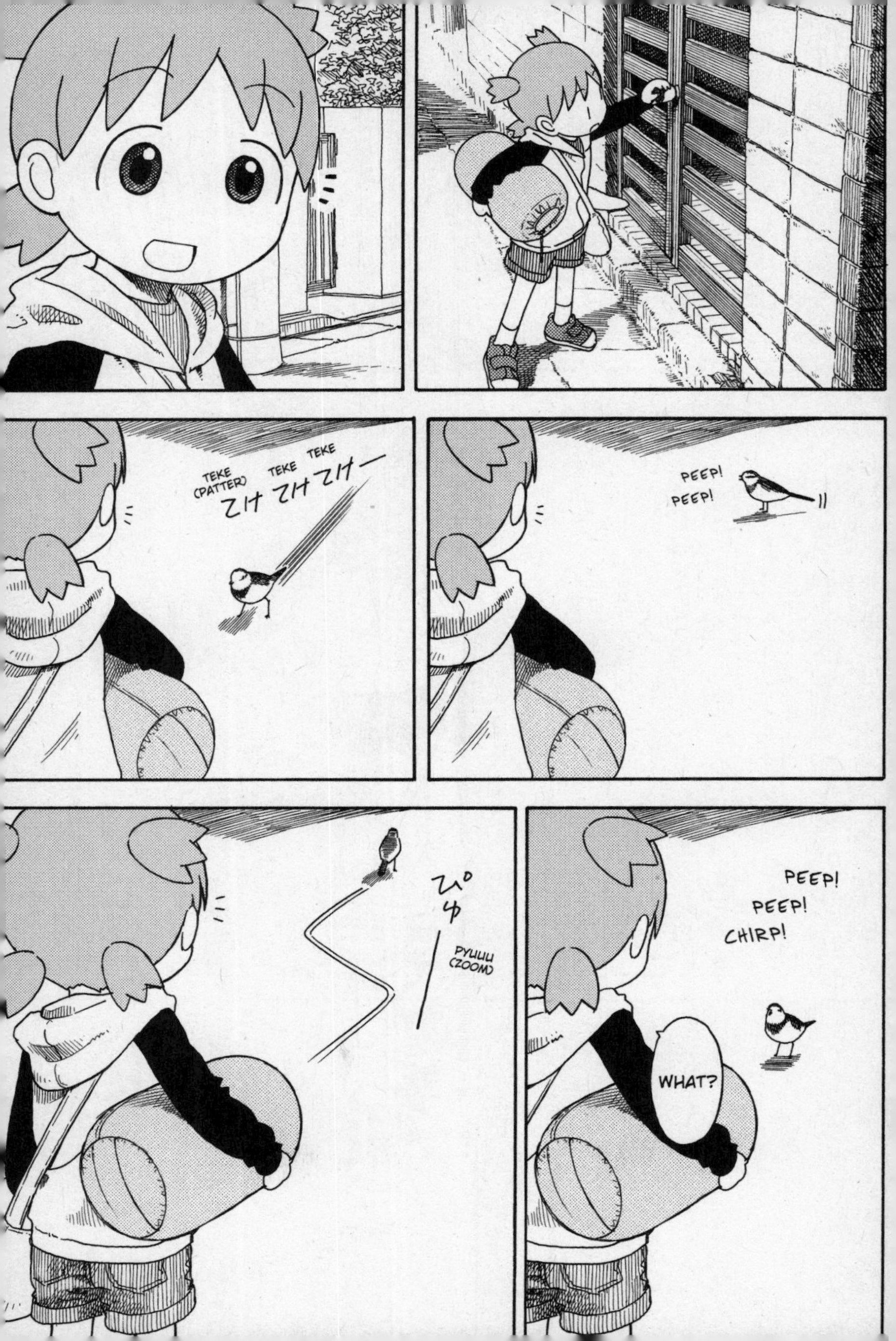
PEEP!
PEEP!
TEKE (PATTER) TEKE TEKE
てけ てけ てけー
PEEP!
PEEP!
CHIRP!
WHAT?
ぴゅ
PYUUU (ZOOM)

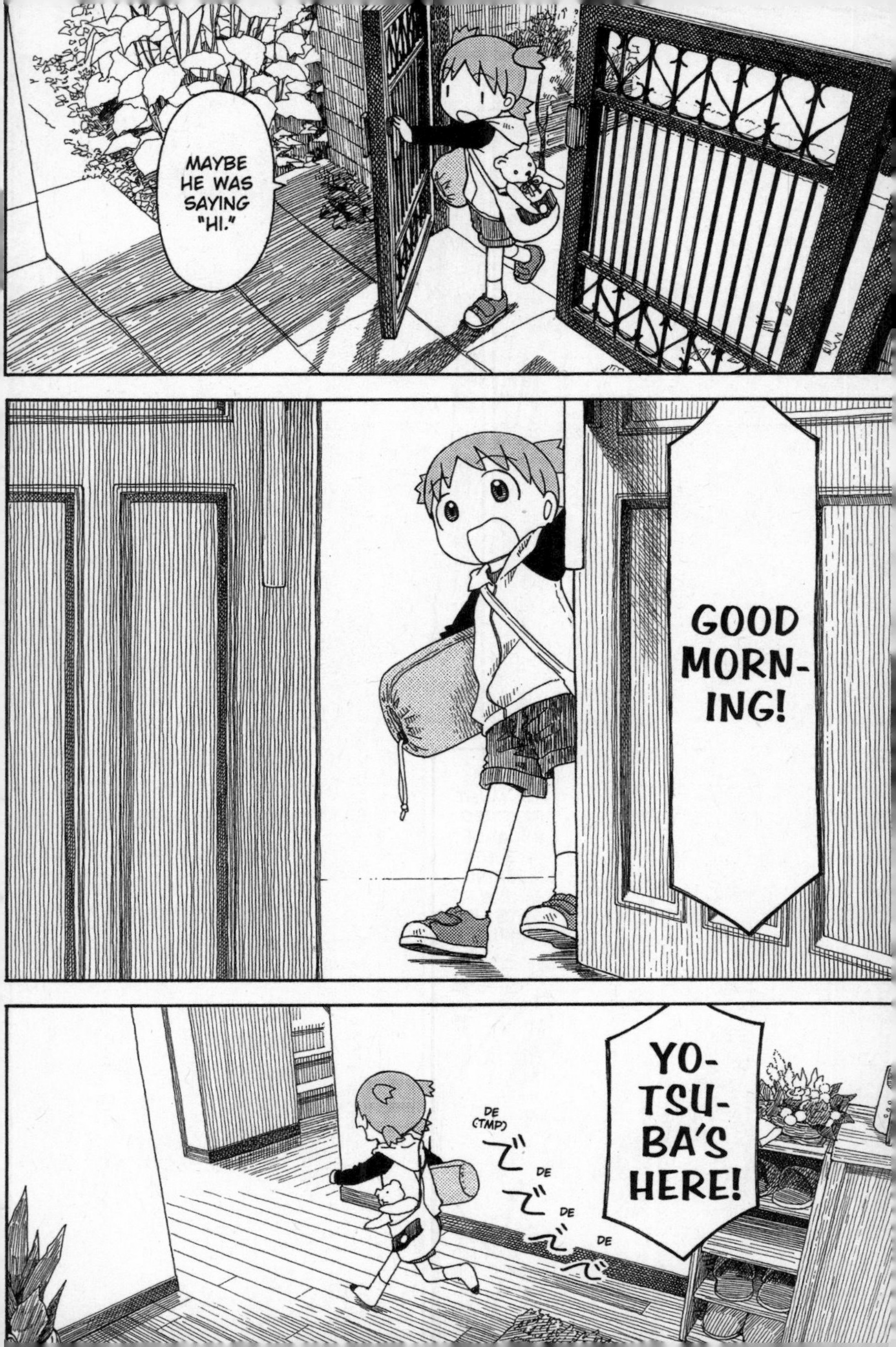
MAYBE HE WAS SAYING "HI."
GOOD MORN-ING!
YO-TSU-BA'S HERE!
DE (TMP) で
DE で
DE で
DE で

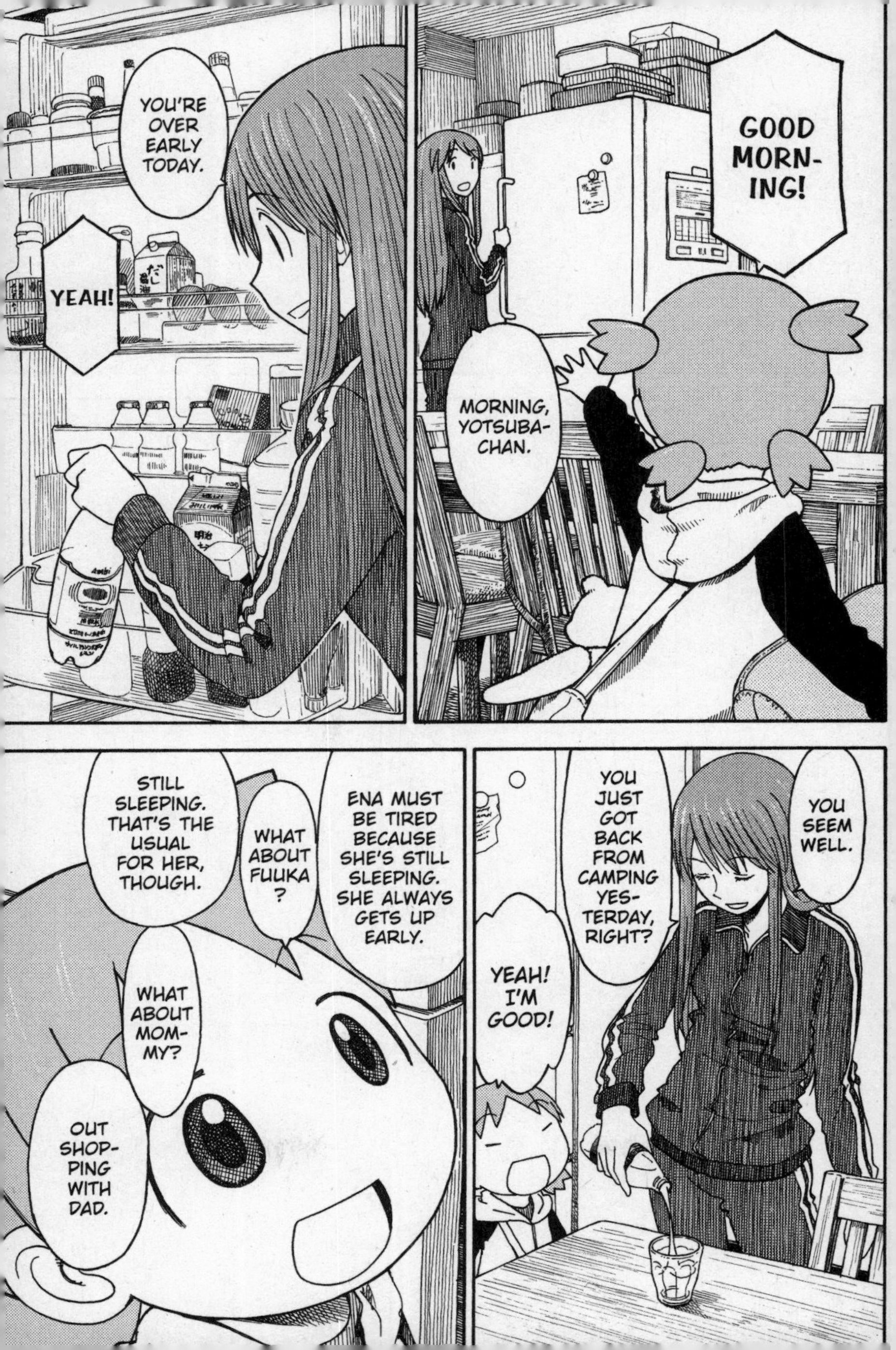
GOOD MORNING!
MORNING, YOTSUBA-CHAN.
YOU'RE OVER EARLY TODAY.
YEAH!
YOU SEEM WELL.
YOU JUST GOT BACK FROM CAMPING YESTERDAY, RIGHT?
YEAH! I'M GOOD!
ENA MUST BE TIRED BECAUSE SHE'S STILL SLEEPING. SHE ALWAYS GETS UP EARLY.
WHAT ABOUT FUUKA?
STILL SLEEPING. THAT'S THE USUAL FOR HER, THOUGH.
WHAT ABOUT MOMMY?
OUT SHOPPING WITH DAD.

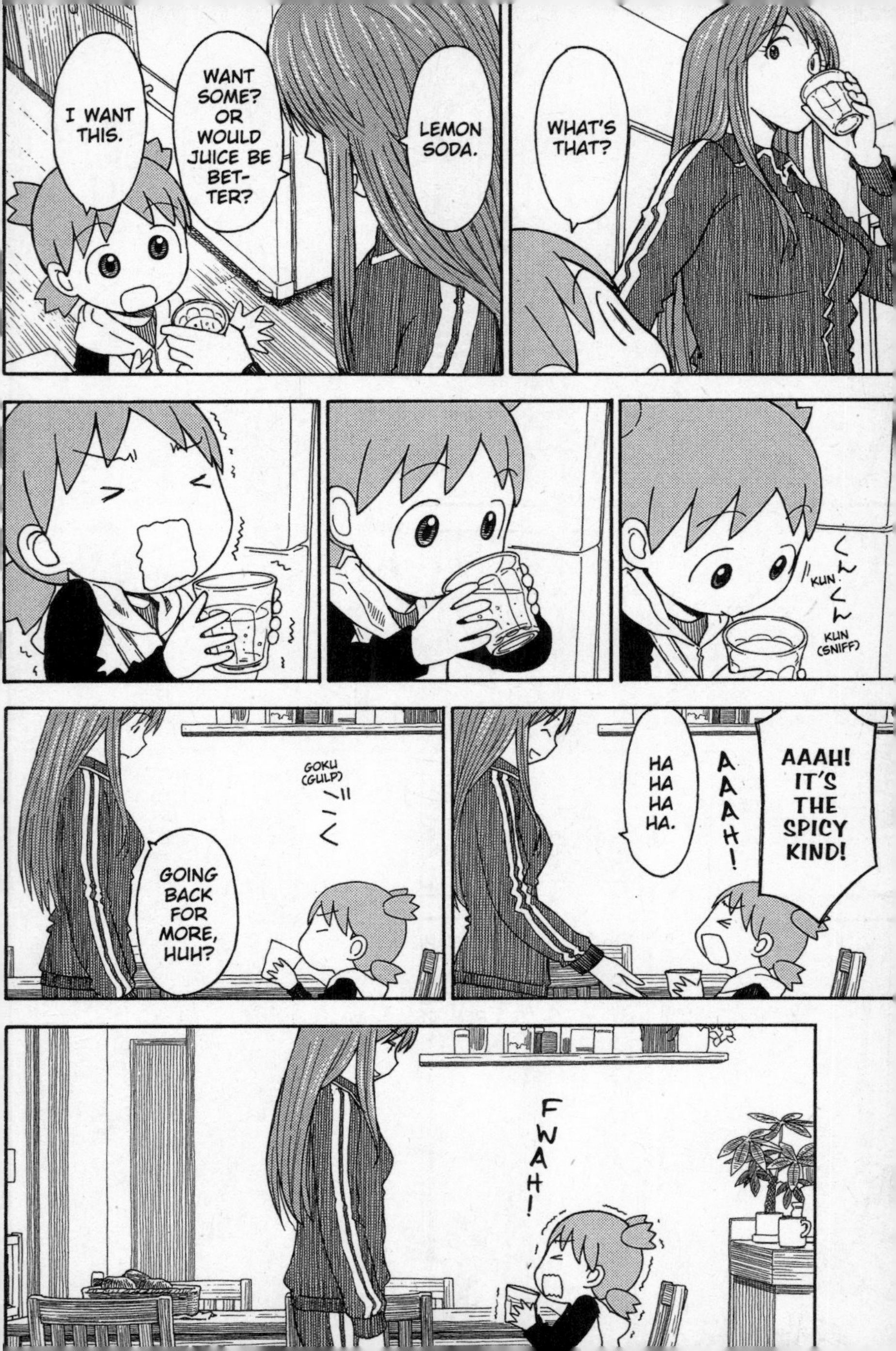
WHAT'S THAT?
LEMON SODA.
WANT SOME? OR WOULD JUICE BE BETTER?
I WANT THIS.
くん くん
KUN KUN (SNIFF)
AAAH! IT'S THE SPICY KIND!
AAAH!
HA HA HA HA.
GOKU (GULP)
GOING BACK FOR MORE, HUH?
FWAH!

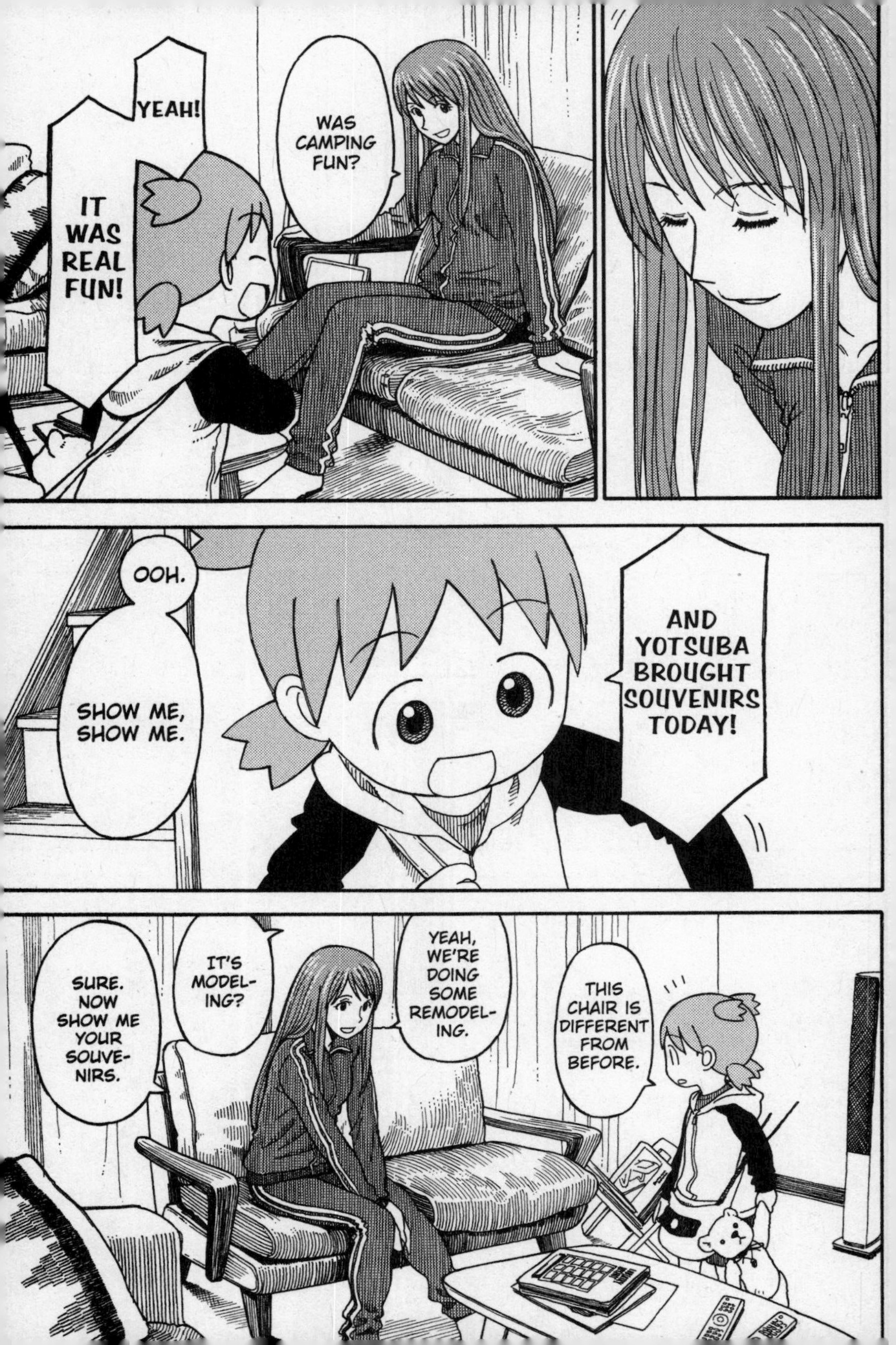
WAS CAMPING FUN?
YEAH! IT WAS REAL FUN!
AND YOTSUBA BROUGHT SOUVENIRS TODAY!
OOH.
SHOW ME, SHOW ME.
THIS CHAIR IS DIFFERENT FROM BEFORE.
YEAH, WE'RE DOING SOME REMODEL-ING.
IT'S MODEL-ING?
SURE. NOW SHOW ME YOUR SOUVE-NIRS.

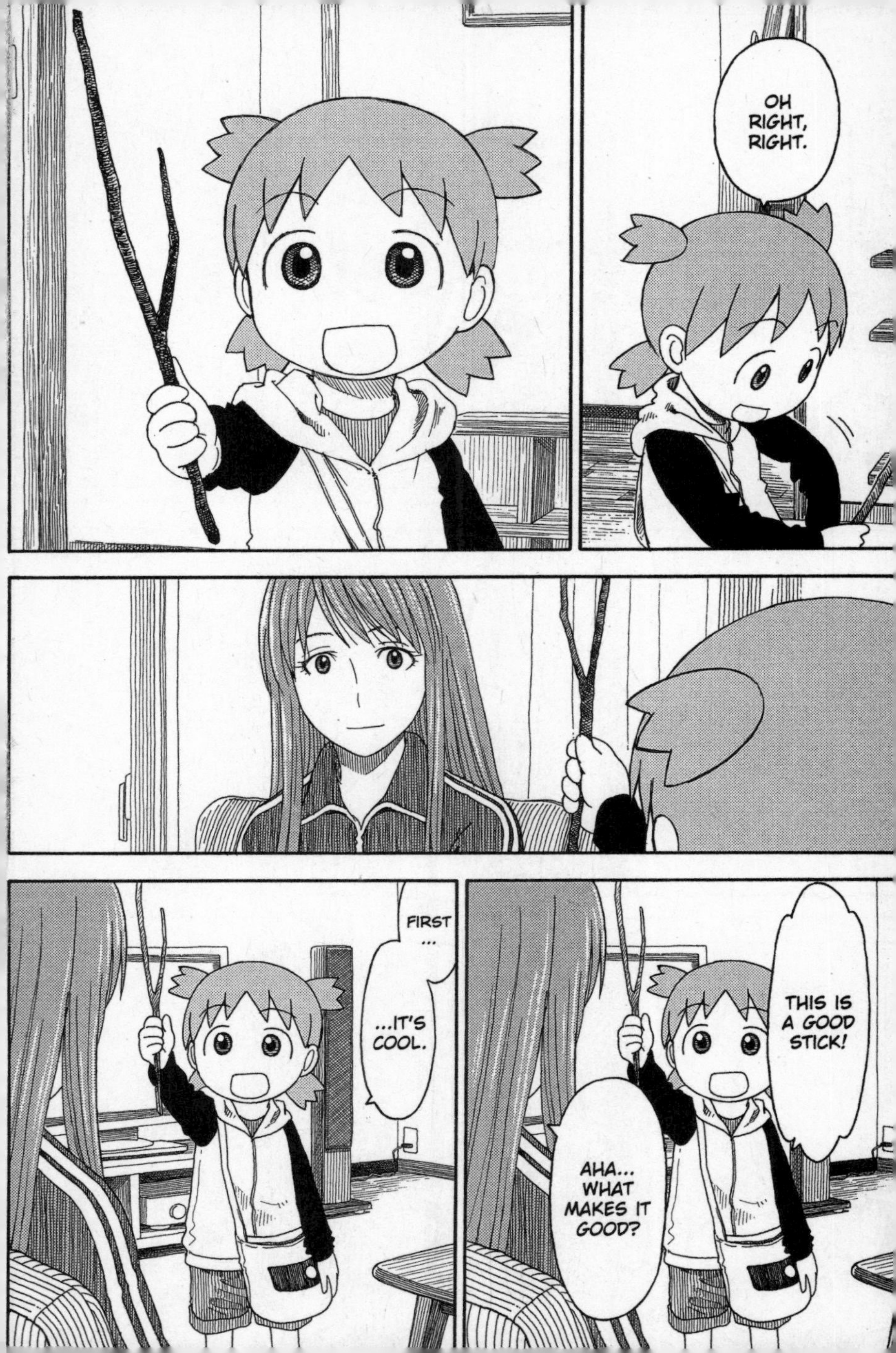
OH RIGHT, RIGHT.
THIS IS A GOOD STICK!
AHA... WHAT MAKES IT GOOD?
FIRST ...
...IT'S COOL.

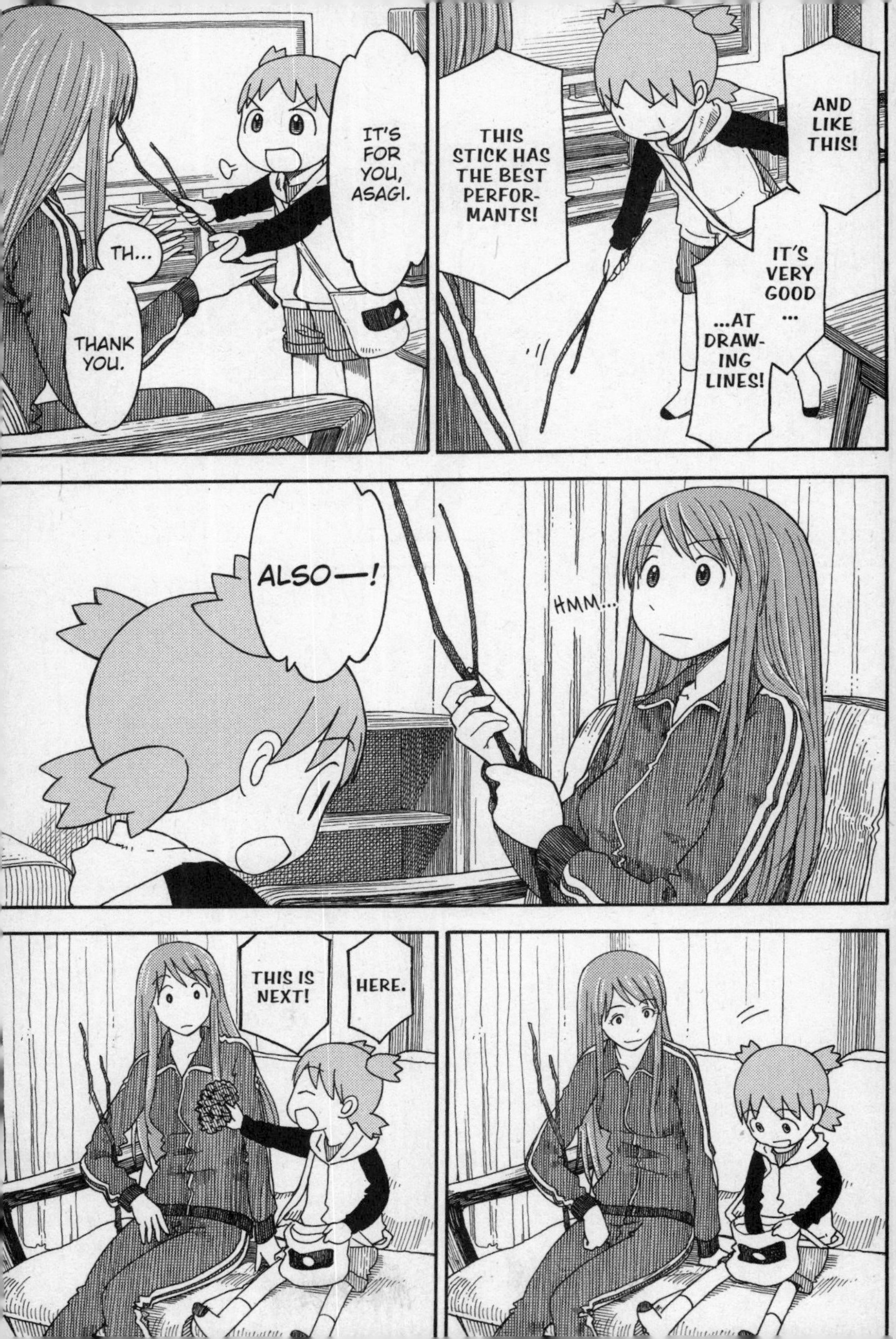
IT'S FOR YOU, ASAGI.
TH...
THANK YOU.
THIS STICK HAS THE BEST PERFORMANTS!
AND LIKE THIS!
IT'S VERY GOOD ...
...AT DRAWING LINES!
ALSO—!
HMM...
THIS IS NEXT!
HERE.

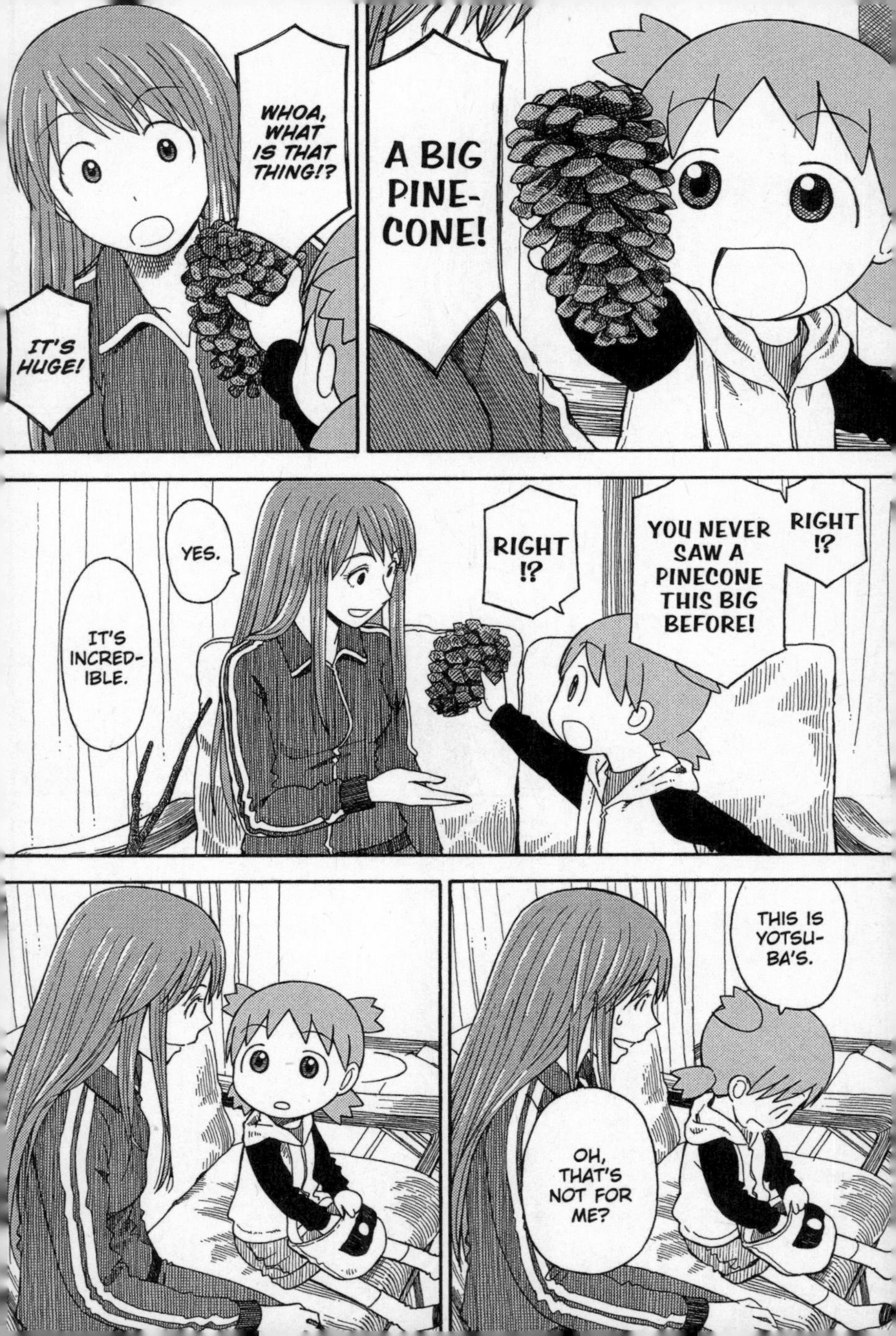
A BIG PINE-CONE!
WHOA, WHAT IS THAT THING!?
IT'S HUGE!
RIGHT !?
YOU NEVER SAW A PINECONE THIS BIG BEFORE!
RIGHT !?
YES.
IT'S INCRED-IBLE.
THIS IS YOTSU-BA'S.
OH, THAT'S NOT FOR ME?

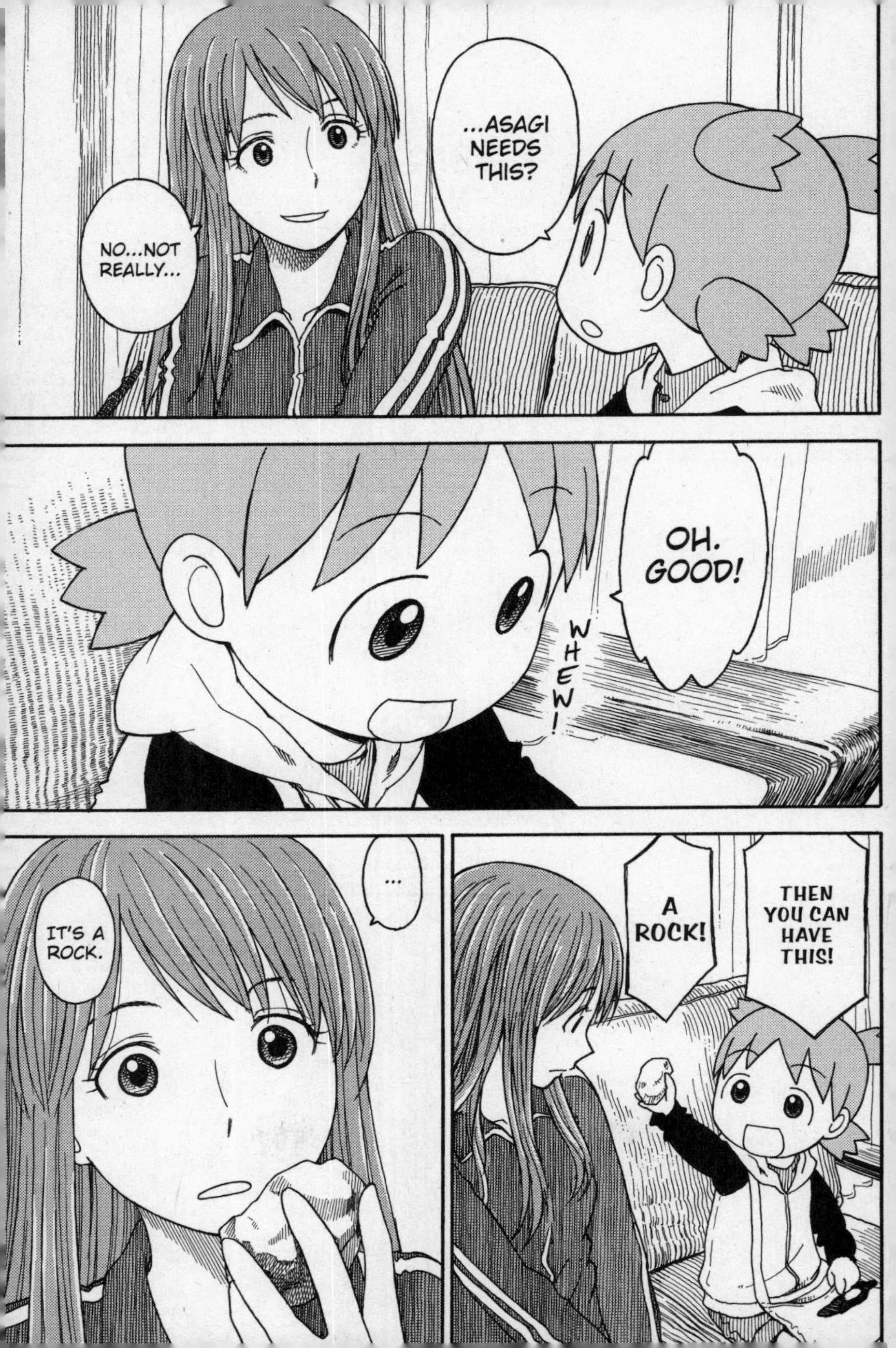

...ASAGI NEEDS THIS?
NO...NOT REALLY...
OH. GOOD!
WHEW!
THEN YOU CAN HAVE THIS!
A ROCK!
...
IT'S A ROCK.

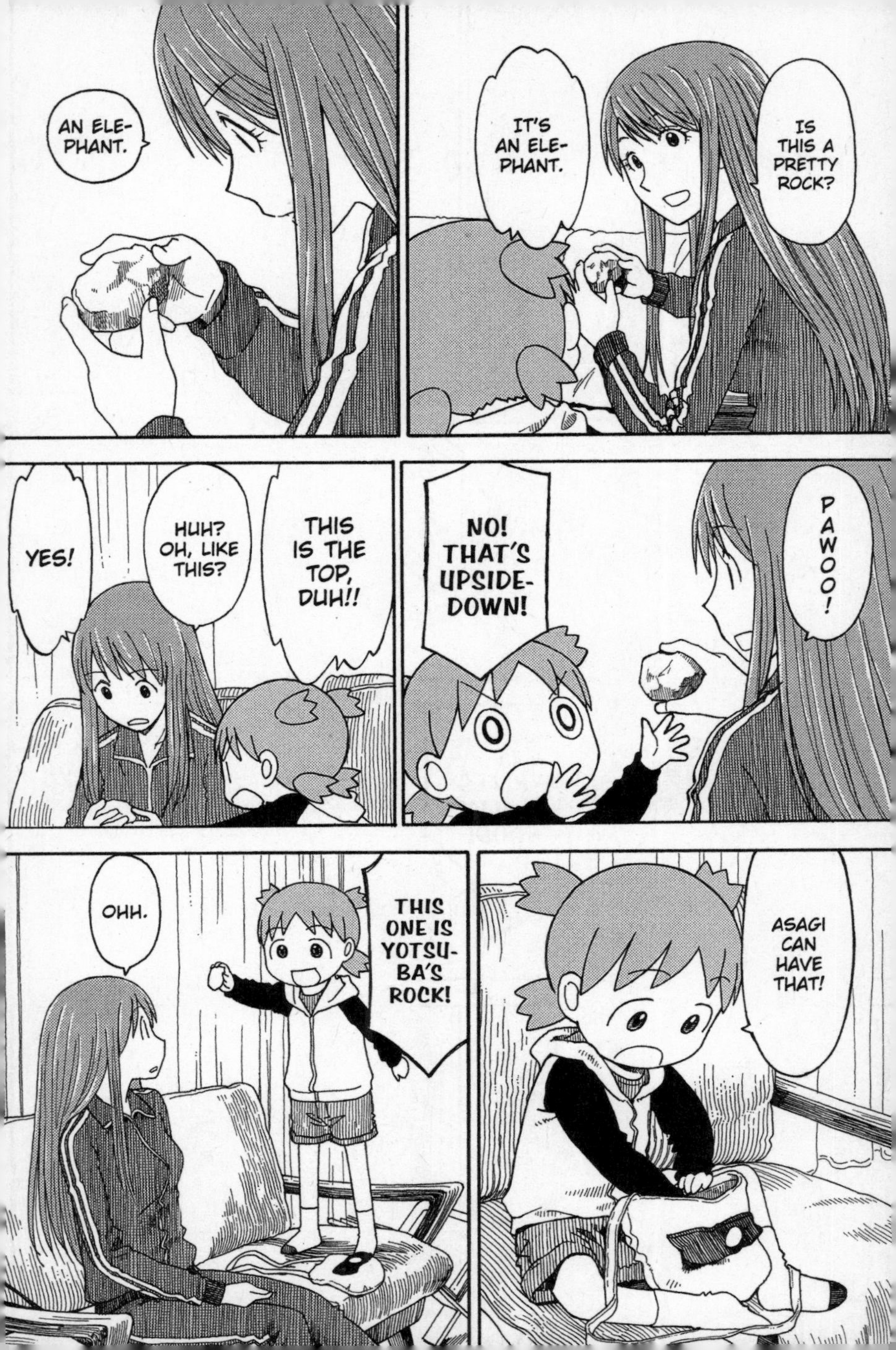
IS THIS A PRETTY ROCK?
IT'S AN ELE-PHANT.
AN ELE-PHANT.
PAWOO!
NO! THAT'S UPSIDE-DOWN!
THIS IS THE TOP, DUH!!
HUH? OH, LIKE THIS?
YES!
ASAGI CAN HAVE THAT!
THIS ONE IS YOTSU-BA'S ROCK!
OHH.

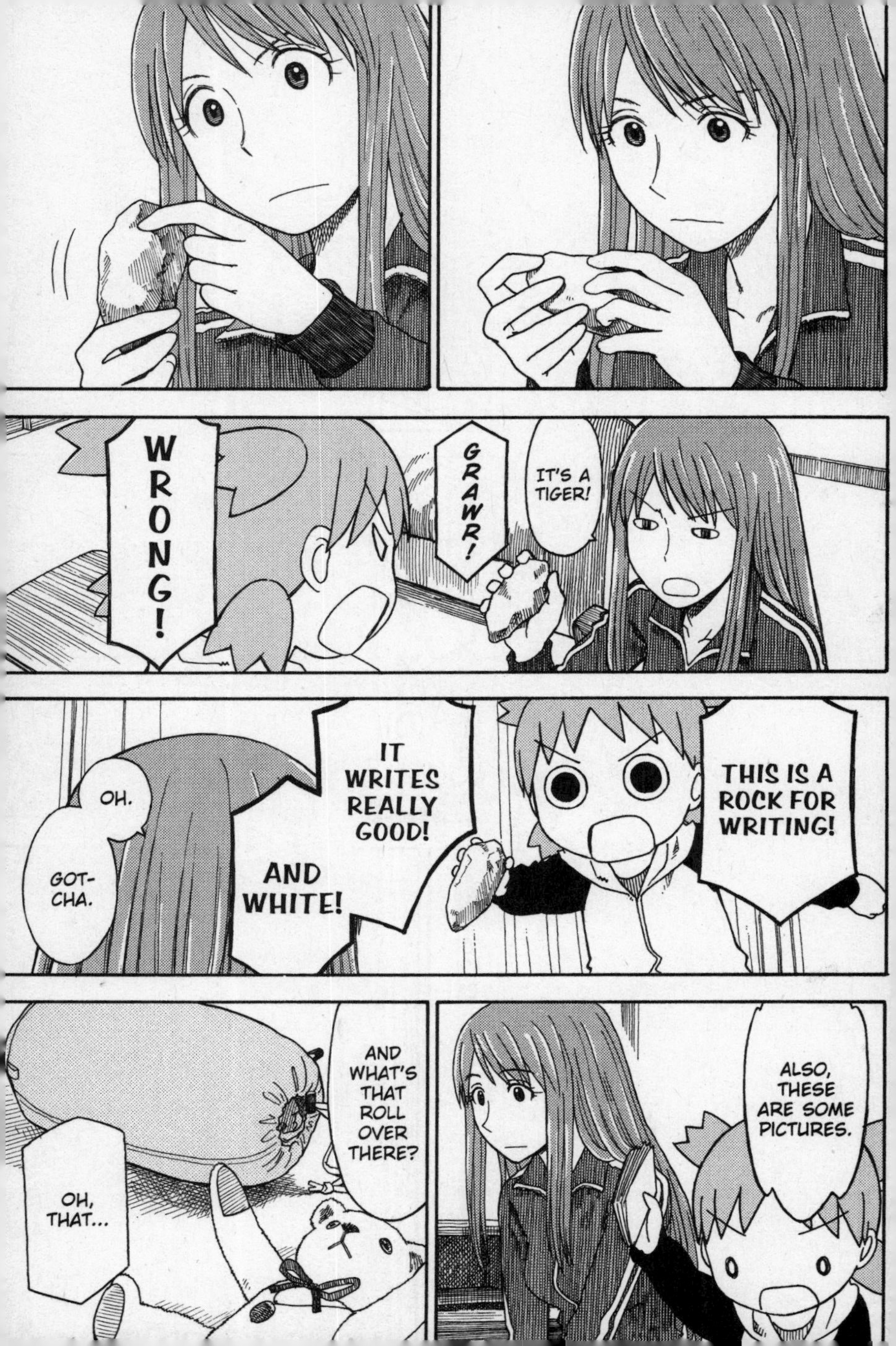
IT'S A TIGER!
GRAWR!
WRONG!
THIS IS A ROCK FOR WRITING!
IT WRITES REALLY GOOD!
AND WHITE!
OH.
GOT-CHA.
ALSO, THESE ARE SOME PICTURES.
AND WHAT'S THAT ROLL OVER THERE?
OH, THAT...

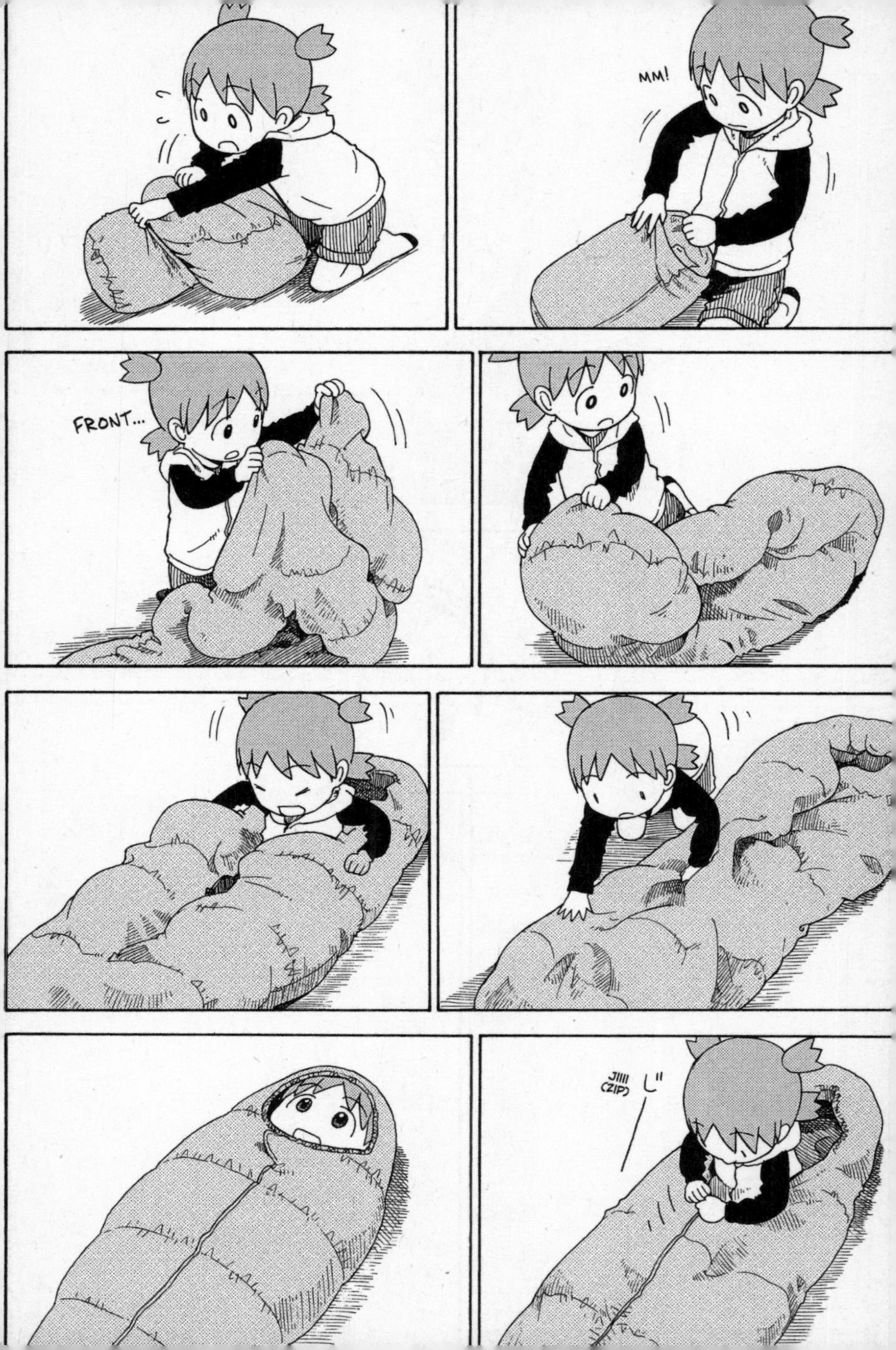
MM!
FRONT...
JIIII
(ZIP)
じ

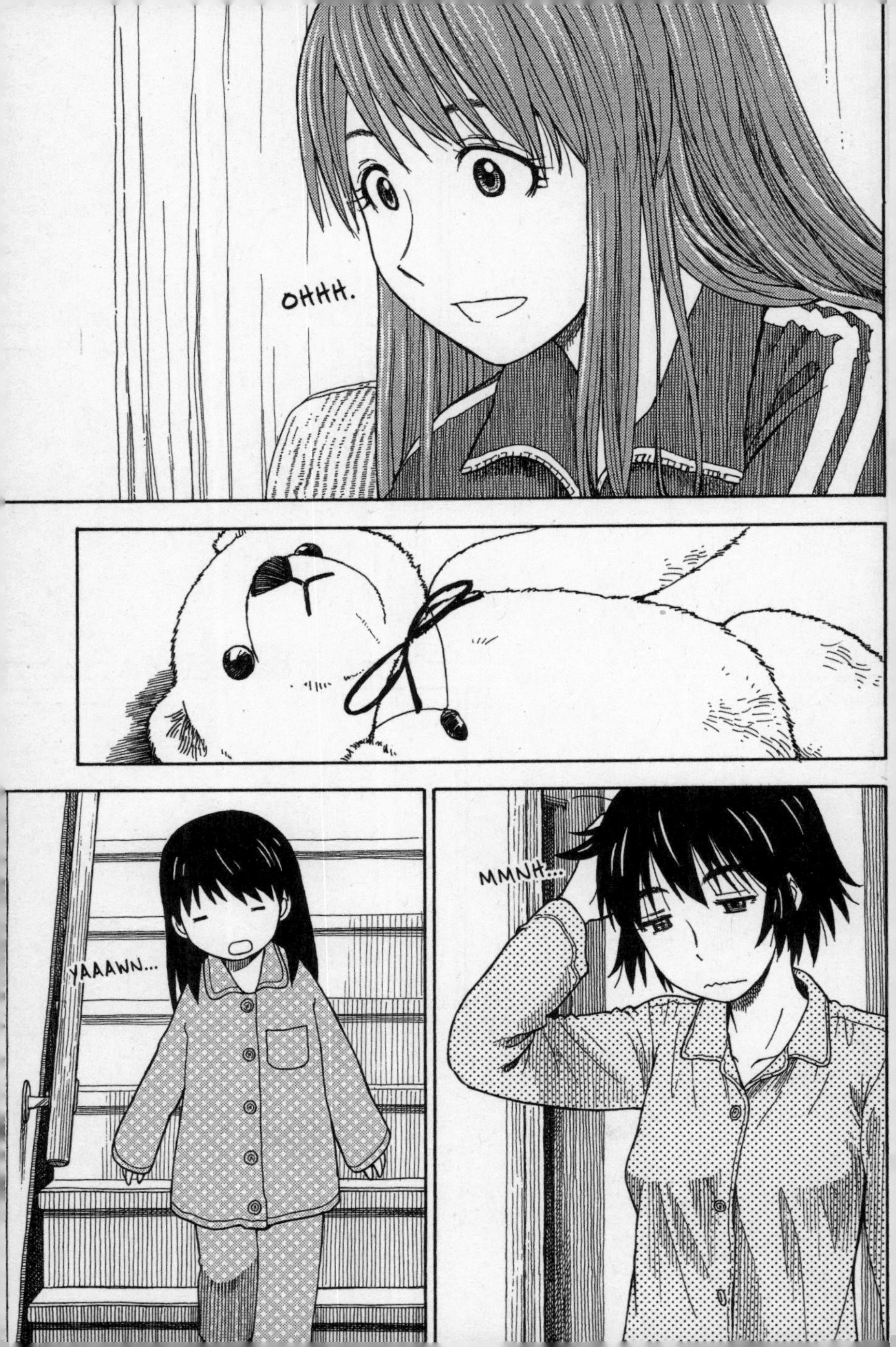
OHHH.
MMNH...
YAAAWN...

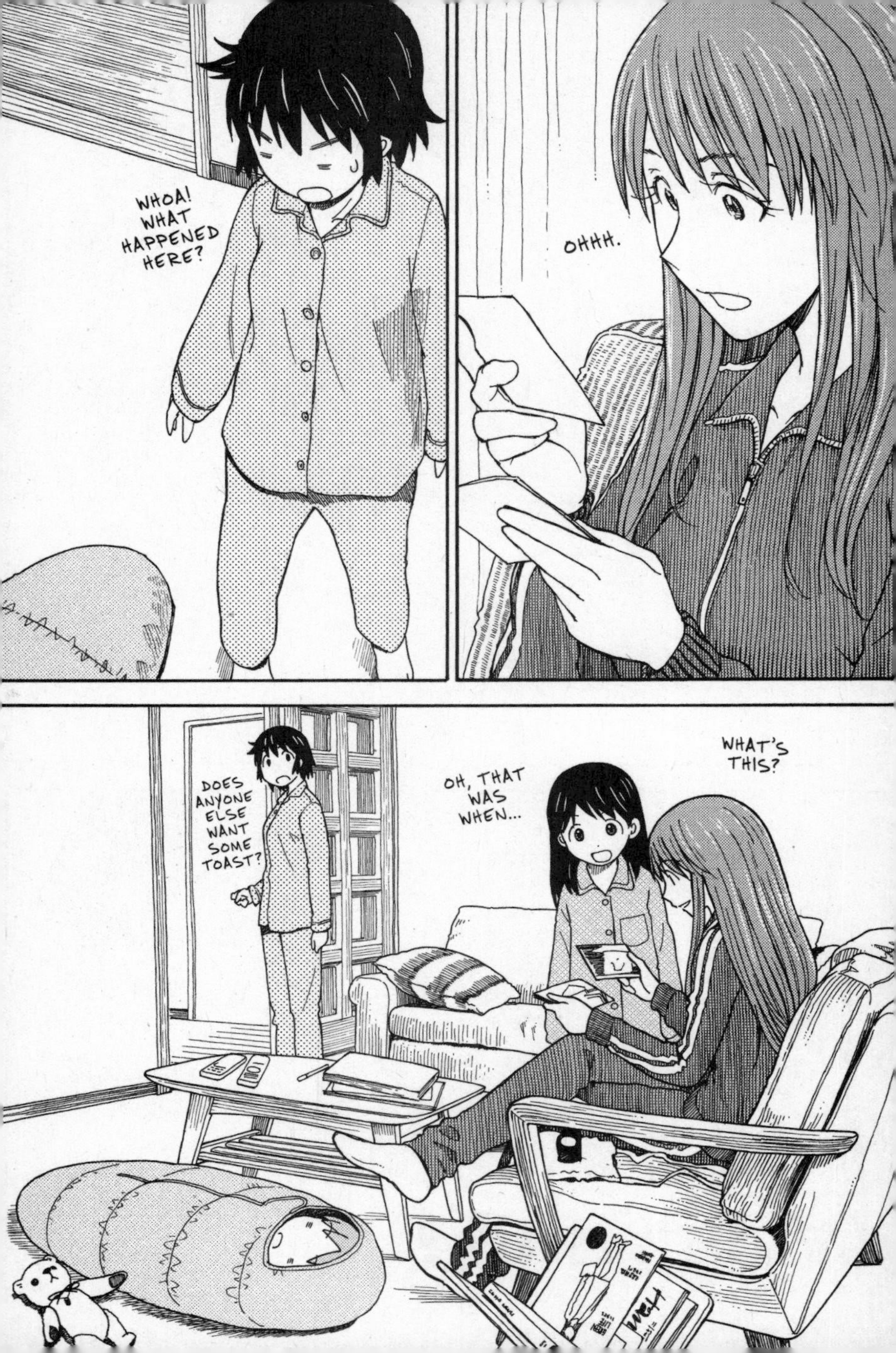
OHHH.
WHOA! WHAT HAPPENED HERE?
WHAT'S THIS?
OH, THAT WAS WHEN...
DOES ANYONE ELSE WANT SOME TOAST?

YOTSUBA&!

HMM.

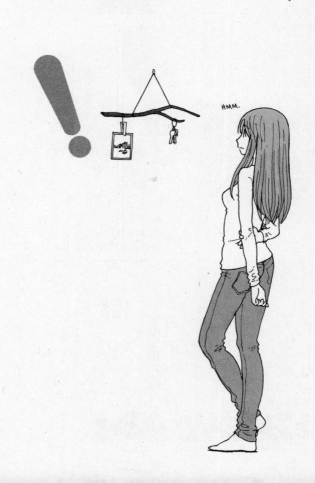

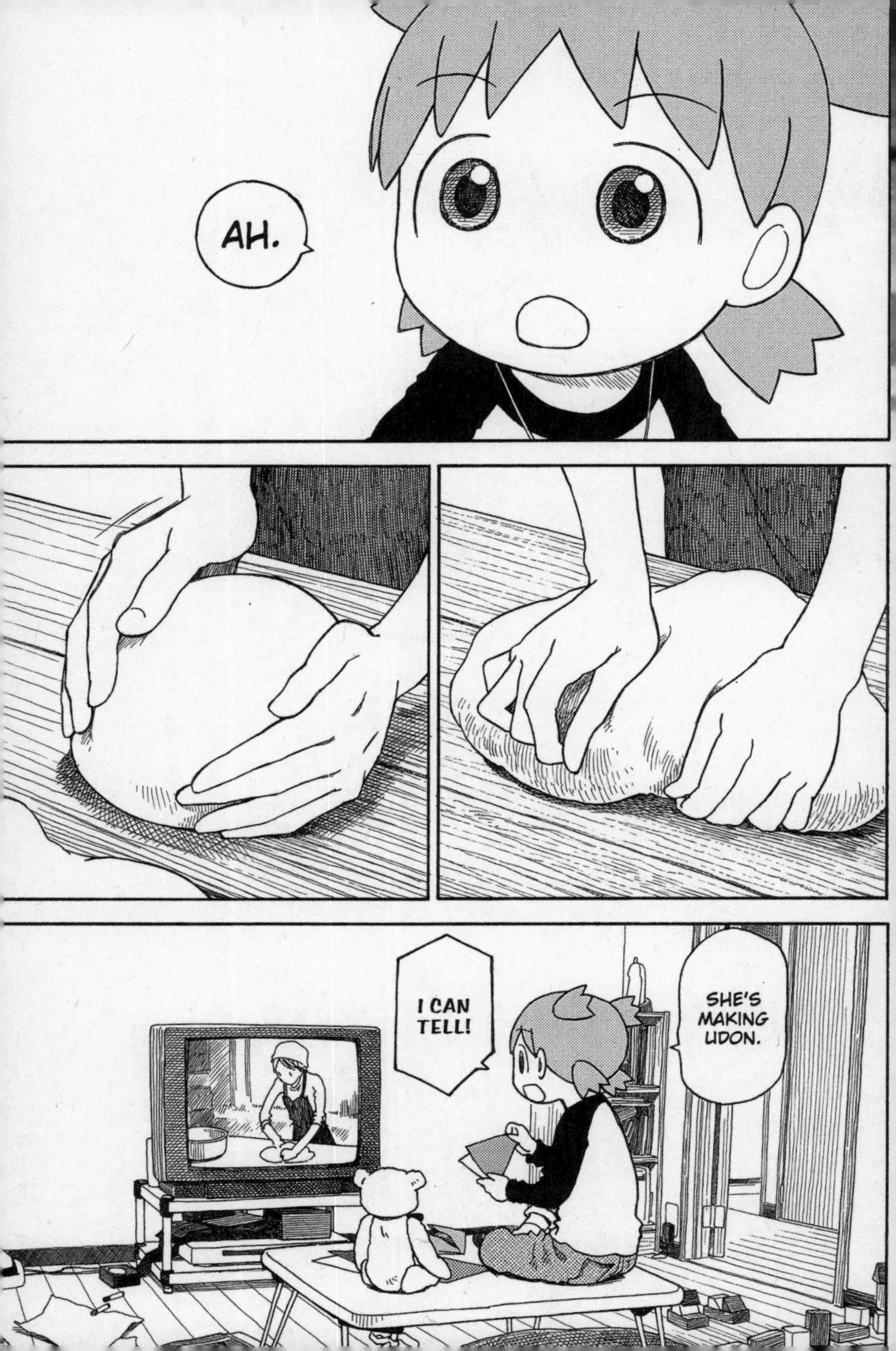
AH.
SHE'S MAKING UDON.
I CAN TELL!

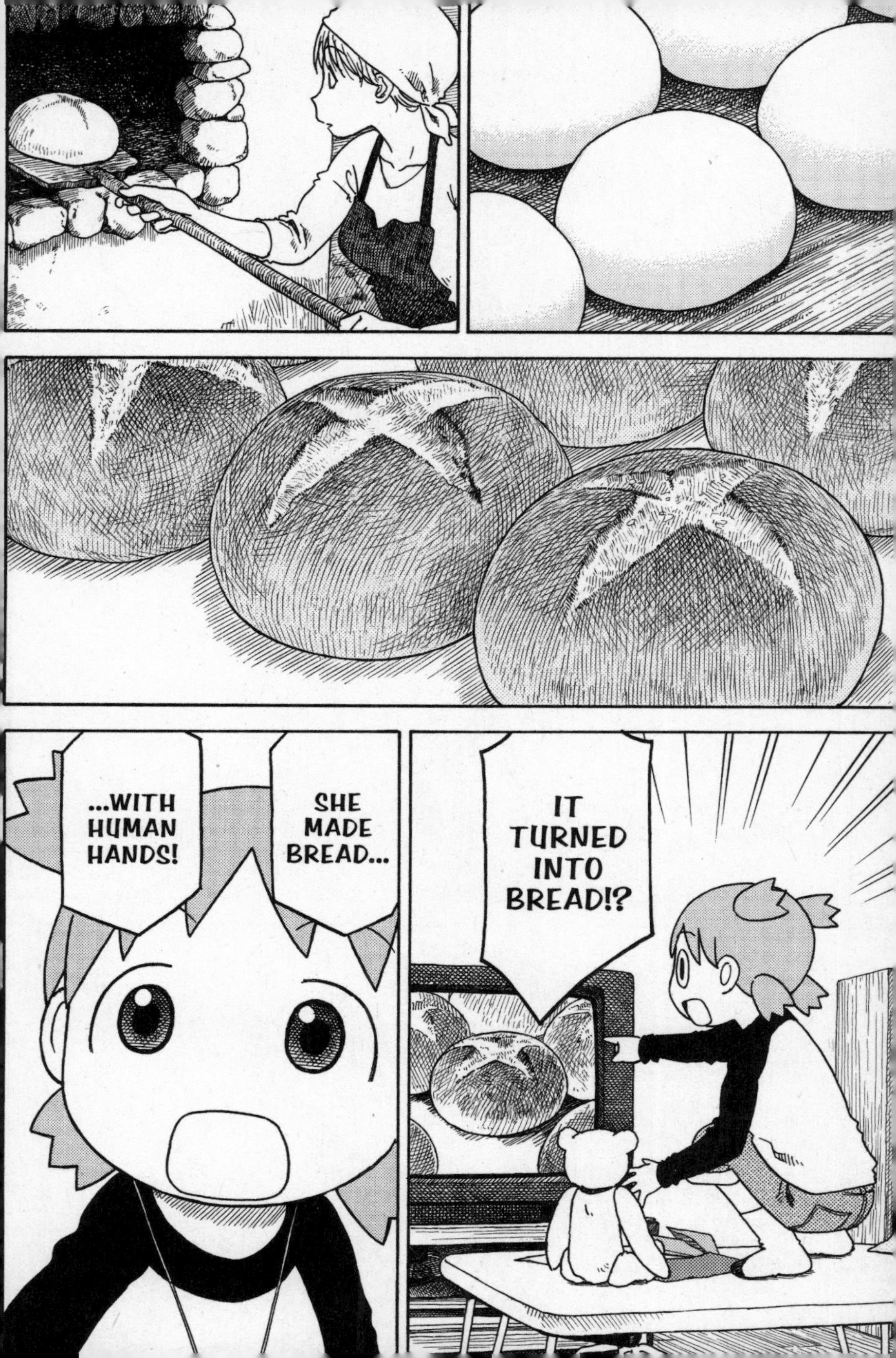
IT TURNED INTO BREAD!?
SHE MADE BREAD...
...WITH HUMAN HANDS!

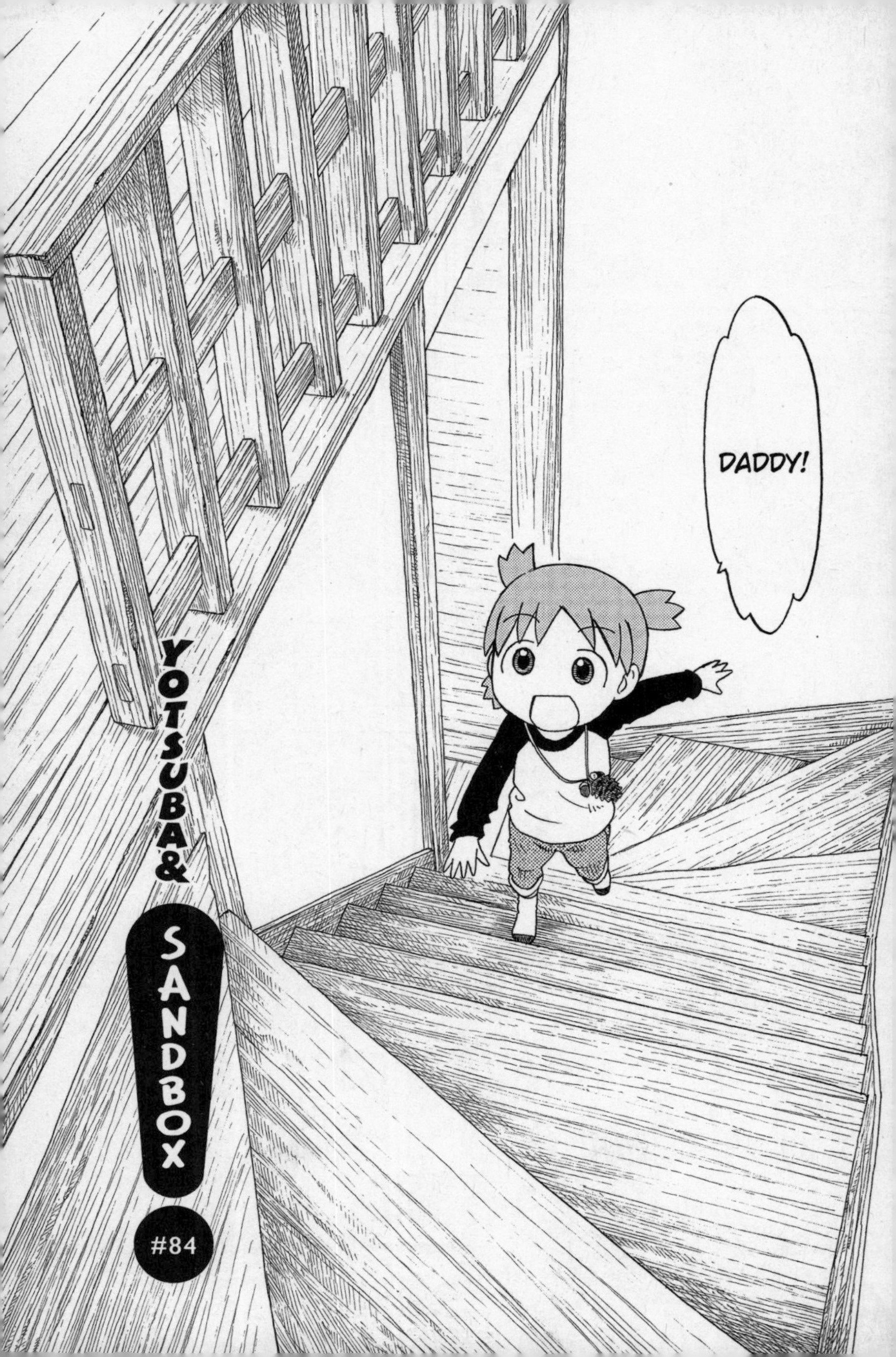
DADDY!
YOTSUBA&
SANDBOX
#84

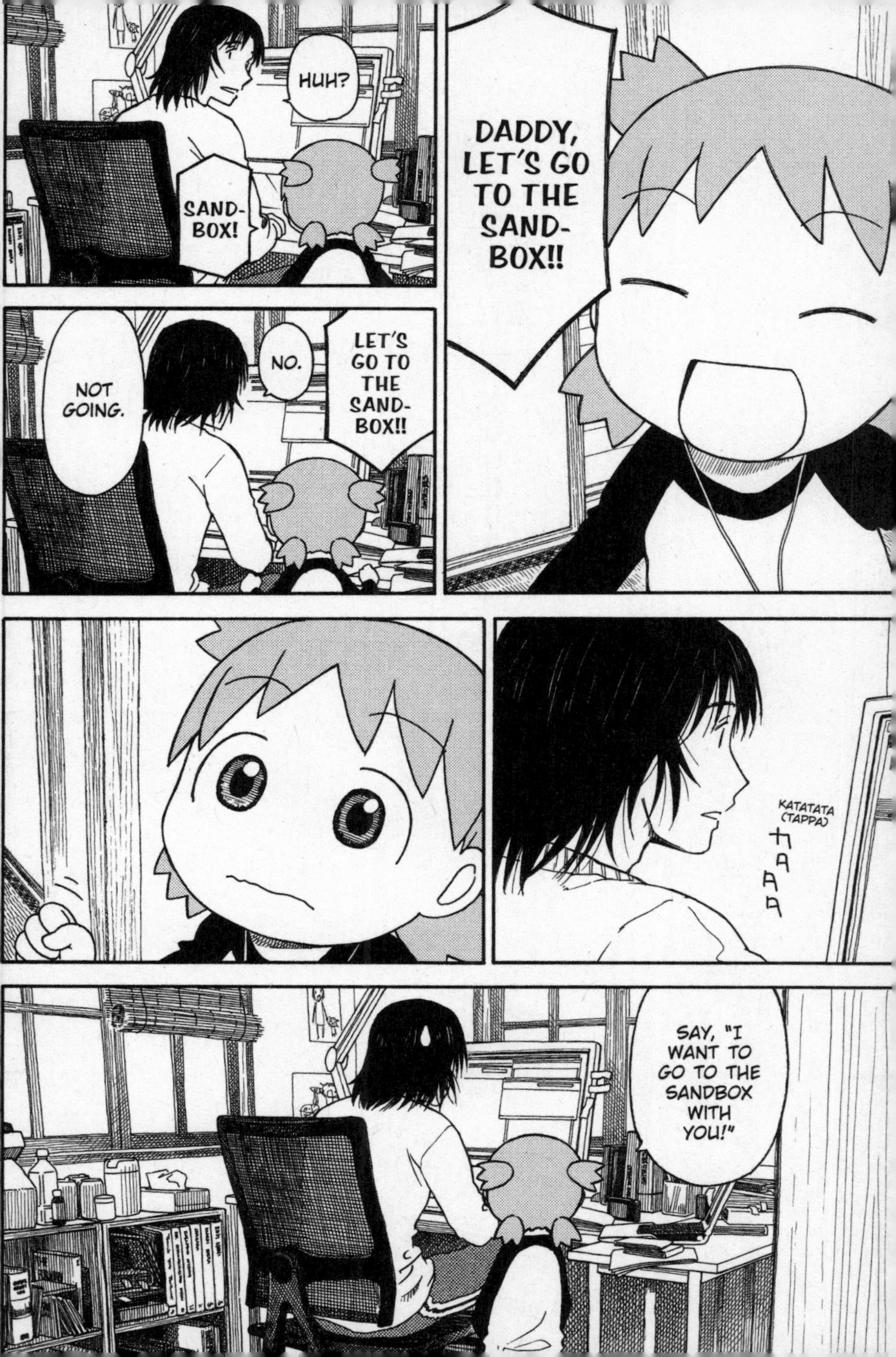
DADDY, LET'S GO TO THE SAND-BOX!!
HUH?
SAND-BOX!
LET'S GO TO THE SAND-BOX!!
NO.
NOT GOING.
KATATATA (TAPPA)
カタタタ
SAY, "I WANT TO GO TO THE SANDBOX WITH YOU!"

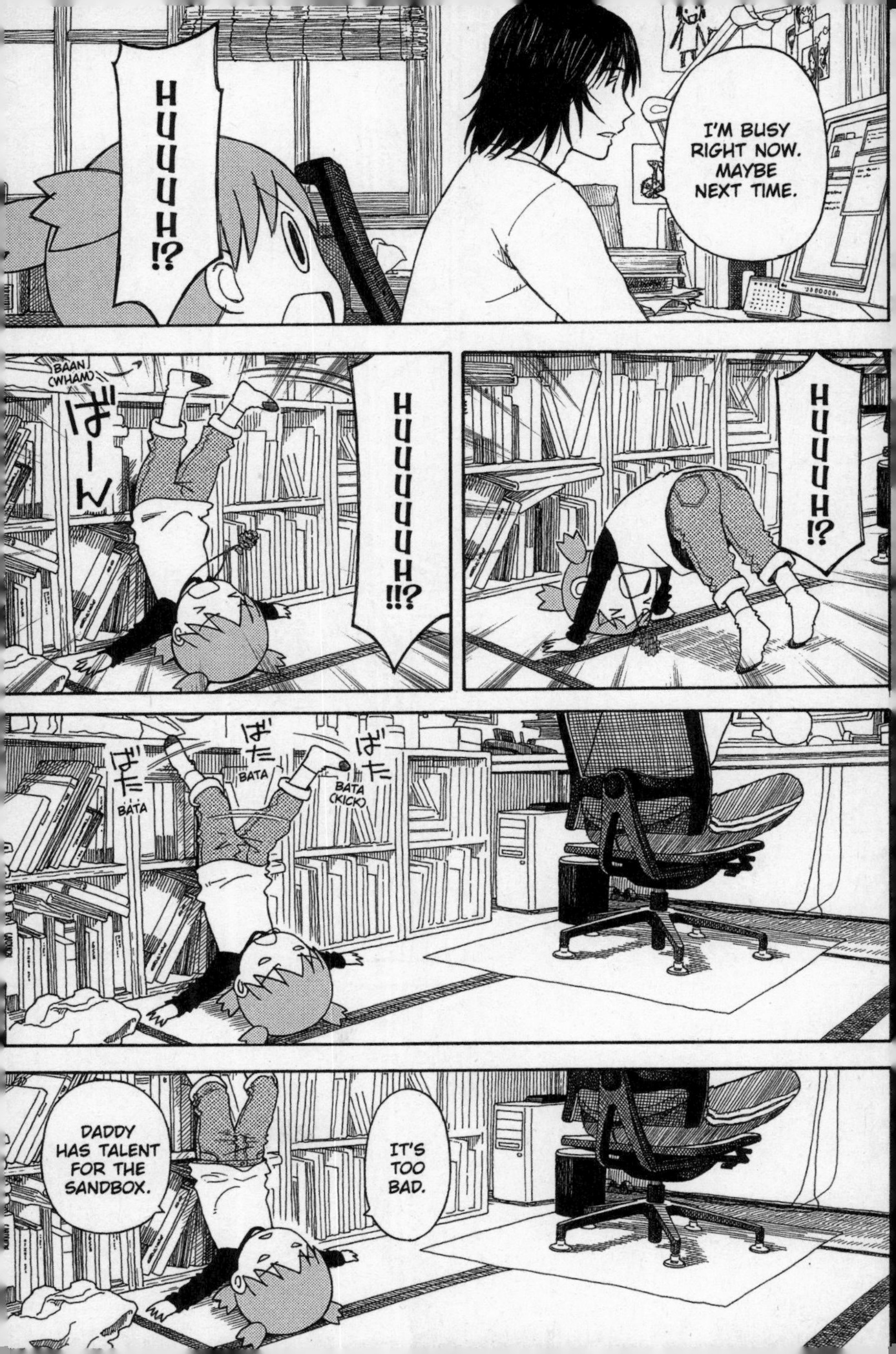
I'M BUSY RIGHT NOW. MAYBE NEXT TIME.
HUUUUH!?
HUUUUH!?
HUUUUUUUH!!?
ばーん
BAAN (WHAM)
ばた
BATA (KICK)
ばた
BATA
ばた
BATA
IT'S TOO BAD.
DADDY HAS TALENT FOR THE SANDBOX.

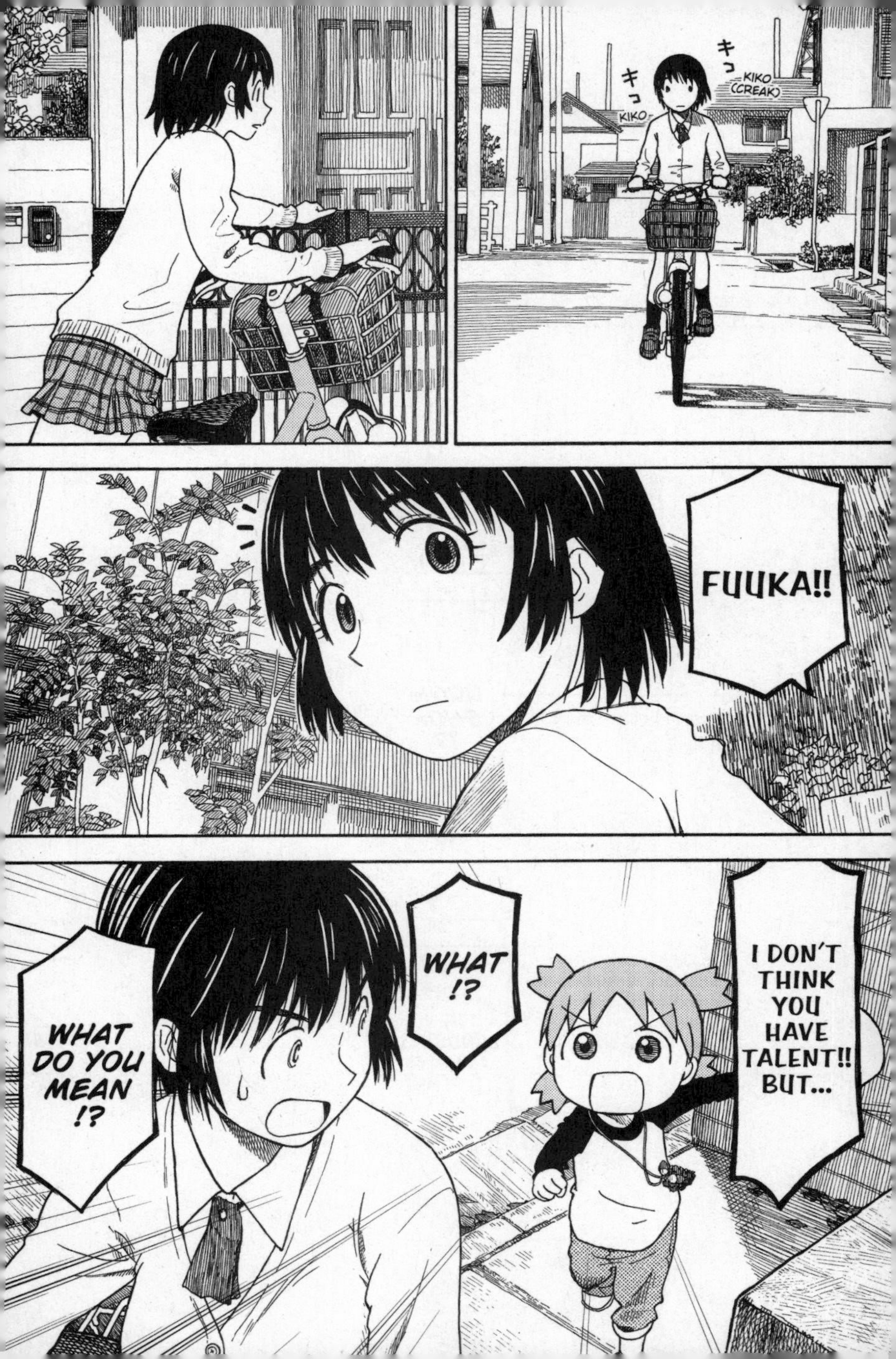
キコ
KIKO (CREAK)
キコ
KIKO
FUUKA!!
I DON'T THINK YOU HAVE TALENT!! BUT...
WHAT !?
WHAT DO YOU MEAN !?

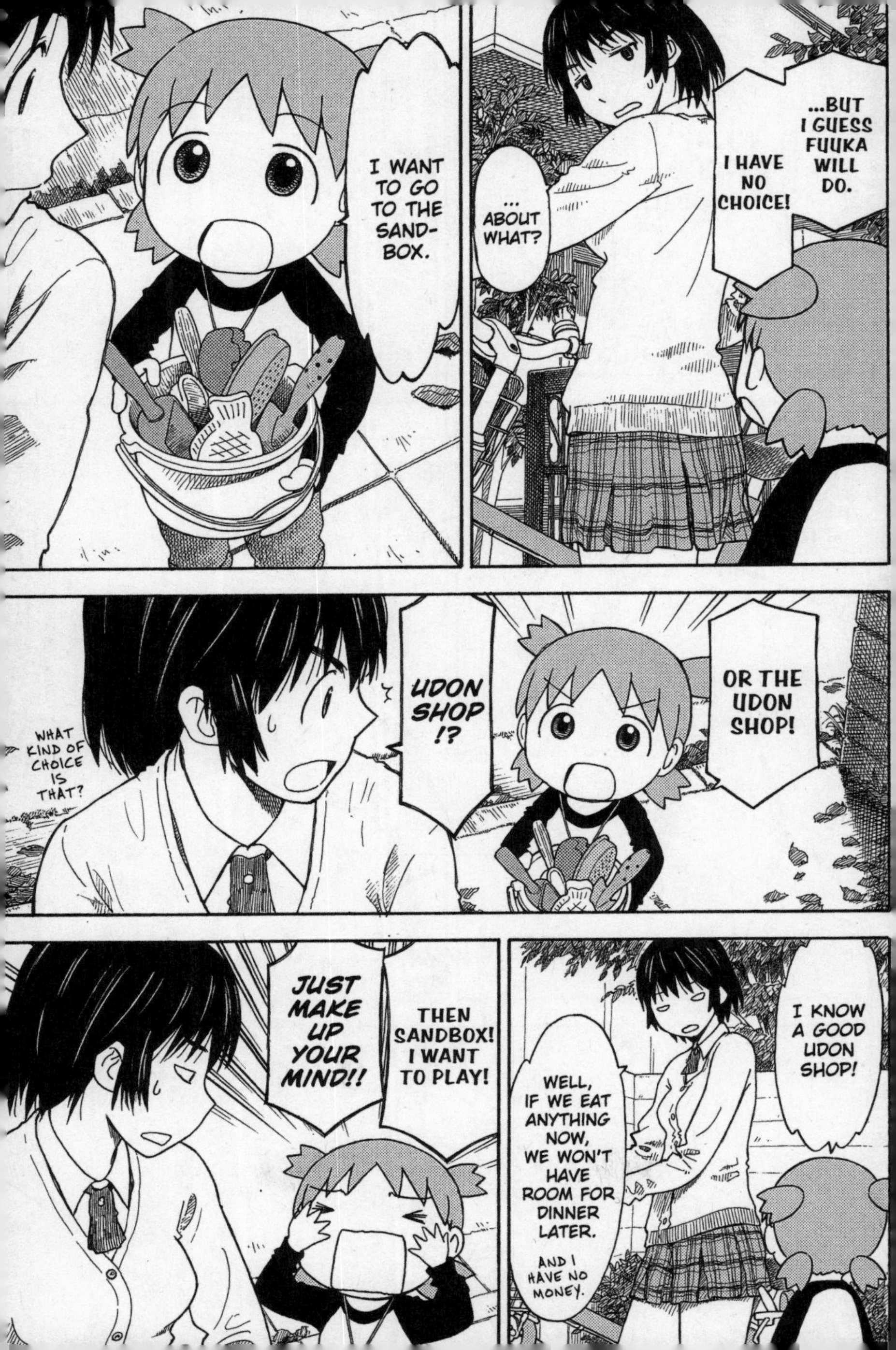
...BUT I GUESS FUUKA WILL DO.
I HAVE NO CHOICE!
... ABOUT WHAT?
I WANT TO GO TO THE SAND-BOX.
OR THE UDON SHOP!
UDON SHOP!?
WHAT KIND OF CHOICE IS THAT?
I KNOW A GOOD UDON SHOP!
WELL, IF WE EAT ANYTHING NOW, WE WON'T HAVE ROOM FOR DINNER LATER.
AND I HAVE NO MONEY.
THEN SANDBOX! I WANT TO PLAY!
JUST MAKE UP YOUR MIND!!

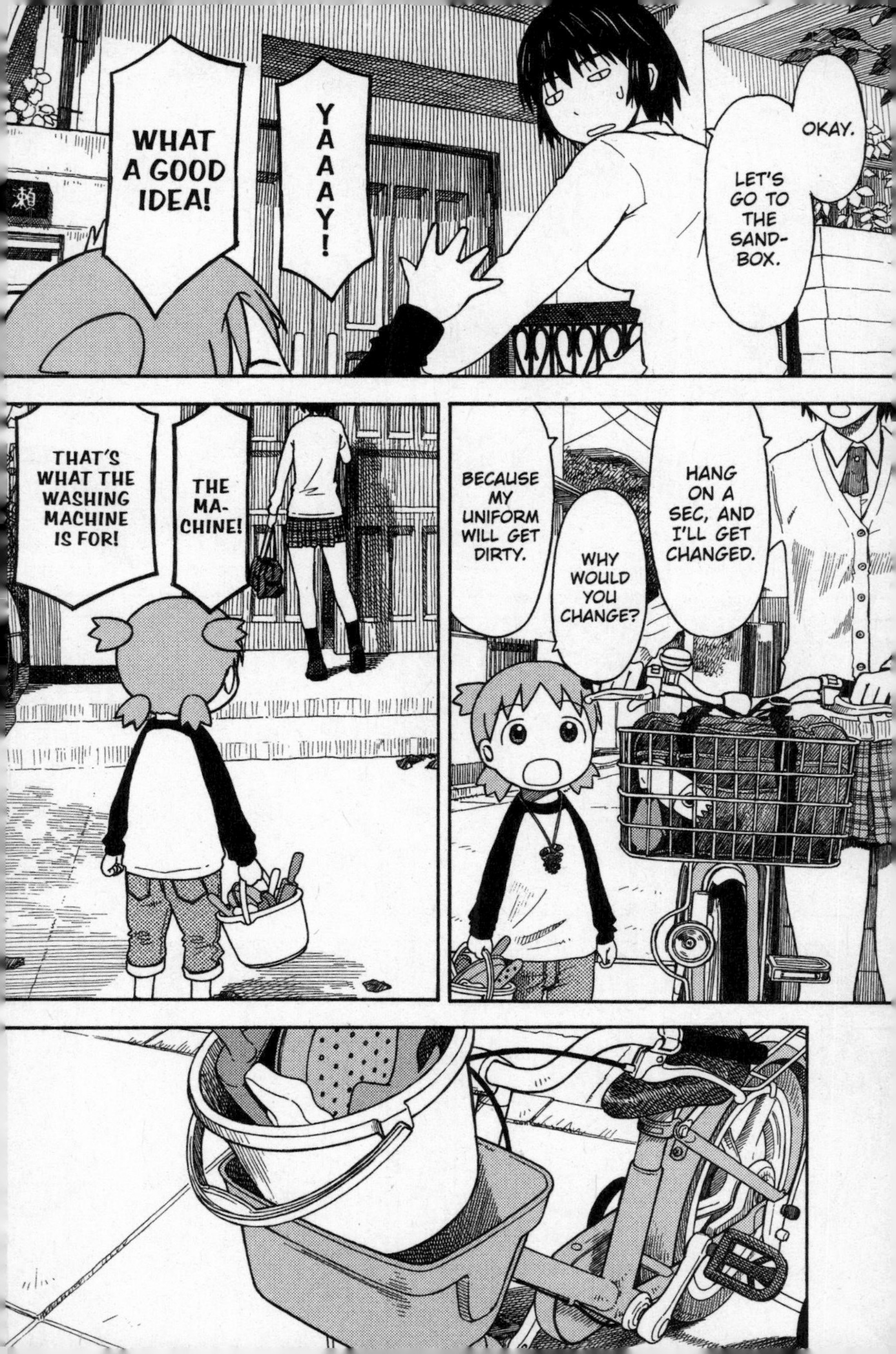

OKAY.
LET'S GO TO THE SANDBOX.
YAAAAY!
WHAT A GOOD IDEA!
HANG ON A SEC, AND I'LL GET CHANGED.
WHY WOULD YOU CHANGE?
BECAUSE MY UNIFORM WILL GET DIRTY.
THE MACHINE!
THAT'S WHAT THE WASHING MACHINE IS FOR!

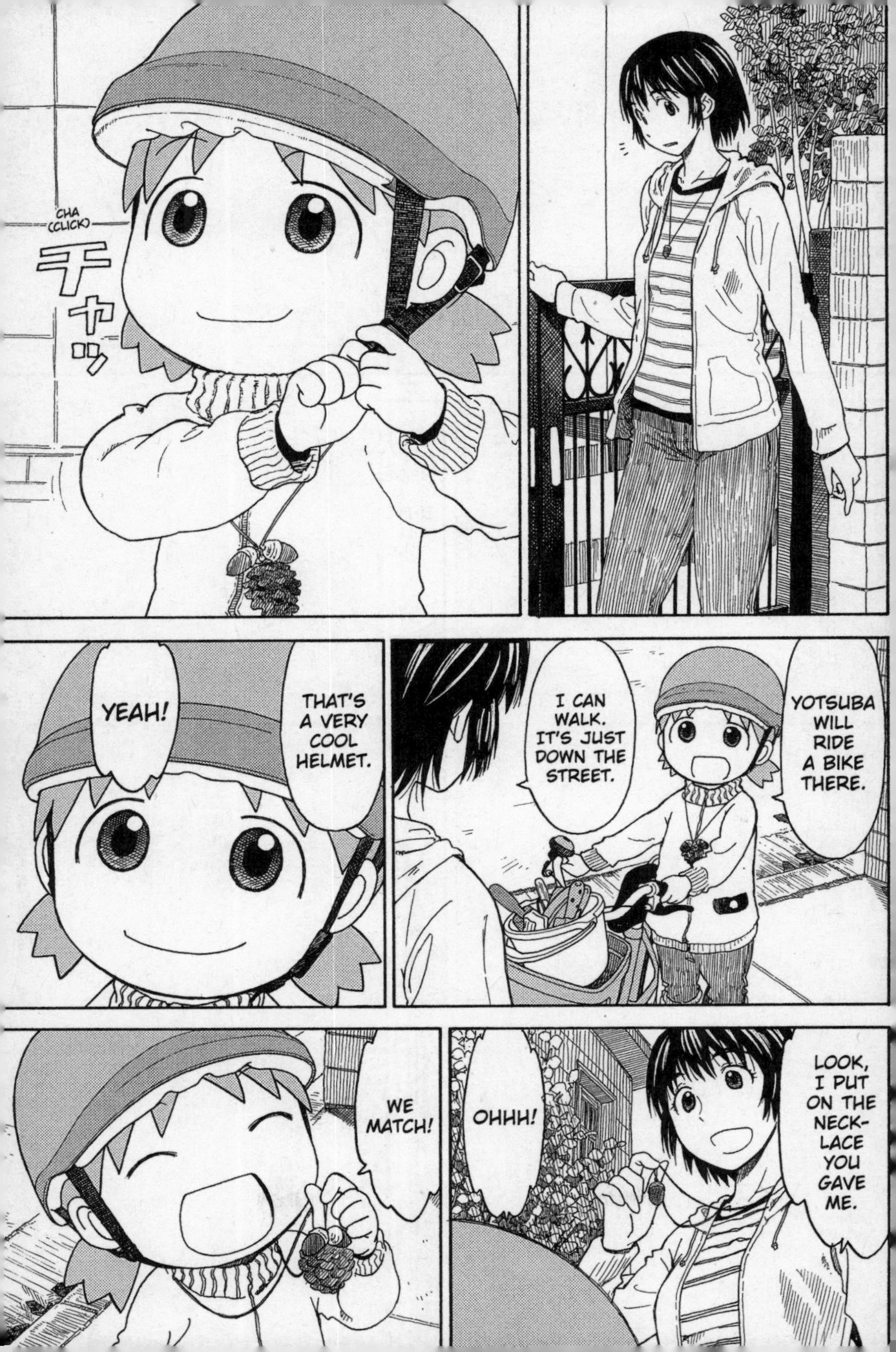
CHA (CLICK)
チャッ
YOTSUBA WILL RIDE A BIKE THERE.
I CAN WALK. IT'S JUST DOWN THE STREET.
THAT'S A VERY COOL HELMET.
YEAH!
LOOK, I PUT ON THE NECKLACE YOU GAVE ME.
OHHH!
WE MATCH!

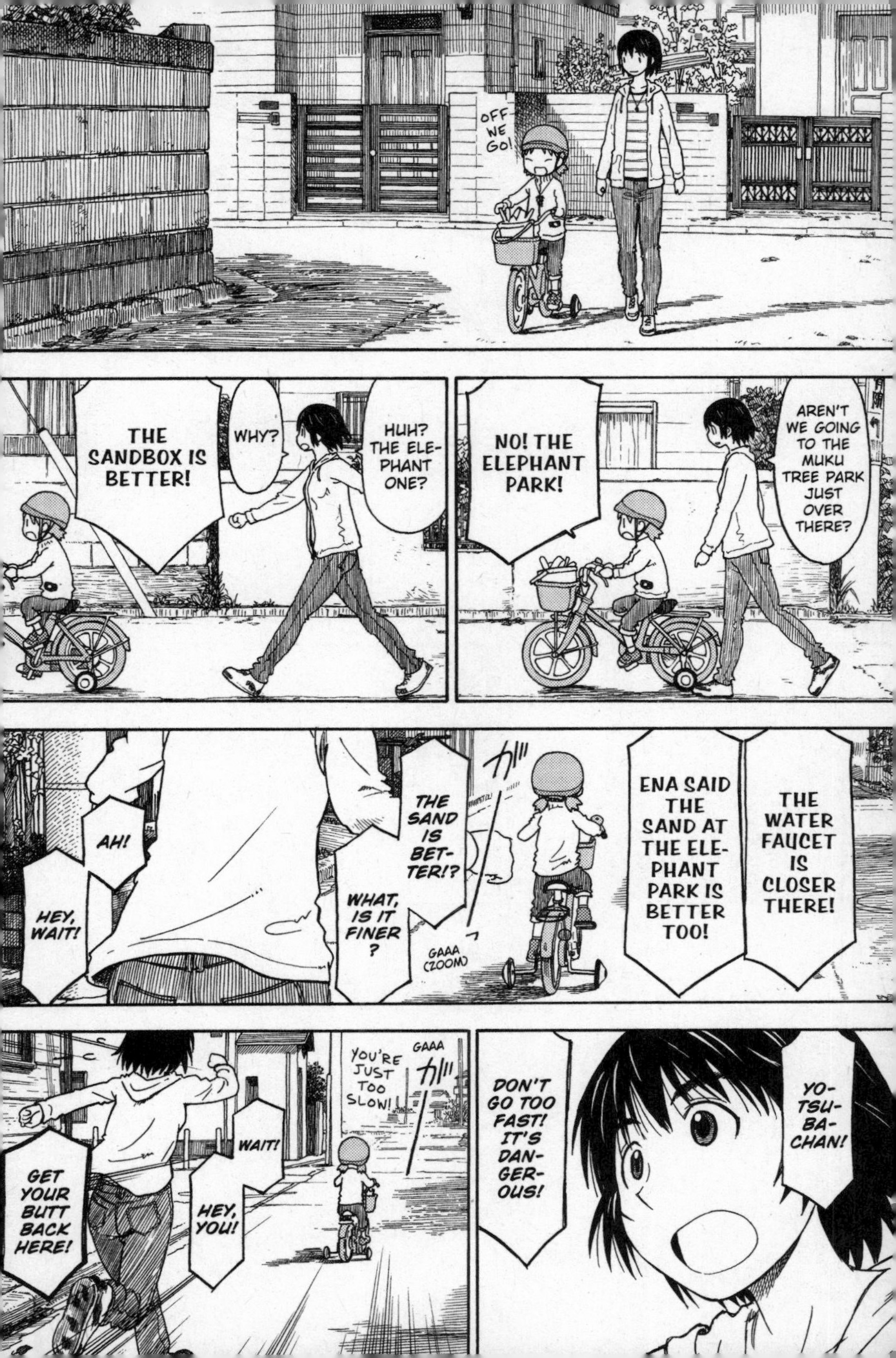
OFF WE GO!
AREN'T WE GOING TO THE MUKU TREE PARK JUST OVER THERE?
NO! THE ELEPHANT PARK!
HUH? THE ELEPHANT ONE?
WHY?
THE SANDBOX IS BETTER!
THE WATER FAUCET IS CLOSER THERE!
ENA SAID THE SAND AT THE ELEPHANT PARK IS BETTER TOO!
GAAA (ZOOM)
THE SAND IS BETTER!?
WHAT, IS IT FINER?
AH!
HEY, WAIT!
YOTSUBA-CHAN!
DON'T GO TOO FAST! IT'S DANGEROUS!
GAAA
YOU'RE JUST TOO SLOW!
WAIT!
HEY, YOU!
GET YOUR BUTT BACK HERE!

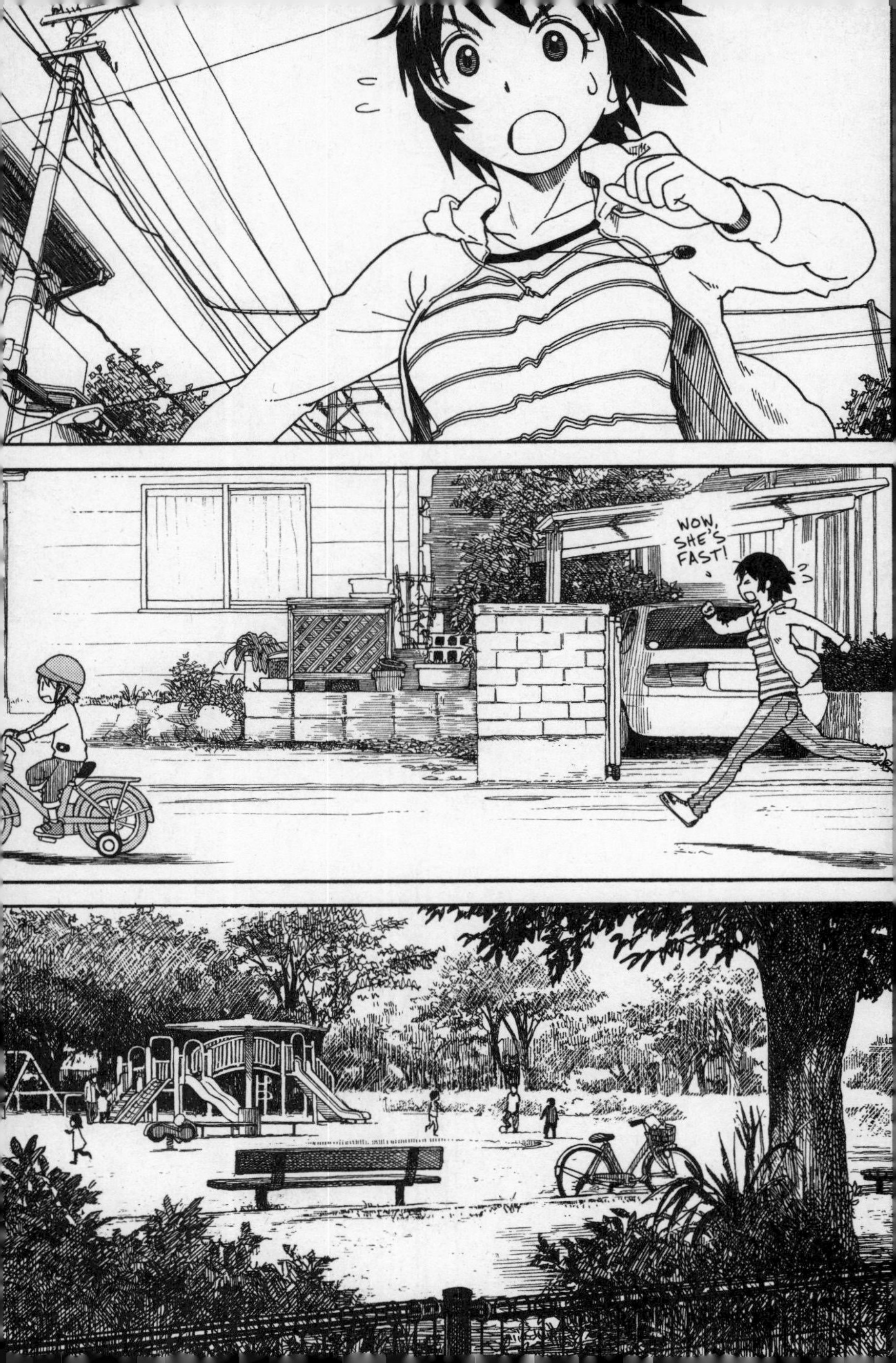
WOW, SHE'S FAST!

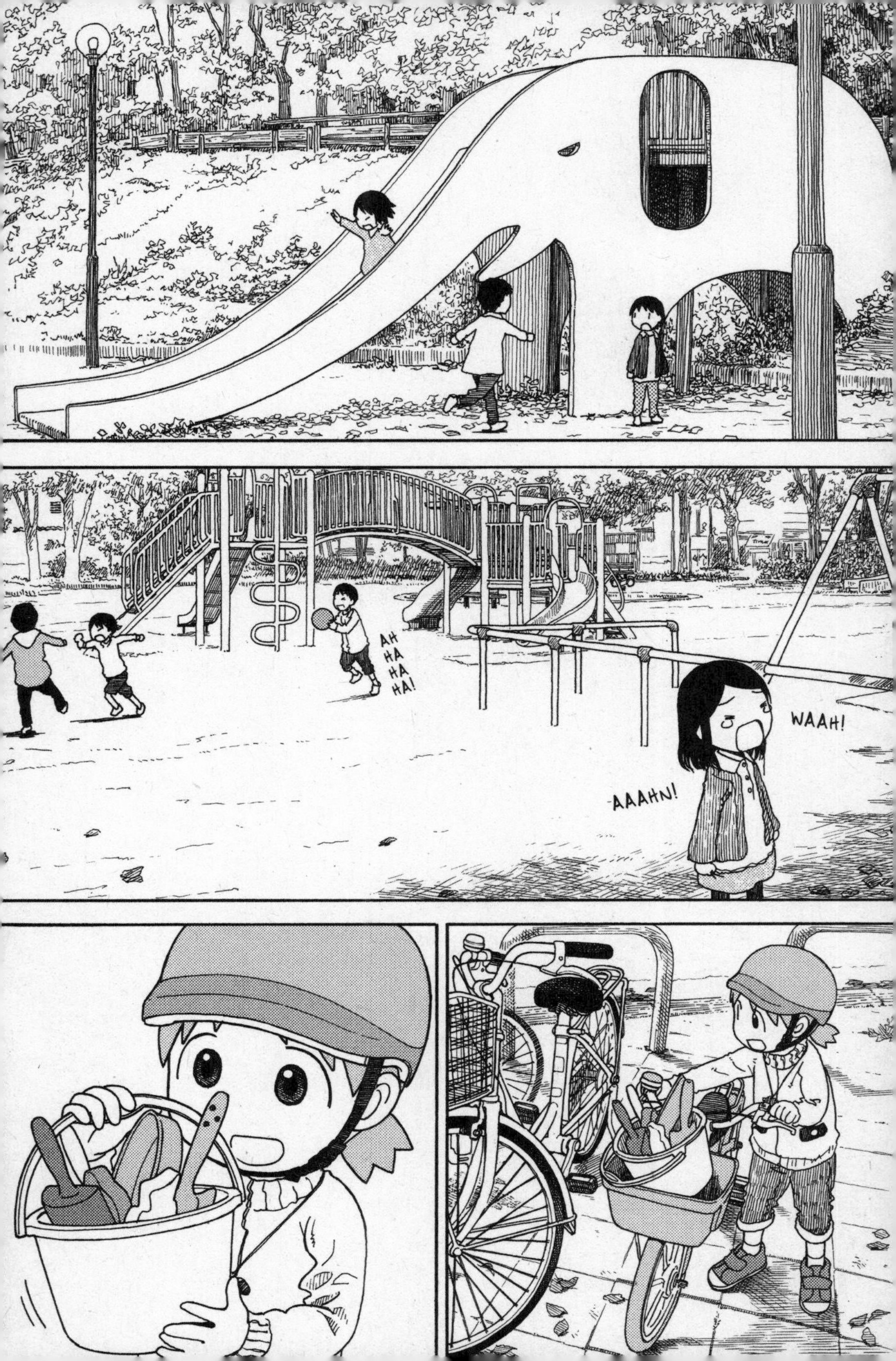
WAAH!
AAAHN!
AH HA HA HA!

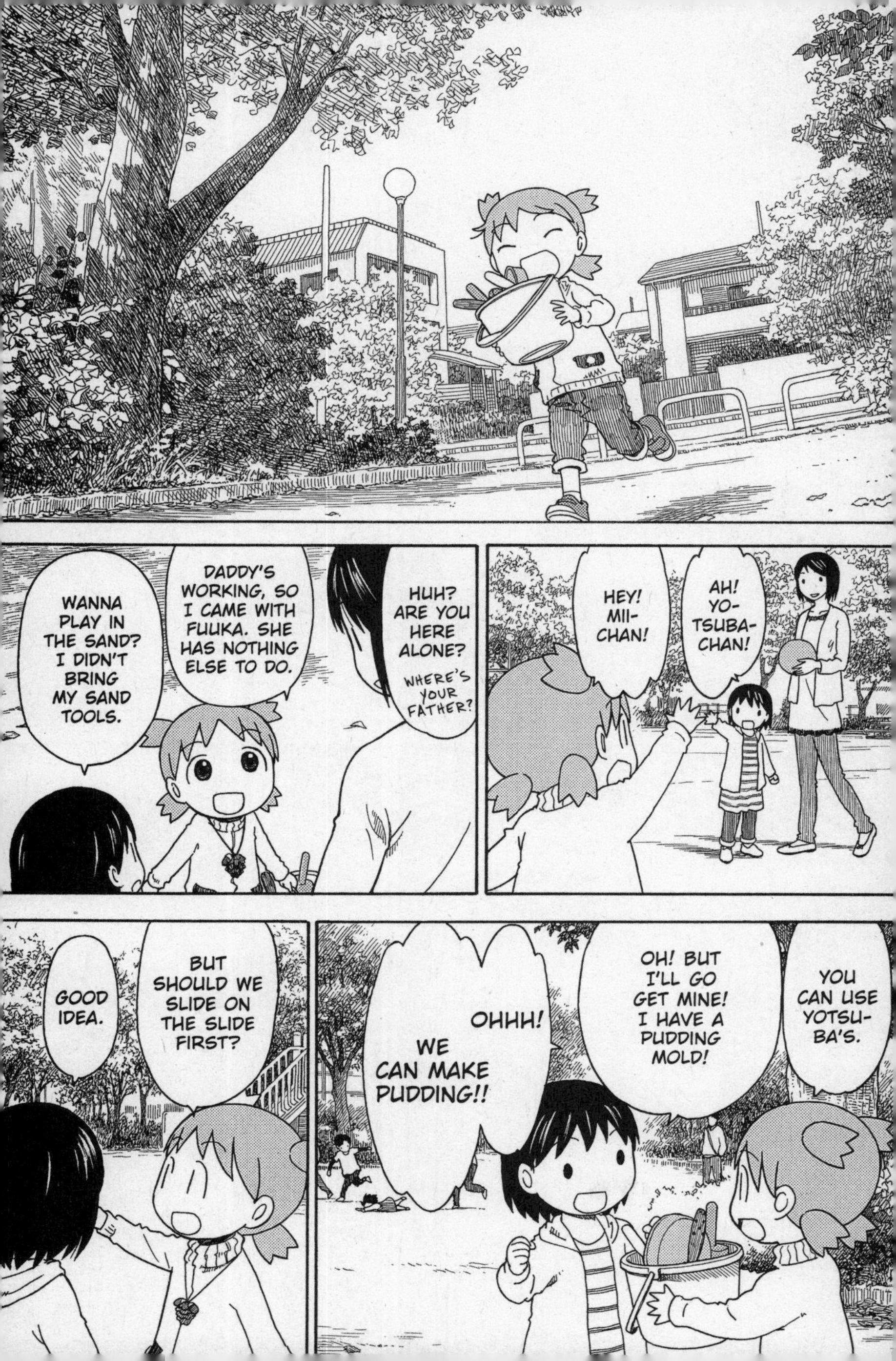
AH! YO-TSUBA-CHAN!
HEY! MII-CHAN!
HUH? ARE YOU HERE ALONE? WHERE'S YOUR FATHER?
DADDY'S WORKING, SO I CAME WITH FUUKA. SHE HAS NOTHING ELSE TO DO.
WANNA PLAY IN THE SAND? I DIDN'T BRING MY SAND TOOLS.
YOU CAN USE YOTSUBA'S.
OH! BUT I'LL GO GET MINE! I HAVE A PUDDING MOLD!
OHHH!
WE CAN MAKE PUDDING!!
BUT SHOULD WE SLIDE ON THE SLIDE FIRST?
GOOD IDEA.

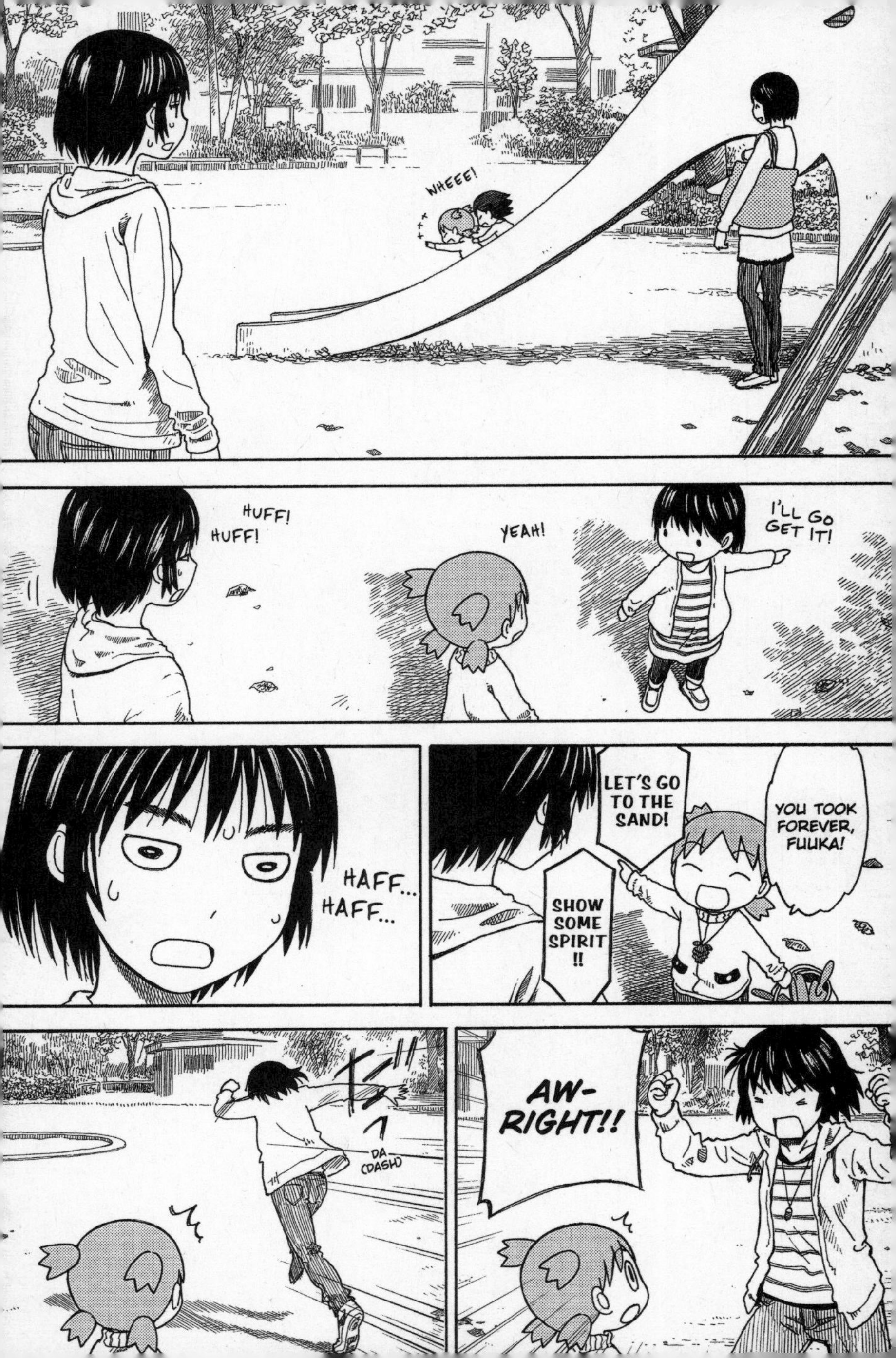
WHEEE!
I'LL GO GET IT!
YEAH!
HUFF! HUFF!
YOU TOOK FOREVER, FUUKA!
LET'S GO TO THE SAND!
SHOW SOME SPIRIT!!
HAFF... HAFF...
AW-RIGHT!!
DA (DASH)

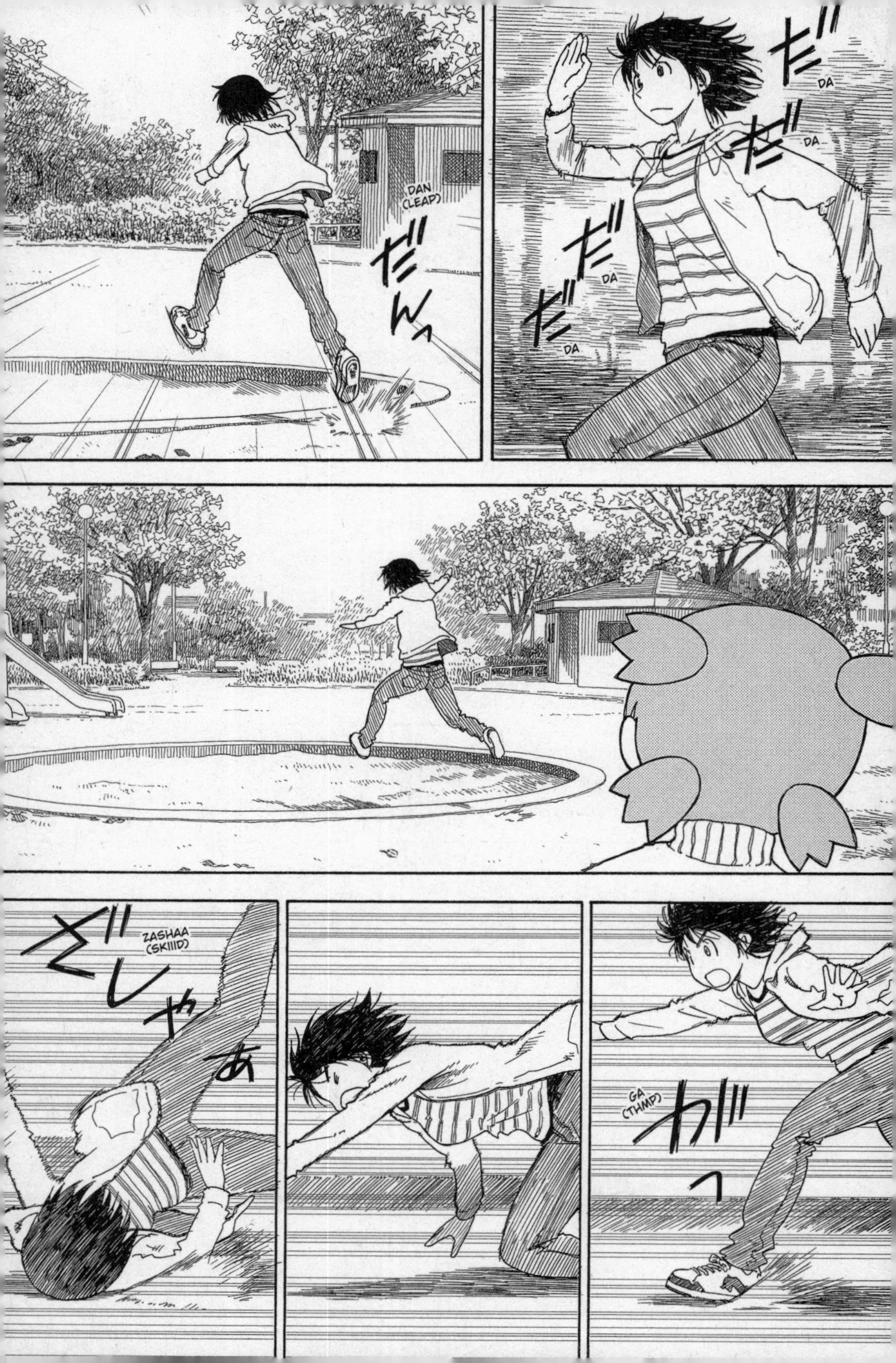

だ
DA
だ
DA
だ
DA
だ
DA
だんっ
DAN (LEAP)
ガッ
GA (THMP)
ざしゃあ
ZASHAA (SKIIID)

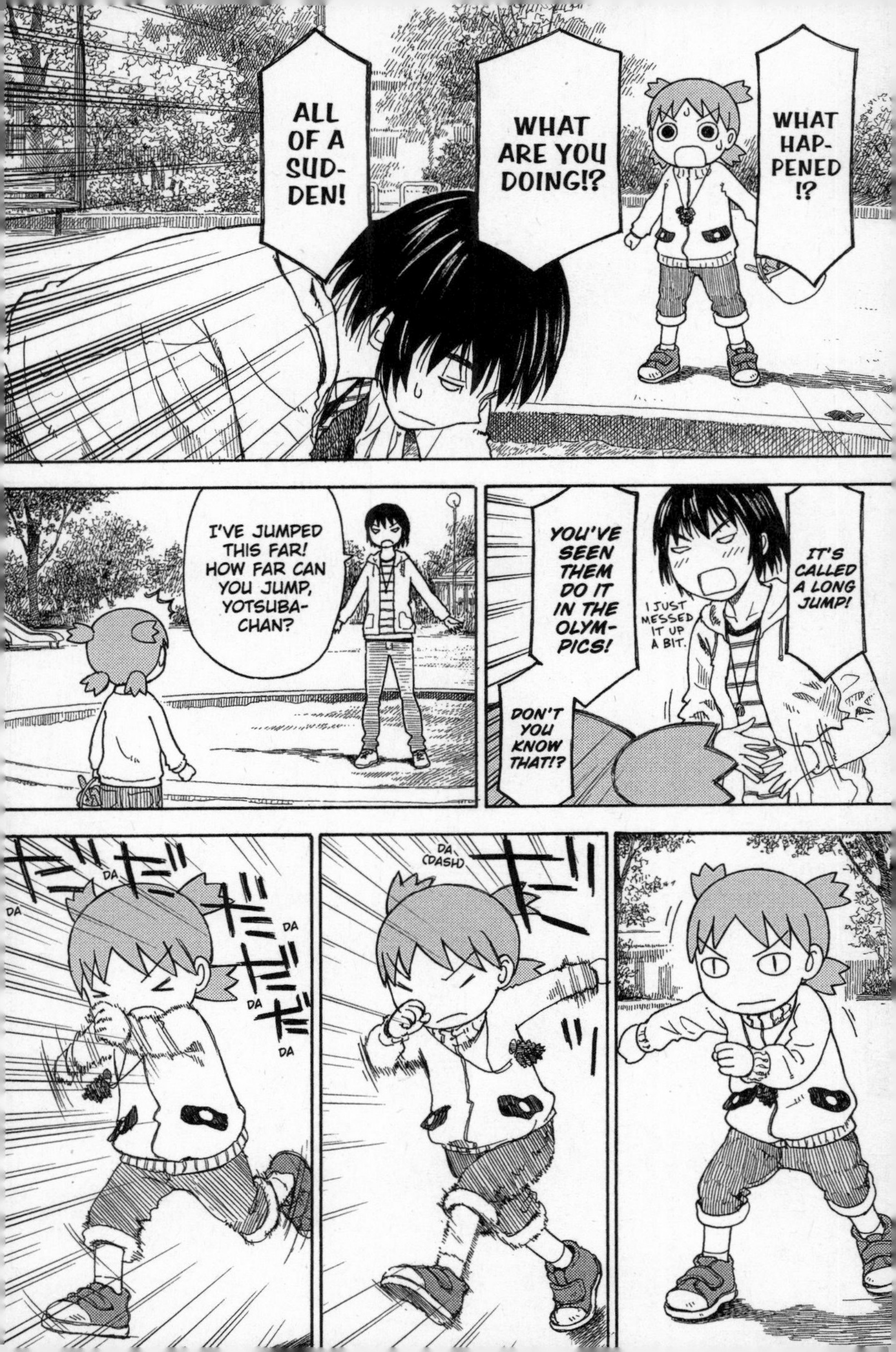
WHAT HAPPENED!?
WHAT ARE YOU DOING!?
ALL OF A SUDDEN!
IT'S CALLED A LONG JUMP!
I JUST MESSED IT UP A BIT.
YOU'VE SEEN THEM DO IT IN THE OLYMPICS!
DON'T YOU KNOW THAT!?
I'VE JUMPED THIS FAR! HOW FAR CAN YOU JUMP, YOTSUBA-CHAN?
DA (DASH)
DA
DA
DA
DA
DA

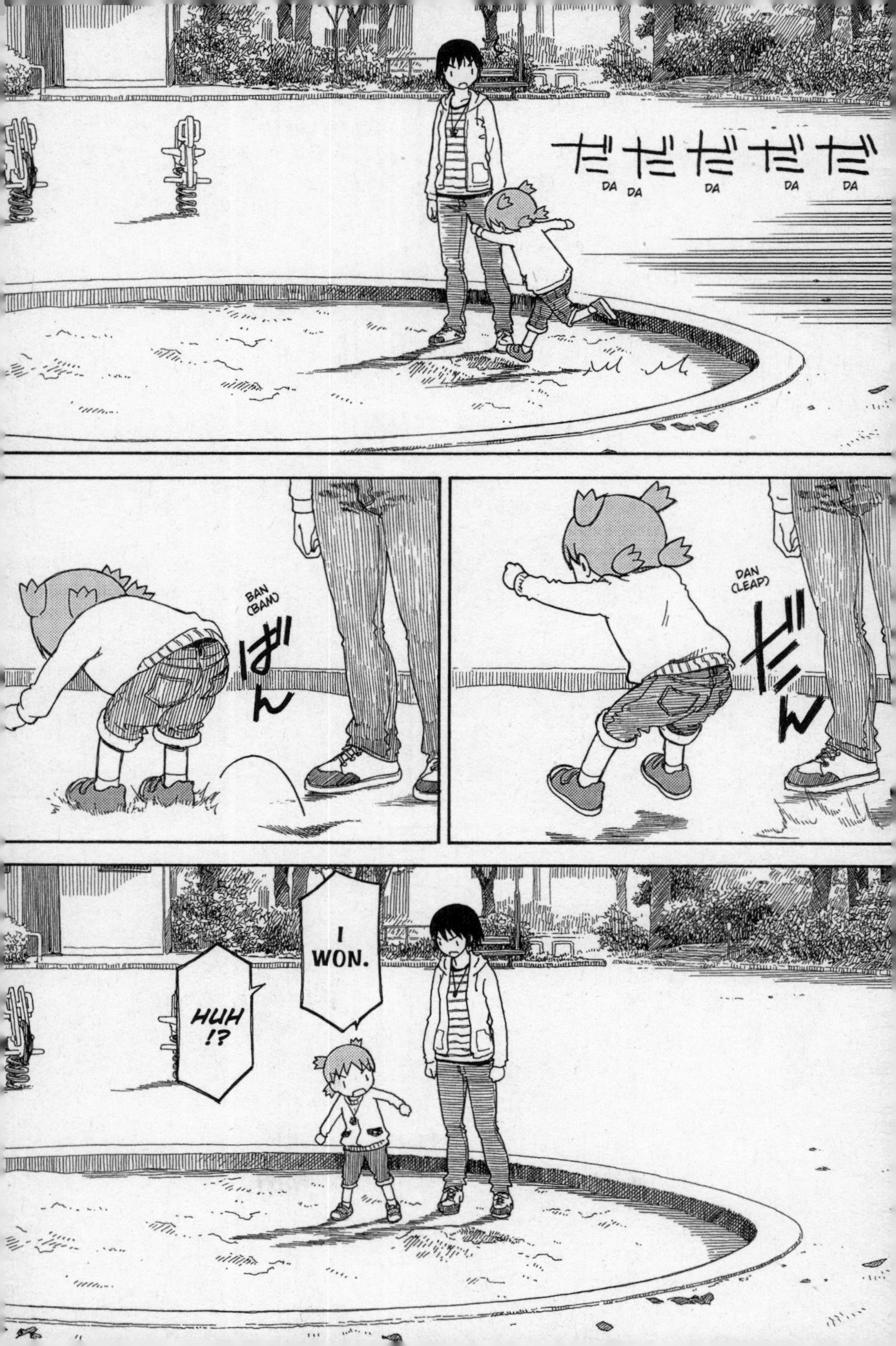
だだだだだ
DA DA DA DA DA
だん
DAN (LEAP)
ばん
BAN (BAM)
I WON.
HUH!?

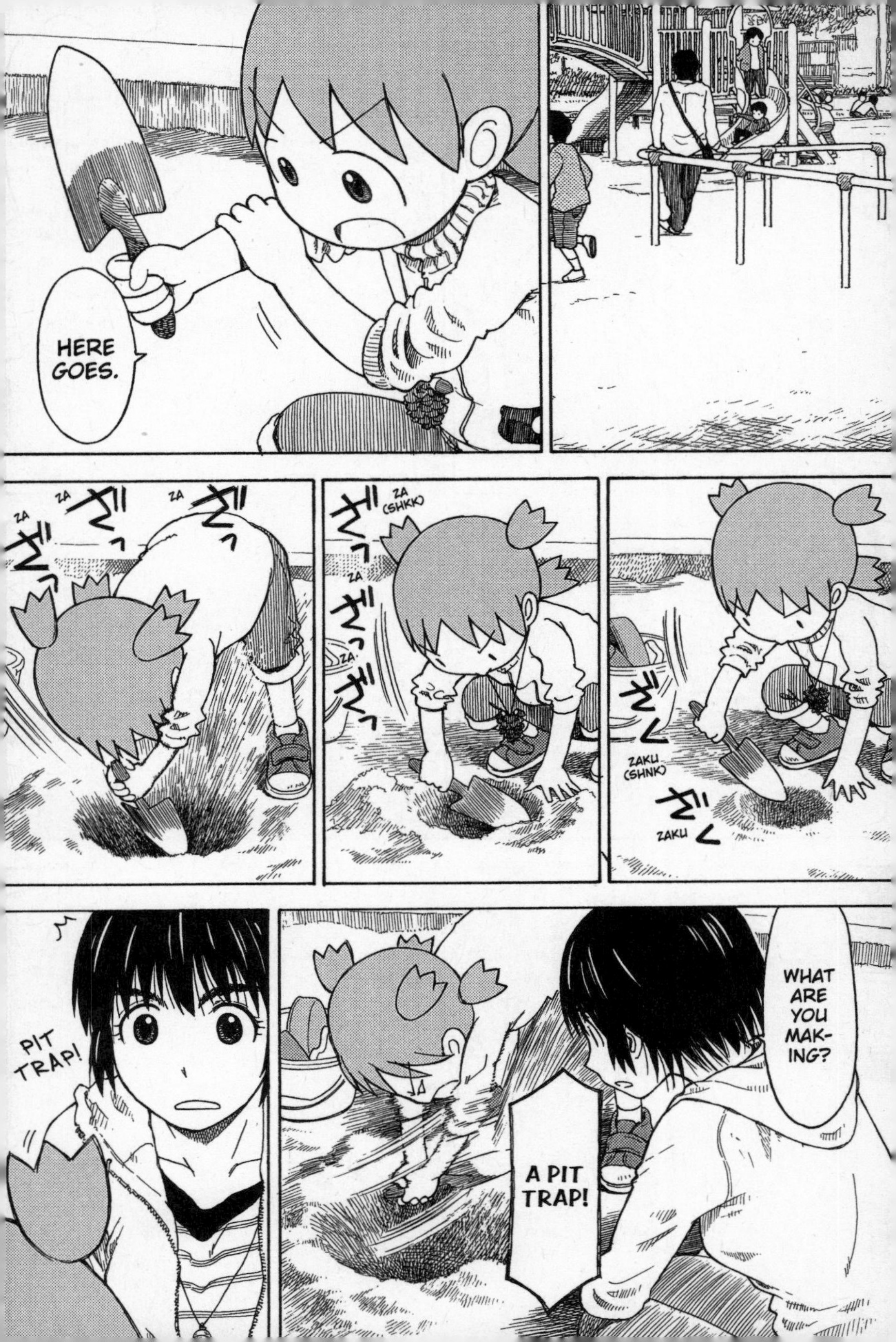
HERE GOES.
ZAKU (SHNK)
ZAKU
ZA (SHKK)
ZA
ZA
ZA
ZA
ZA
WHAT ARE YOU MAK-ING?
A PIT TRAP!
PIT TRAP!

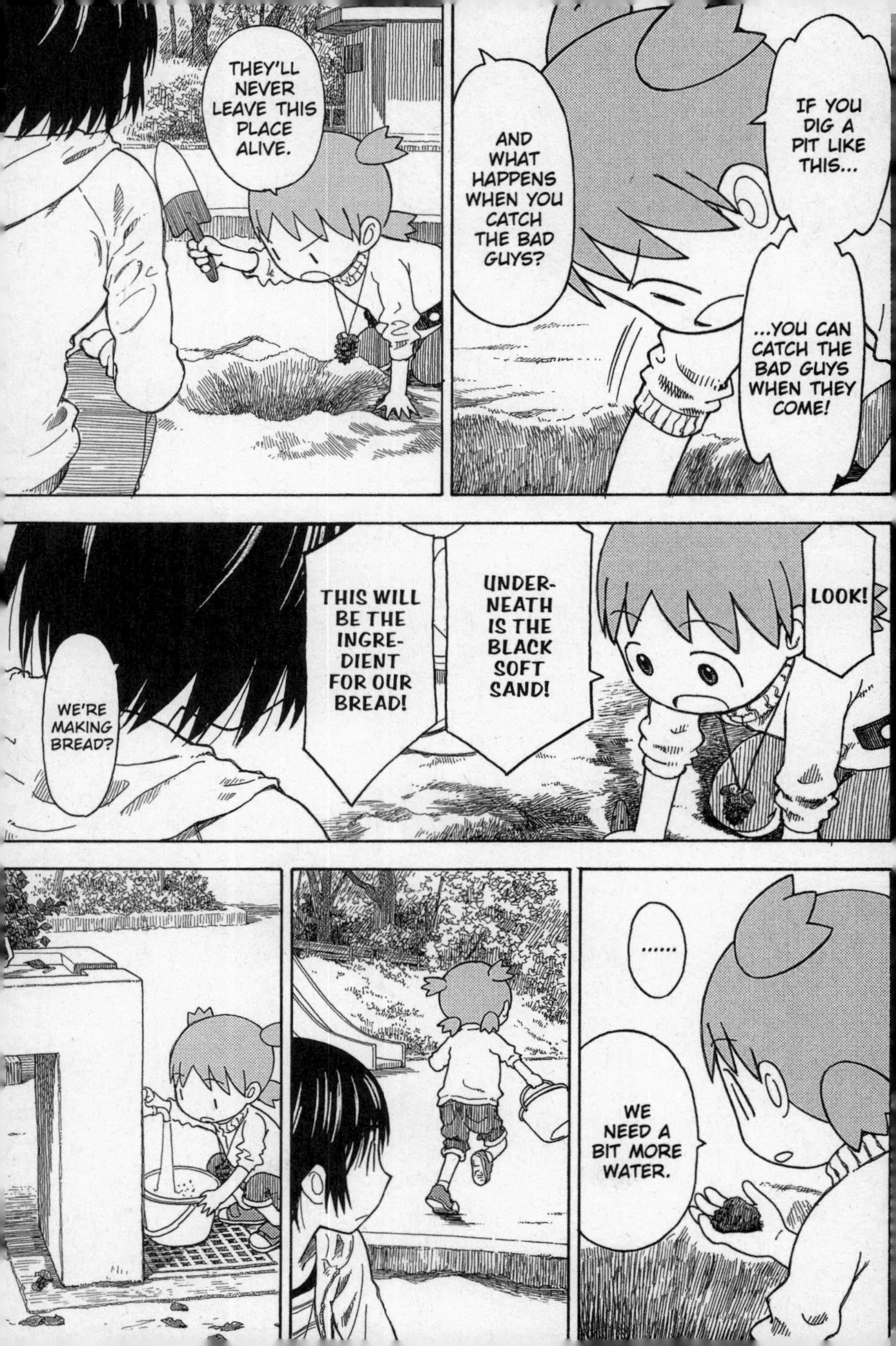
IF YOU DIG A PIT LIKE THIS...
...YOU CAN CATCH THE BAD GUYS WHEN THEY COME!
AND WHAT HAPPENS WHEN YOU CATCH THE BAD GUYS?
THEY'LL NEVER LEAVE THIS PLACE ALIVE.
LOOK!
UNDER-NEATH IS THE BLACK SOFT SAND!
THIS WILL BE THE INGRE-DIENT FOR OUR BREAD!
WE'RE MAKING BREAD?
......
WE NEED A BIT MORE WATER.

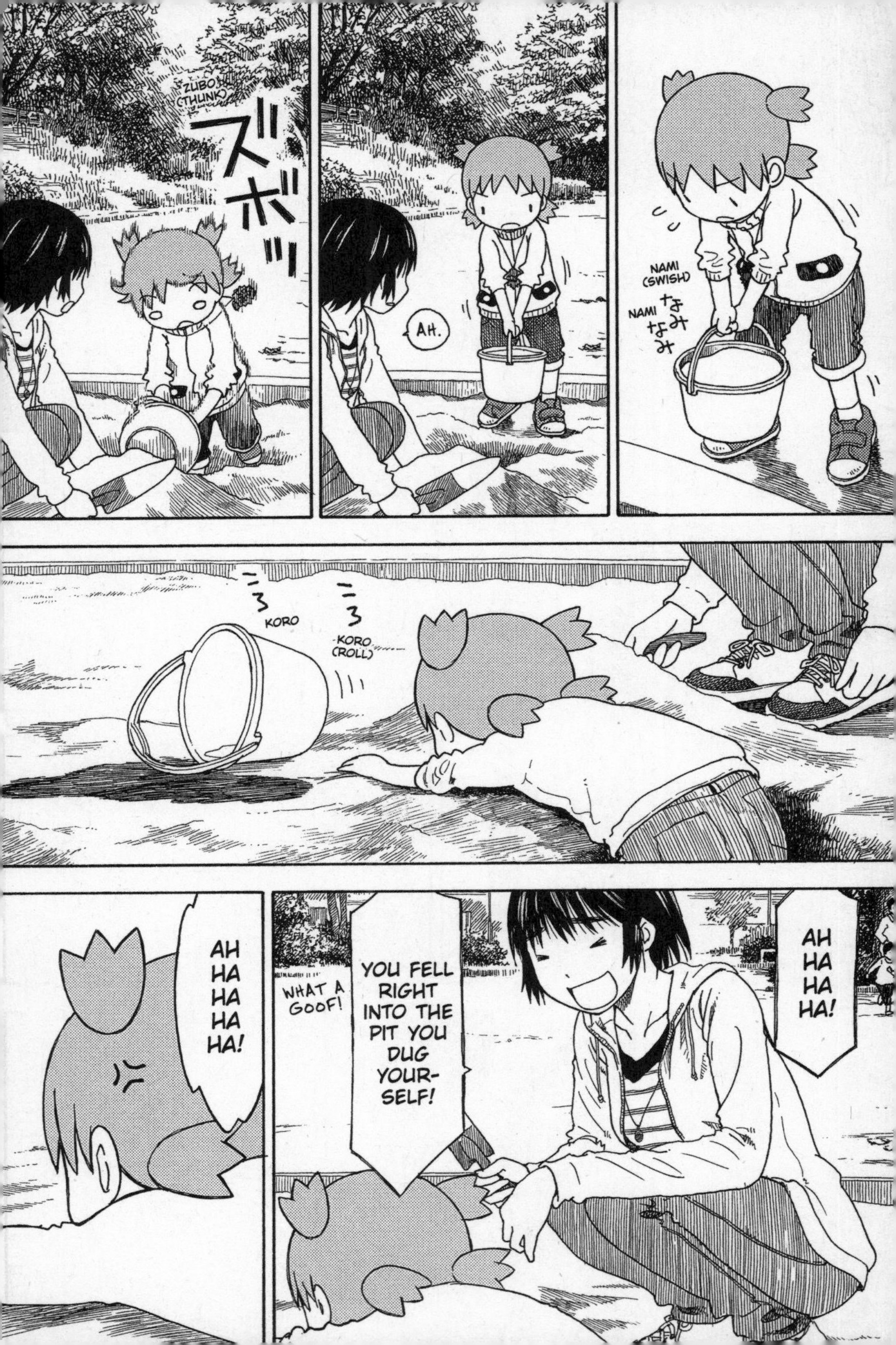
NAMI (SWISH)
NAMI
なみなみ
AH.
ZUBO (THUNK)
ズボッ
ころ
ころ
KORO
KORO (ROLL)
AH HA HA HA HA!
YOU FELL RIGHT INTO THE PIT YOU DUG YOURSELF!
WHAT A GOOF!
AH HA HA HA HA!

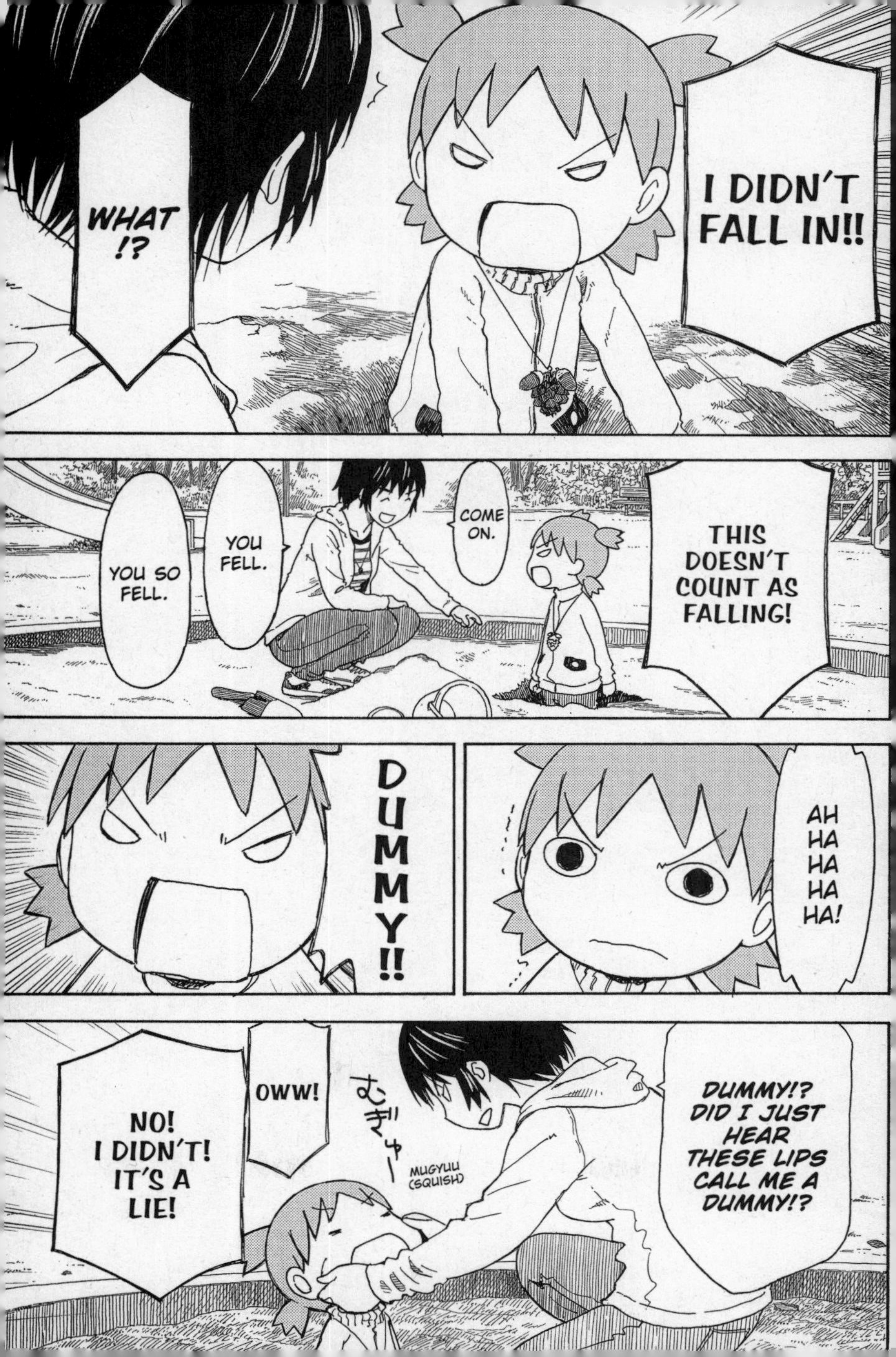
I DIDN'T FALL IN!!
WHAT !?
THIS DOESN'T COUNT AS FALLING!
COME ON.
YOU FELL.
YOU SO FELL.
AH HA HA HA HA!
DUMMY!!
DUMMY!? DID I JUST HEAR THESE LIPS CALL ME A DUMMY!?
むぎゅー
MUGYUU (SQUISH)
OWW!
NO! I DIDN'T! IT'S A LIE!

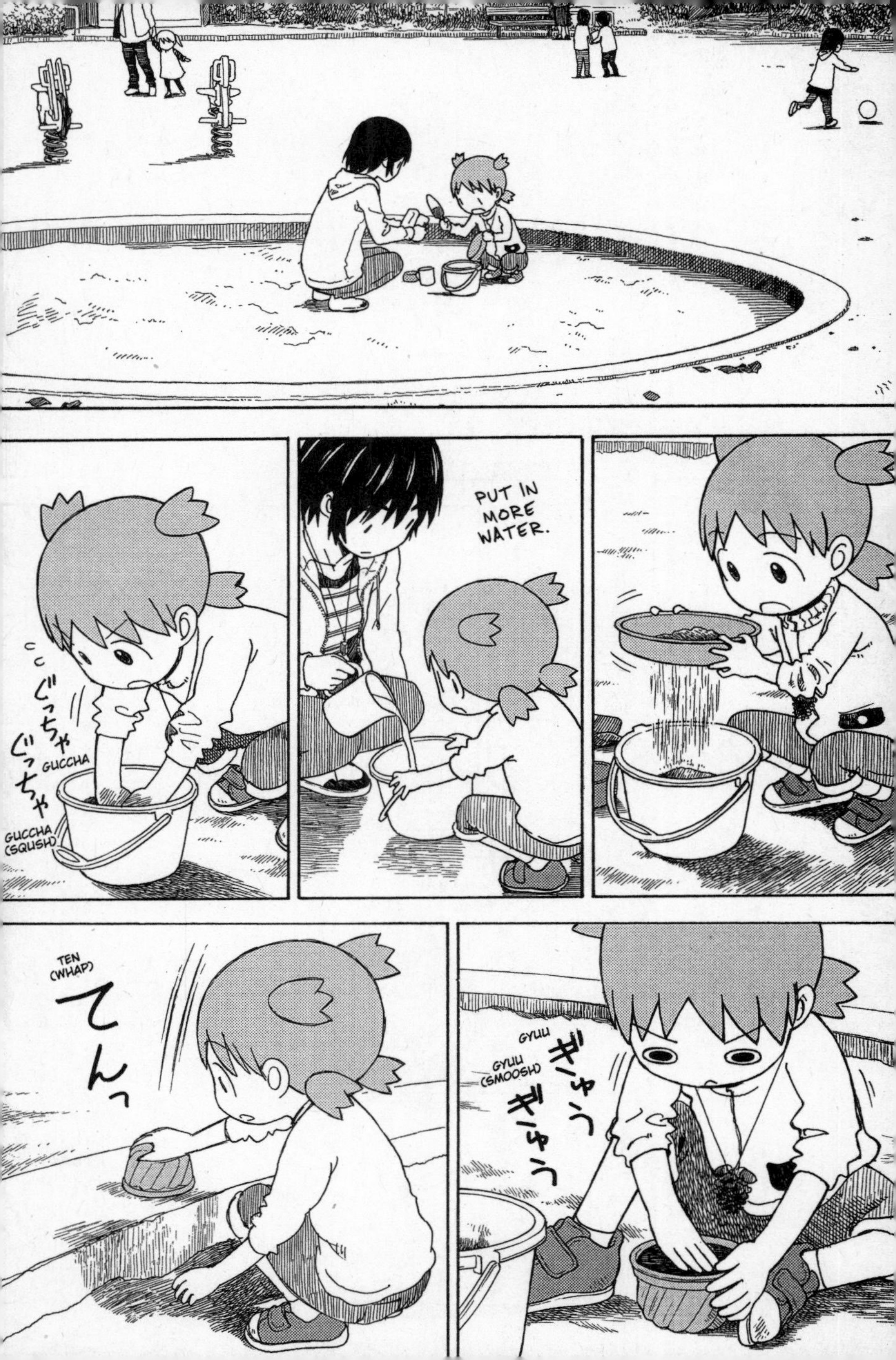
PUT IN MORE WATER.
ぐっちゃ ぐっちゃ
GUCCHA
GUCCHA (SQUSH)
ぎゅう ぎゅう
GYUU
GYUU (SMOOSH)
てんっ
TEN (WHAP)

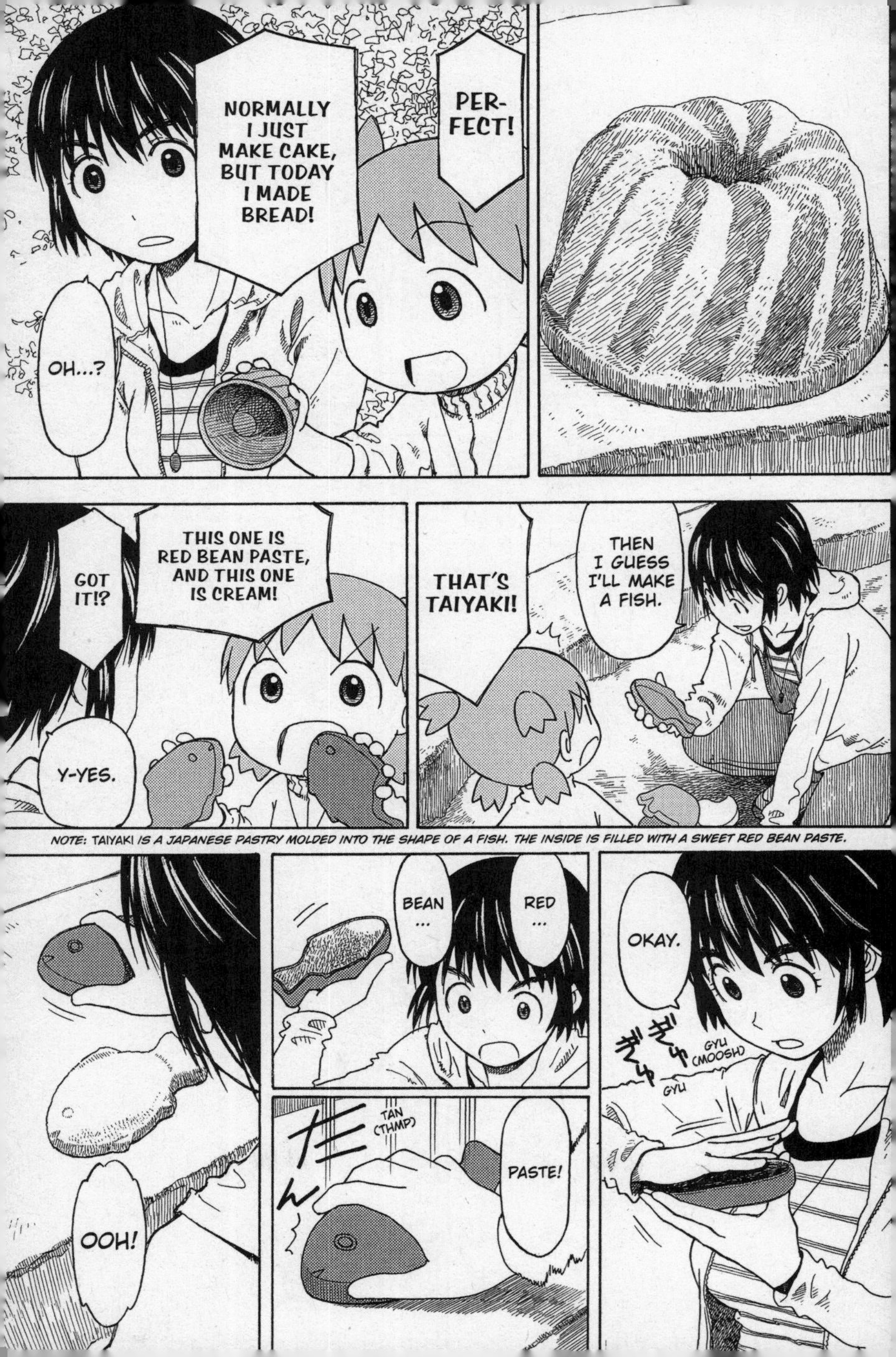
PER-FECT!
NORMALLY I JUST MAKE CAKE, BUT TODAY I MADE BREAD!
OH...?
THEN I GUESS I'LL MAKE A FISH.
THAT'S TAIYAKI!
THIS ONE IS RED BEAN PASTE, AND THIS ONE IS CREAM!
GOT IT!?
Y-YES.
NOTE: TAIYAKI IS A JAPANESE PASTRY MOLDED INTO THE SHAPE OF A FISH. THE INSIDE IS FILLED WITH A SWEET RED BEAN PASTE.
OKAY.
ぎゅ
GYU (MOOSH)
ぎゅ
GYU
RED ...
BEAN ...
TAN (THMP)
PASTE!
OOH!

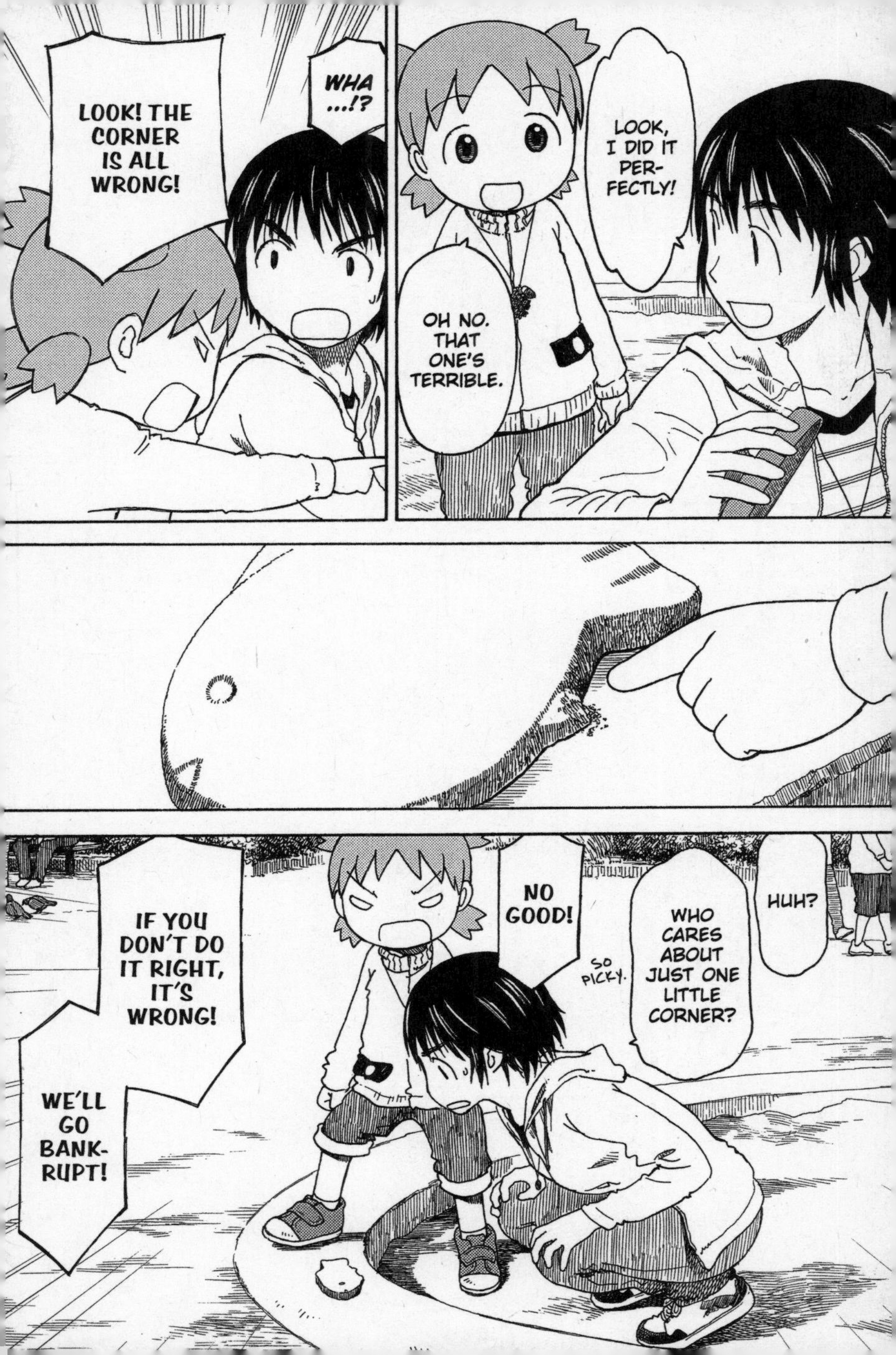
LOOK, I DID IT PER-FECTLY!
OH NO. THAT ONE'S TERRIBLE.
WHA ...!?
LOOK! THE CORNER IS ALL WRONG!
HUH?
WHO CARES ABOUT JUST ONE LITTLE CORNER?
SO PICKY.
NO GOOD!
IF YOU DON'T DO IT RIGHT, IT'S WRONG!
WE'LL GO BANK-RUPT!

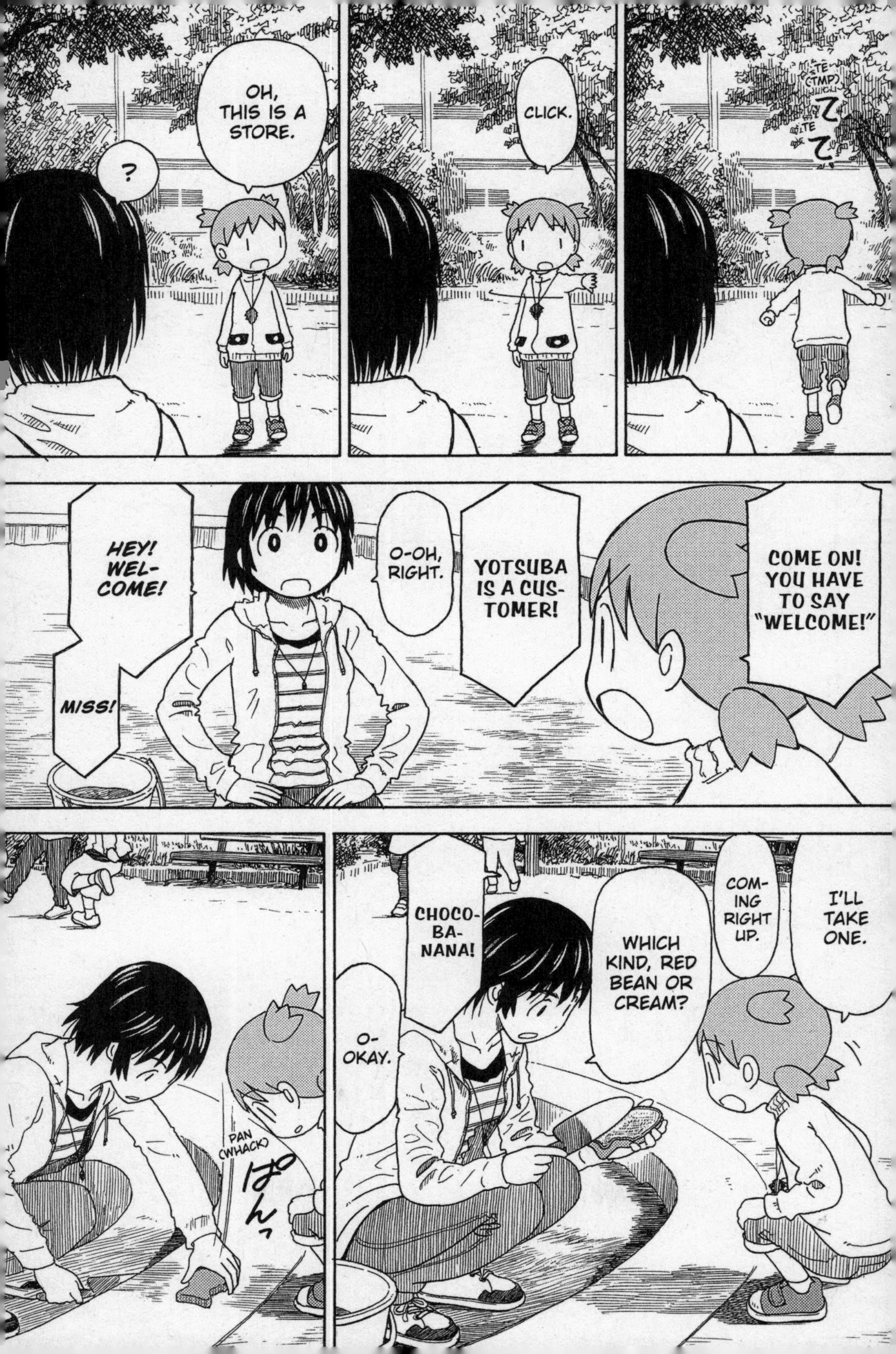
TE (TMP) て
TE て
CLICK.
OH, THIS IS A STORE.
?
COME ON! YOU HAVE TO SAY "WELCOME!"
YOTSUBA IS A CUS-TOMER!
O-OH, RIGHT.
HEY! WEL-COME!
MISS!
I'LL TAKE ONE.
COM-ING RIGHT UP.
WHICH KIND, RED BEAN OR CREAM?
CHOCO-BA-NANA!
O-OKAY.
PAN (WHACK) ぱん

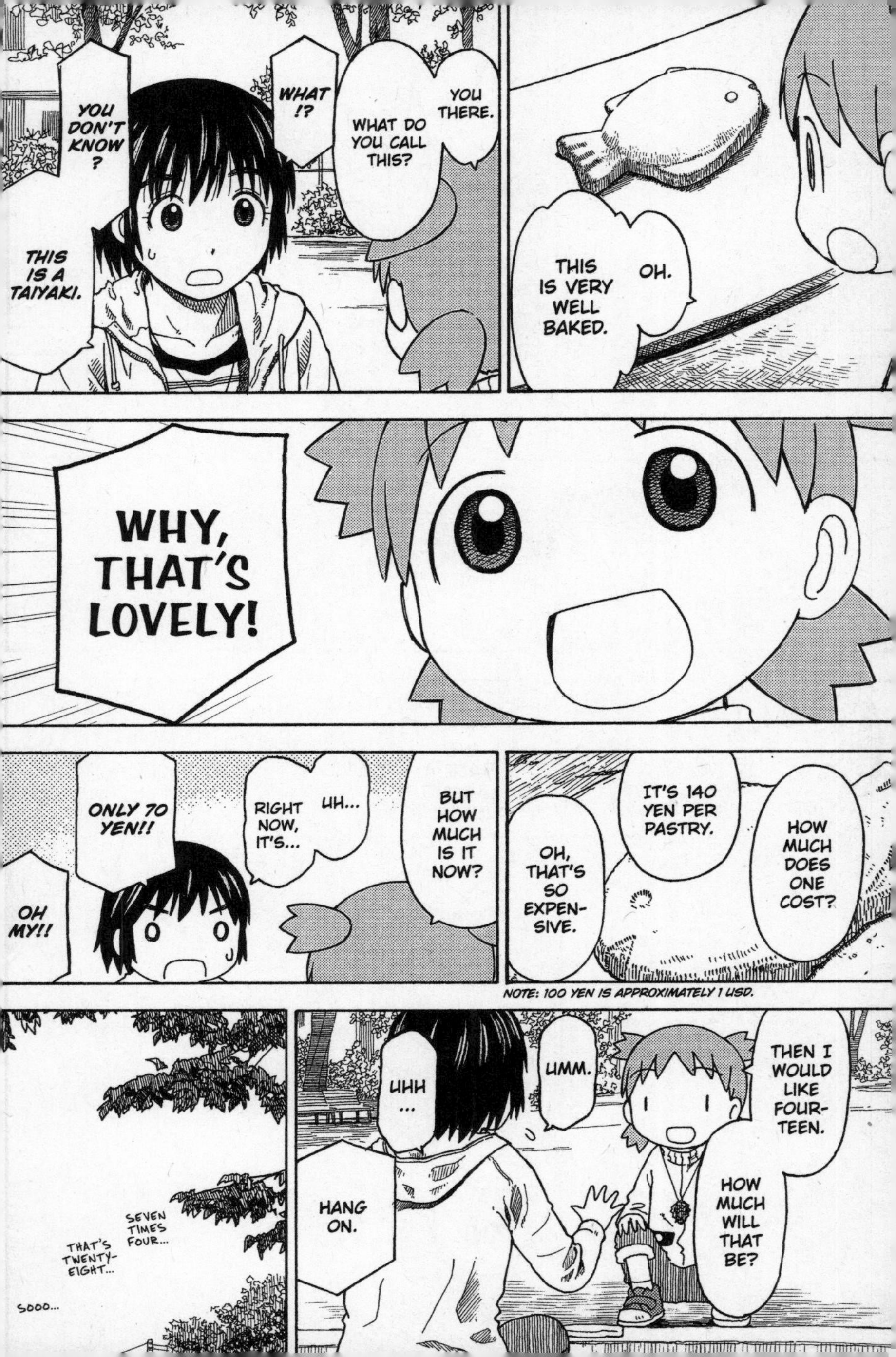
OH.
THIS IS VERY WELL BAKED.
YOU THERE.
WHAT DO YOU CALL THIS?
WHAT!?
YOU DON'T KNOW?
THIS IS A TAIYAKI.
WHY, THAT'S LOVELY!
HOW MUCH DOES ONE COST?
IT'S 140 YEN PER PASTRY.
OH, THAT'S SO EXPENSIVE.
BUT HOW MUCH IS IT NOW?
UH...
RIGHT NOW, IT'S...
ONLY 70 YEN!!
OH MY!!
NOTE: 100 YEN IS APPROXIMATELY 1 USD.
THEN I WOULD LIKE FOURTEEN.
HOW MUCH WILL THAT BE?
UMM.
UHH...
HANG ON.
SEVEN TIMES FOUR...
THAT'S TWENTY-EIGHT...
SOOO...

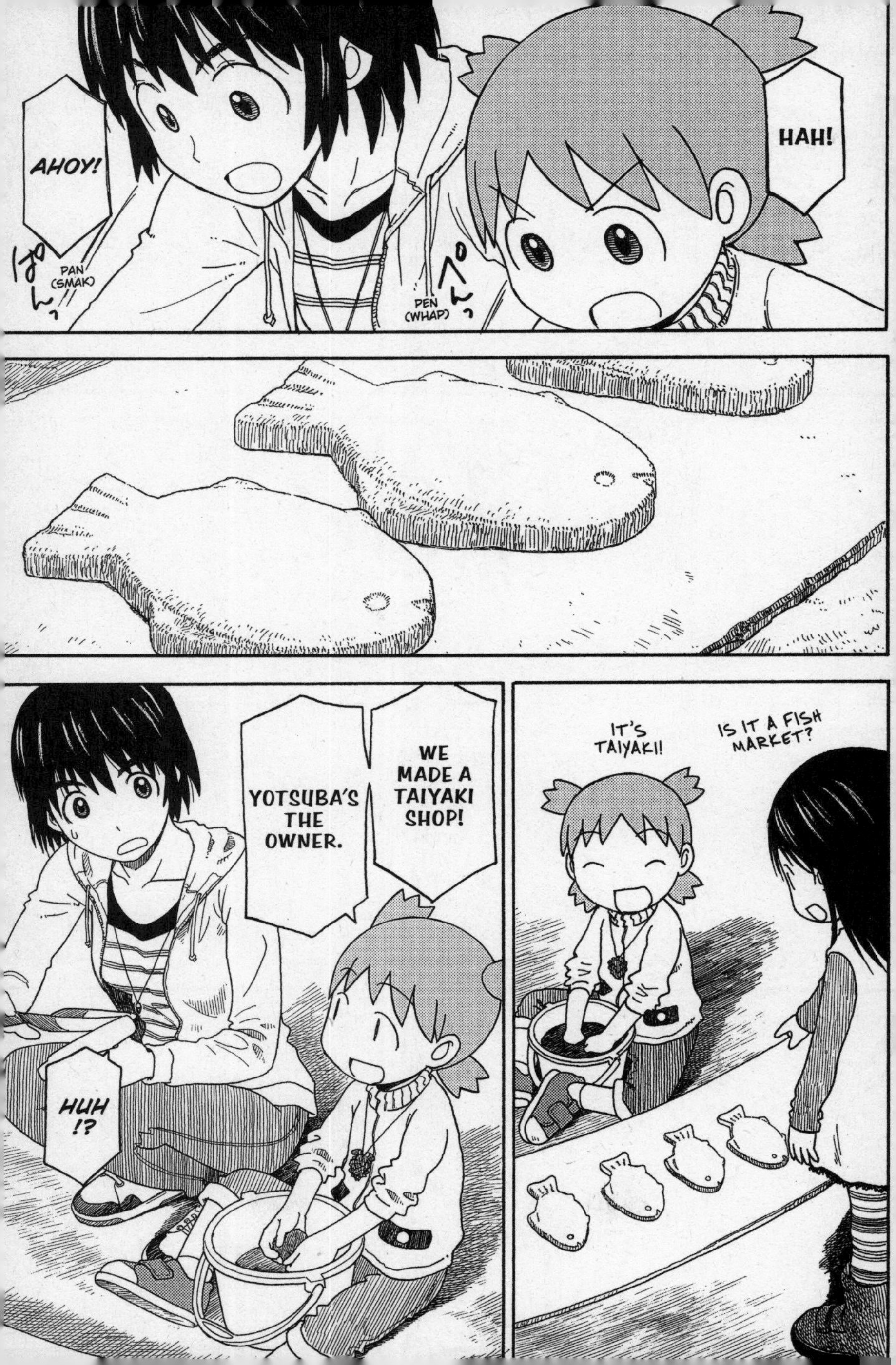
HAH!
AHOY!
ぺん
PEN (WHAP)
ぱん
PAN (SMAK)
IS IT A FISH MARKET?
IT'S TAIYAKI!
WE MADE A TAIYAKI SHOP!
YOTSUBA'S THE OWNER.
HUH!?

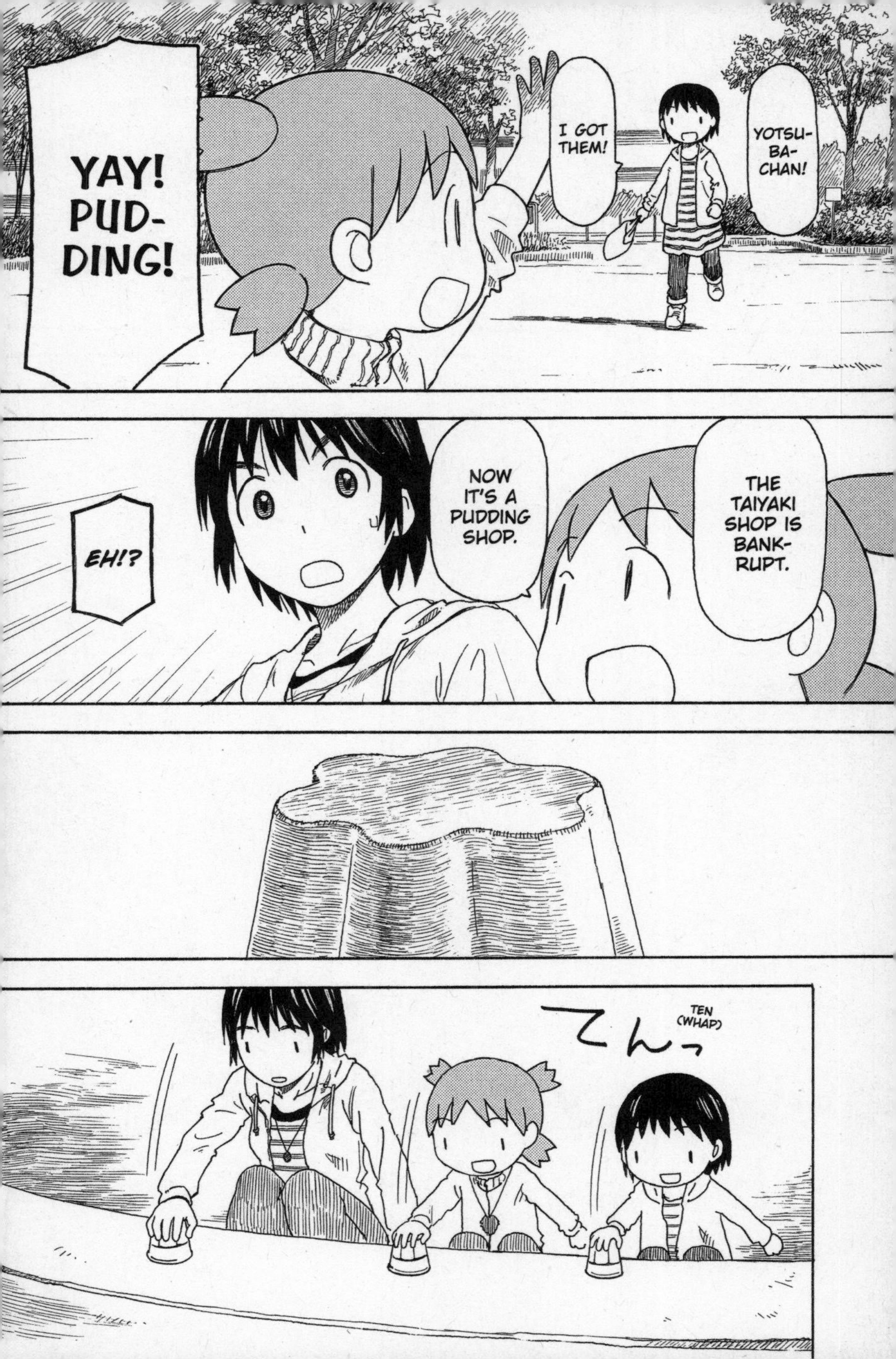
YOTSU-BA-CHAN!
I GOT THEM!
YAY! PUD-DING!
THE TAIYAKI SHOP IS BANK-RUPT.
NOW IT'S A PUDDING SHOP.
EH!?
てんっ
TEN (WHAP)

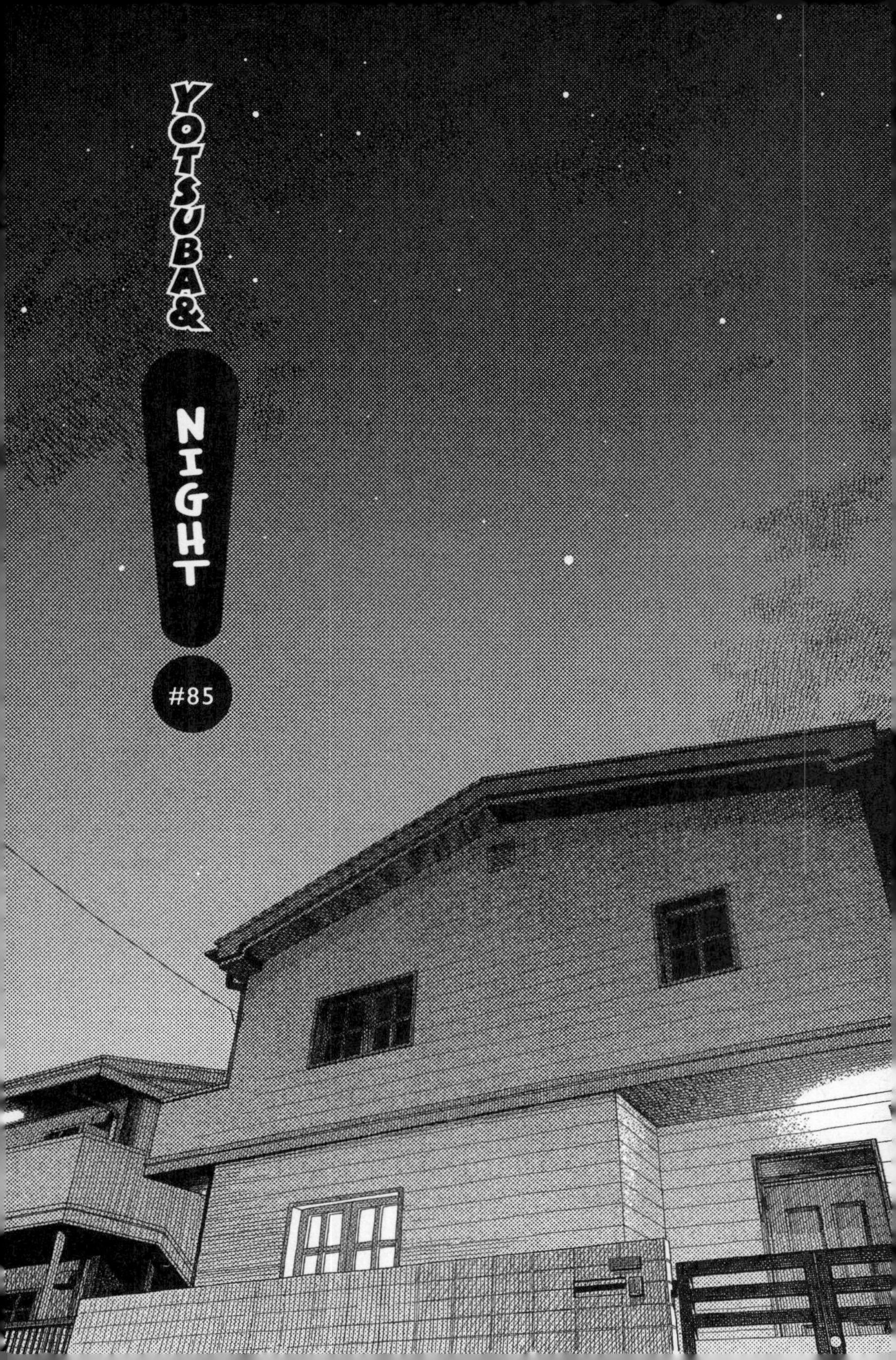
YOTSUBA&
NIGHT
#85

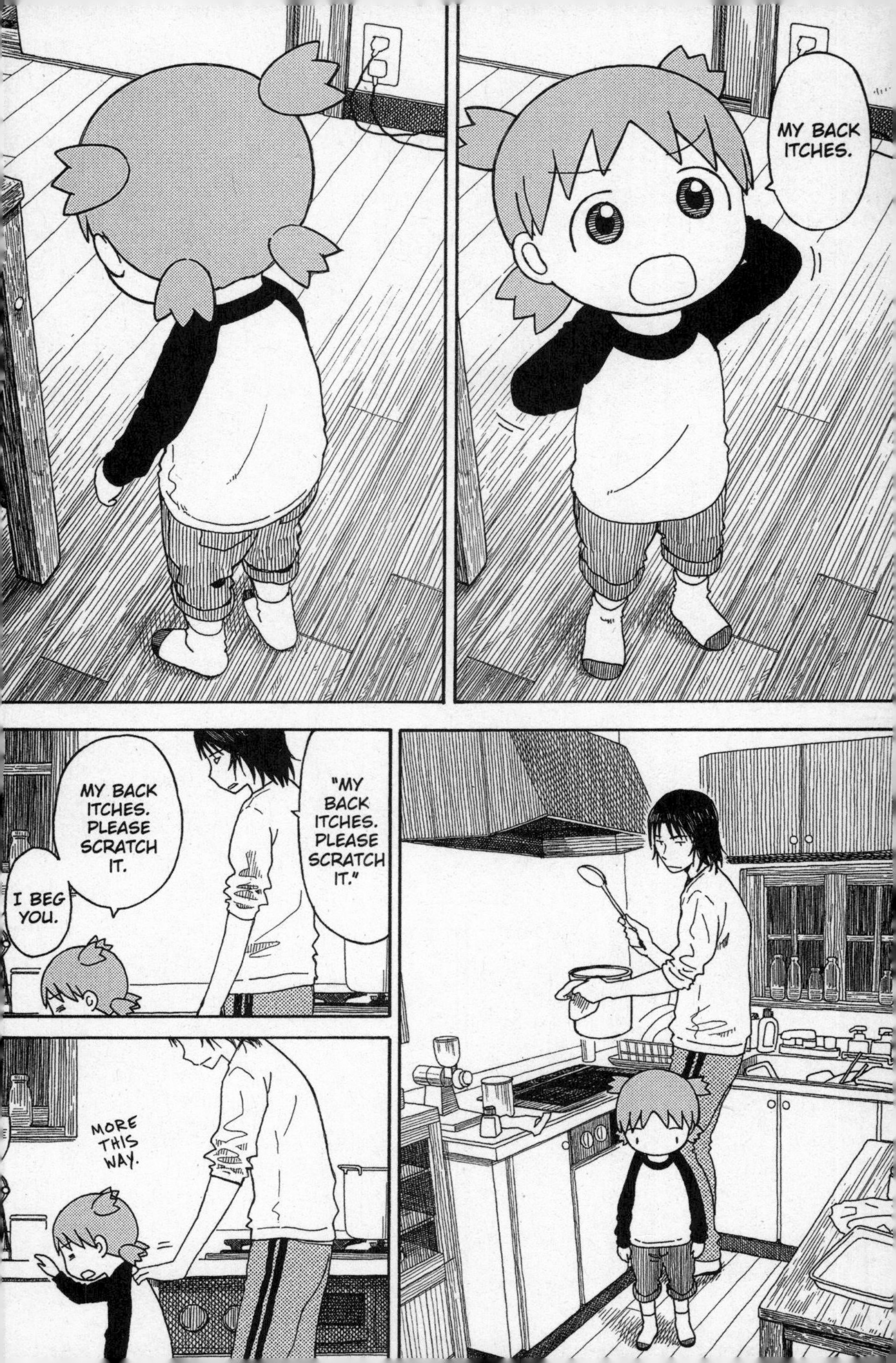
MY BACK ITCHES.
"MY BACK ITCHES. PLEASE SCRATCH IT."
MY BACK ITCHES. PLEASE SCRATCH IT.
I BEG YOU.
MORE THIS WAY.

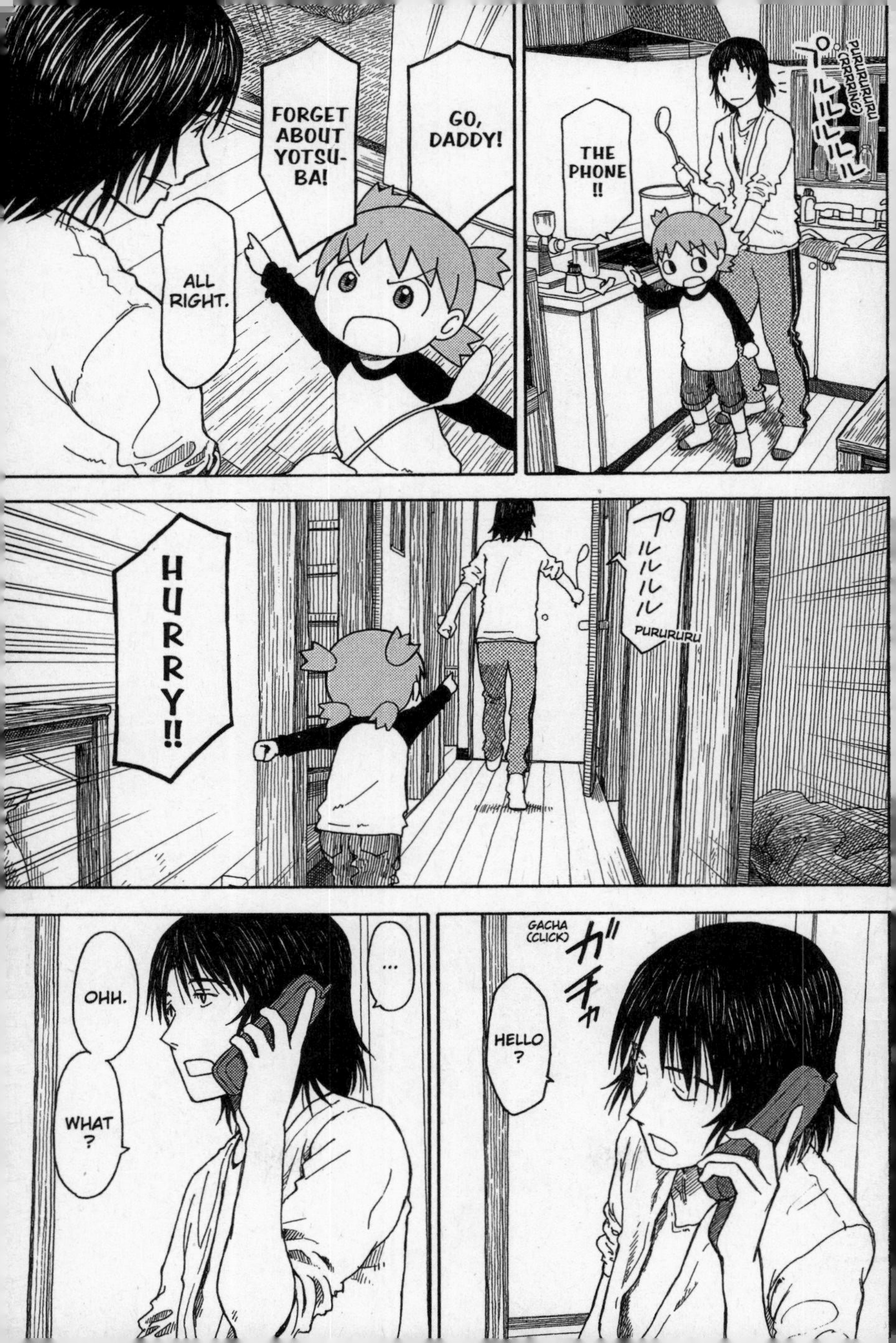
プルルルルル
PURURURURU (RRRRING)
THE PHONE !!
GO, DADDY!
FORGET ABOUT YOTSU-BA!
ALL RIGHT.
プルルルル
PURURURU
HURRY!!
GACHA (CLICK)
ガチャ
HELLO ?
...
OHH.
WHAT ?

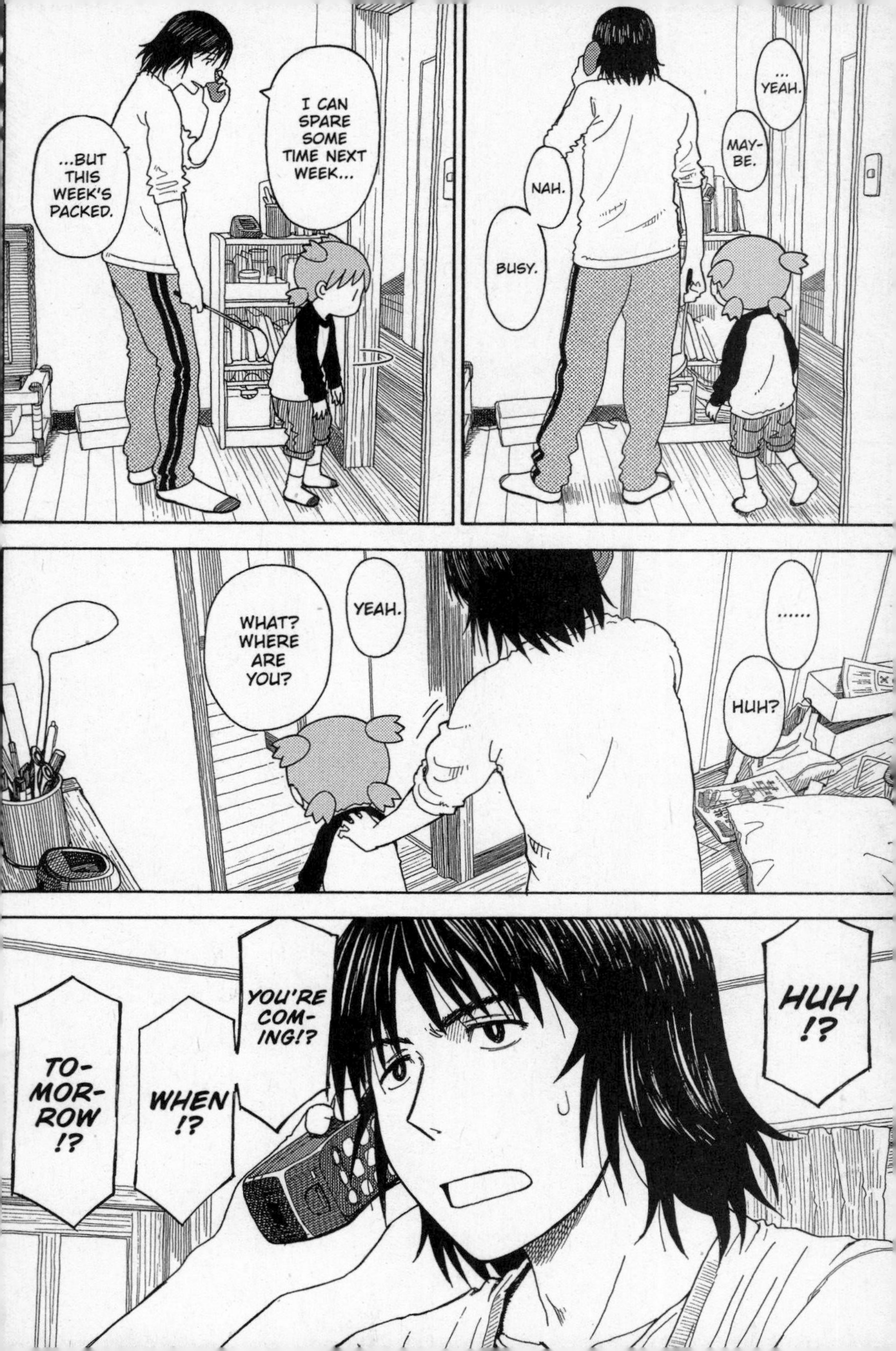

... YEAH.
MAY-BE.
NAH.
BUSY.
I CAN SPARE SOME TIME NEXT WEEK...
...BUT THIS WEEK'S PACKED.
......
HUH?
YEAH.
WHAT? WHERE ARE YOU?
HUH!?
YOU'RE COM-ING!?
WHEN!?
TO-MOR-ROW!?

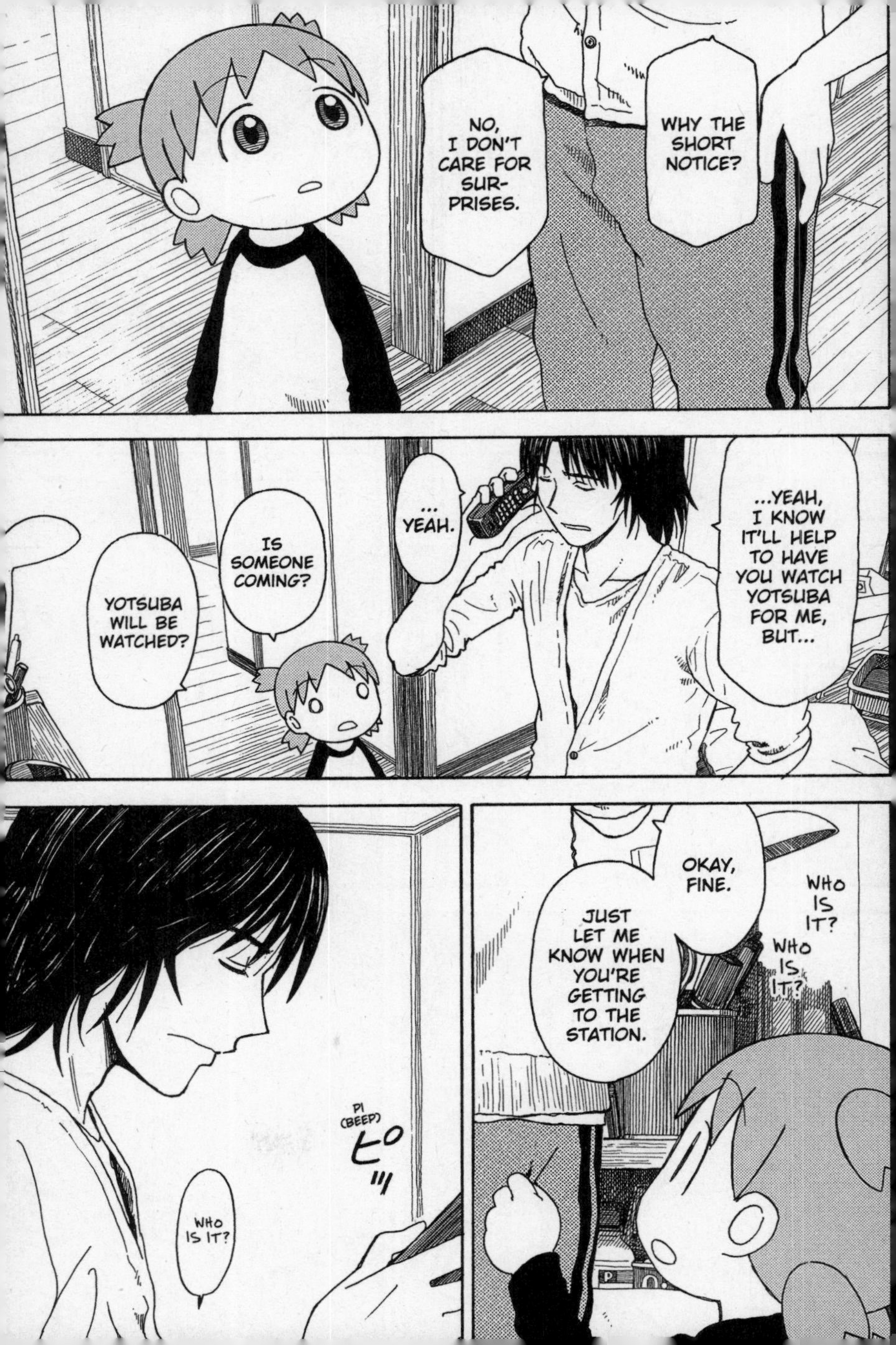
WHY THE SHORT NOTICE?
NO, I DON'T CARE FOR SUR-PRISES.
...YEAH, I KNOW IT'LL HELP TO HAVE YOU WATCH YOTSUBA FOR ME, BUT...
... YEAH.
IS SOMEONE COMING?
YOTSUBA WILL BE WATCHED?
OKAY, FINE.
JUST LET ME KNOW WHEN YOU'RE GETTING TO THE STATION.
WHO IS IT?
WHO IS IT?
PI (BEEP)
ピッ
WHO IS IT?

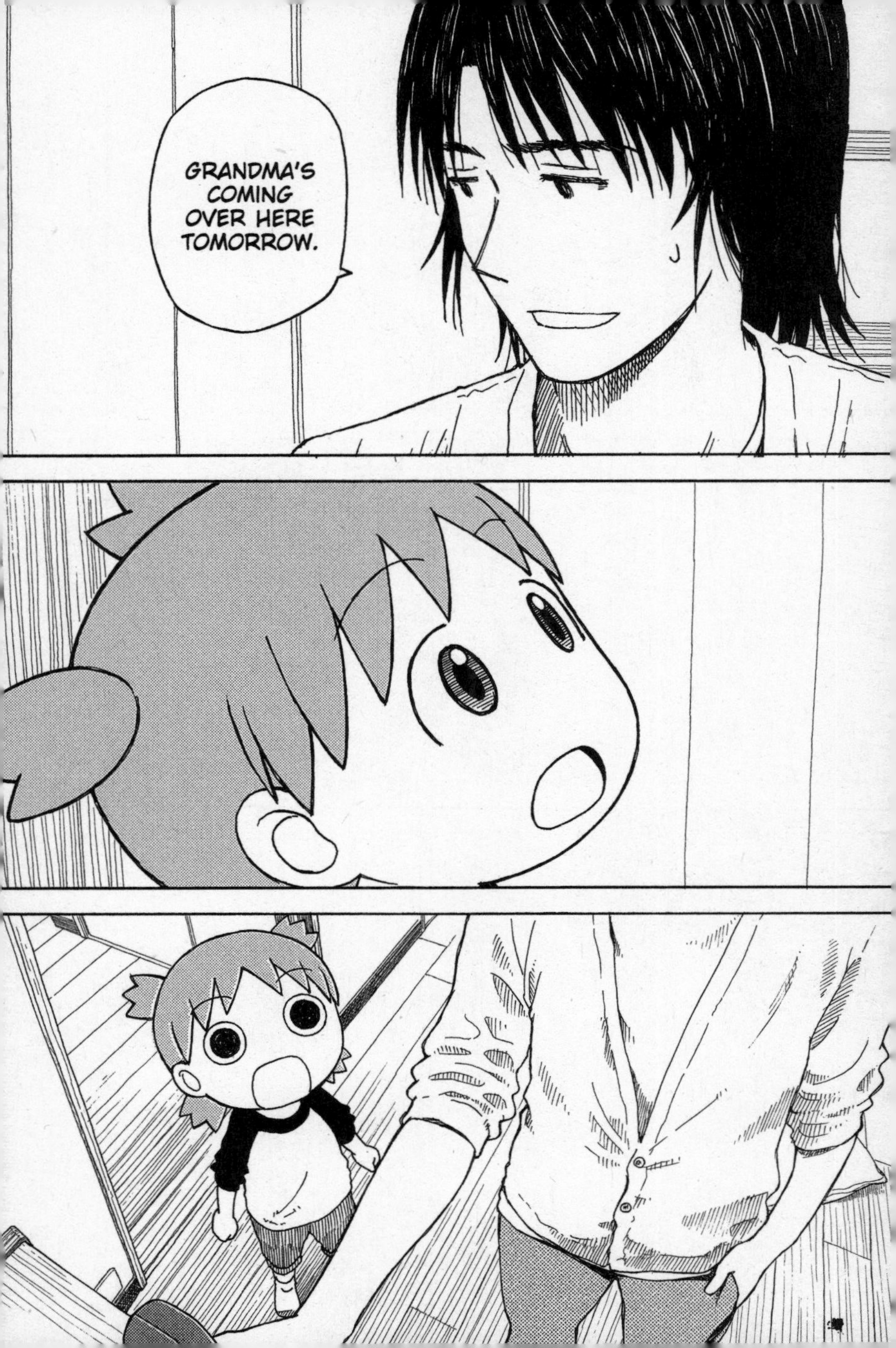
GRANDMA'S COMING OVER HERE TOMORROW.

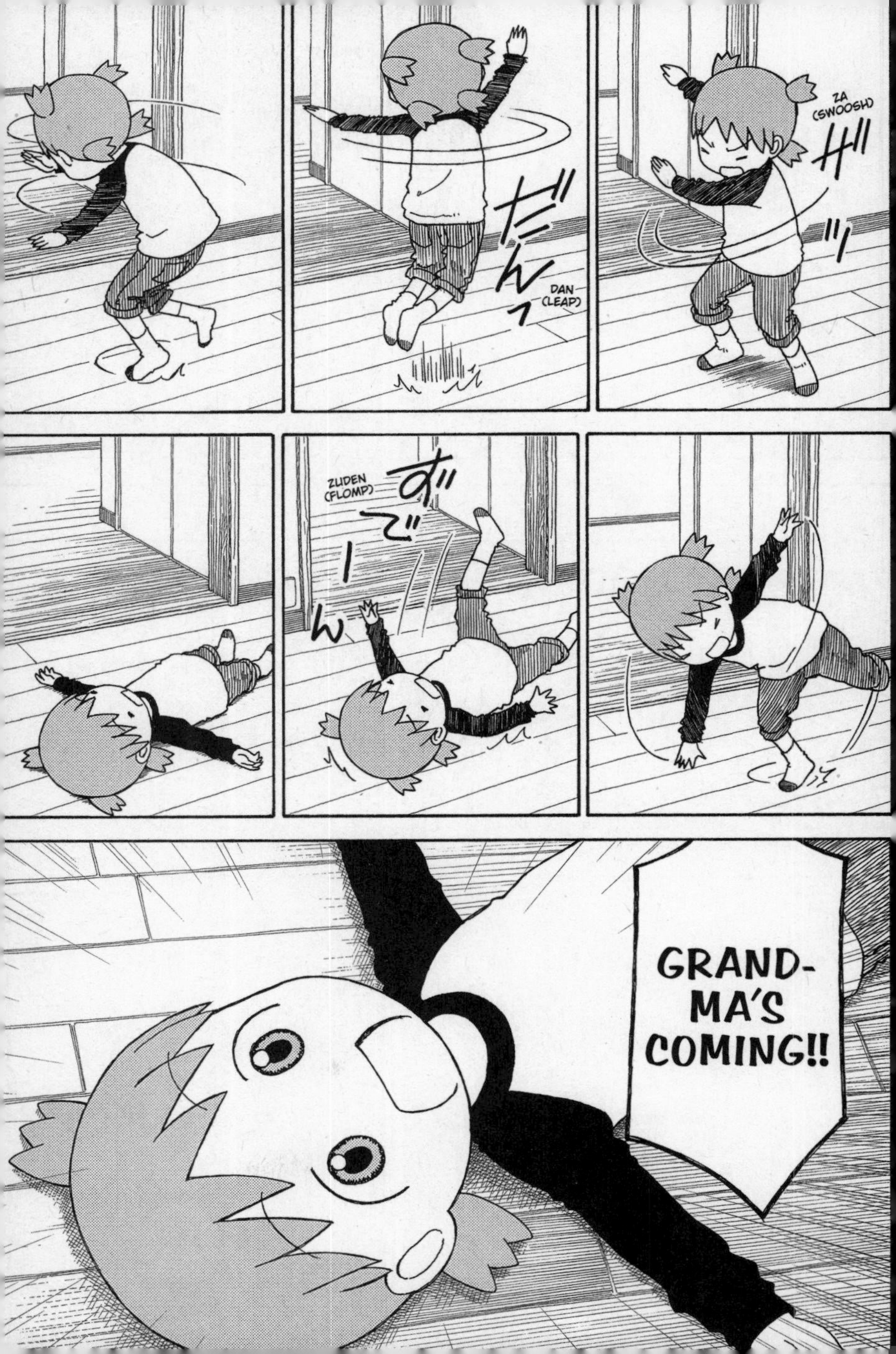
ザッ
ZA (SWOOSH)
だんっ
DAN (LEAP)
ずでーん
ZUDEN (FLOMP)
GRAND-MA'S COMING!!

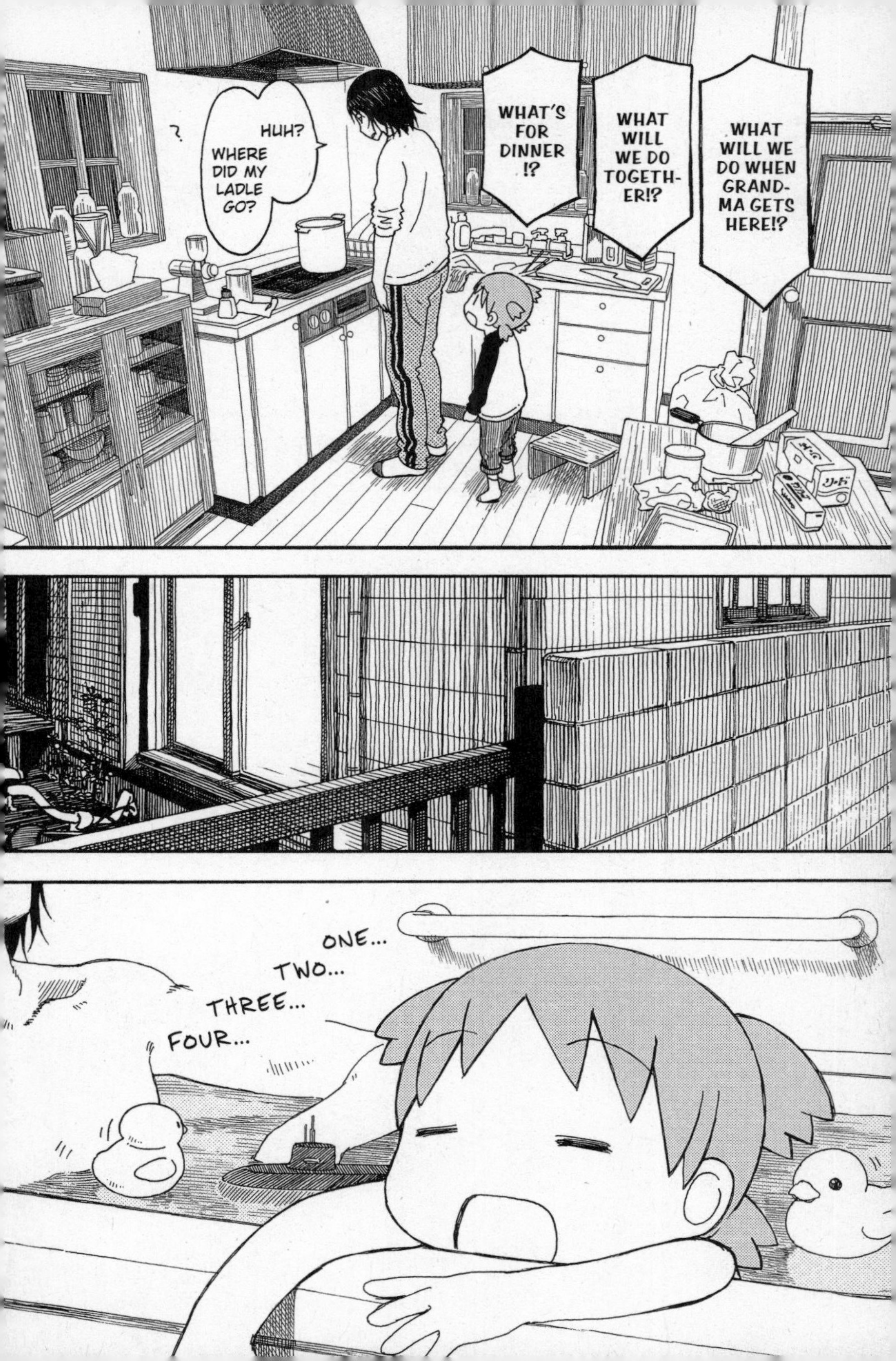
WHAT WILL WE DO WHEN GRAND-MA GETS HERE!?
WHAT WILL WE DO TOGETH-ER!?
WHAT'S FOR DINNER !?
HUH? WHERE DID MY LADLE GO?
?
ONE...
TWO...
THREE...
FOUR...

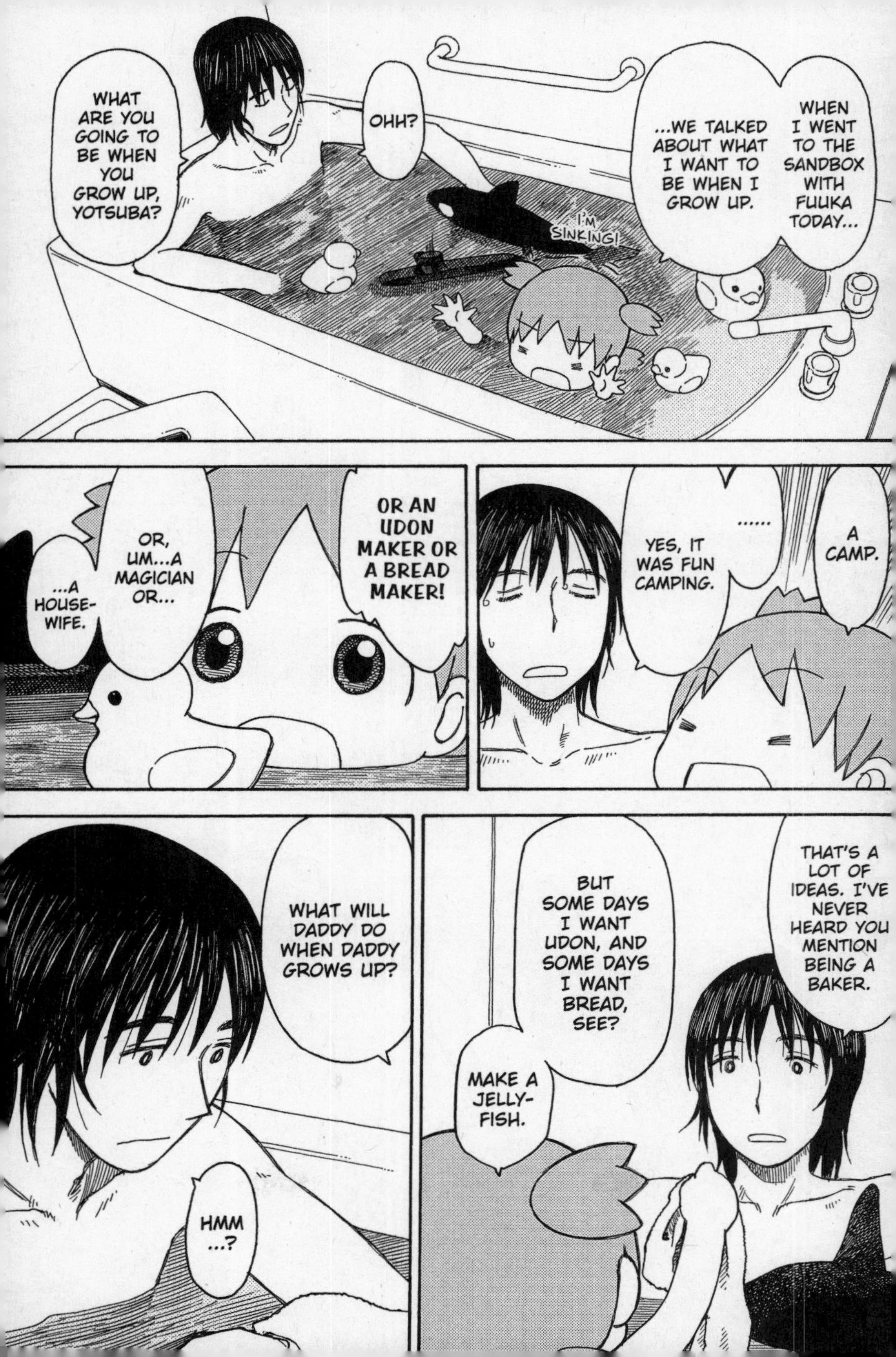
WHEN I WENT TO THE SANDBOX WITH FUUKA TODAY...
...WE TALKED ABOUT WHAT I WANT TO BE WHEN I GROW UP.
OHH?
WHAT ARE YOU GOING TO BE WHEN YOU GROW UP, YOTSUBA?
I'M SINKING!
A CAMP.
......
YES, IT WAS FUN CAMPING.
OR AN UDON MAKER OR A BREAD MAKER!
OR, UM...A MAGICIAN OR...
...A HOUSE-WIFE.
THAT'S A LOT OF IDEAS. I'VE NEVER HEARD YOU MENTION BEING A BAKER.
BUT SOME DAYS I WANT UDON, AND SOME DAYS I WANT BREAD, SEE?
MAKE A JELLY-FISH.
WHAT WILL DADDY DO WHEN DADDY GROWS UP?
HMM ...?

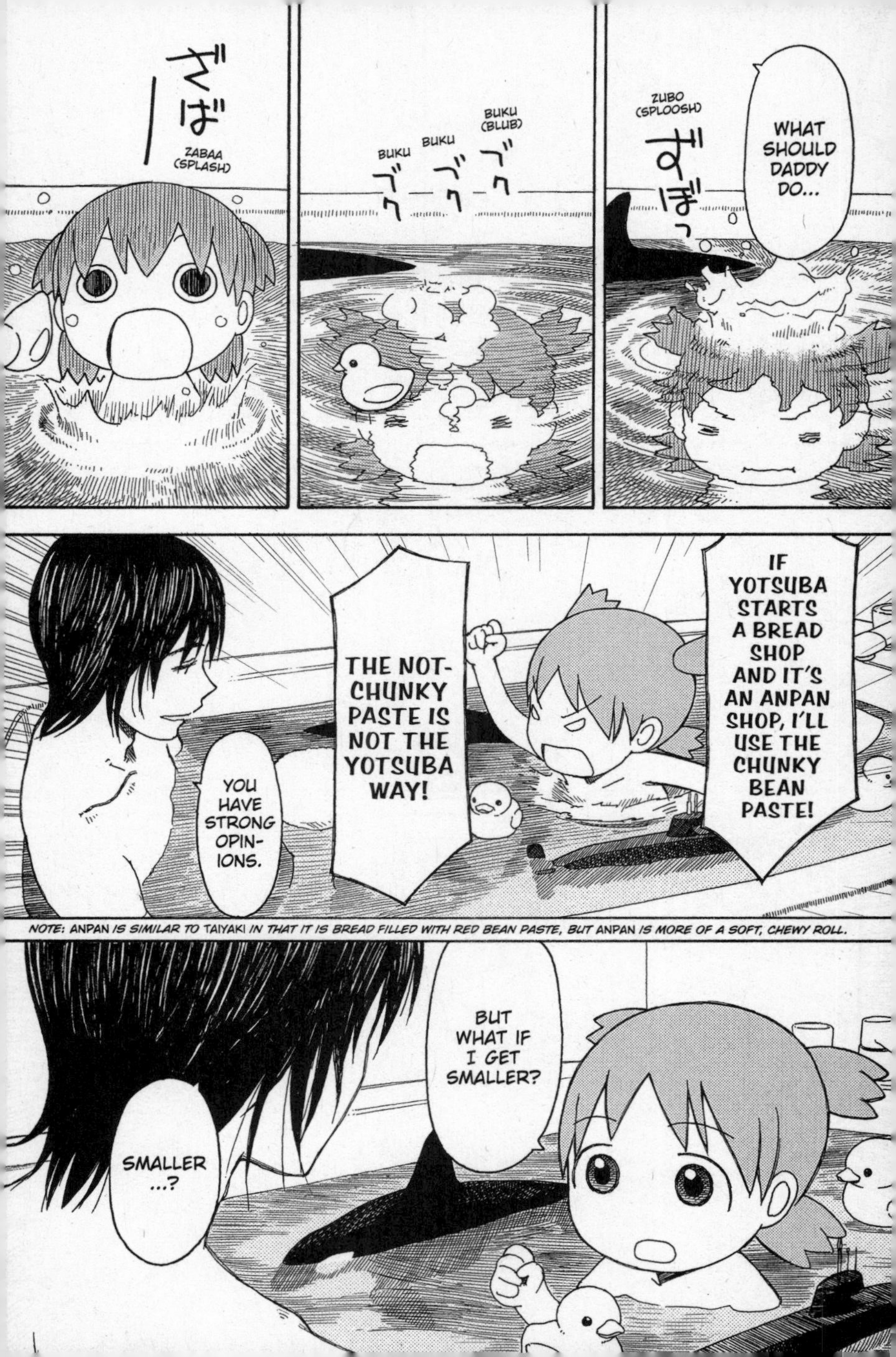
WHAT SHOULD DADDY DO...
ずぼっ
ZUBO (SPLOOSH)
ブク
BUKU (BLUB)
ブク
BUKU
ブク
BUKU
ざばー
ZABAA (SPLASH)
IF YOTSUBA STARTS A BREAD SHOP AND IT'S AN ANPAN SHOP, I'LL USE THE CHUNKY BEAN PASTE!
THE NOT-CHUNKY PASTE IS NOT THE YOTSUBA WAY!
YOU HAVE STRONG OPIN-IONS.
NOTE: ANPAN IS SIMILAR TO TAIYAKI IN THAT IT IS BREAD FILLED WITH RED BEAN PASTE, BUT ANPAN IS MORE OF A SOFT, CHEWY ROLL.
BUT WHAT IF I GET SMALLER?
SMALLER ...?

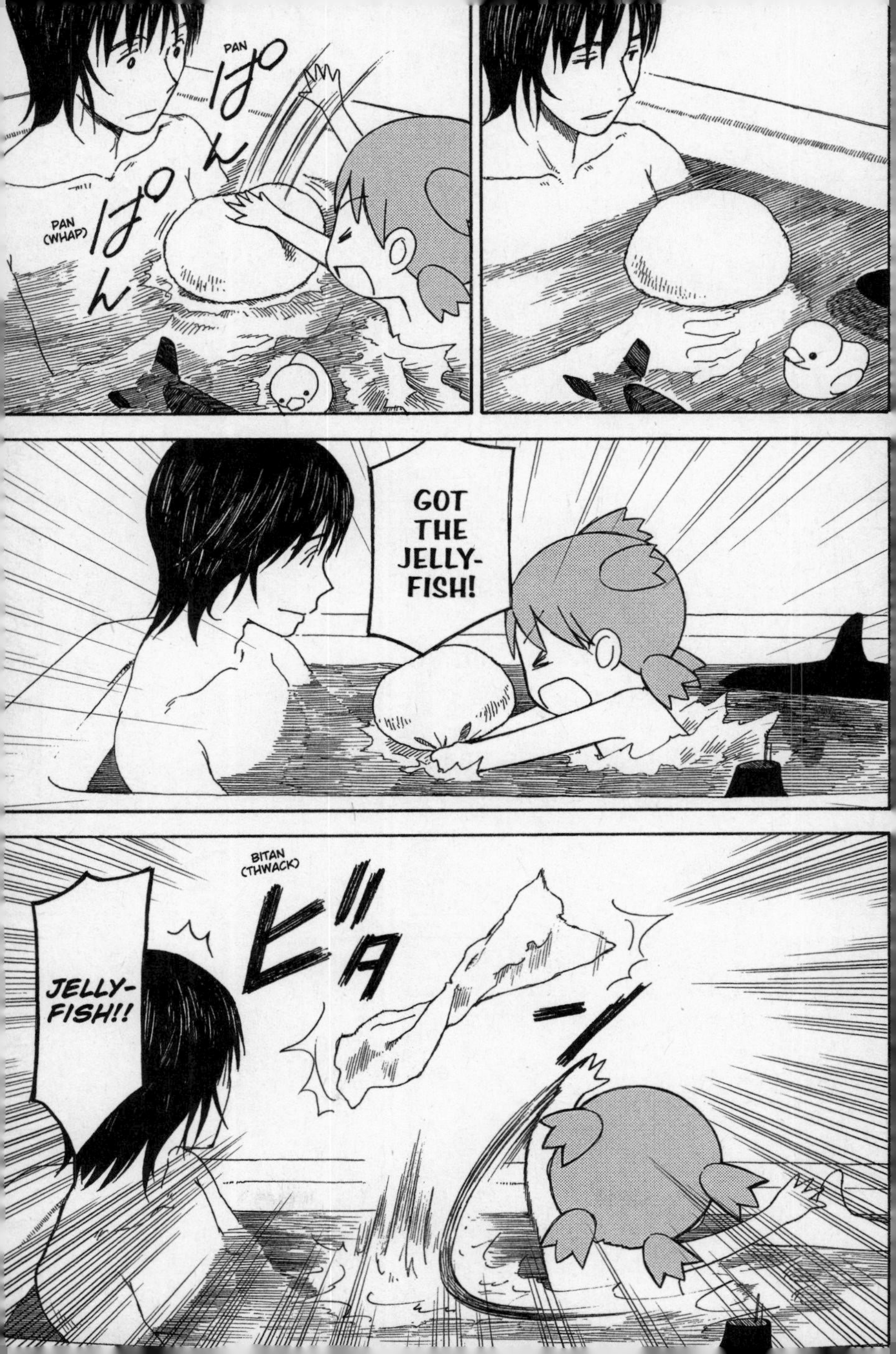
PAN
ぱん
PAN (WHAP)
ぱん
GOT THE JELLY-FISH!
BITAN (THWACK)
ビタン
JELLY-FISH!!

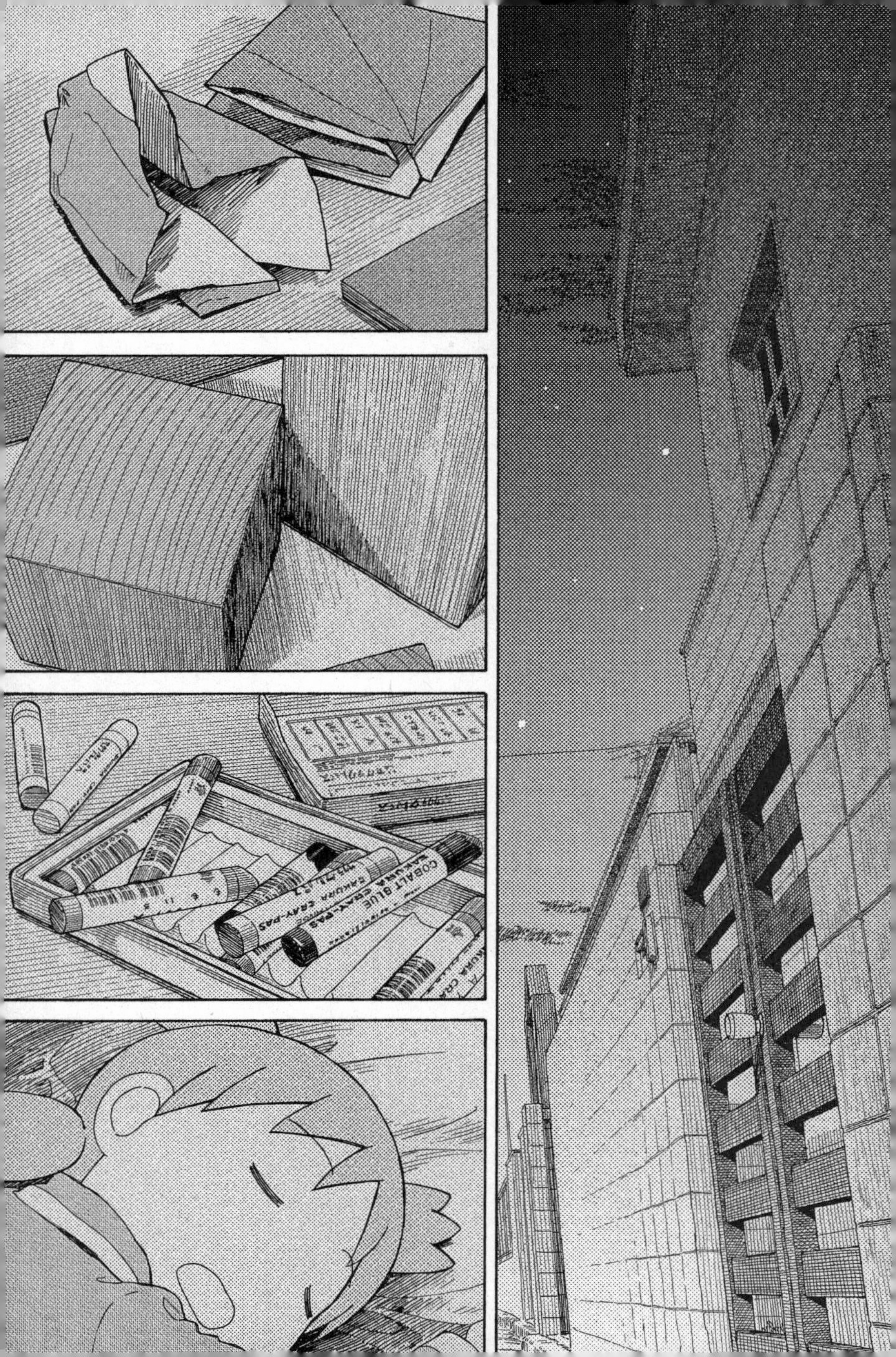
COBALT BLUE
SAKURA CRAY-PAS
SAKURA CRAY-PAS

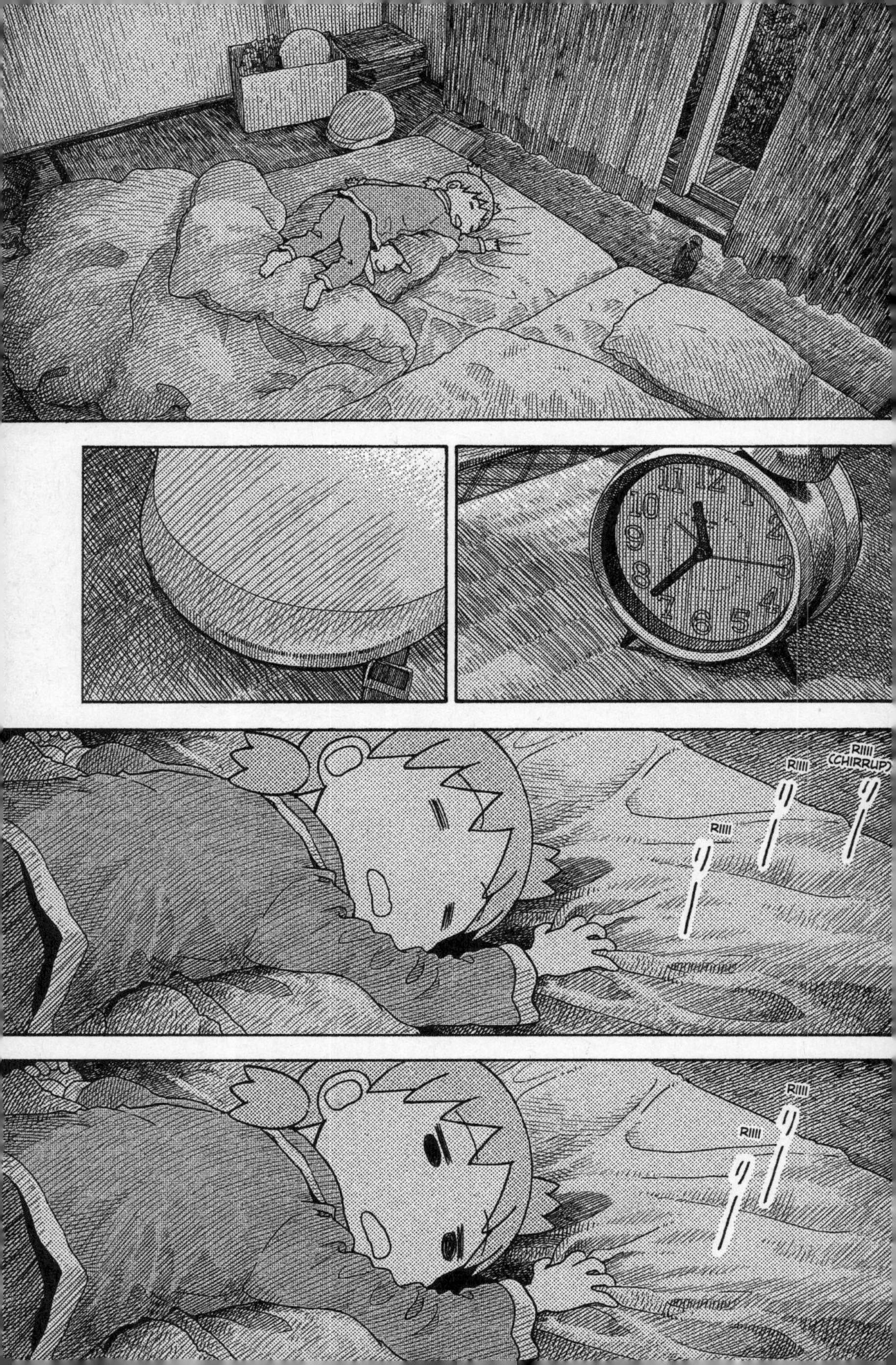
RIIII (CHIRRUP)
RIIII
RIIII
RIIII
RIIII

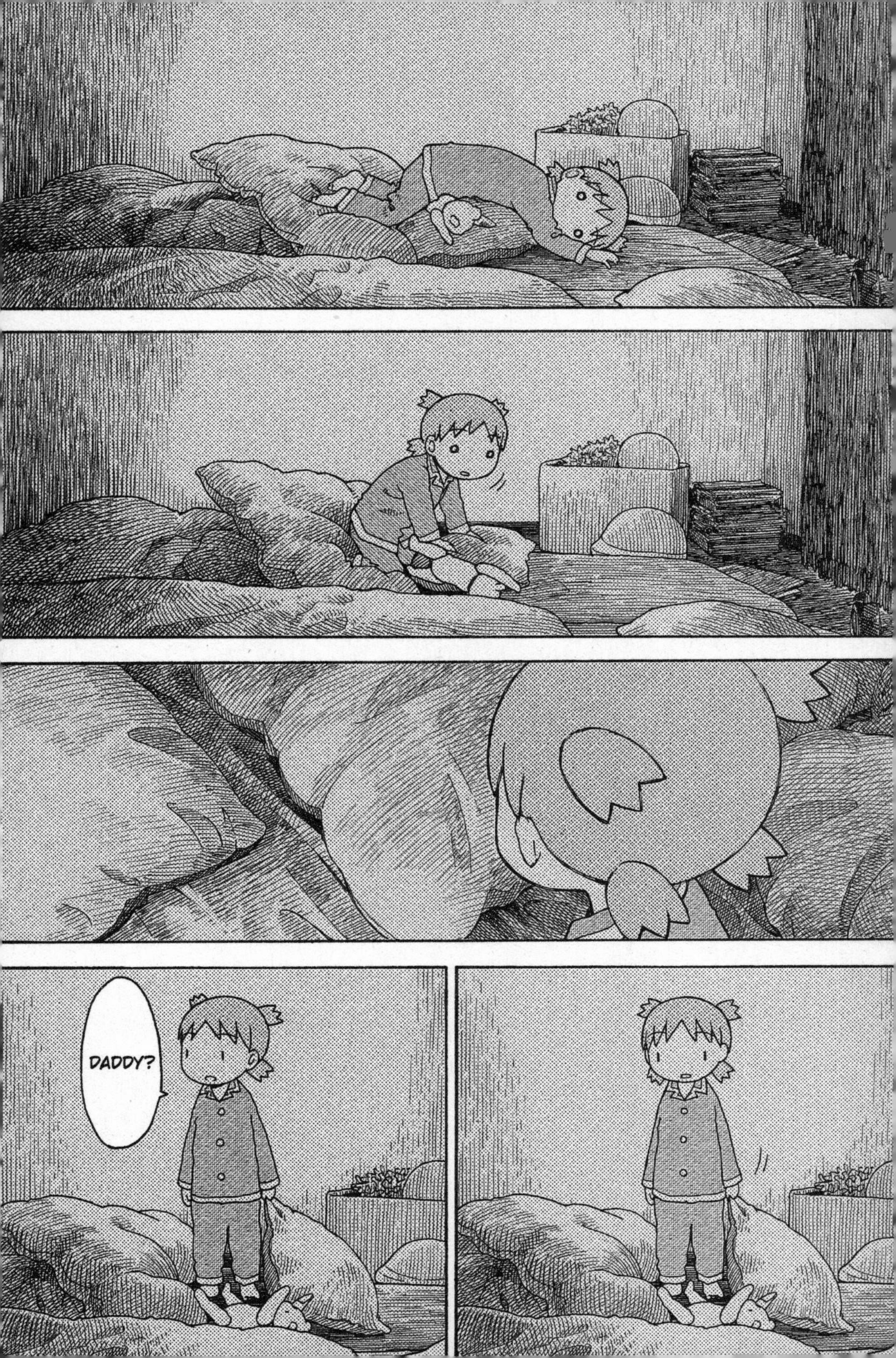
DADDY?

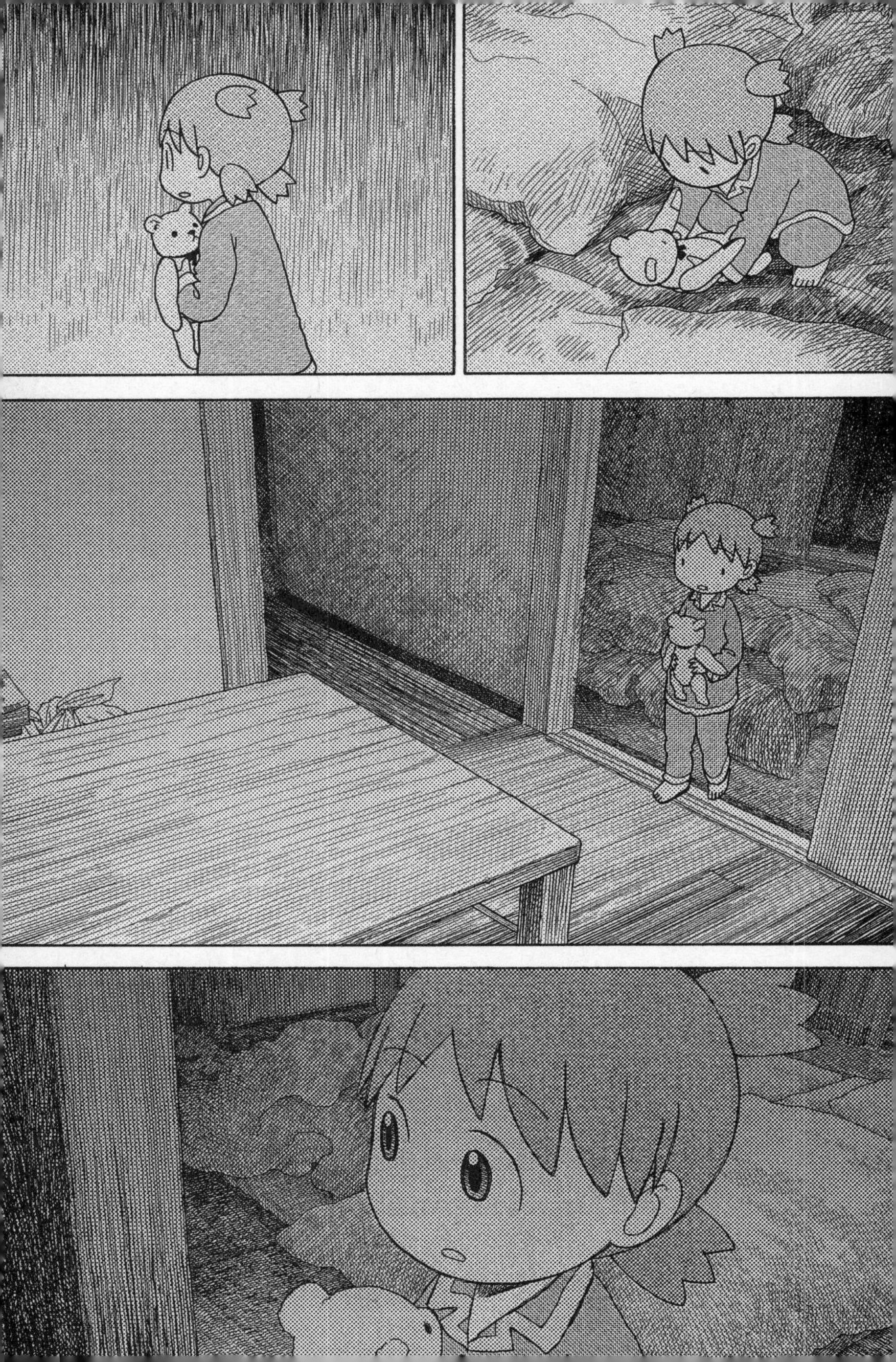

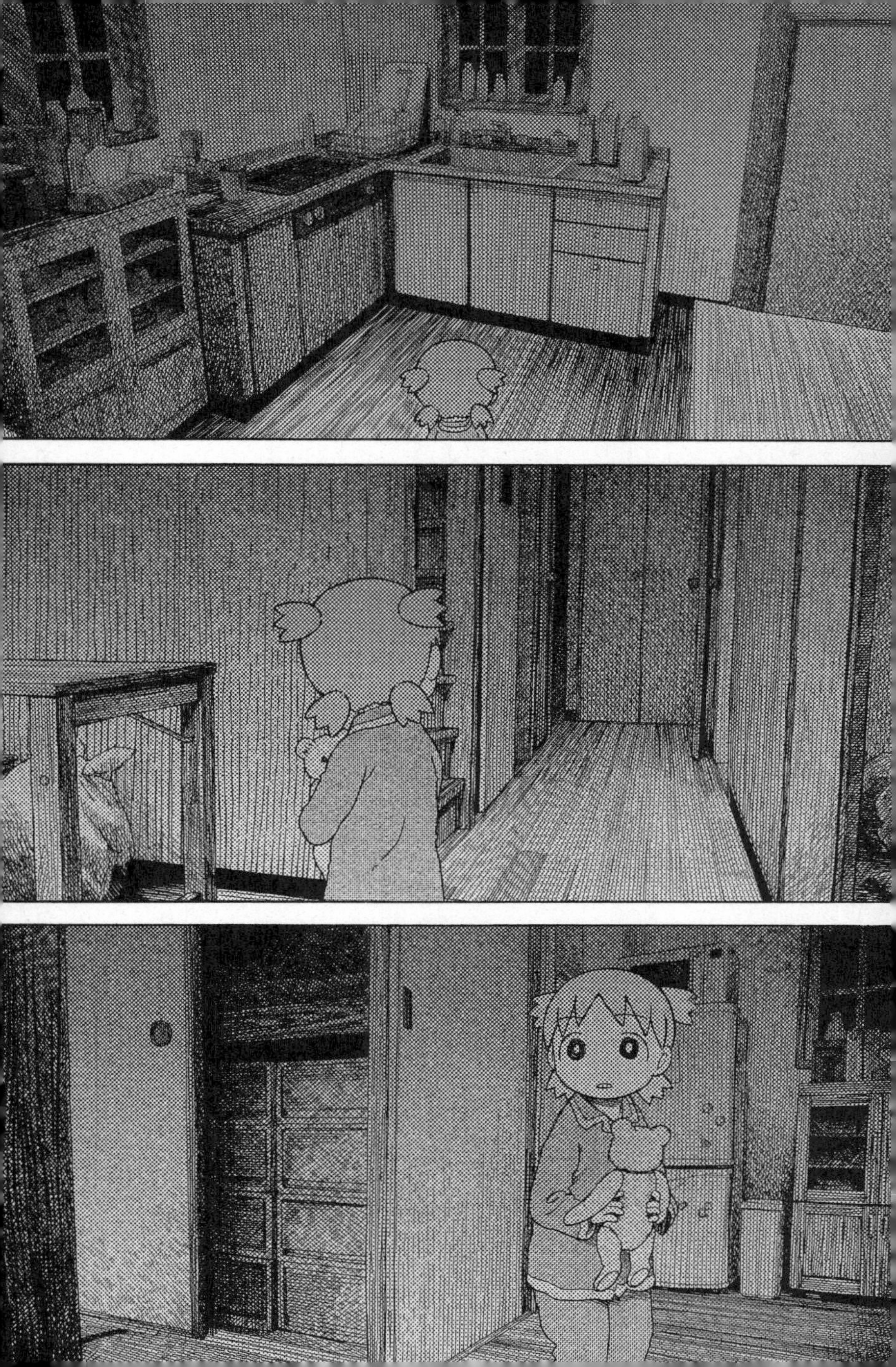

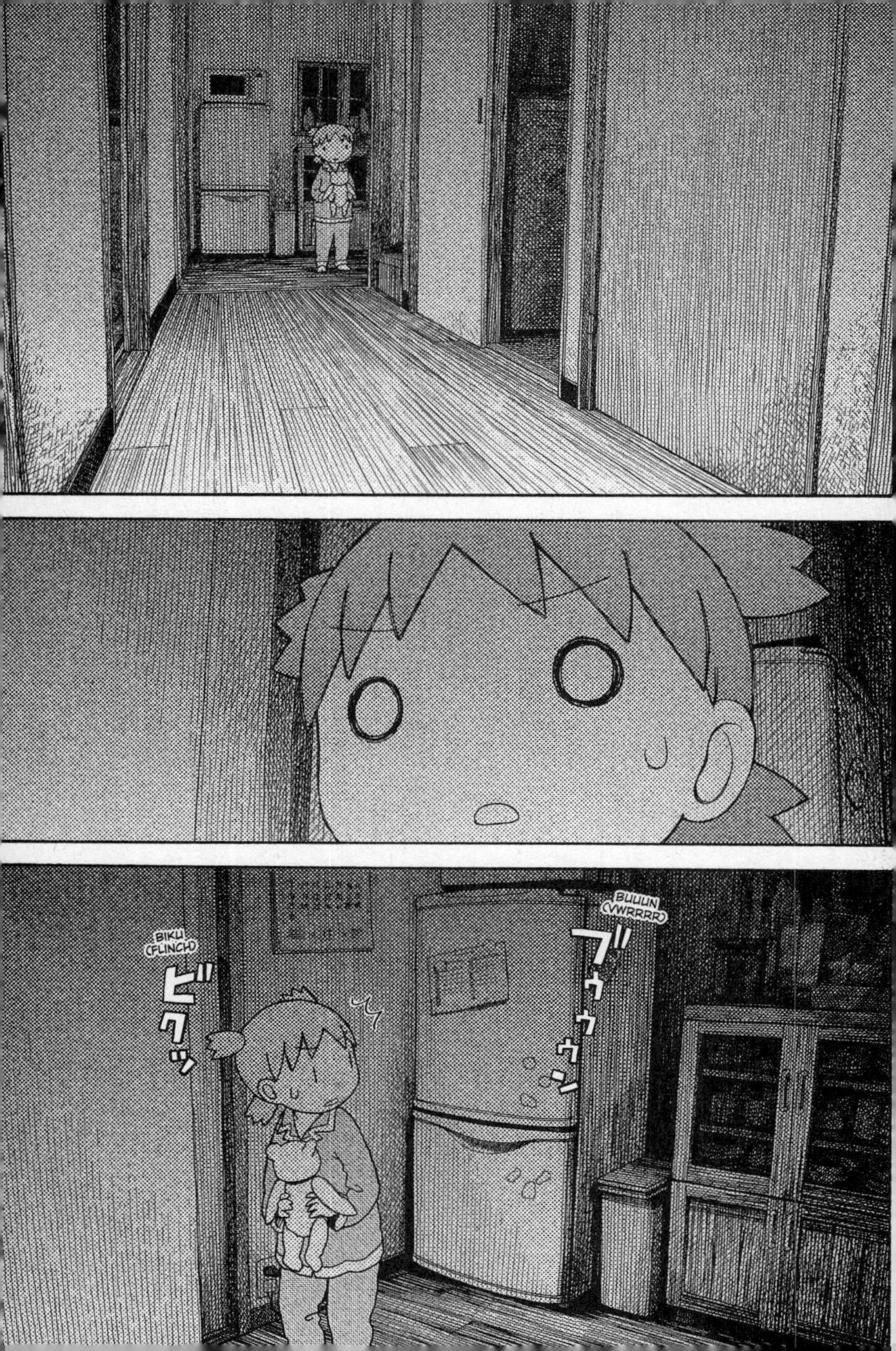
BUUUN (VWRRRR)
ブウゥウン
BIKU (FLINCH)
ビクッ

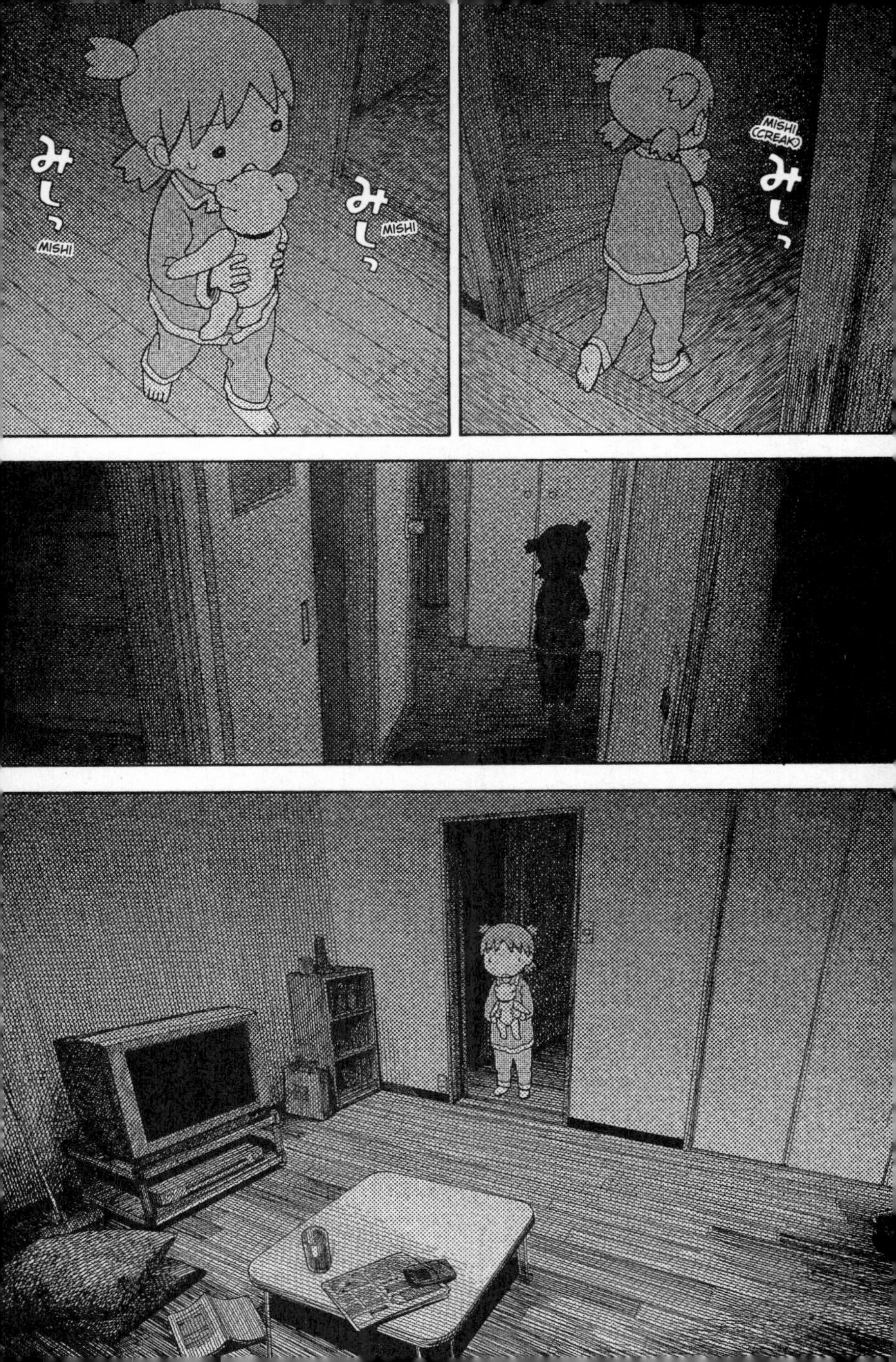
MISHI
(CREAK)
みしっ
みしっ
MISHI
みしっ
MISHI

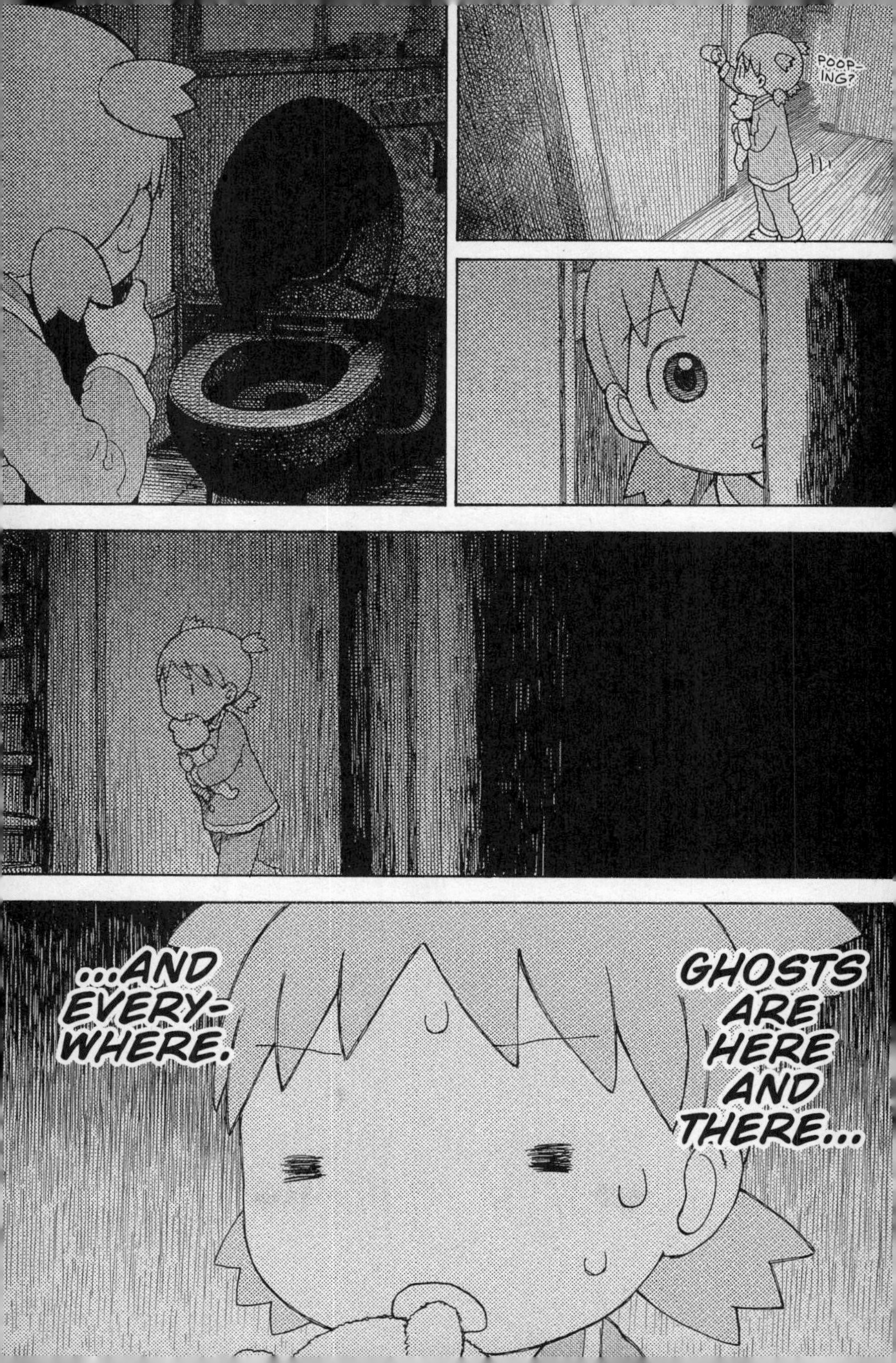
POOP-ING?
GHOSTS ARE HERE AND THERE...
...AND EVERY-WHERE.

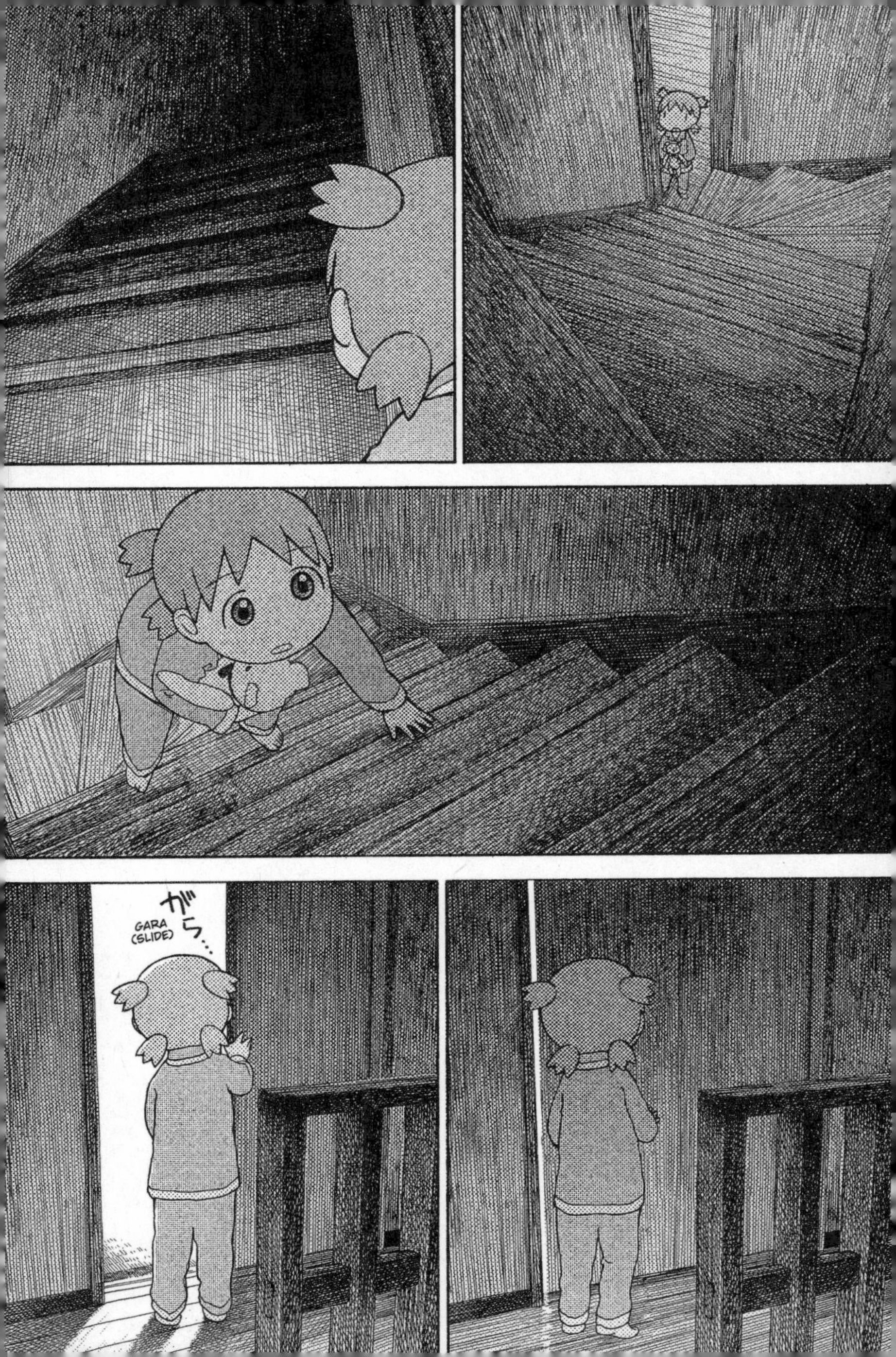
がら…
GARA (SLIDE)

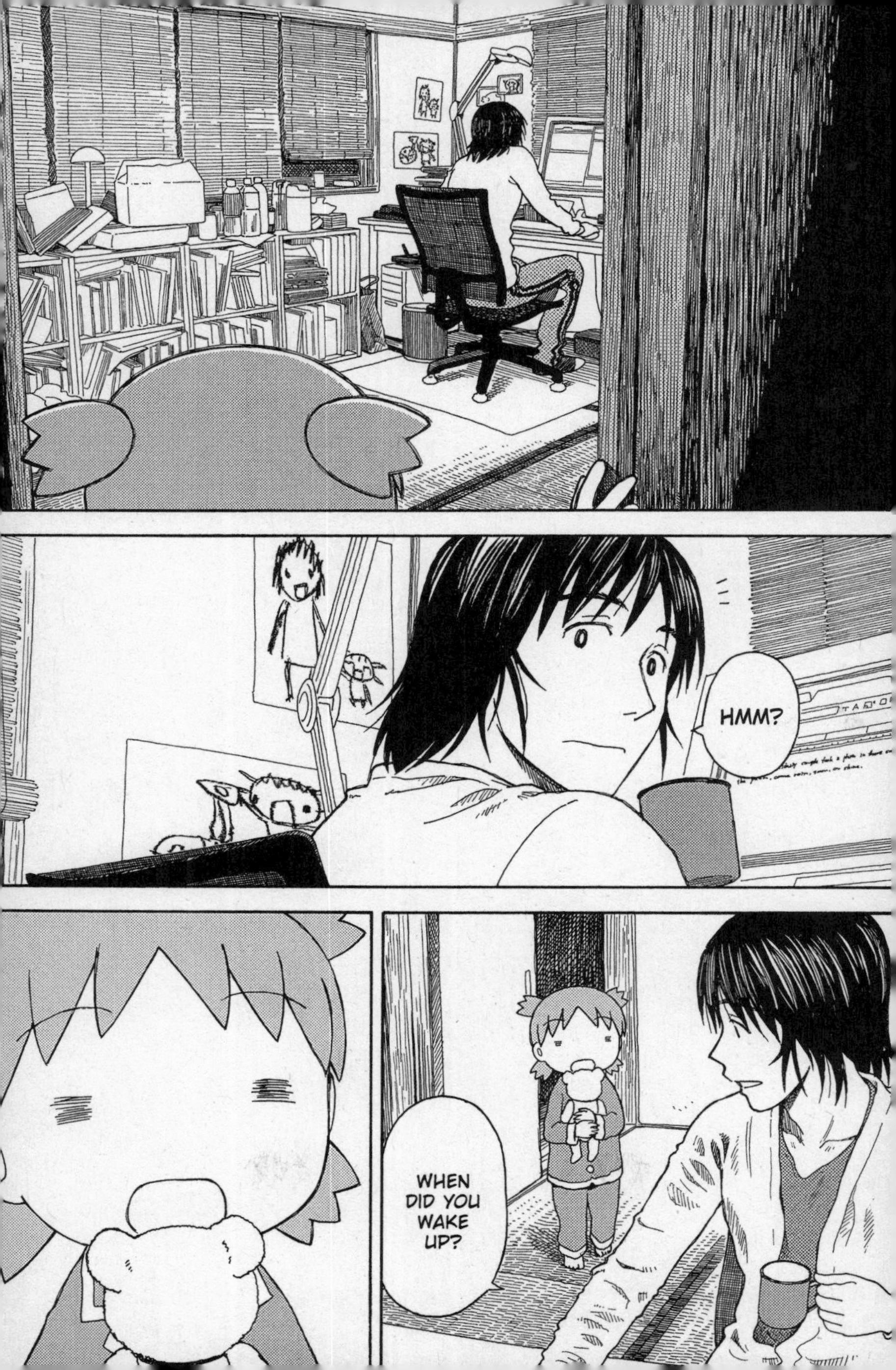
HMM?
WHEN DID YOU WAKE UP?

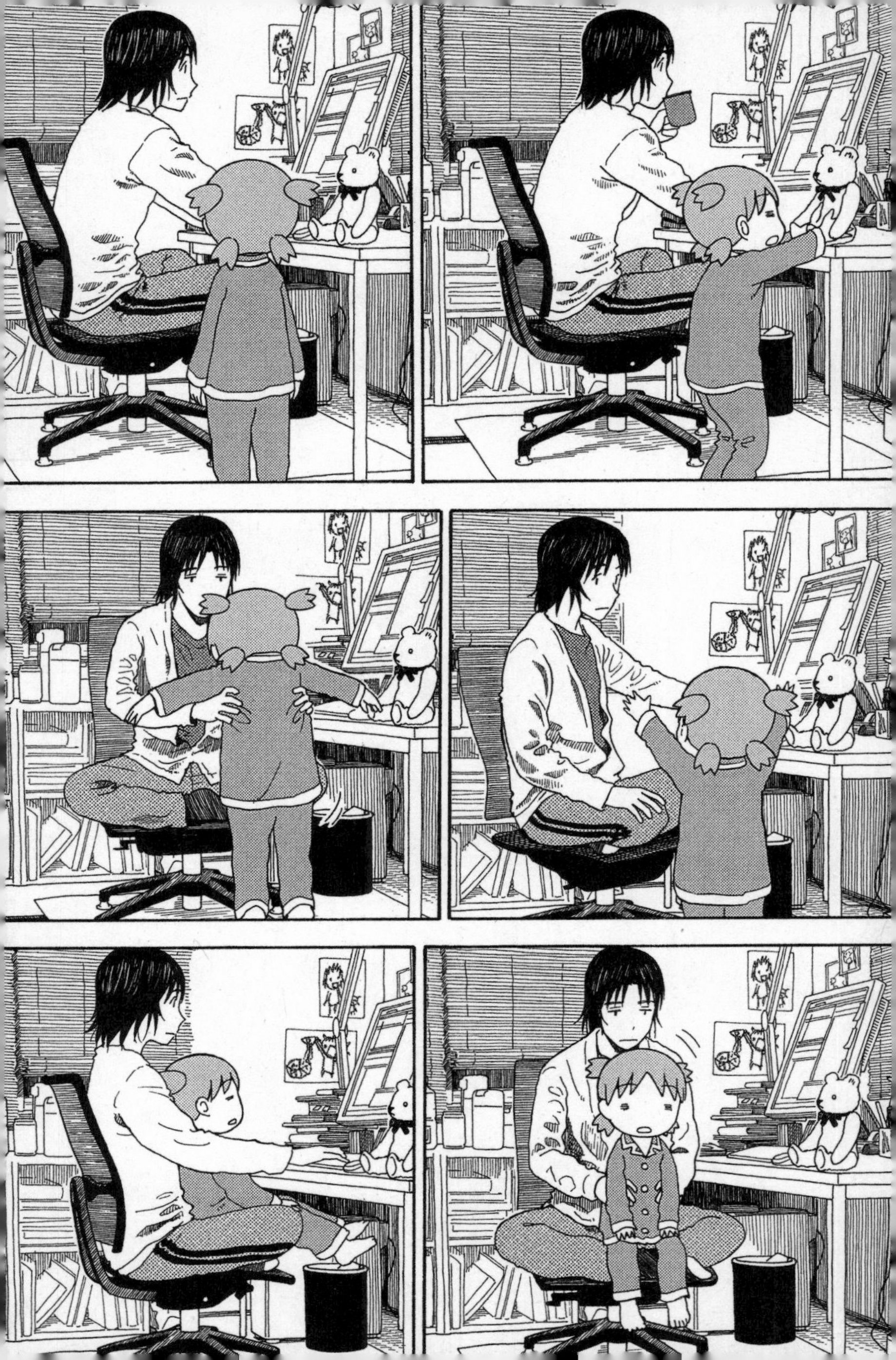

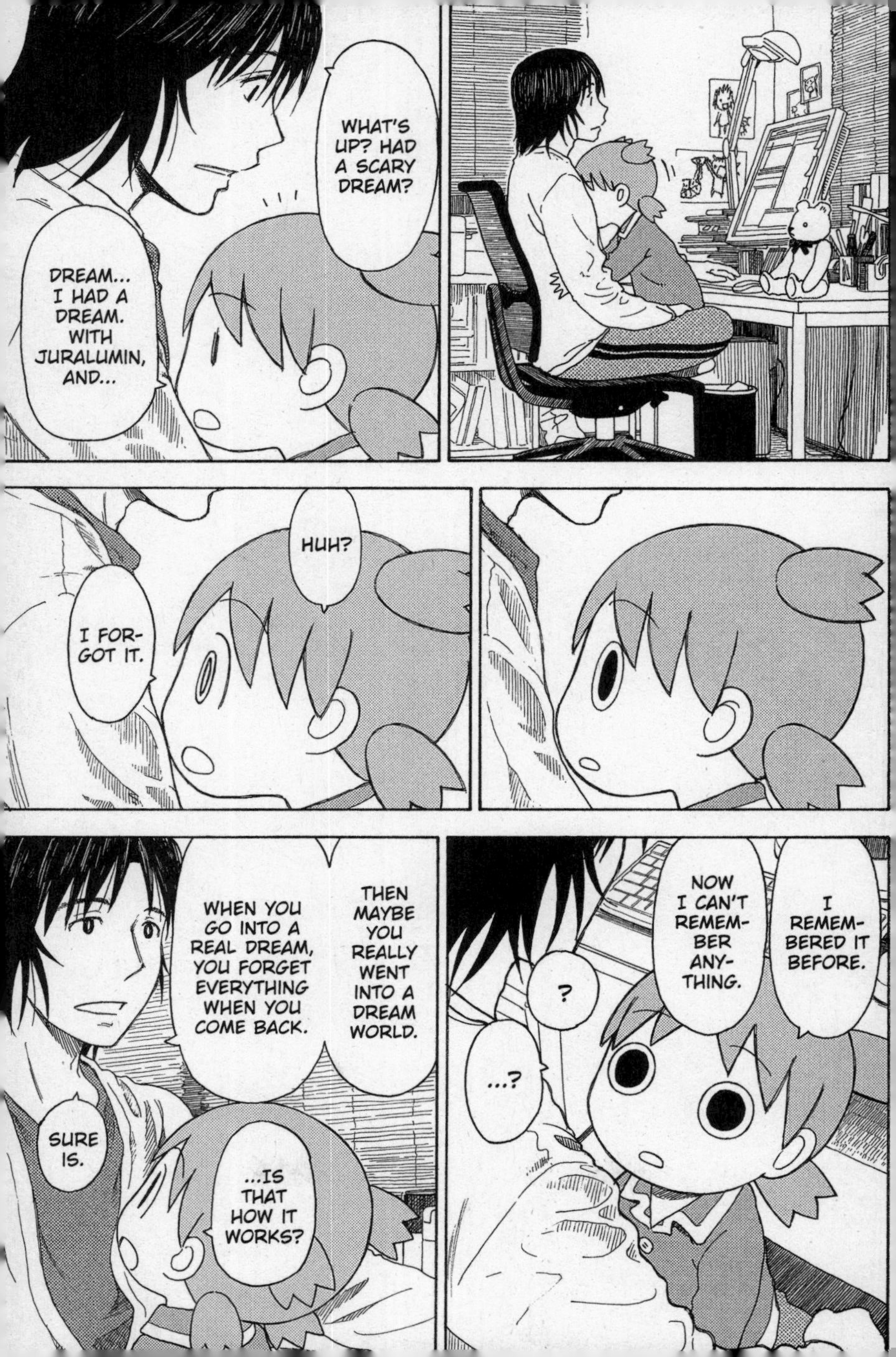
WHAT'S UP? HAD A SCARY DREAM?
DREAM... I HAD A DREAM. WITH JURALUMIN, AND...
HUH?
I FORGOT IT.
I REMEMBERED IT BEFORE.
NOW I CAN'T REMEMBER ANYTHING.
?
...?
THEN MAYBE YOU REALLY WENT INTO A DREAM WORLD.
WHEN YOU GO INTO A REAL DREAM, YOU FORGET EVERYTHING WHEN YOU COME BACK.
...IS THAT HOW IT WORKS?
SURE IS.

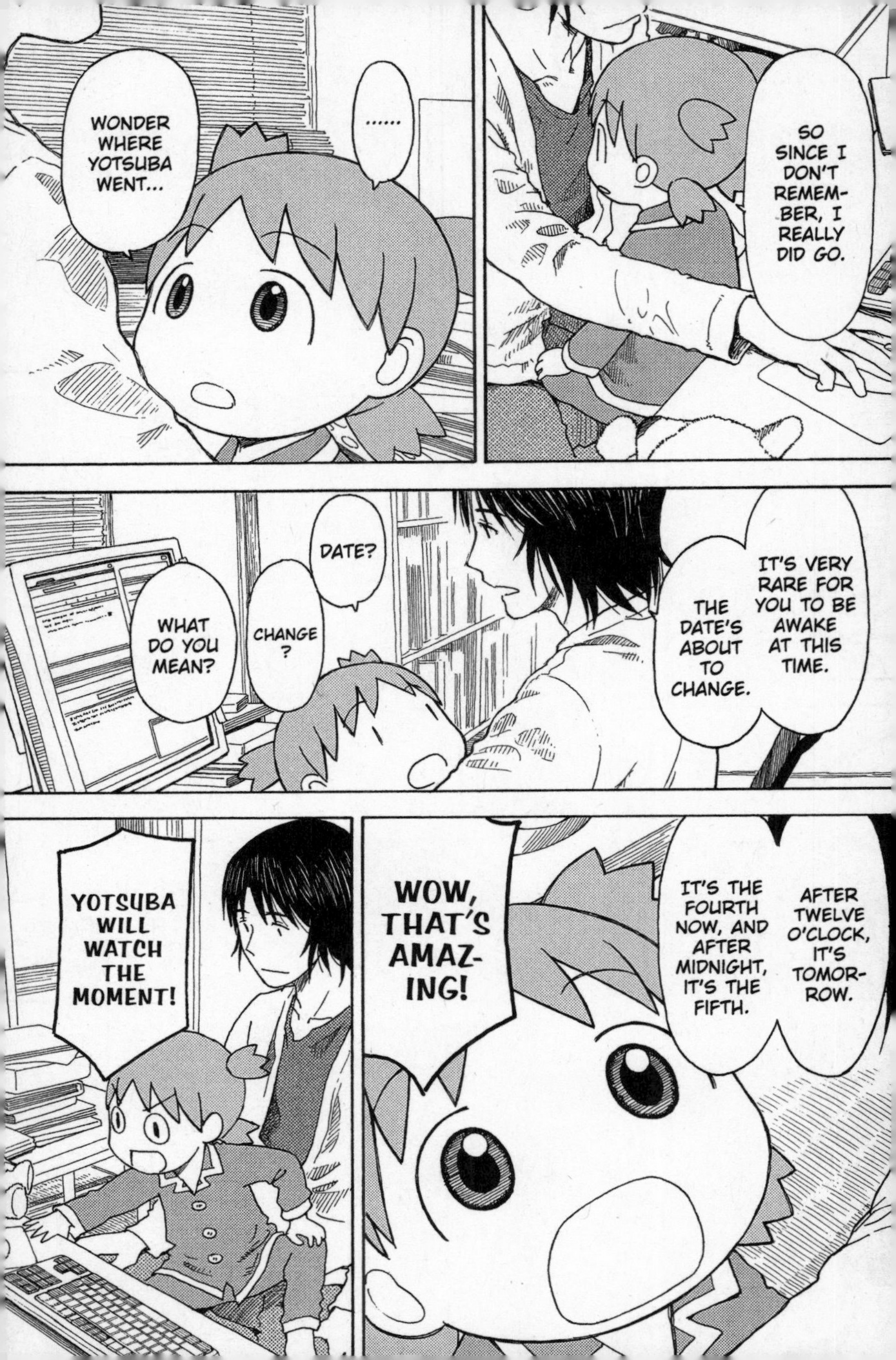
SO SINCE I DON'T REMEMBER, I REALLY DID GO.
......
WONDER WHERE YOTSUBA WENT...
IT'S VERY RARE FOR YOU TO BE AWAKE AT THIS TIME.
THE DATE'S ABOUT TO CHANGE.
DATE?
CHANGE?
WHAT DO YOU MEAN?
AFTER TWELVE O'CLOCK, IT'S TOMORROW.
IT'S THE FOURTH NOW, AND AFTER MIDNIGHT, IT'S THE FIFTH.
WOW, THAT'S AMAZING!
YOTSUBA WILL WATCH THE MOMENT!

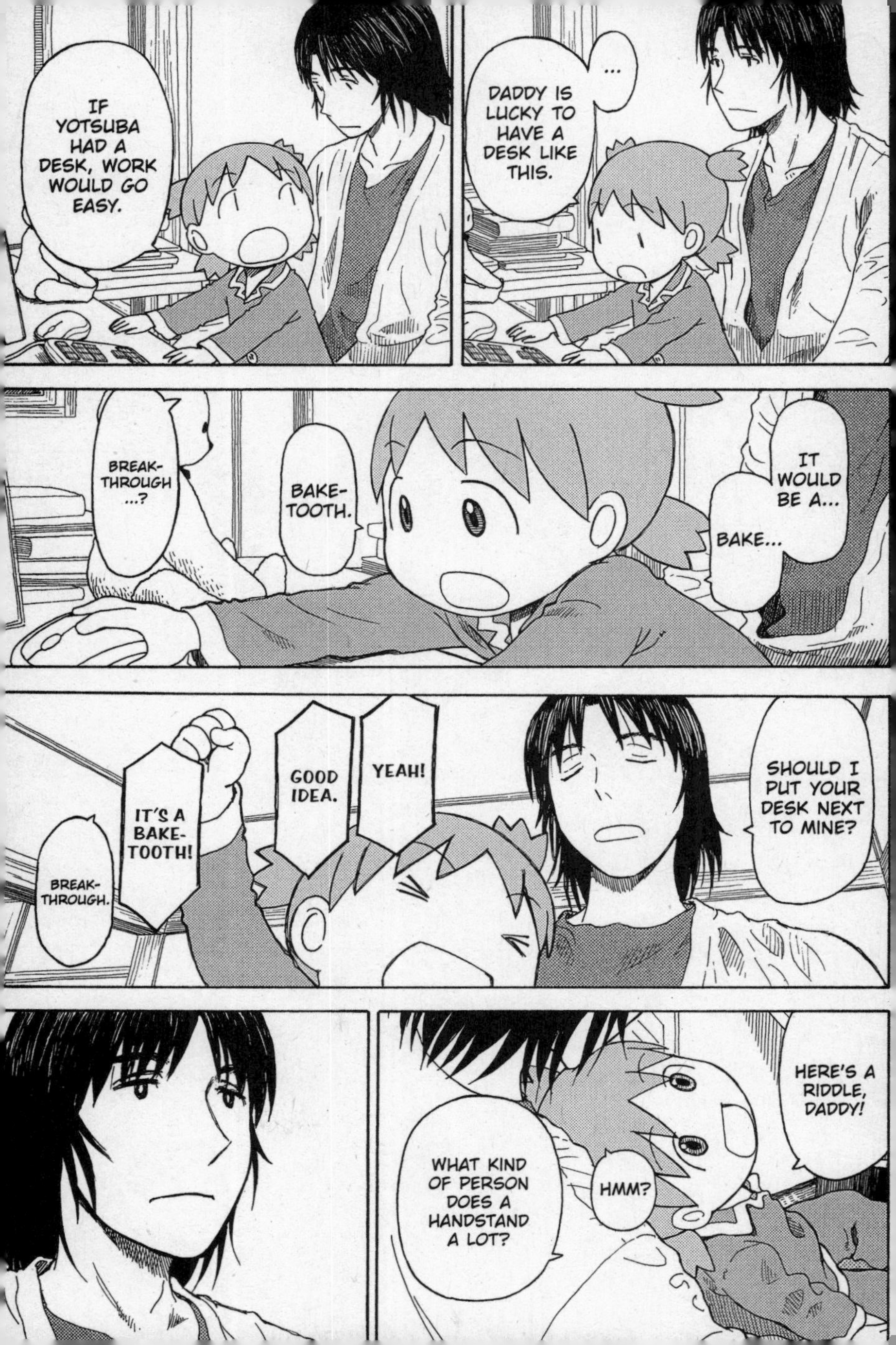
...
DADDY IS LUCKY TO HAVE A DESK LIKE THIS.
IF YOTSUBA HAD A DESK, WORK WOULD GO EASY.
IT WOULD BE A...
BAKE...
BAKE-TOOTH.
BREAK-THROUGH...?
SHOULD I PUT YOUR DESK NEXT TO MINE?
YEAH!
GOOD IDEA.
IT'S A BAKE-TOOTH!
BREAK-THROUGH.
HERE'S A RIDDLE, DADDY!
HMM?
WHAT KIND OF PERSON DOES A HANDSTAND A LOT?

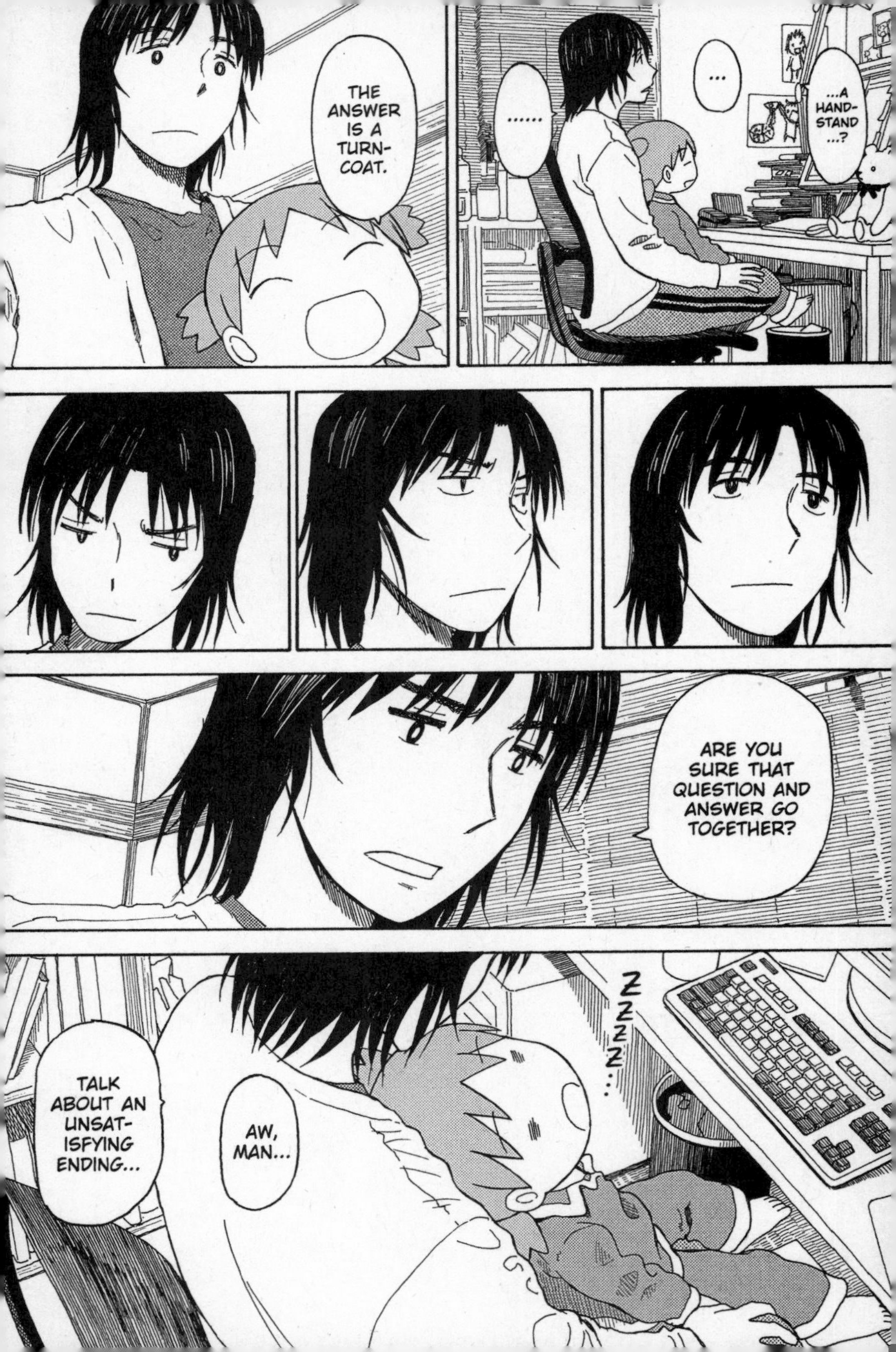
...A HANDSTAND...?
...
......
THE ANSWER IS A TURNCOAT.
ARE YOU SURE THAT QUESTION AND ANSWER GO TOGETHER?
ZZZZ...
AW, MAN...
TALK ABOUT AN UNSATISFYING ENDING...

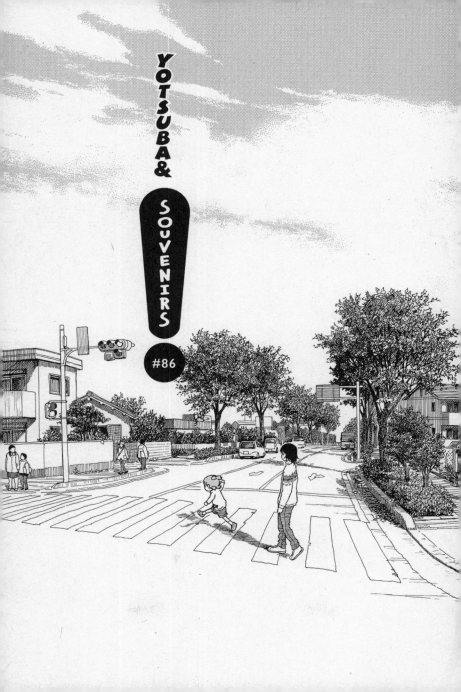

YOTSUBA&
SOUVENIRS!
#86

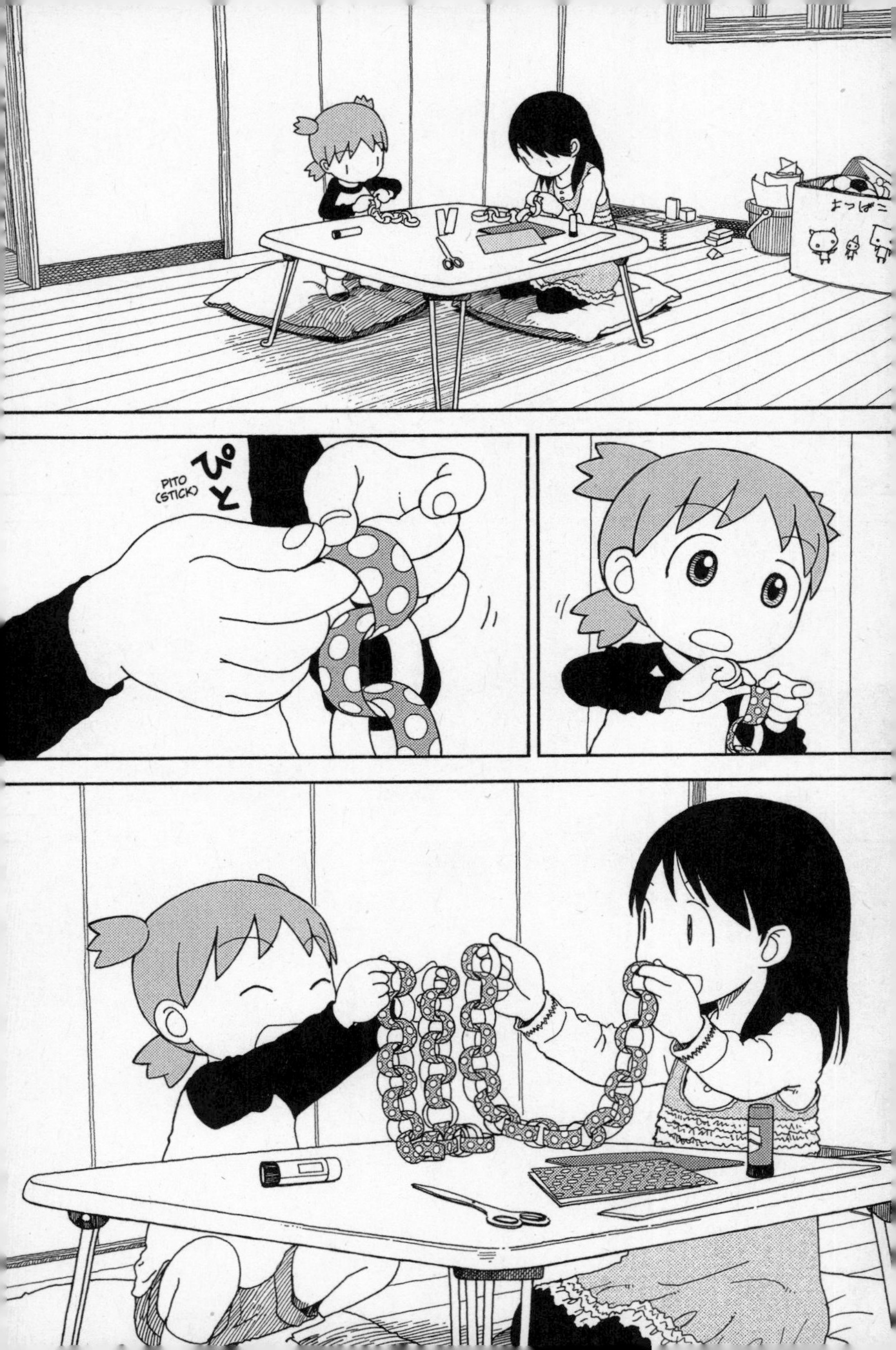
ぴと
PITO (STICK)

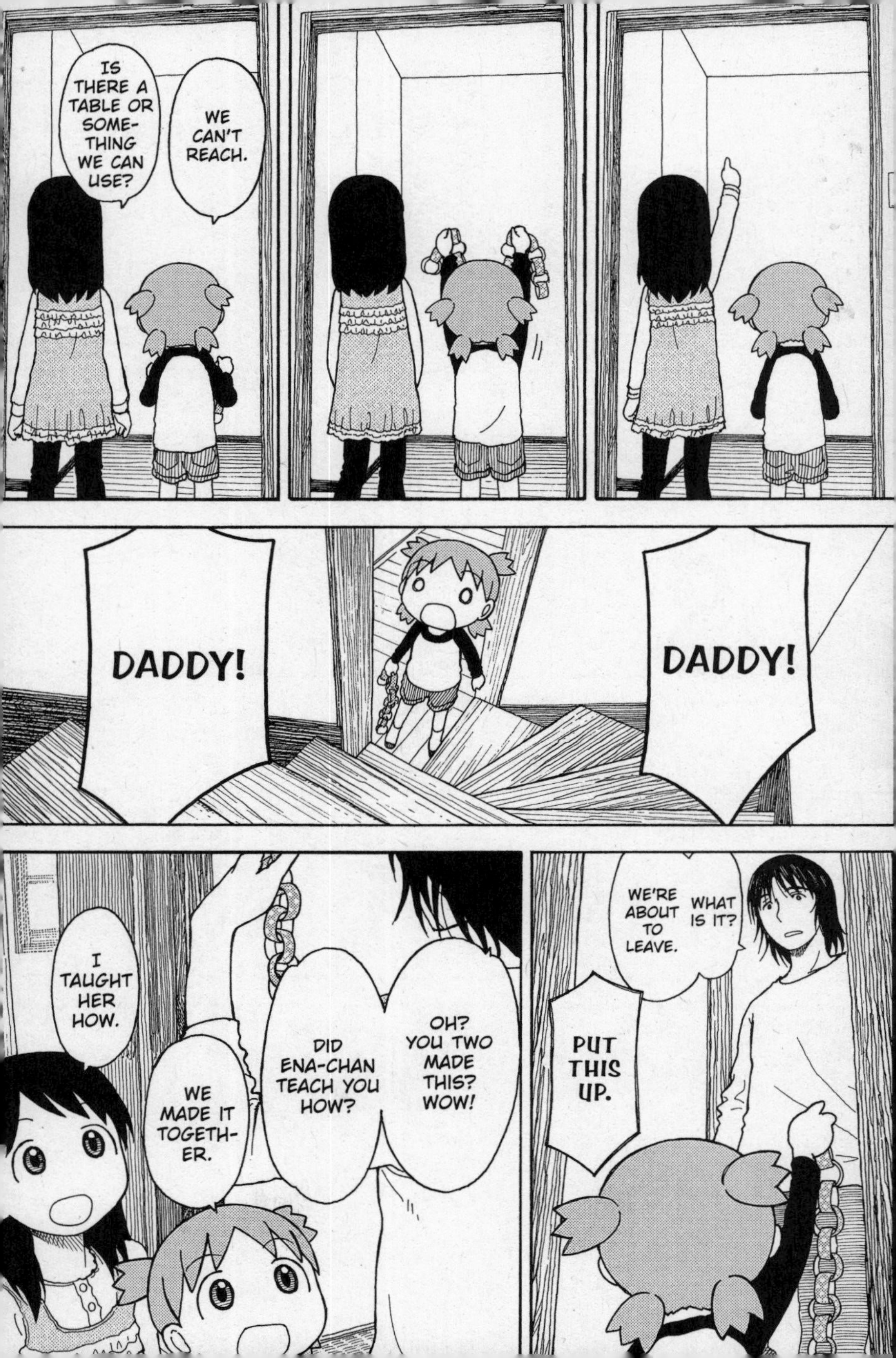
WE CAN'T REACH.
IS THERE A TABLE OR SOME-THING WE CAN USE?
DADDY!
DADDY!
WHAT IS IT?
WE'RE ABOUT TO LEAVE.
PUT THIS UP.
OH? YOU TWO MADE THIS? WOW!
DID ENA-CHAN TEACH YOU HOW?
WE MADE IT TOGETH-ER.
I TAUGHT HER HOW.

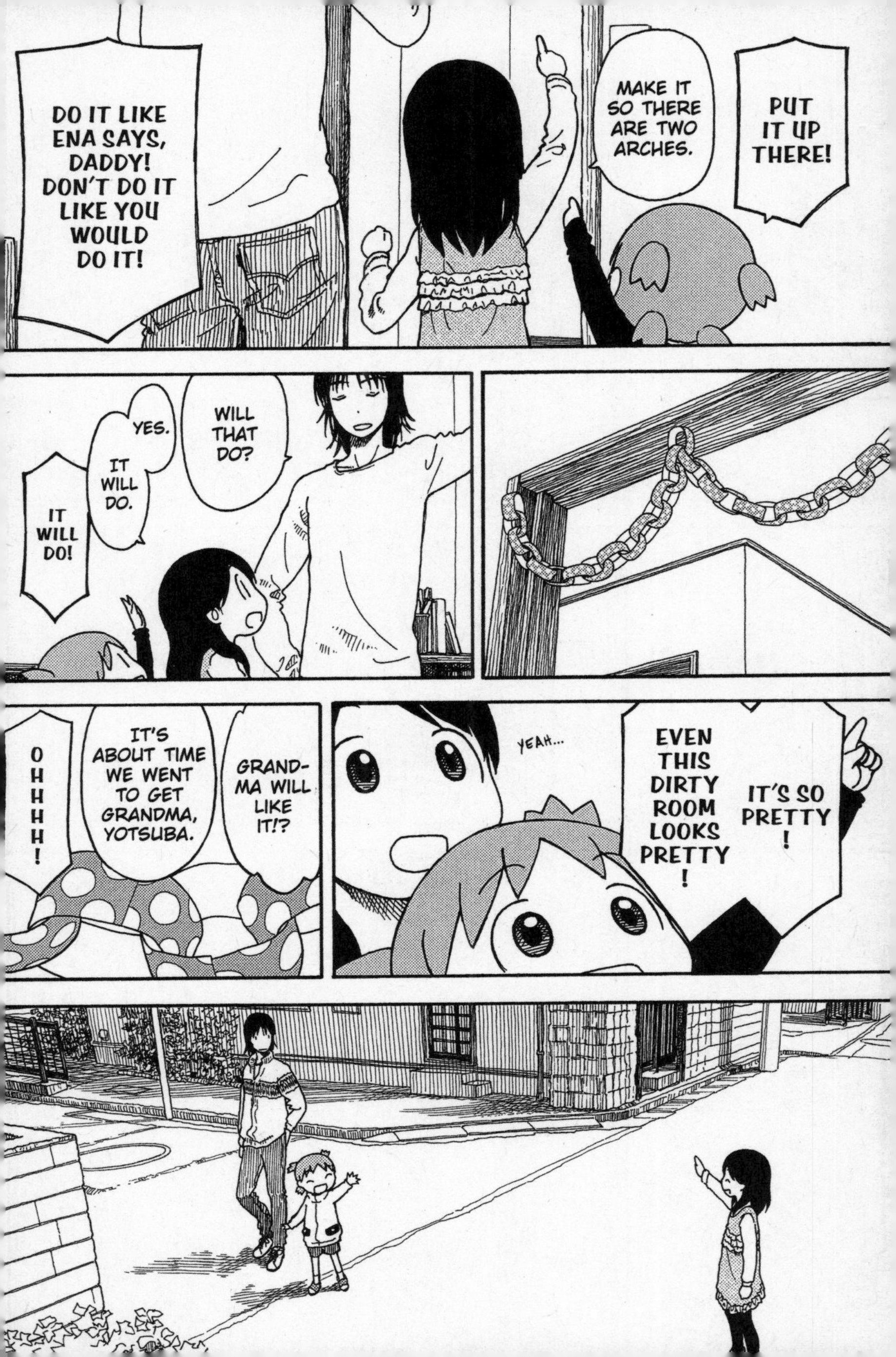
PUT IT UP THERE!
MAKE IT SO THERE ARE TWO ARCHES.
DO IT LIKE ENA SAYS, DADDY! DON'T DO IT LIKE YOU WOULD DO IT!
WILL THAT DO?
YES. IT WILL DO.
IT WILL DO!
IT'S SO PRETTY!
EVEN THIS DIRTY ROOM LOOKS PRETTY!
YEAH...
GRANDMA WILL LIKE IT!?
IT'S ABOUT TIME WE WENT TO GET GRANDMA, YOTSUBA.
OHHHHH!

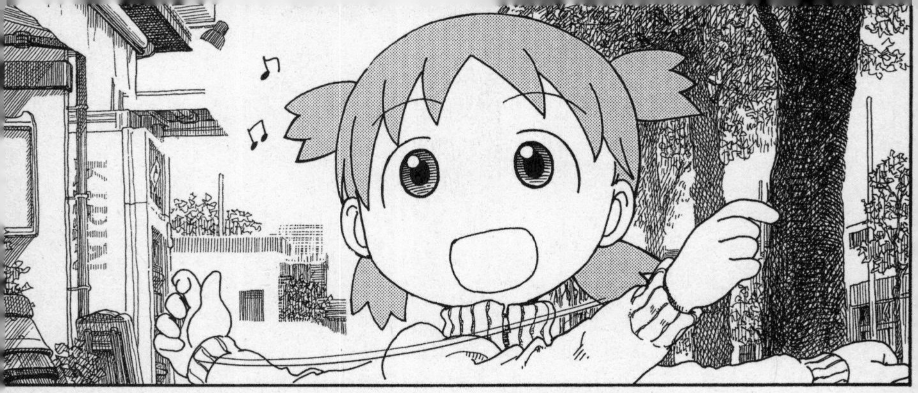

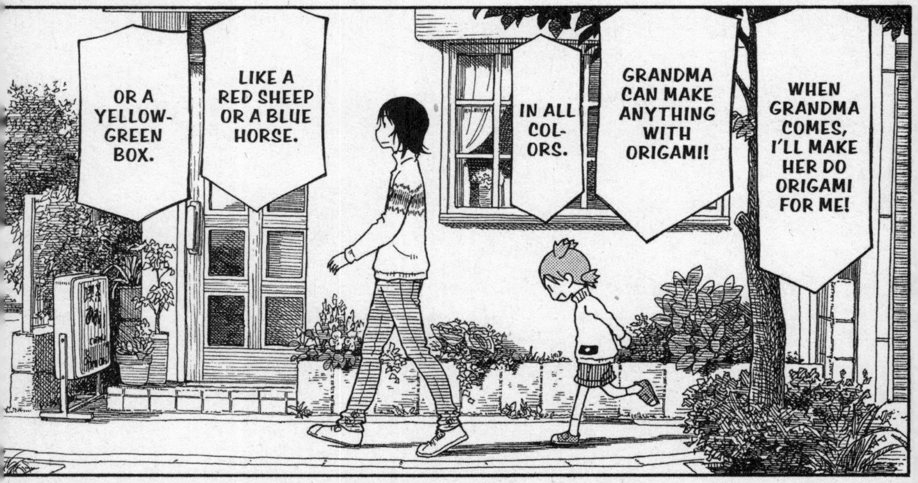
WHEN GRANDMA COMES, I'LL MAKE HER DO ORIGAMI FOR ME!
GRANDMA CAN MAKE ANYTHING WITH ORIGAMI!
IN ALL COL-ORS.
LIKE A RED SHEEP OR A BLUE HORSE.
OR A YELLOW-GREEN BOX.

NOTE: KYARI PAMYU PAMYU IS A JAPANESE POP SINGER KNOWN FOR HER ECCENTRIC FASHION SENSE AND BIZARRE MUSIC VIDEOS.

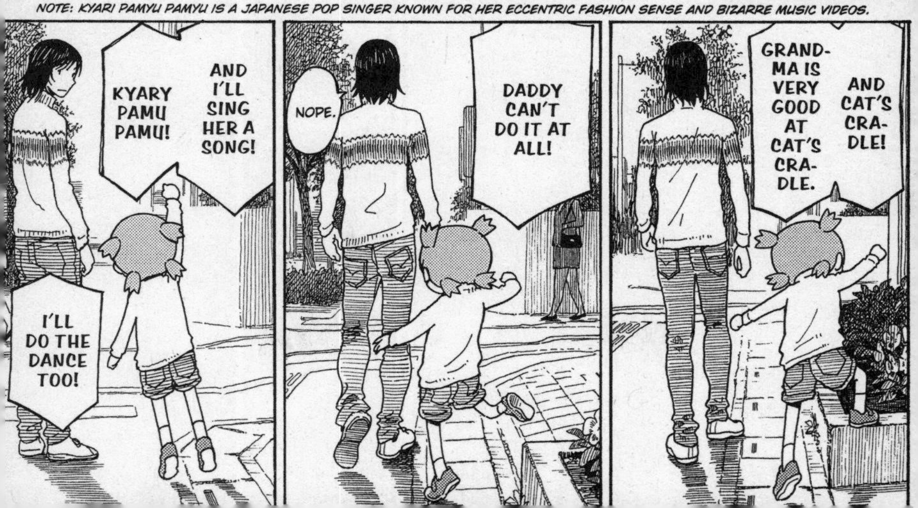
AND CAT'S CRA-DLE!
GRAND-MA IS VERY GOOD AT CAT'S CRA-DLE.
DADDY CAN'T DO IT AT ALL!
NOPE.
AND I'LL SING HER A SONG!
KYARY PAMU PAMU!
I'LL DO THE DANCE TOO!

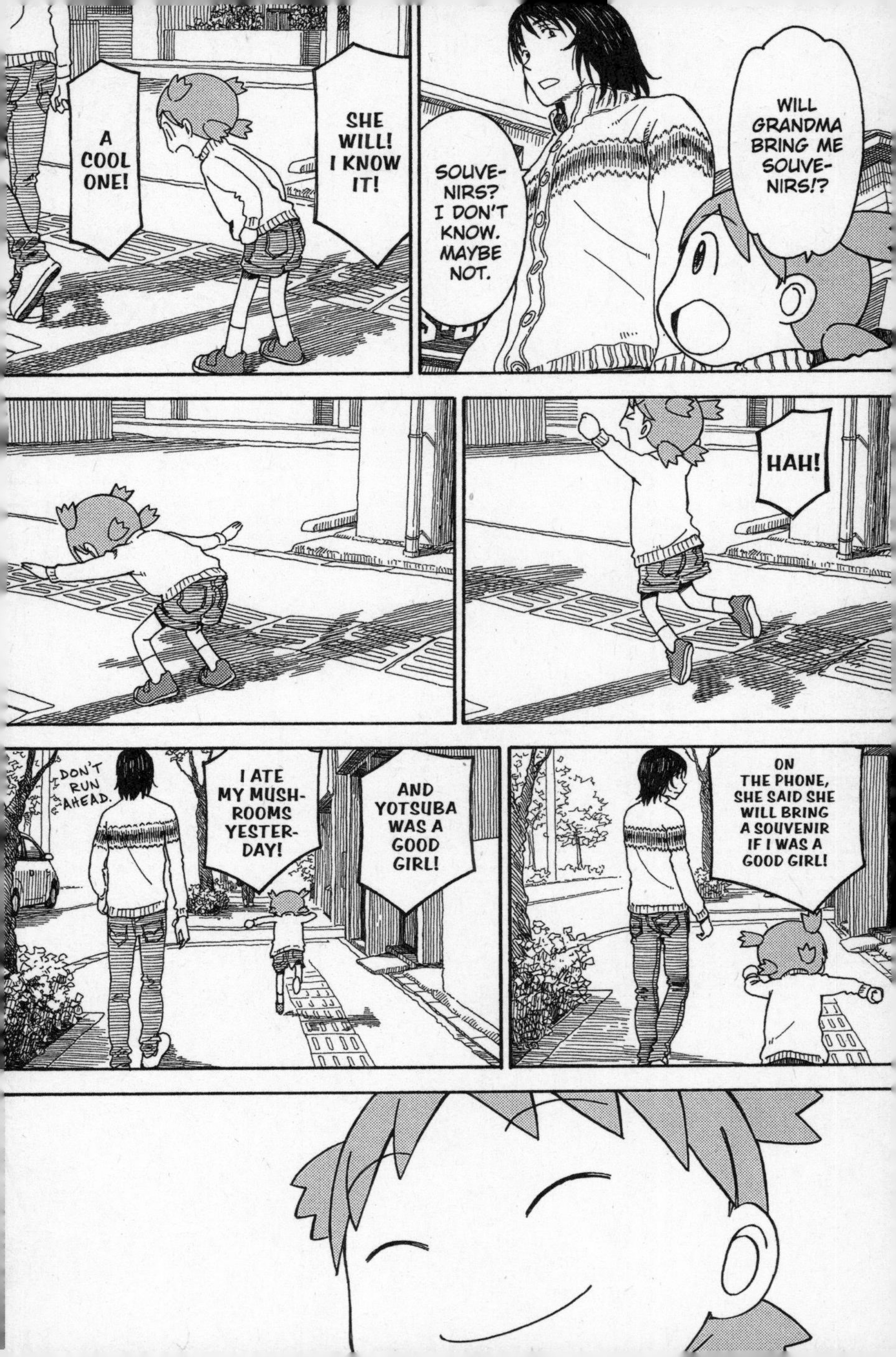
WILL GRANDMA BRING ME SOUVENIRS!?
SOUVENIRS? I DON'T KNOW. MAYBE NOT.
SHE WILL! I KNOW IT!
A COOL ONE!
HAH!
ON THE PHONE, SHE SAID SHE WILL BRING A SOUVENIR IF I WAS A GOOD GIRL!
AND YOTSUBA WAS A GOOD GIRL!
I ATE MY MUSHROOMS YESTERDAY!
DON'T RUN AHEAD.

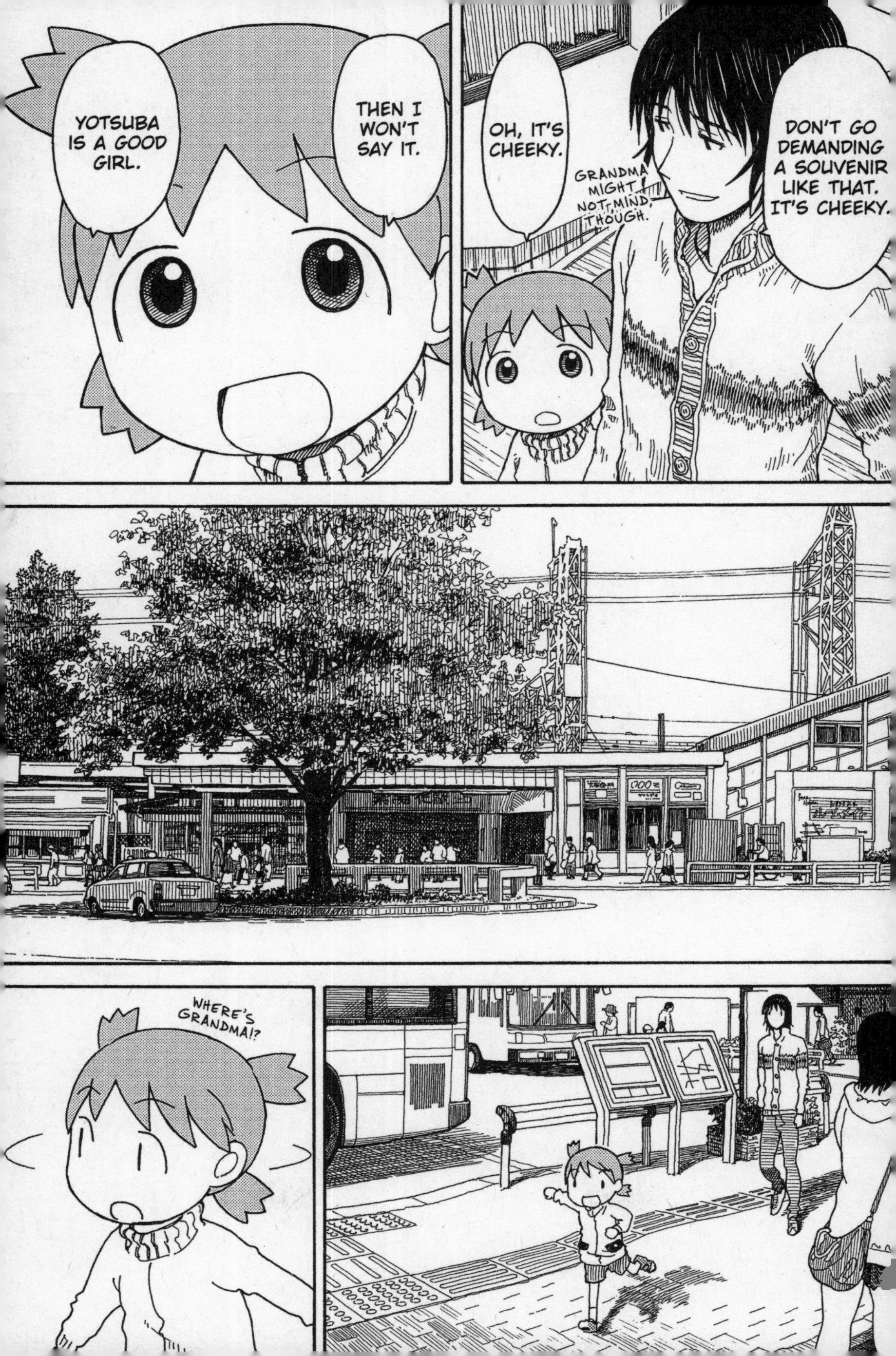
DON'T GO DEMANDING A SOUVENIR LIKE THAT. IT'S CHEEKY.
OH, IT'S CHEEKY.
GRANDMA MIGHT NOT MIND, THOUGH.
THEN I WON'T SAY IT.
YOTSUBA IS A GOOD GIRL.
WHERE'S GRANDMA!?

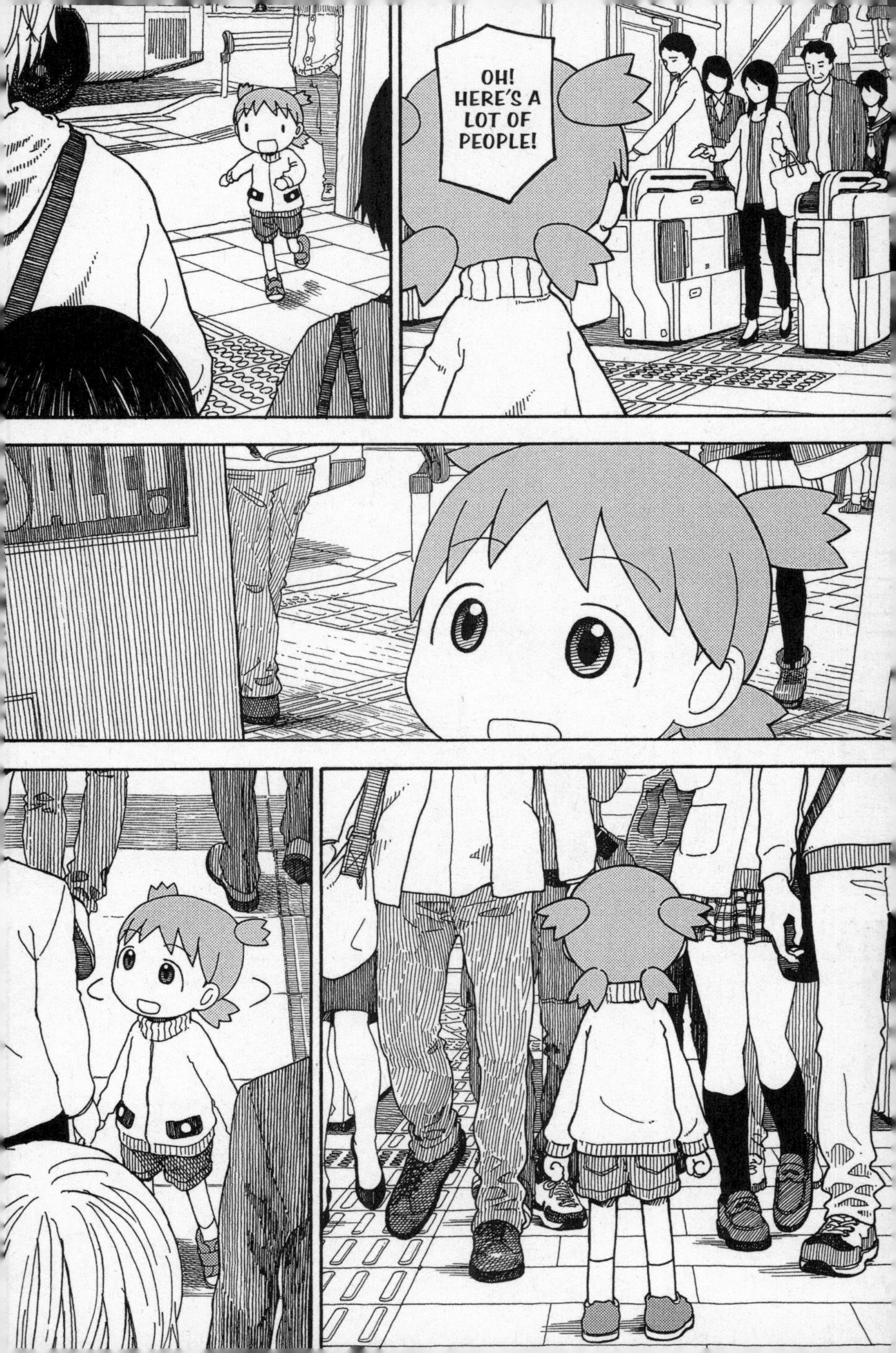
OH! HERE'S A LOT OF PEOPLE!

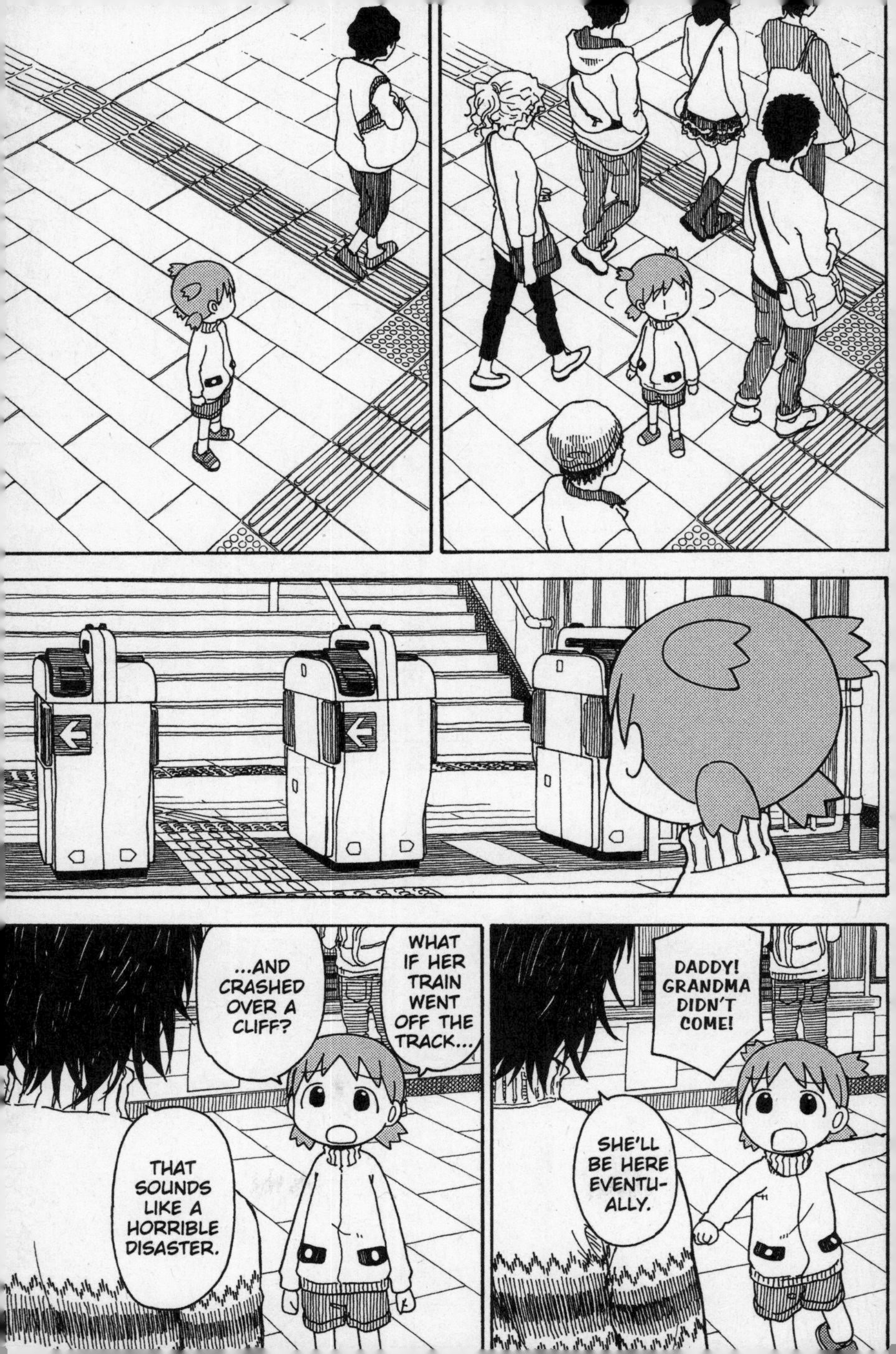
DADDY! GRANDMA DIDN'T COME!
SHE'LL BE HERE EVENTU-ALLY.
WHAT IF HER TRAIN WENT OFF THE TRACK...
...AND CRASHED OVER A CLIFF?
THAT SOUNDS LIKE A HORRIBLE DISASTER.

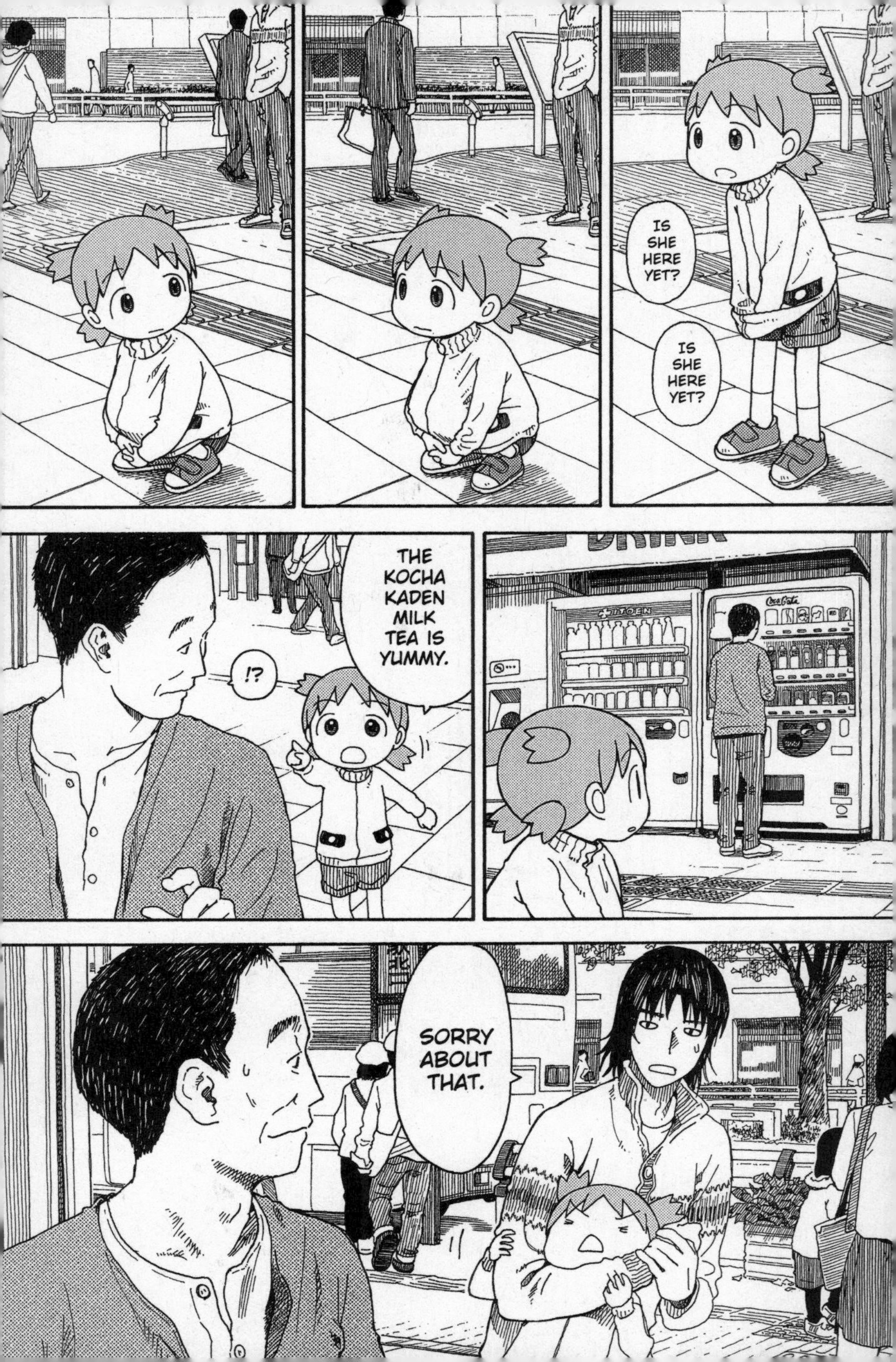
IS SHE HERE YET?
IS SHE HERE YET?
THE KOCHA KADEN MILK TEA IS YUMMY.
!?
SORRY ABOUT THAT.

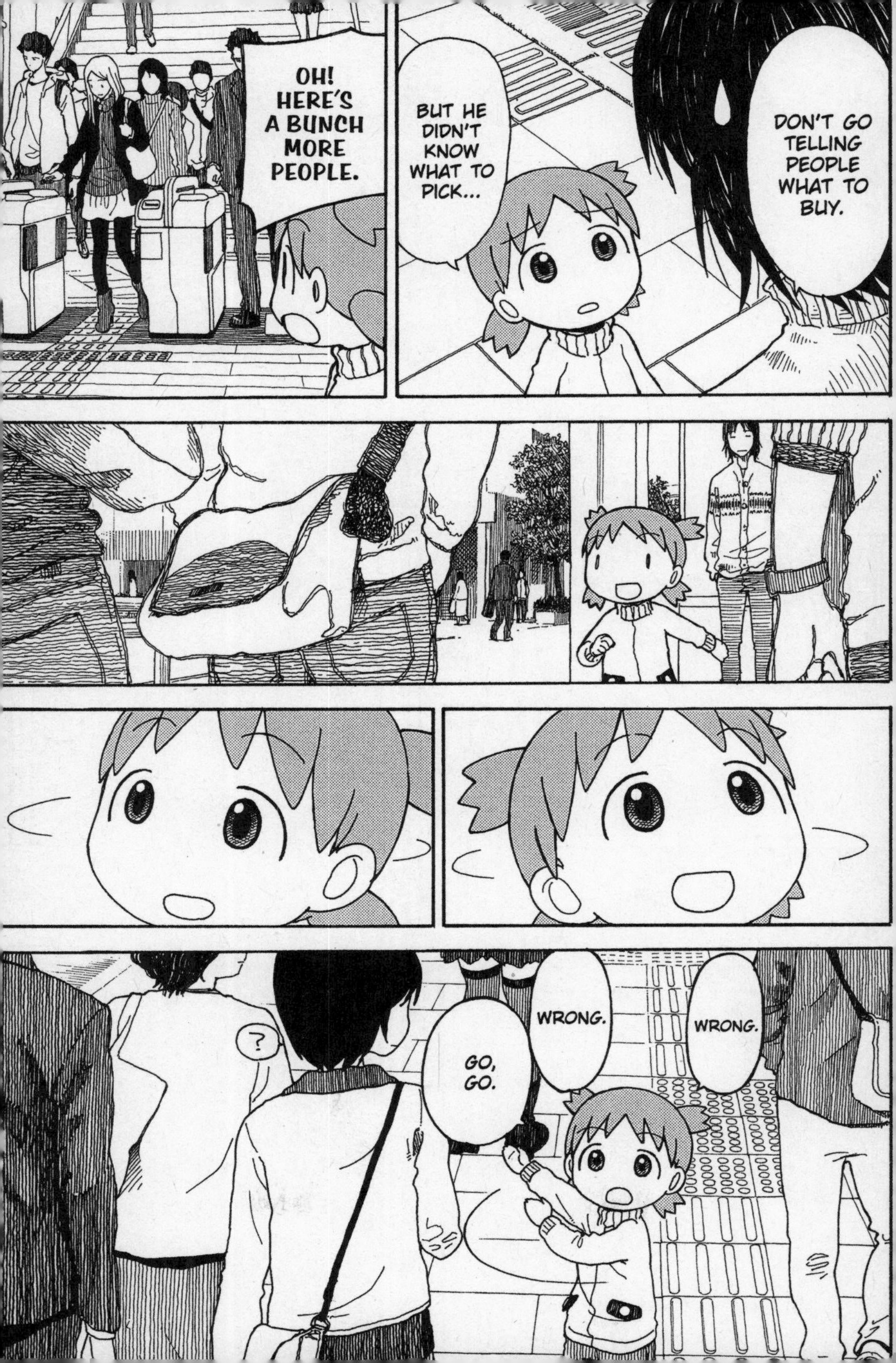
DON'T GO TELLING PEOPLE WHAT TO BUY.
BUT HE DIDN'T KNOW WHAT TO PICK...
OH! HERE'S A BUNCH MORE PEOPLE.
WRONG.
WRONG.
GO, GO.
?

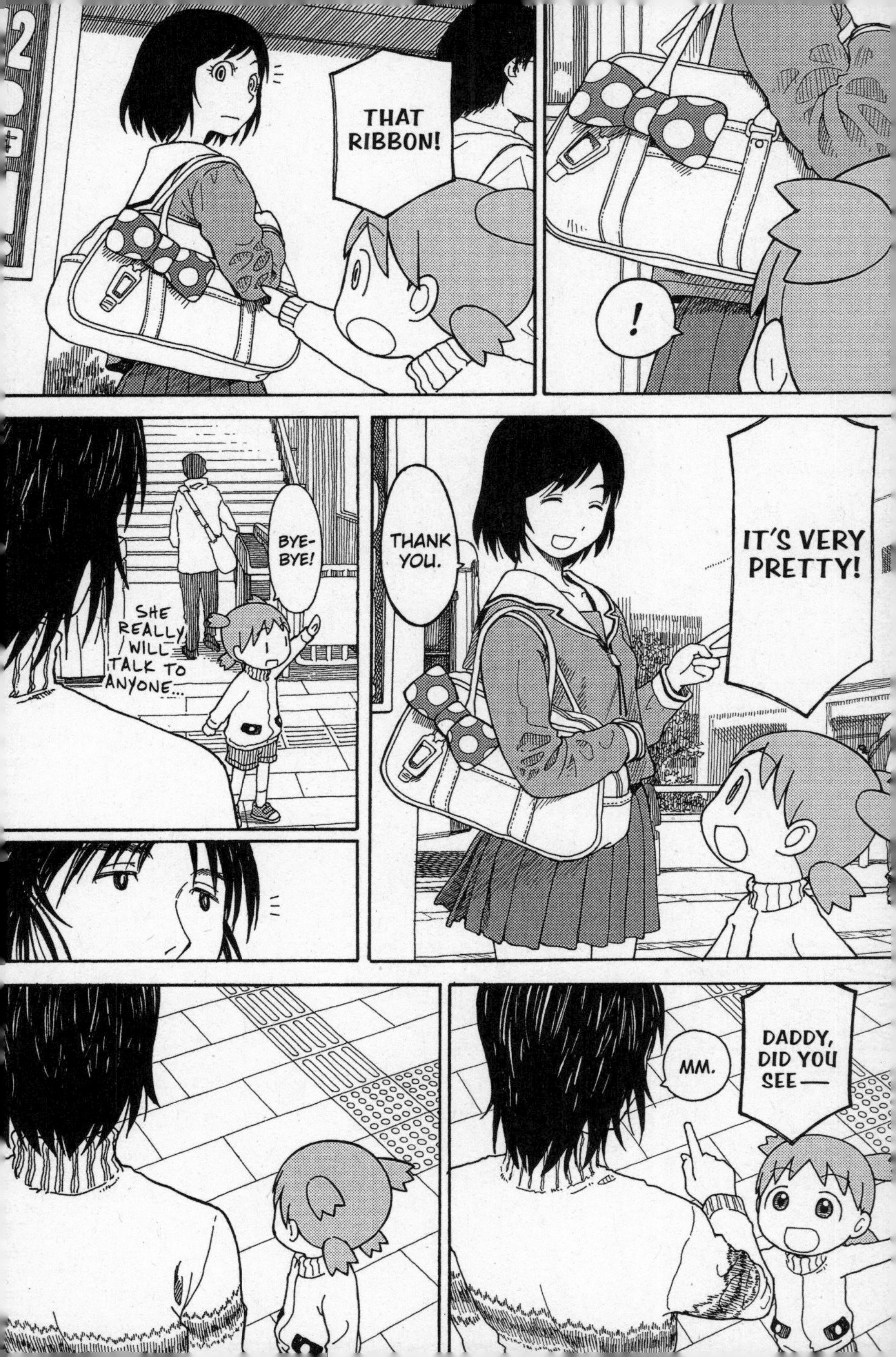
!
THAT RIBBON!
IT'S VERY PRETTY!
THANK YOU.
BYE-BYE!
SHE REALLY WILL TALK TO ANYONE...
DADDY, DID YOU SEE—
MM.

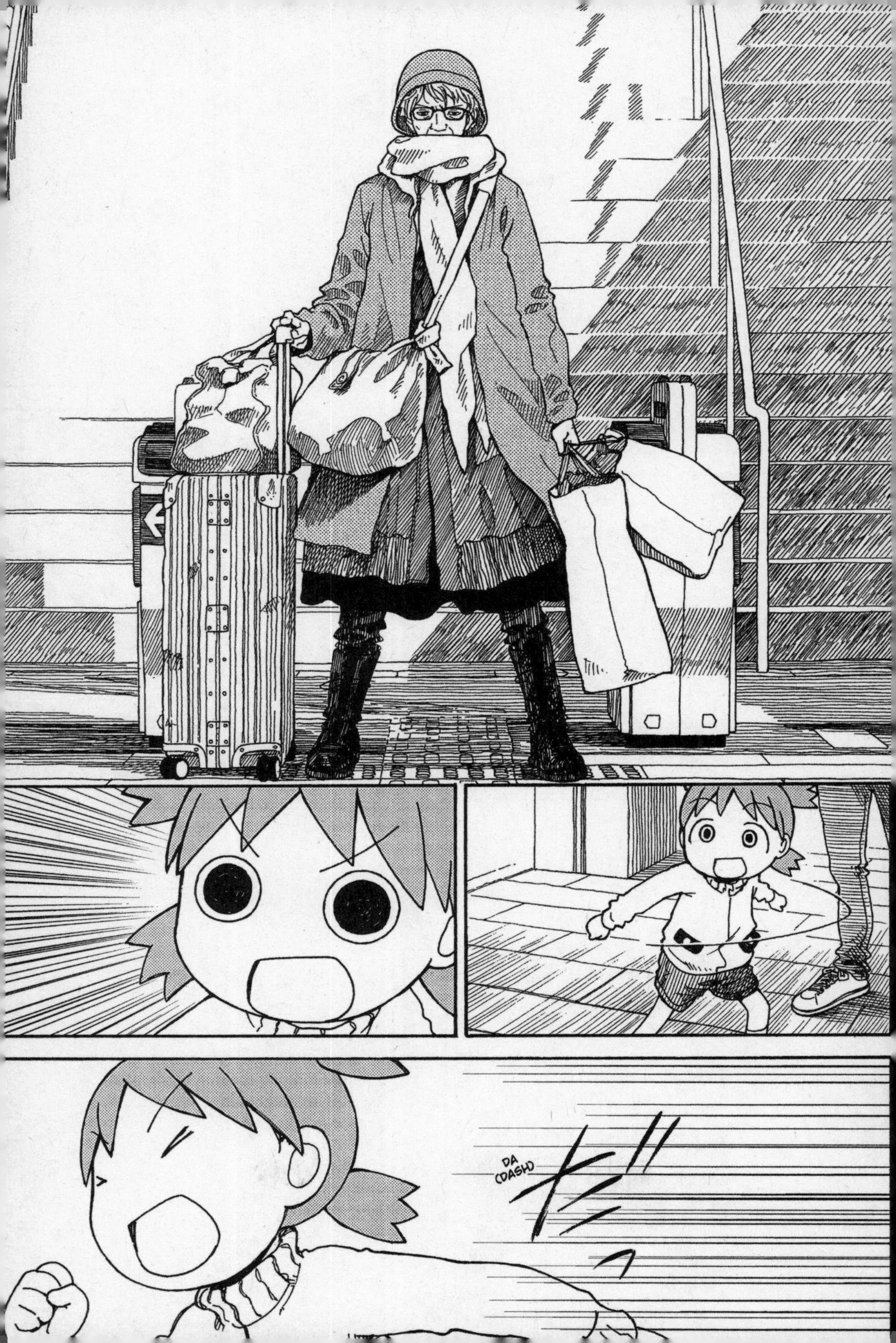
DA
(DASH)

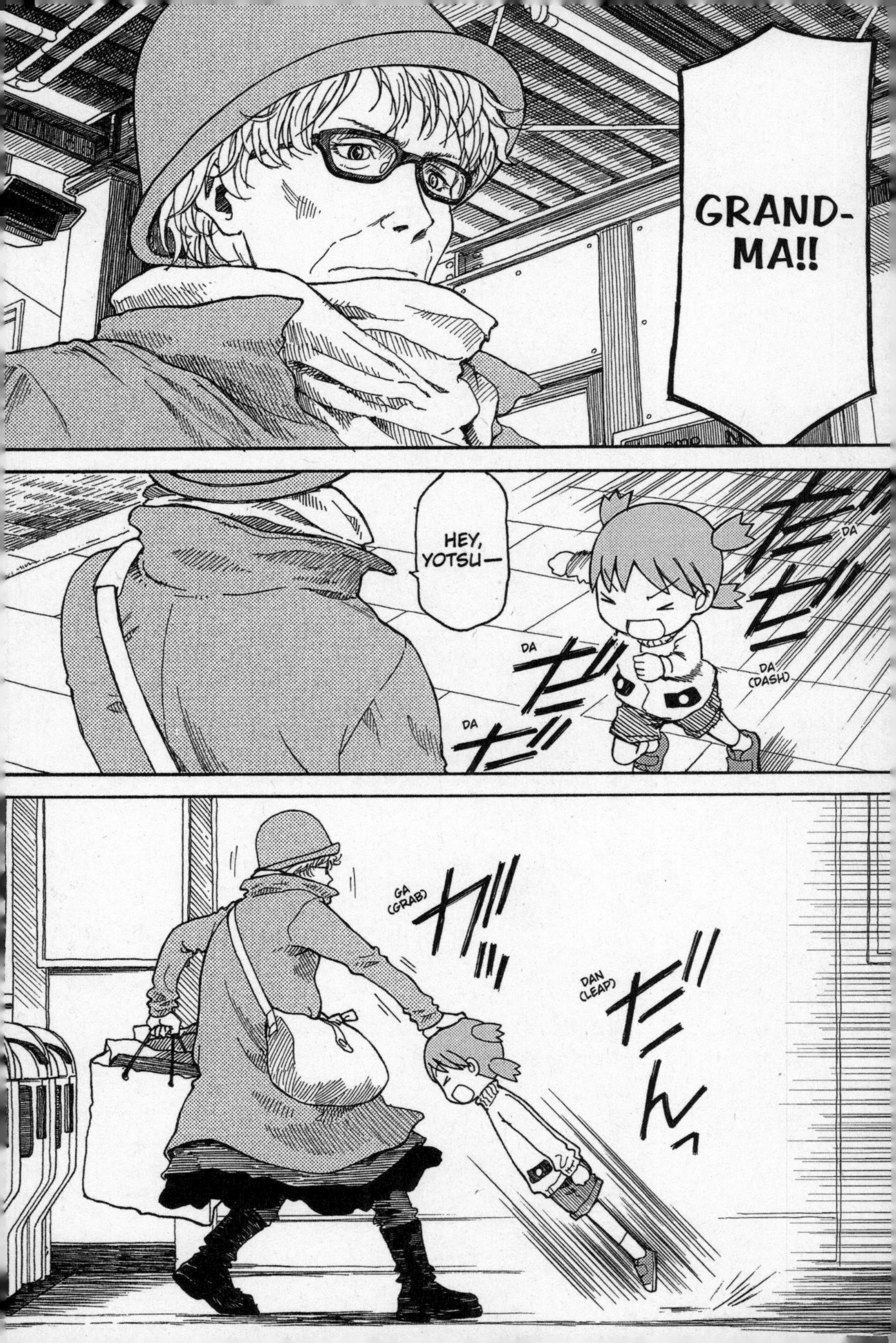
GRAND-MA!!
DA
HEY, YOTSU—
DA
DA (DASH)
DA
GA (GRAB)
DAN (LEAP)

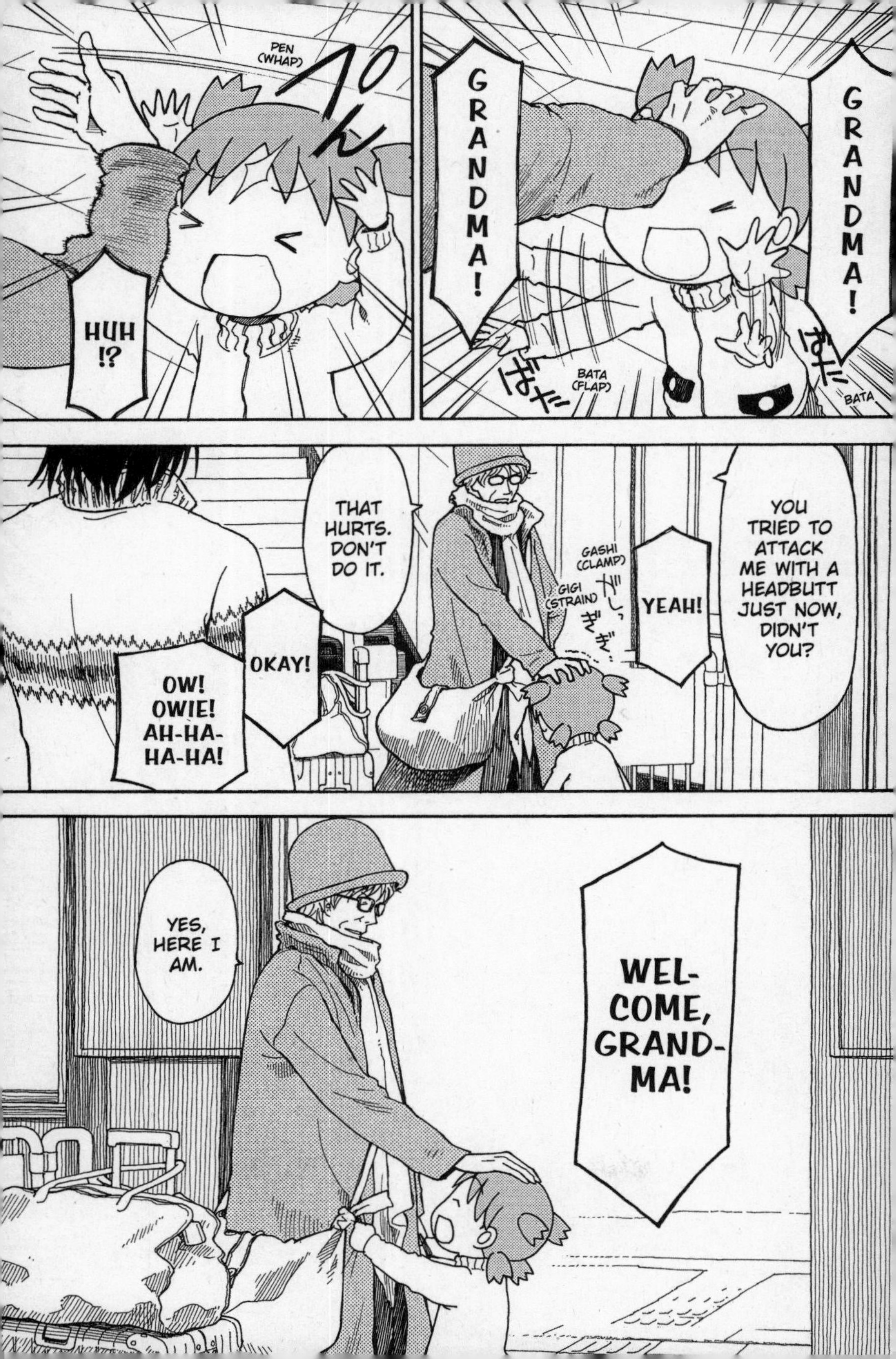
GRANDMA!
GRANDMA!
BATA
BATA (FLAP)
PEN (WHAP)
HUH!?
YOU TRIED TO ATTACK ME WITH A HEADBUTT JUST NOW, DIDN'T YOU?
YEAH!
GASHI (CLAMP)
GIGI (STRAIN)
THAT HURTS. DON'T DO IT.
OKAY!
OW! OWIE! AH-HA-HA-HA!
WEL-COME, GRAND-MA!
YES, HERE I AM.

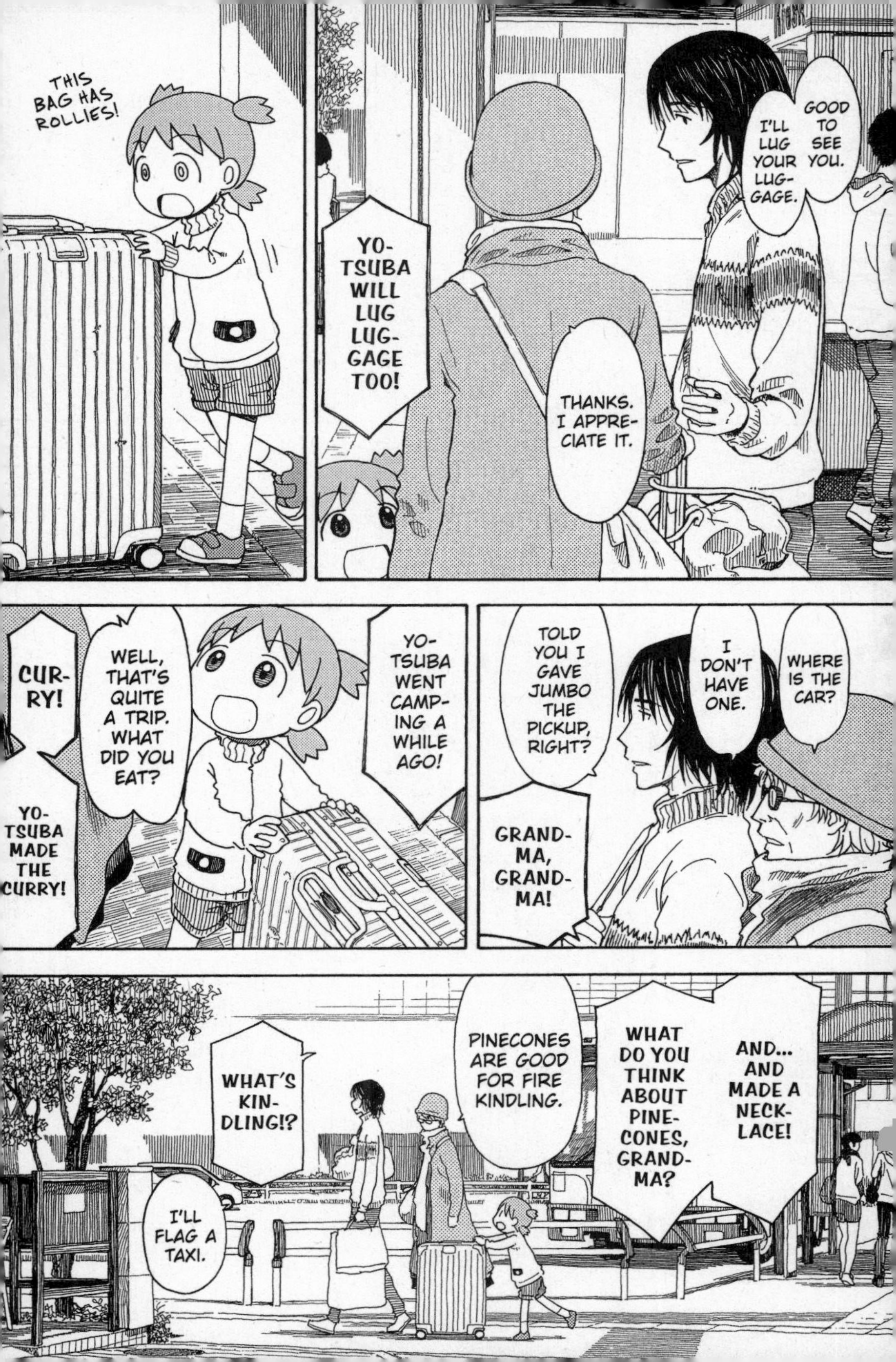
GOOD TO SEE YOU.
I'LL LUG YOUR LUGGAGE.
THANKS. I APPRECIATE IT.
YOTSUBA WILL LUG LUGGAGE TOO!
THIS BAG HAS ROLLIES!
WHERE IS THE CAR?
I DON'T HAVE ONE.
TOLD YOU I GAVE JUMBO THE PICKUP, RIGHT?
GRANDMA, GRANDMA!
YOTSUBA WENT CAMPING A WHILE AGO!
WELL, THAT'S QUITE A TRIP. WHAT DID YOU EAT?
CURRY!
YOTSUBA MADE THE CURRY!
AND... AND MADE A NECKLACE!
WHAT DO YOU THINK ABOUT PINECONES, GRANDMA?
PINECONES ARE GOOD FOR FIRE KINDLING.
WHAT'S KINDLING!?
I'LL FLAG A TAXI.

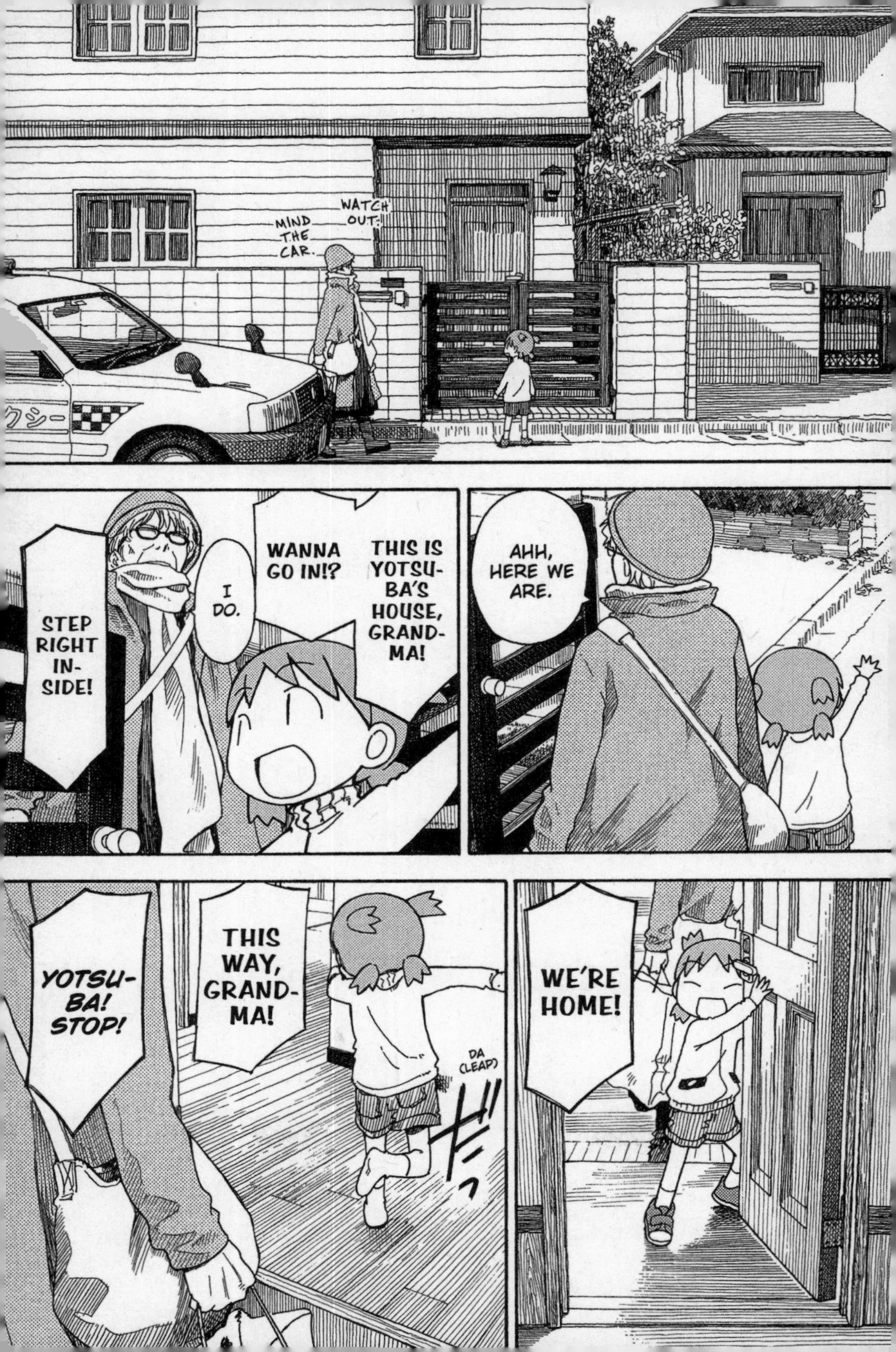

WATCH OUT.
MIND THE CAR.
クシー
AHH, HERE WE ARE.
THIS IS YOTSUBA'S HOUSE, GRANDMA!
WANNA GO IN!?
I DO.
STEP RIGHT INSIDE!
WE'RE HOME!
DA (LEAP)
THIS WAY, GRANDMA!
YOTSUBA! STOP!

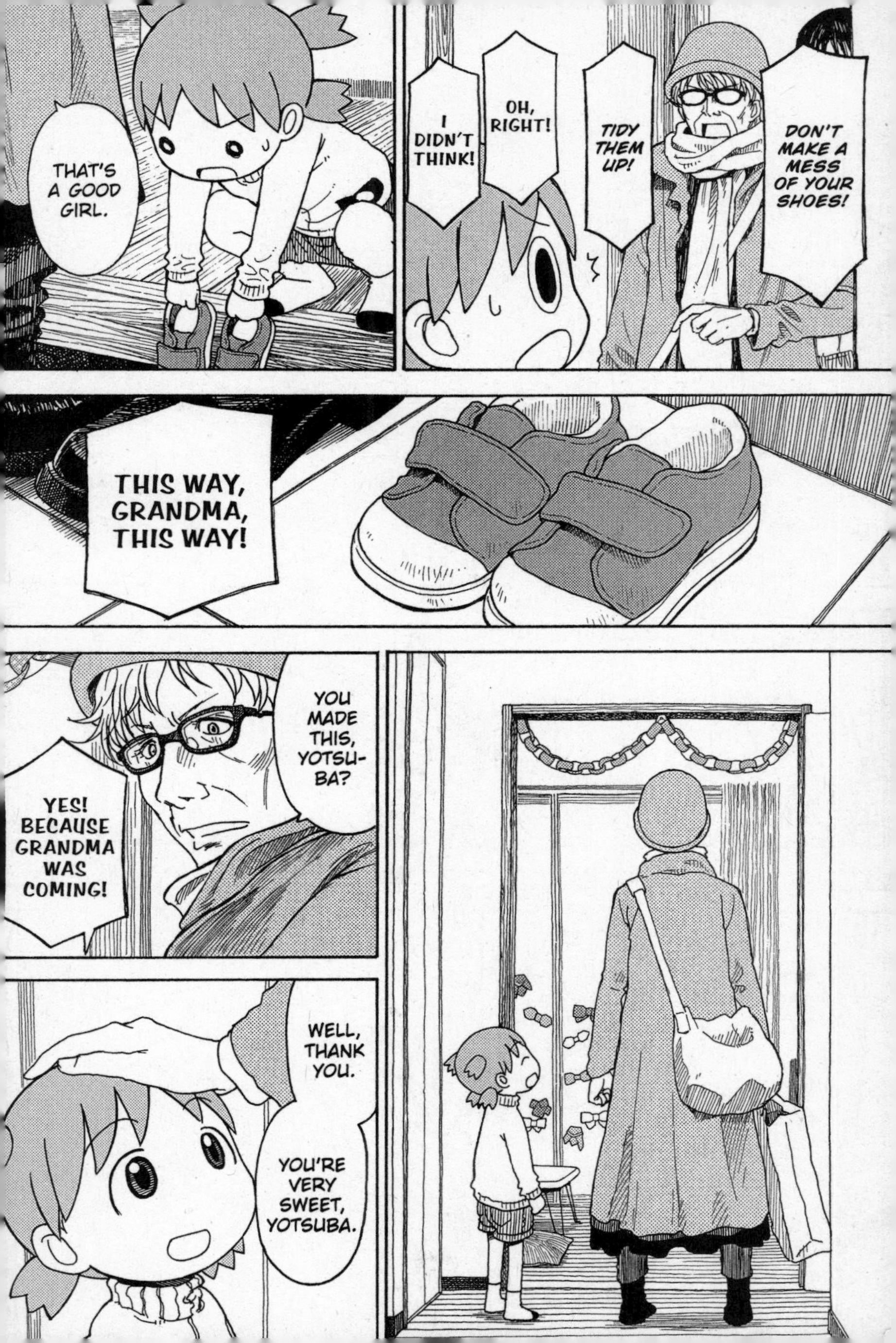
DON'T MAKE A MESS OF YOUR SHOES!
TIDY THEM UP!
OH, RIGHT!
I DIDN'T THINK!
THAT'S A GOOD GIRL.
THIS WAY, GRANDMA, THIS WAY!
YOU MADE THIS, YOTSUBA?
YES! BECAUSE GRANDMA WAS COMING!
WELL, THANK YOU.
YOU'RE VERY SWEET, YOTSUBA.

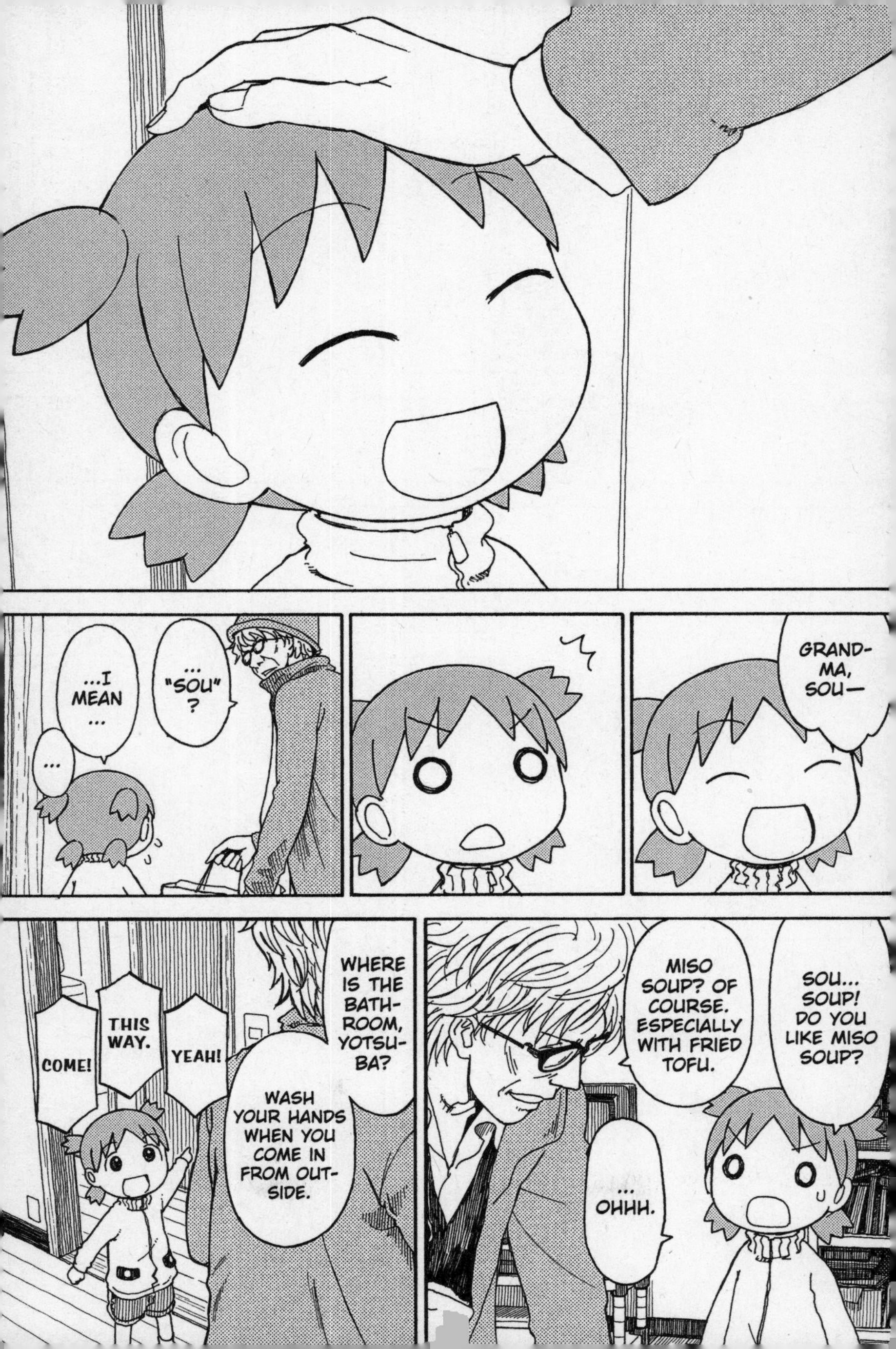
GRAND-MA, SOU—
... "SOU" ?
...I MEAN ...
...
SOU... SOUP! DO YOU LIKE MISO SOUP?
MISO SOUP? OF COURSE. ESPECIALLY WITH FRIED TOFU.
... OHHH.
WHERE IS THE BATH-ROOM, YOTSU-BA?
WASH YOUR HANDS WHEN YOU COME IN FROM OUT-SIDE.
YEAH!
THIS WAY.
COME!

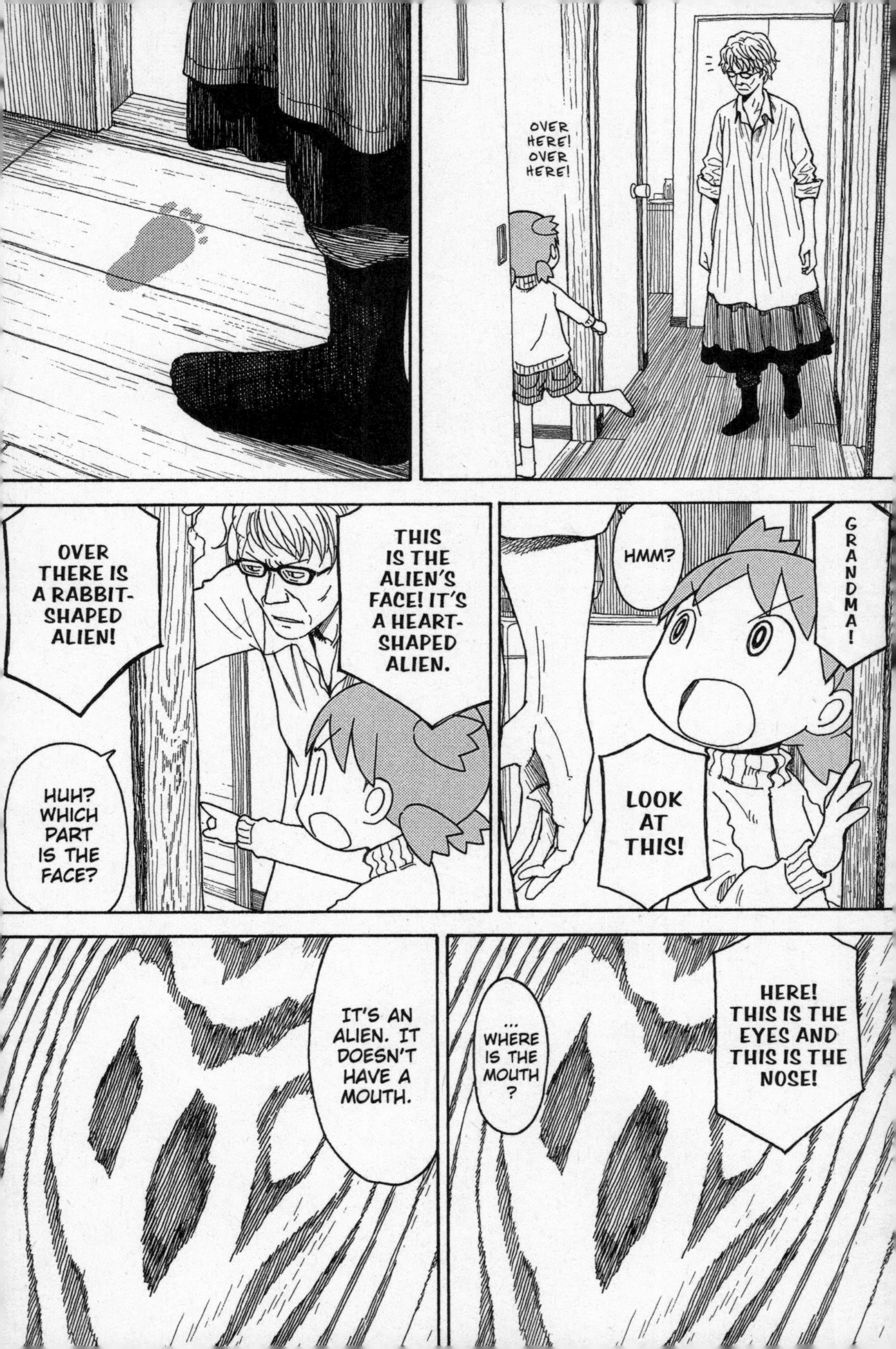
OVER HERE! OVER HERE!
GRANDMA!
HMM?
LOOK AT THIS!
THIS IS THE ALIEN'S FACE! IT'S A HEART-SHAPED ALIEN.
OVER THERE IS A RABBIT-SHAPED ALIEN!
HUH? WHICH PART IS THE FACE?
HERE! THIS IS THE EYES AND THIS IS THE NOSE!
... WHERE IS THE MOUTH?
IT'S AN ALIEN. IT DOESN'T HAVE A MOUTH.

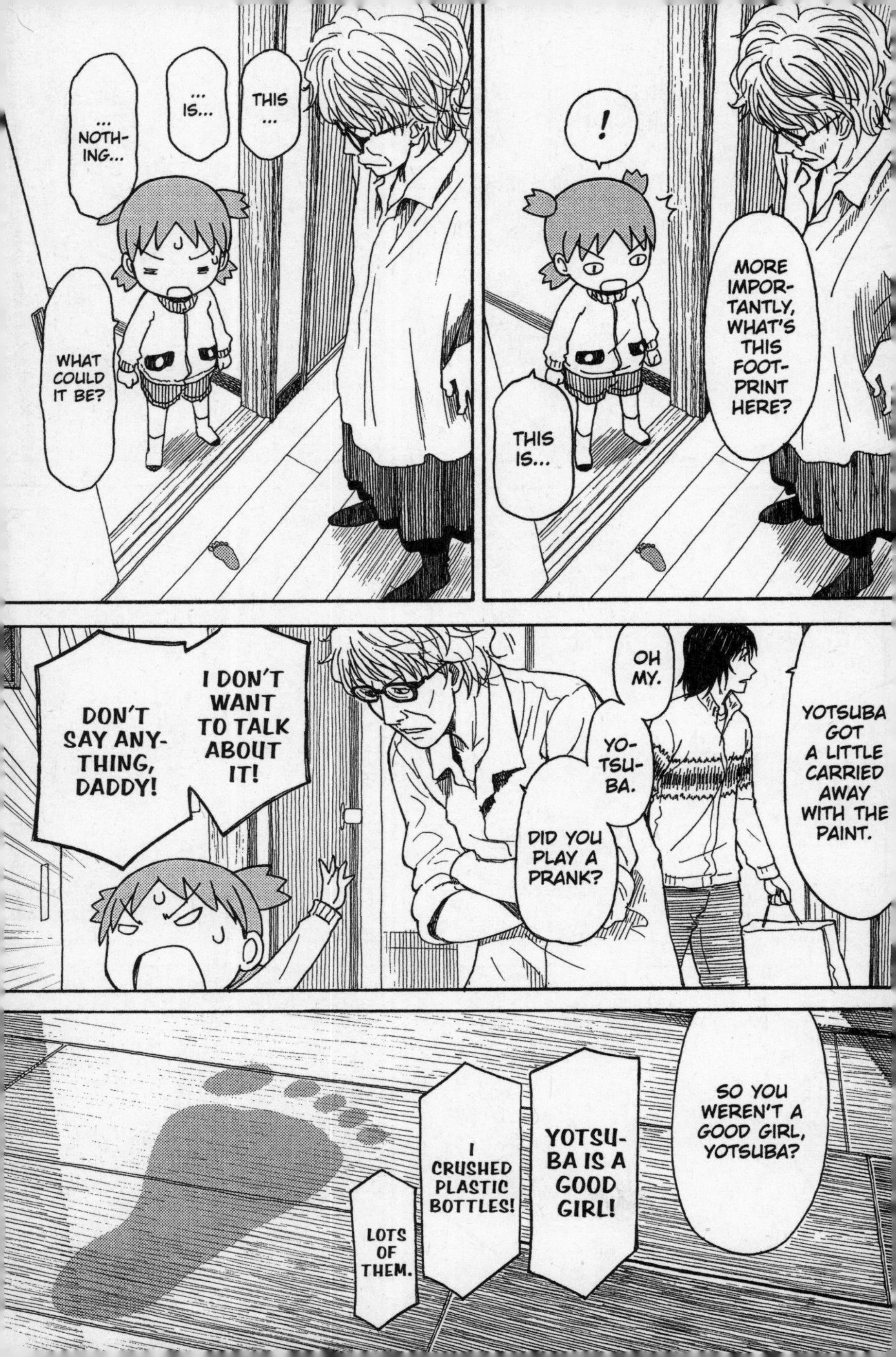
MORE IMPORTANTLY, WHAT'S THIS FOOTPRINT HERE?
!
THIS IS...
THIS ...
... IS...
... NOTHING...
WHAT COULD IT BE?
YOTSUBA GOT A LITTLE CARRIED AWAY WITH THE PAINT.
OH MY.
YOTSUBA.
DID YOU PLAY A PRANK?
I DON'T WANT TO TALK ABOUT IT!
DON'T SAY ANYTHING, DADDY!
SO YOU WEREN'T A GOOD GIRL, YOTSUBA?
YOTSUBA IS A GOOD GIRL!
I CRUSHED PLASTIC BOTTLES!
LOTS OF THEM.

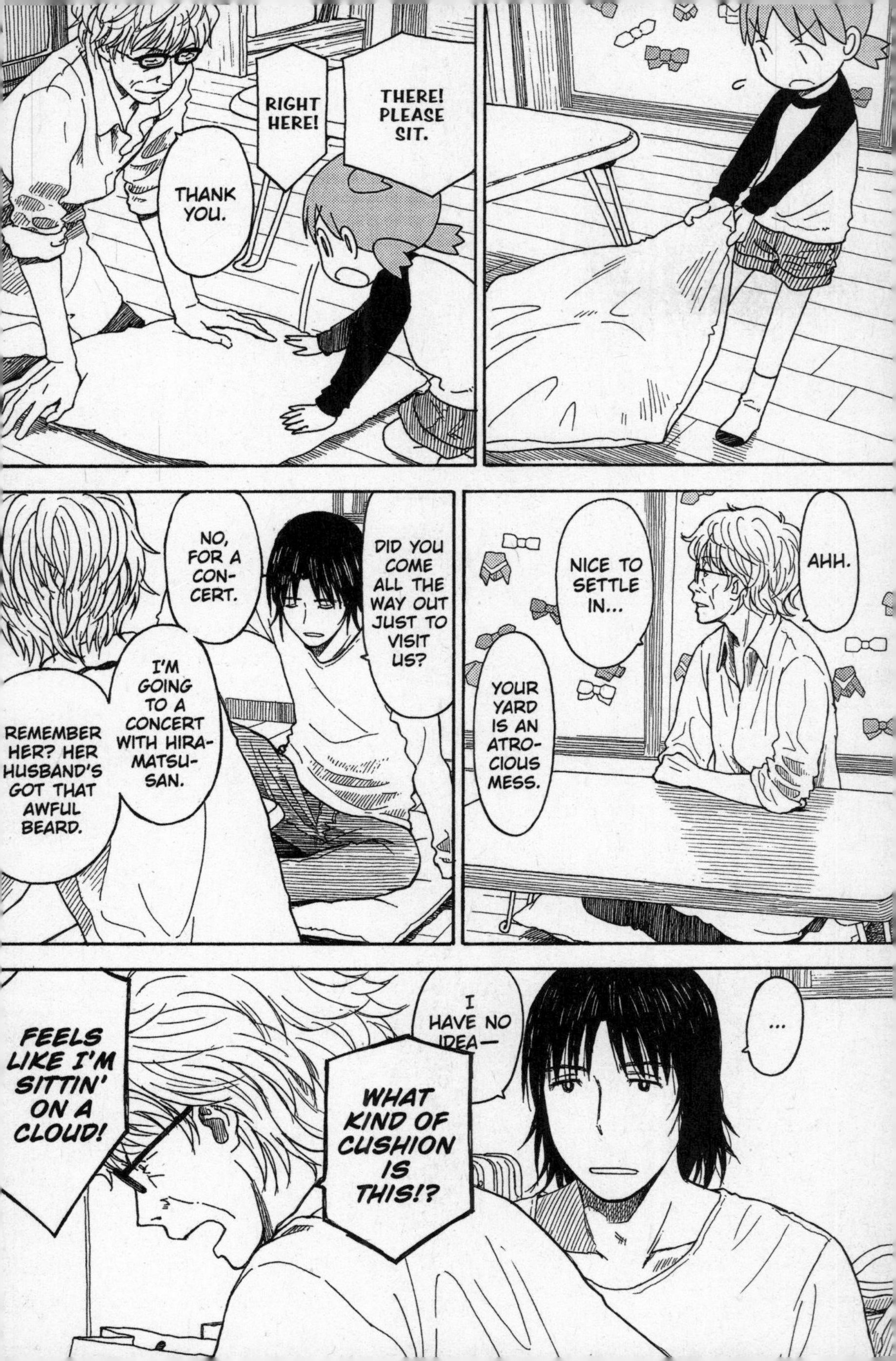
THERE! PLEASE SIT.
RIGHT HERE!
THANK YOU.
AHH.
NICE TO SETTLE IN...
YOUR YARD IS AN ATROCIOUS MESS.
DID YOU COME ALL THE WAY OUT JUST TO VISIT US?
NO, FOR A CON-CERT.
I'M GOING TO A CONCERT WITH HIRA-MATSU-SAN.
REMEMBER HER? HER HUSBAND'S GOT THAT AWFUL BEARD.
...
I HAVE NO IDEA—
WHAT KIND OF CUSHION IS THIS!?
FEELS LIKE I'M SITTIN' ON A CLOUD!

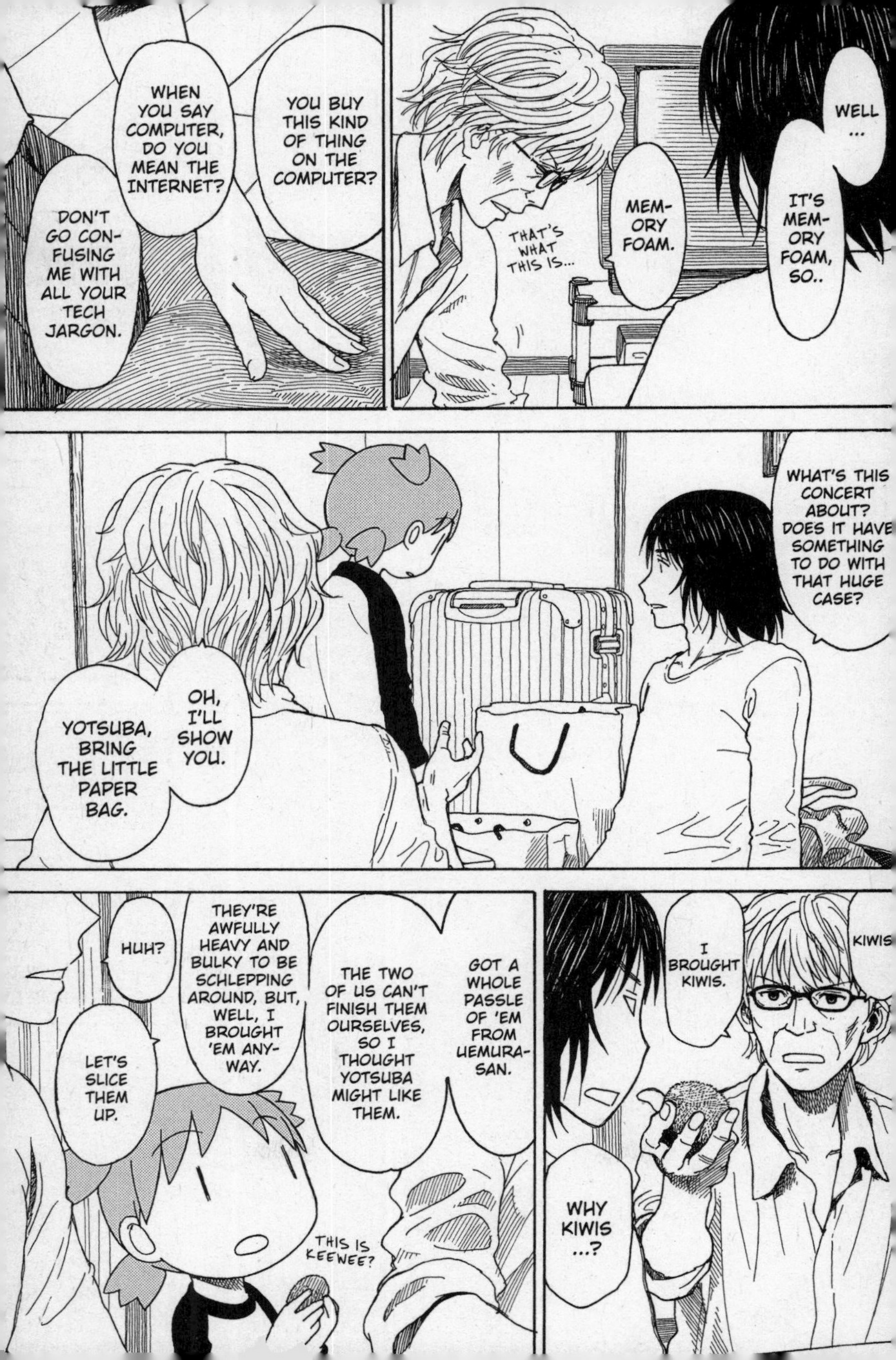

WELL ...
IT'S MEMORY FOAM, SO..
MEMORY FOAM.
THAT'S WHAT THIS IS...
YOU BUY THIS KIND OF THING ON THE COMPUTER?
WHEN YOU SAY COMPUTER, DO YOU MEAN THE INTERNET?
DON'T GO CONFUSING ME WITH ALL YOUR TECH JARGON.
WHAT'S THIS CONCERT ABOUT? DOES IT HAVE SOMETHING TO DO WITH THAT HUGE CASE?
OH, I'LL SHOW YOU.
YOTSUBA, BRING THE LITTLE PAPER BAG.
KIWIS
I BROUGHT KIWIS.
WHY KIWIS ...?
GOT A WHOLE PASSLE OF 'EM FROM UEMURA-SAN.
THE TWO OF US CAN'T FINISH THEM OURSELVES, SO I THOUGHT YOTSUBA MIGHT LIKE THEM.
THEY'RE AWFULLY HEAVY AND BULKY TO BE SCHLEPPING AROUND, BUT, WELL, I BROUGHT 'EM ANYWAY.
HUH?
THIS IS KEEWEE?
LET'S SLICE THEM UP.

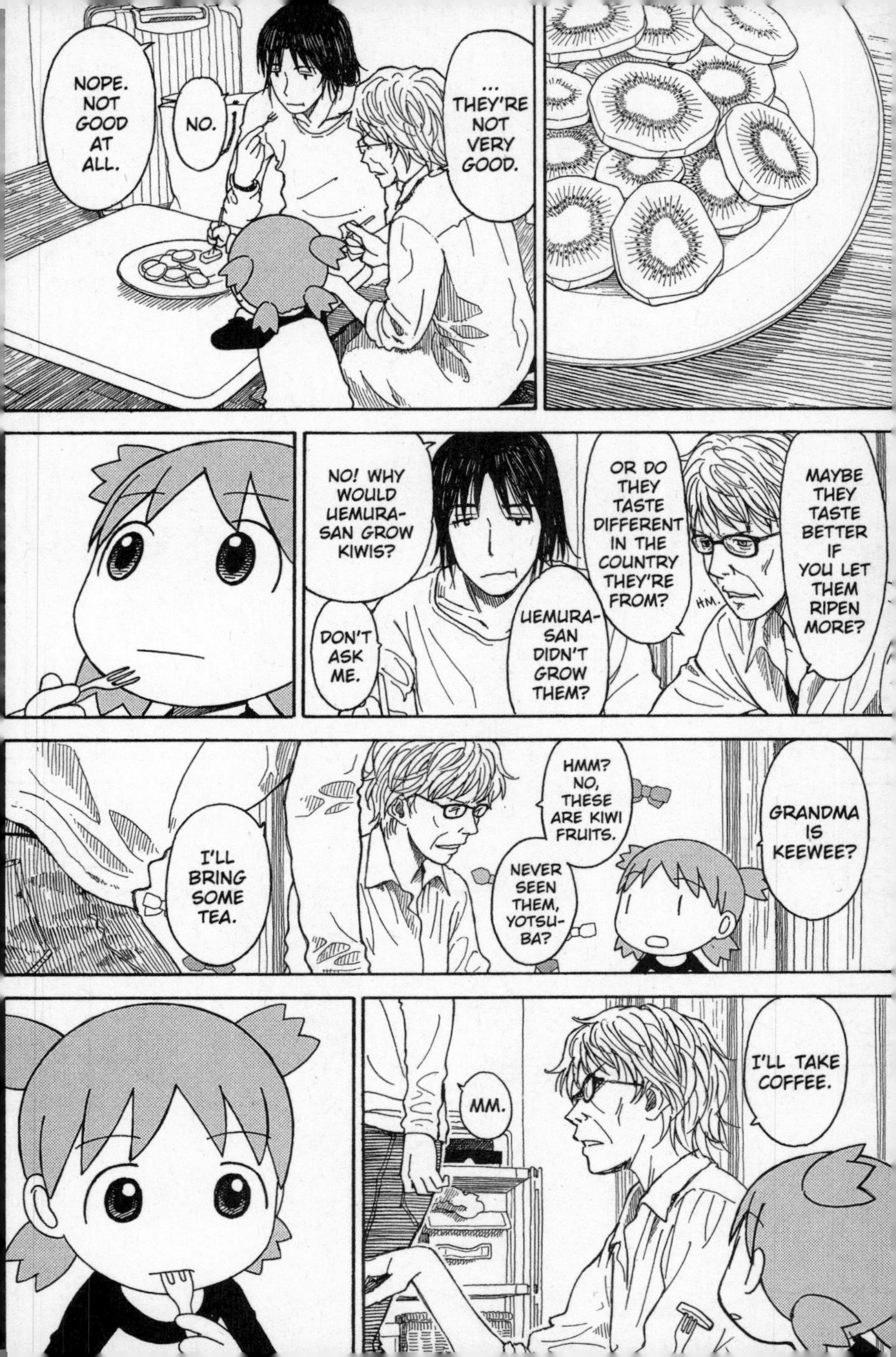
... THEY'RE NOT VERY GOOD.
NO.
NOPE. NOT GOOD AT ALL.
MAYBE THEY TASTE BETTER IF YOU LET THEM RIPEN MORE?
HM.
OR DO THEY TASTE DIFFERENT IN THE COUNTRY THEY'RE FROM?
UEMURA-SAN DIDN'T GROW THEM?
NO! WHY WOULD UEMURA-SAN GROW KIWIS?
DON'T ASK ME.
GRANDMA IS KEEWEE?
HMM? NO, THESE ARE KIWI FRUITS.
NEVER SEEN THEM, YOTSUBA?
I'LL BRING SOME TEA.
I'LL TAKE COFFEE.
MM.

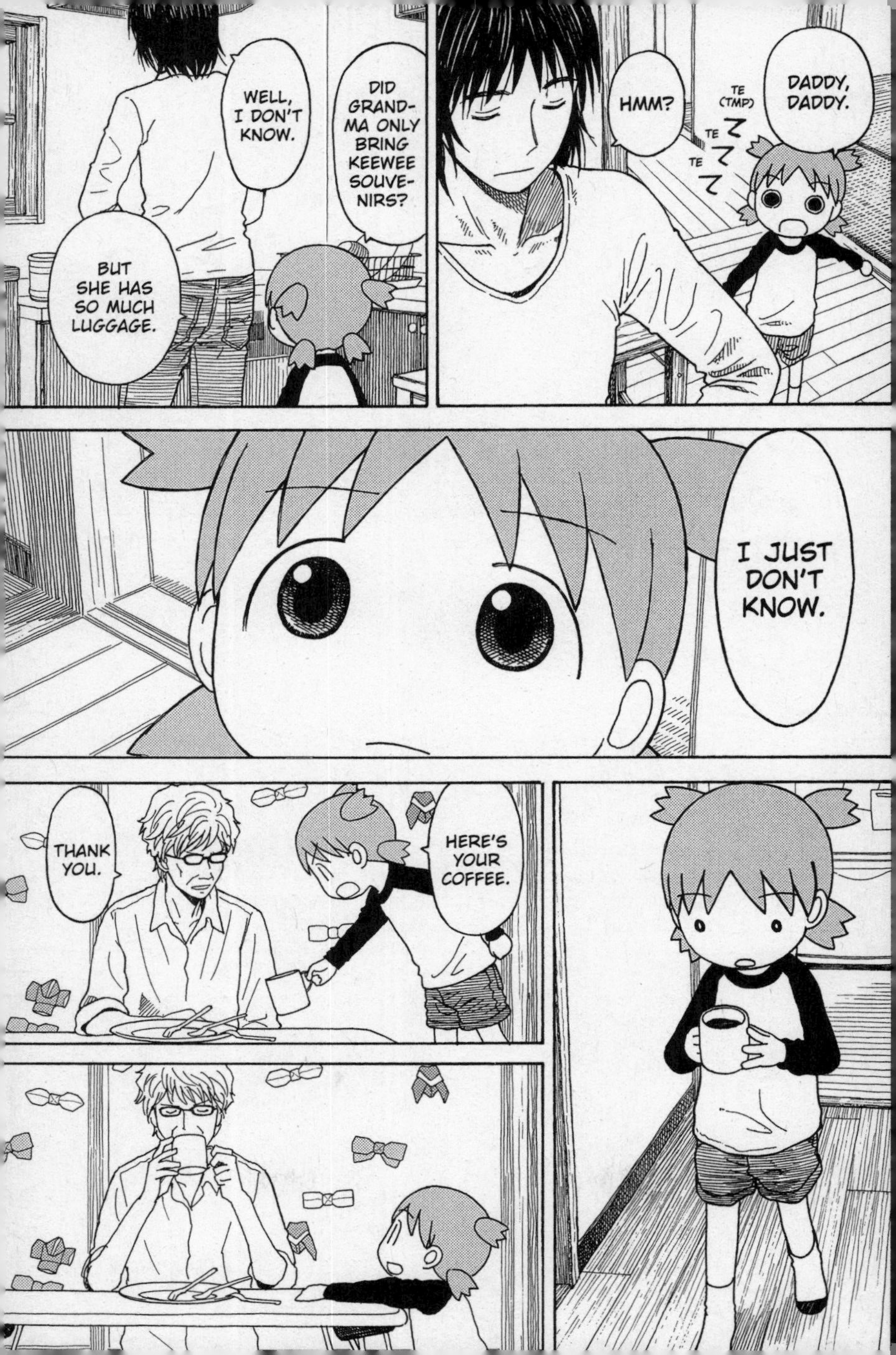
DADDY, DADDY.
TE (TMP) TE TE
HMM?
DID GRANDMA ONLY BRING KEEWEE SOUVENIRS?
WELL, I DON'T KNOW.
BUT SHE HAS SO MUCH LUGGAGE.
I JUST DON'T KNOW.
HERE'S YOUR COFFEE.
THANK YOU.

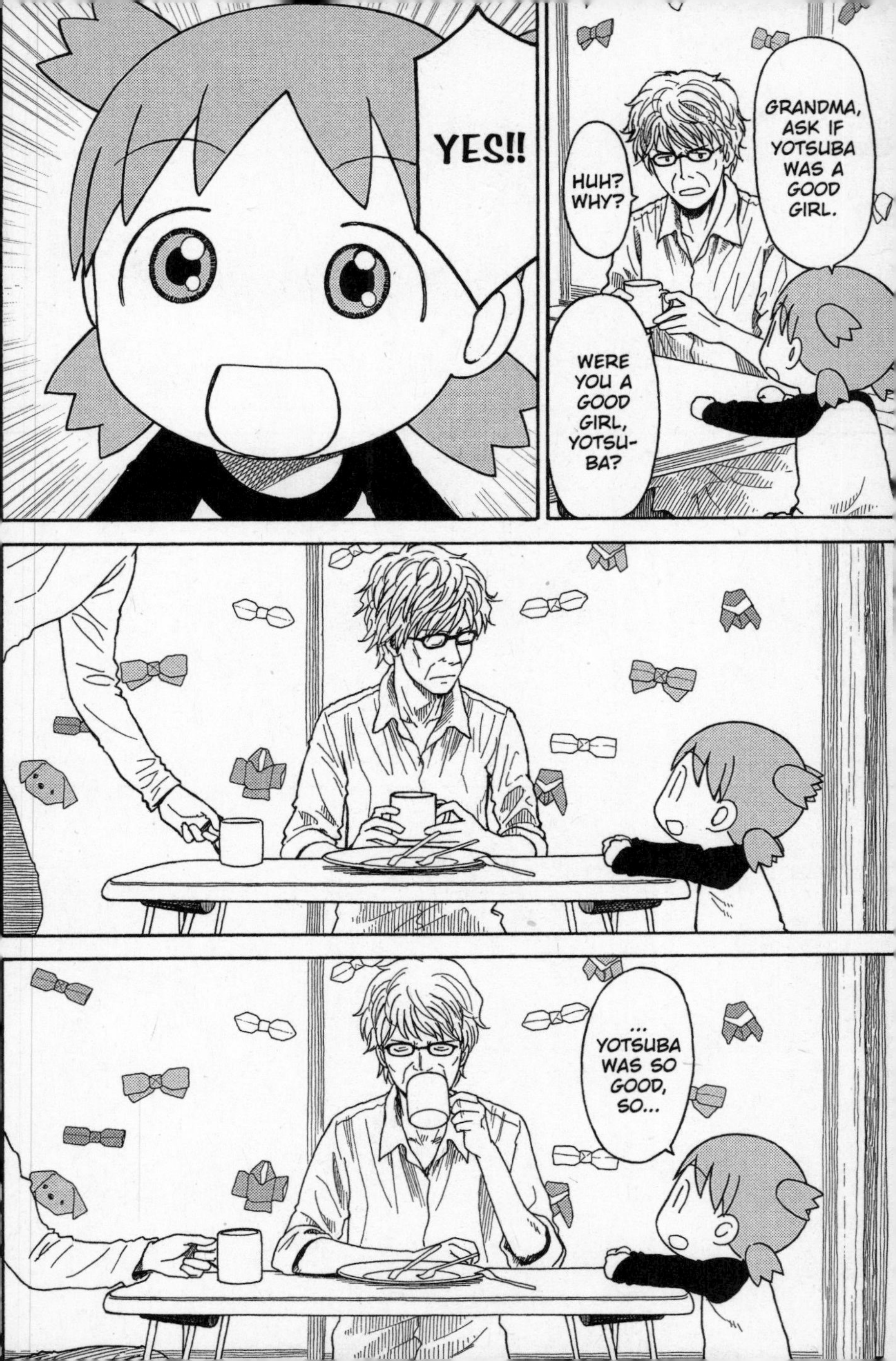
GRANDMA, ASK IF YOTSUBA WAS A GOOD GIRL.
HUH? WHY?
WERE YOU A GOOD GIRL, YOTSU-BA?
YES!!
... YOTSUBA WAS SO GOOD, SO...

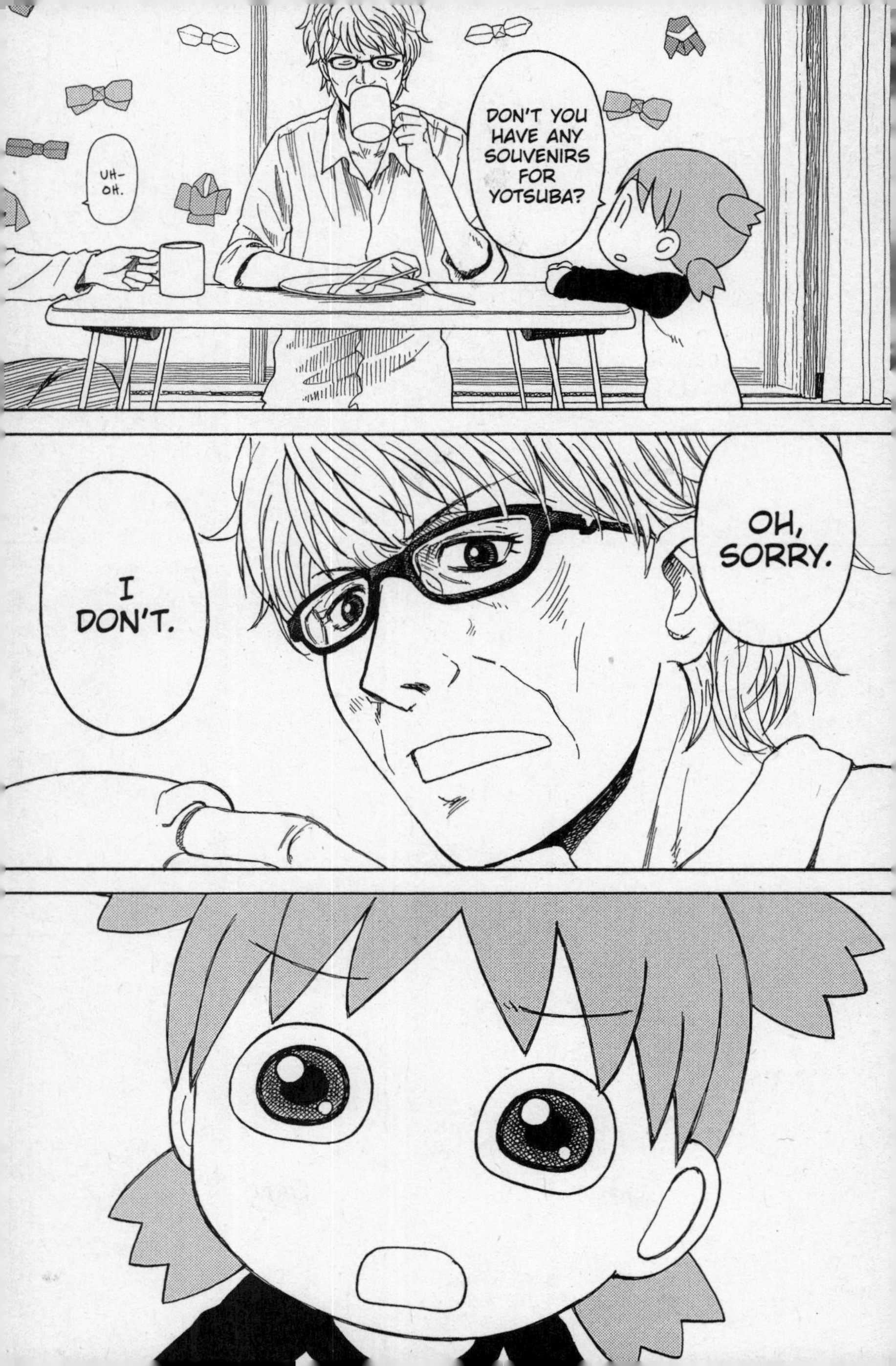
DON'T YOU HAVE ANY SOUVENIRS FOR YOTSUBA?
UH-OH.
OH, SORRY.
I DON'T.

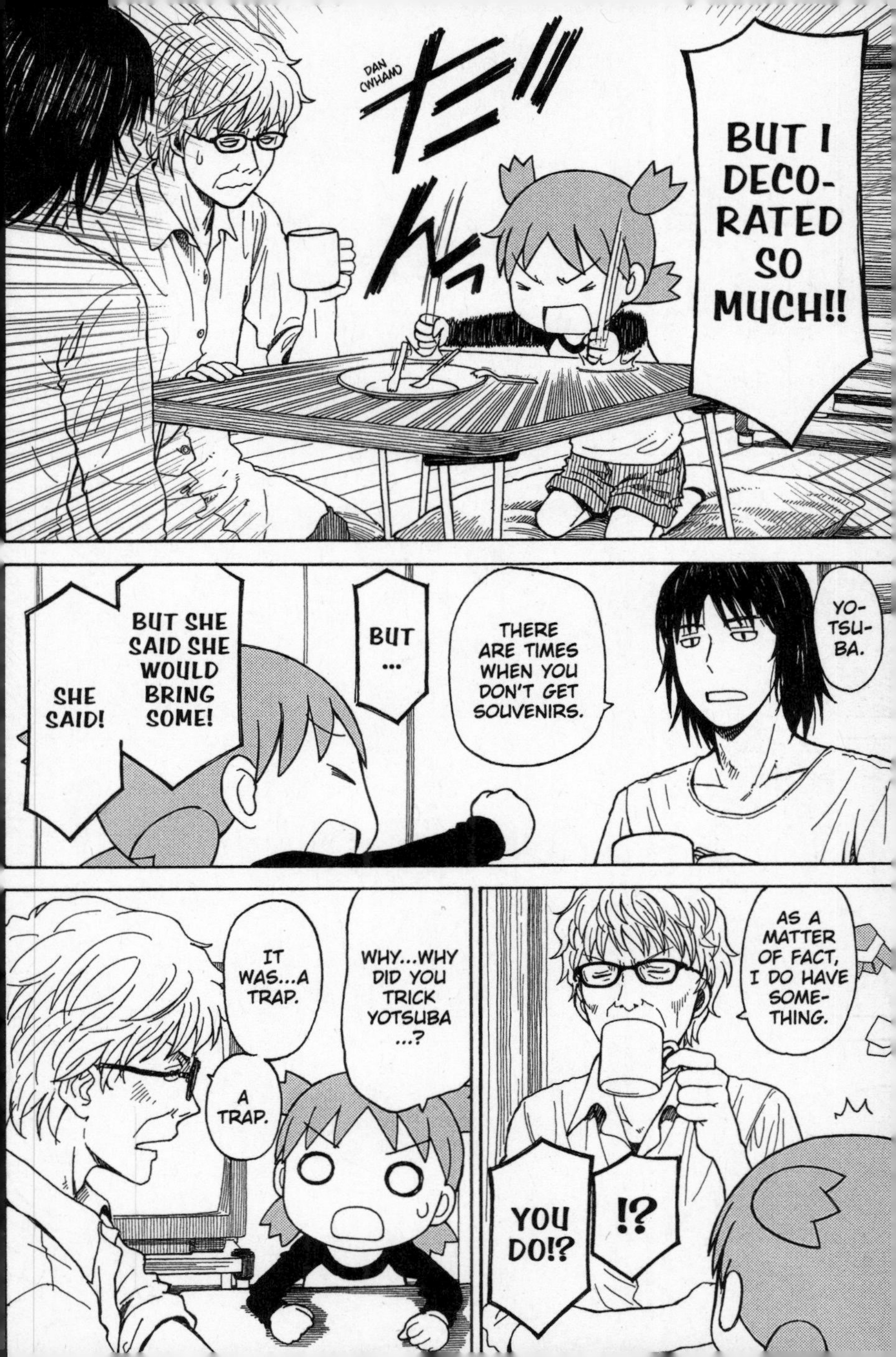
BUT I DECORATED SO MUCH!!
DAN (WHAM)
YO-TSU-BA.
THERE ARE TIMES WHEN YOU DON'T GET SOUVENIRS.
BUT ...
BUT SHE SAID SHE WOULD BRING SOME!
SHE SAID!
AS A MATTER OF FACT, I DO HAVE SOME-THING.
!?
YOU DO!?
WHY...WHY DID YOU TRICK YOTSUBA ...?
IT WAS...A TRAP.
A TRAP.

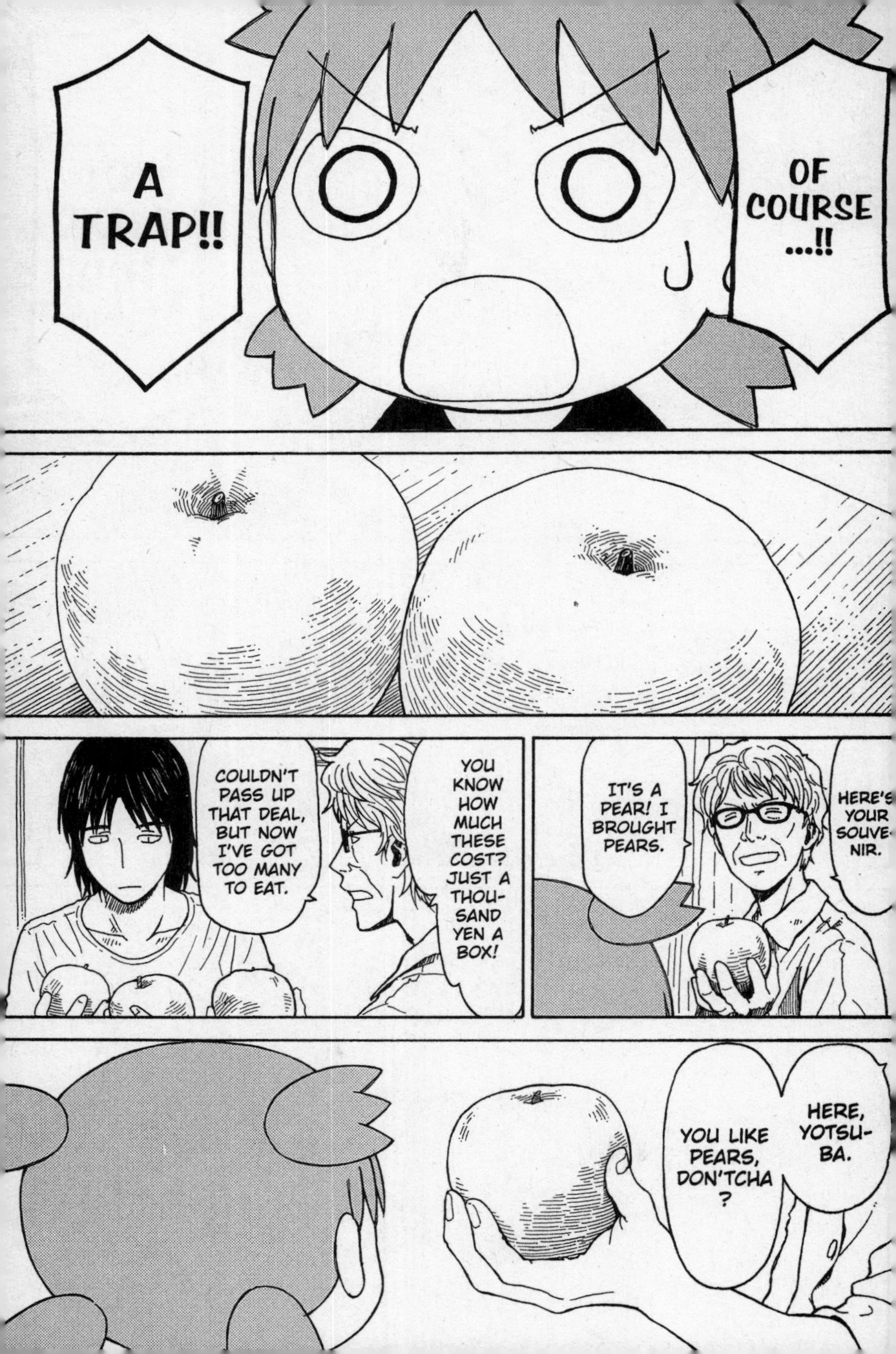
OF COURSE ...!!
A TRAP!!
HERE'S YOUR SOUVENIR.
IT'S A PEAR! I BROUGHT PEARS.
YOU KNOW HOW MUCH THESE COST? JUST A THOUSAND YEN A BOX!
COULDN'T PASS UP THAT DEAL, BUT NOW I'VE GOT TOO MANY TO EAT.
HERE, YOTSUBA.
YOU LIKE PEARS, DON'TCHA?

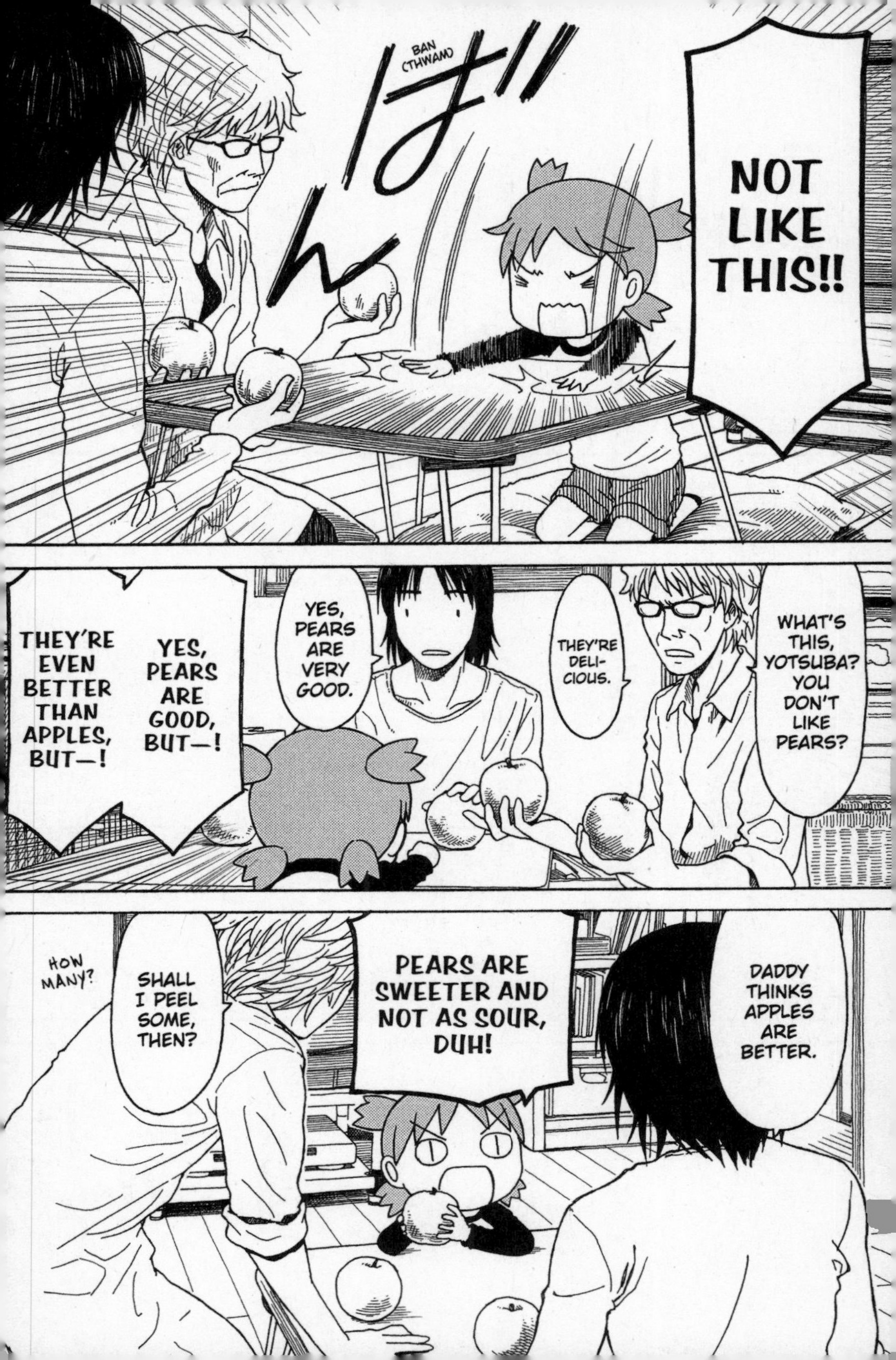
NOT LIKE THIS!!
ばん
BAN (THWAM)
WHAT'S THIS, YOTSUBA? YOU DON'T LIKE PEARS?
THEY'RE DELICIOUS.
YES, PEARS ARE VERY GOOD.
YES, PEARS ARE GOOD, BUT—!
THEY'RE EVEN BETTER THAN APPLES, BUT—!
DADDY THINKS APPLES ARE BETTER.
PEARS ARE SWEETER AND NOT AS SOUR, DUH!
SHALL I PEEL SOME, THEN?
HOW MANY?

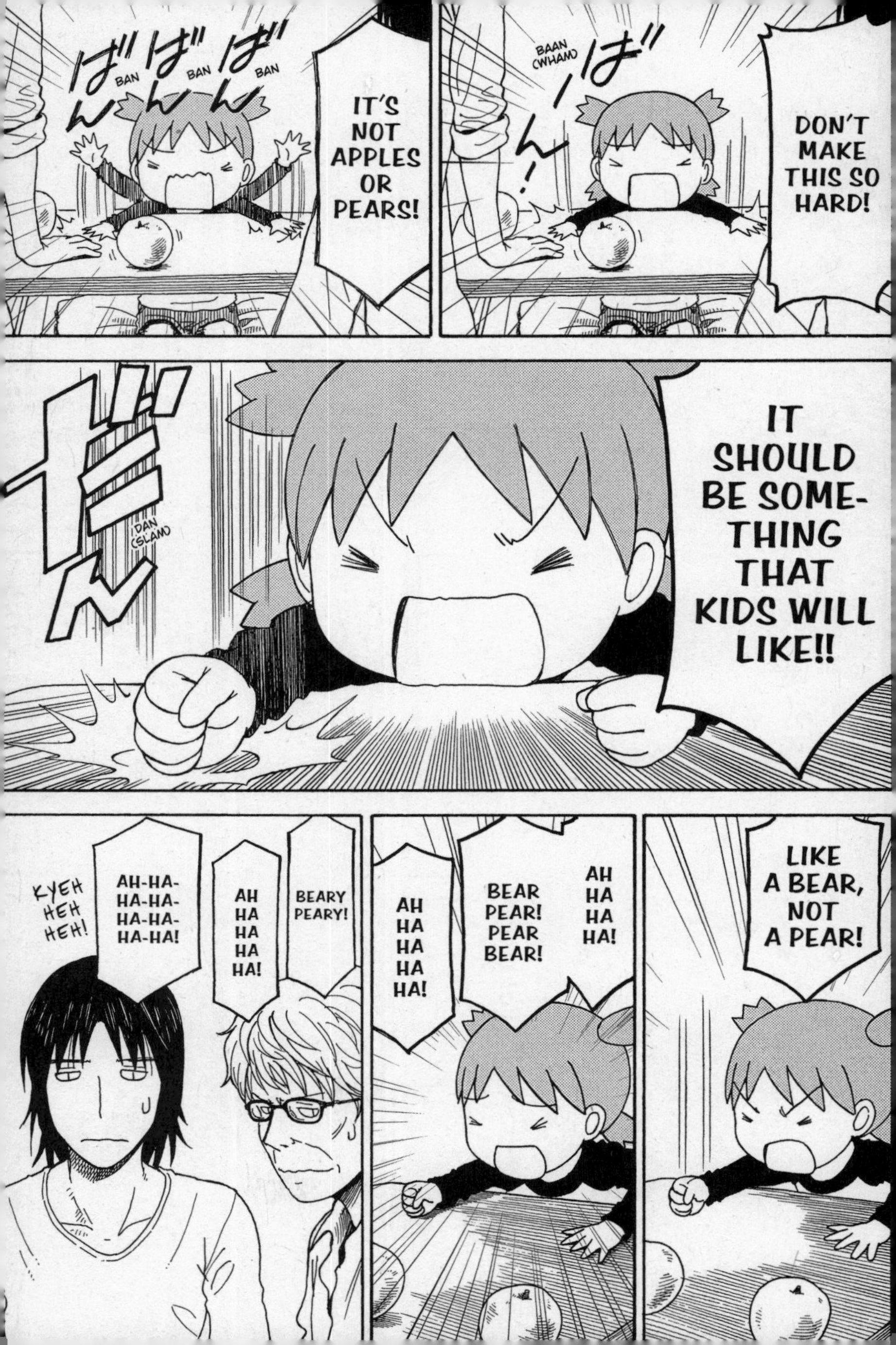

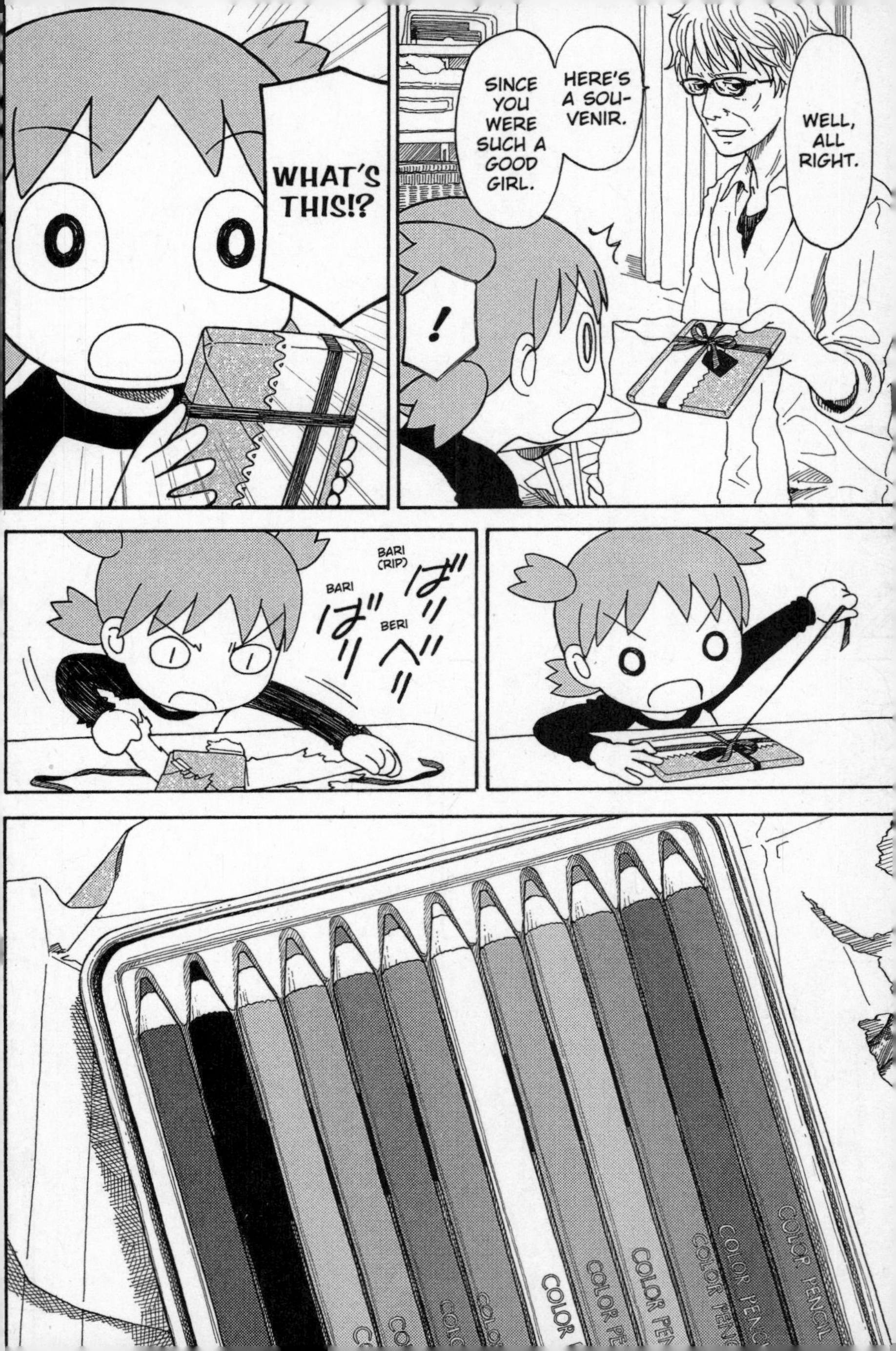
WELL, ALL RIGHT.
HERE'S A SOU-VENIR.
SINCE YOU WERE SUCH A GOOD GIRL.
!
WHAT'S THIS!?
ばりっ
BARI (RIP)
ばりっ
BARI
べりっ
BERI
COLOR PENCIL

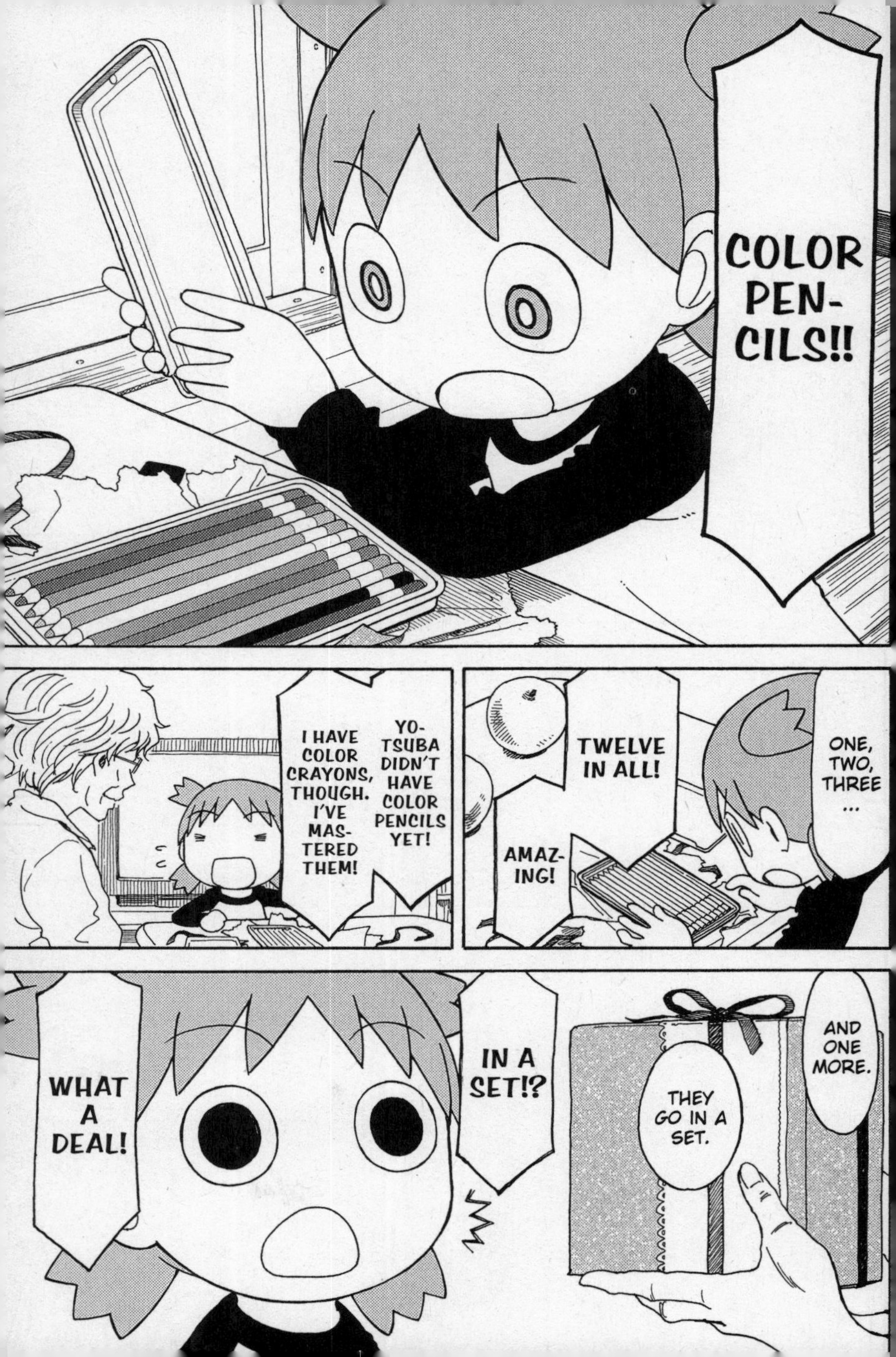
COLOR PEN-CILS!!
ONE, TWO, THREE ...
TWELVE IN ALL!
AMAZ-ING!
YO-TSUBA DIDN'T HAVE COLOR PENCILS YET!
I HAVE COLOR CRAYONS, THOUGH. I'VE MAS-TERED THEM!
AND ONE MORE.
THEY GO IN A SET.
IN A SET!?
WHAT A DEAL!

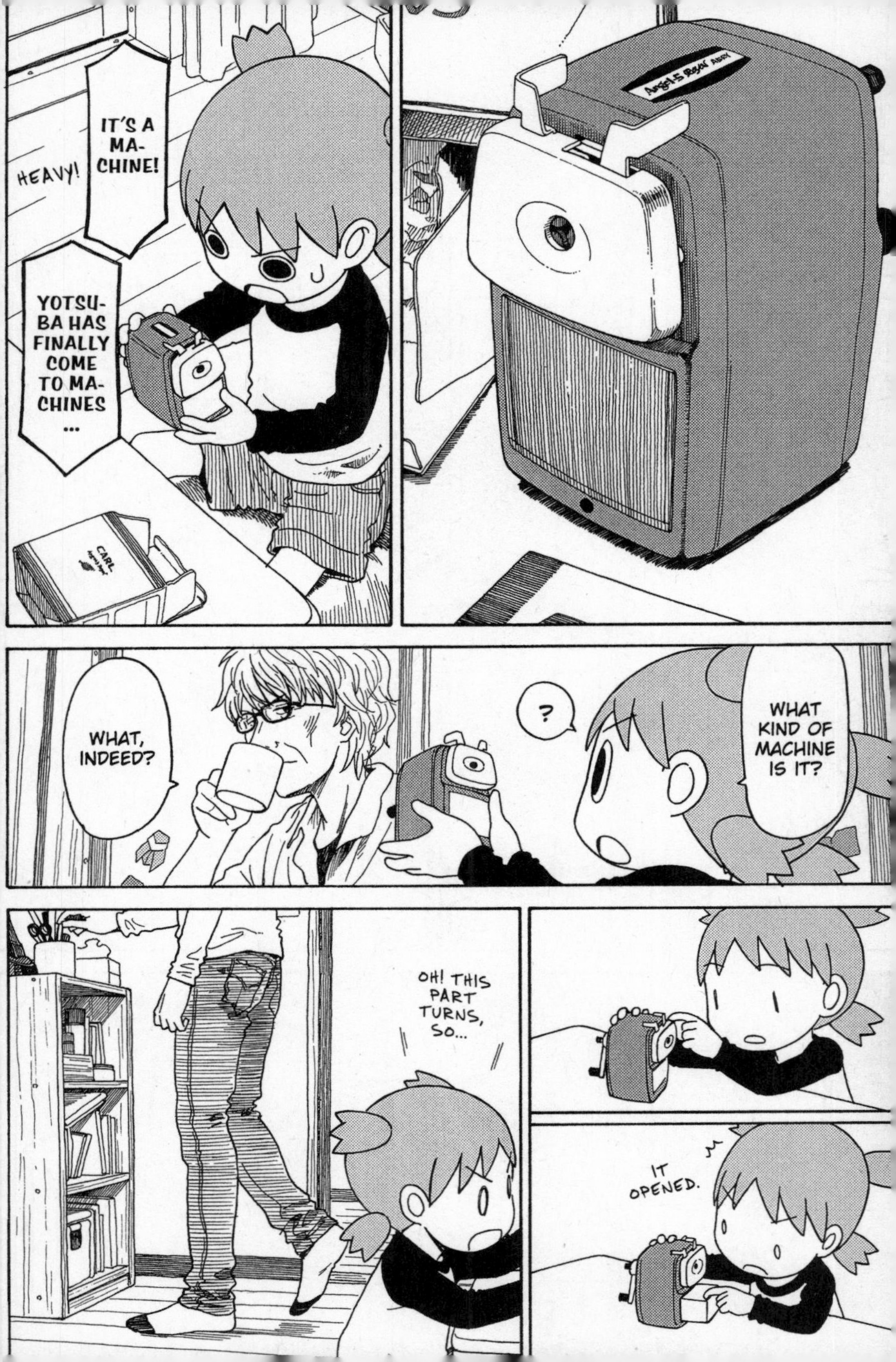
IT'S A MA-CHINE!
HEAVY!
YOTSU-BA HAS FINALLY COME TO MA-CHINES ...
CARL
WHAT KIND OF MACHINE IS IT?
?
WHAT, INDEED?
IT OPENED.
OH! THIS PART TURNS, SO...

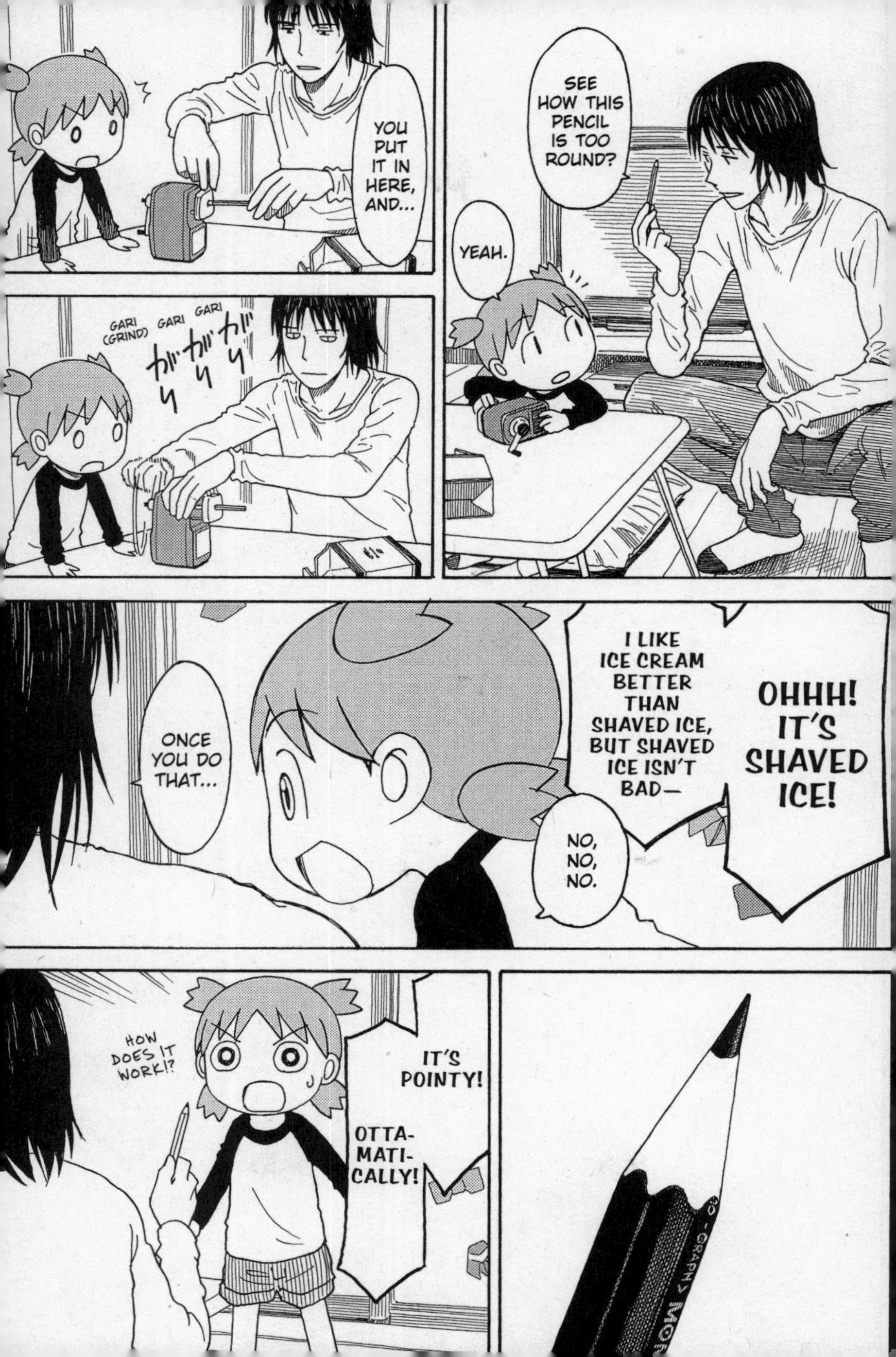
SEE HOW THIS PENCIL IS TOO ROUND?
YEAH.
YOU PUT IT IN HERE, AND...
GARI (GRIND) GARI GARI
ガリガリガリ
OHHH! IT'S SHAVED ICE!
I LIKE ICE CREAM BETTER THAN SHAVED ICE, BUT SHAVED ICE ISN'T BAD—
NO, NO, NO.
ONCE YOU DO THAT...
IT'S POINTY!
OTTA-MATI-CALLY!
HOW DOES IT WORK!?

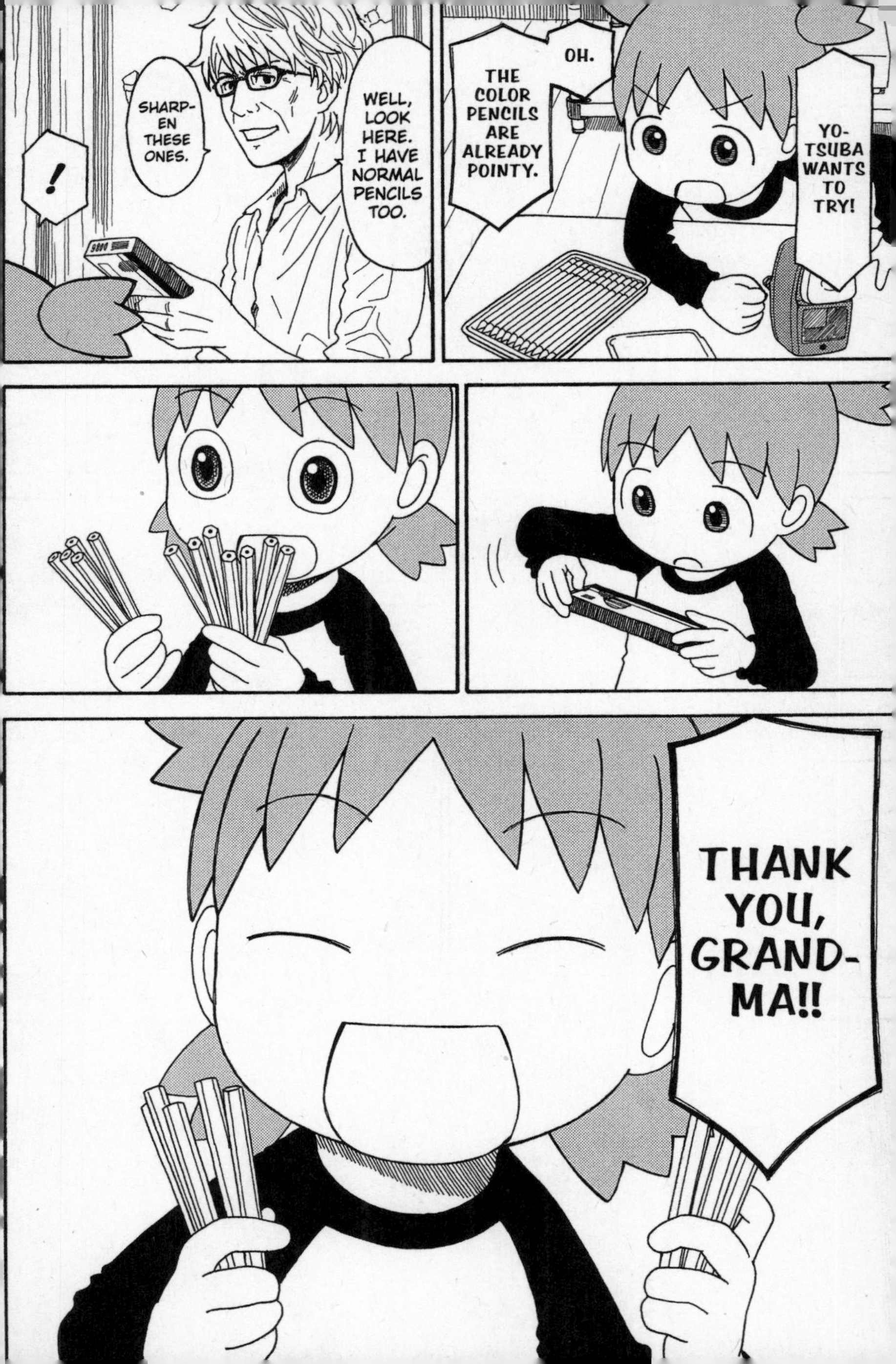
YO-TSUBA WANTS TO TRY!
OH.
THE COLOR PENCILS ARE ALREADY POINTY.
WELL, LOOK HERE. I HAVE NORMAL PENCILS TOO.
SHARP-EN THESE ONES.
!
THANK YOU, GRAND-MA!!

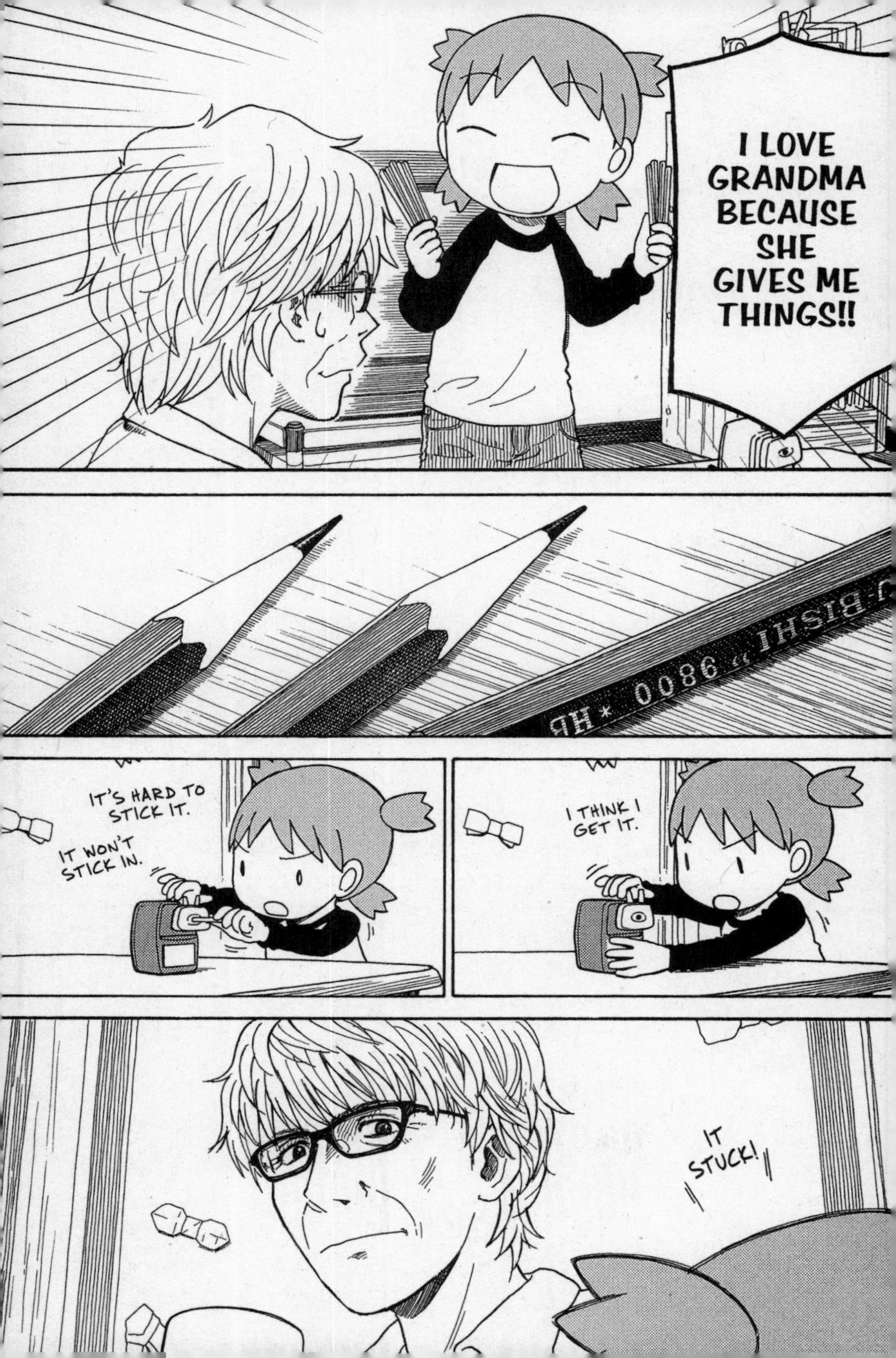
I LOVE GRANDMA BECAUSE SHE GIVES ME THINGS!!
I THINK I GET IT.
IT'S HARD TO STICK IT.
IT WON'T STICK IN.
IT STUCK!

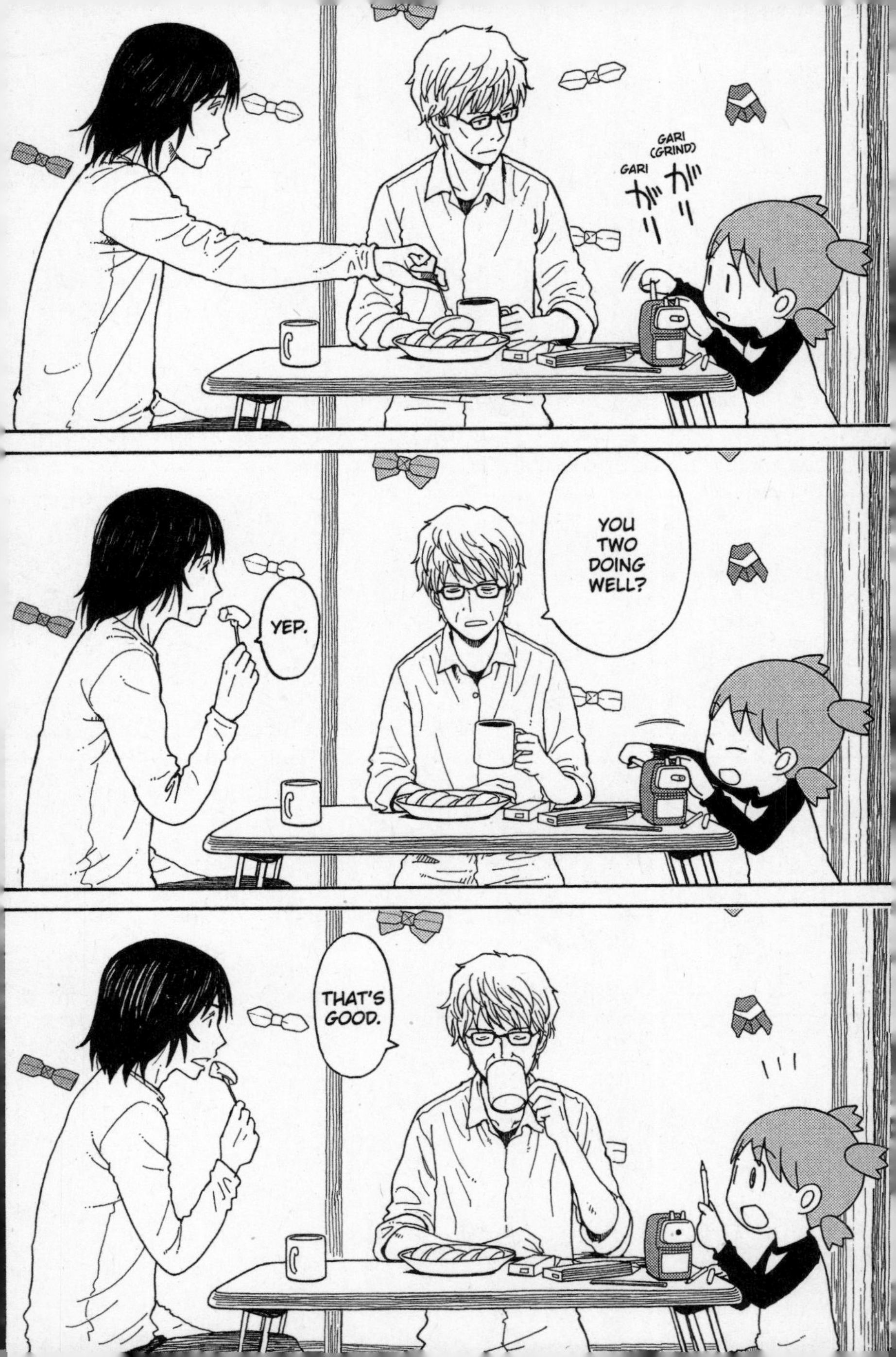

GARI (GRIND)
GARI
がり
がり
YOU TWO DOING WELL?
YEP.
THAT'S GOOD.

YOTSUBA&!

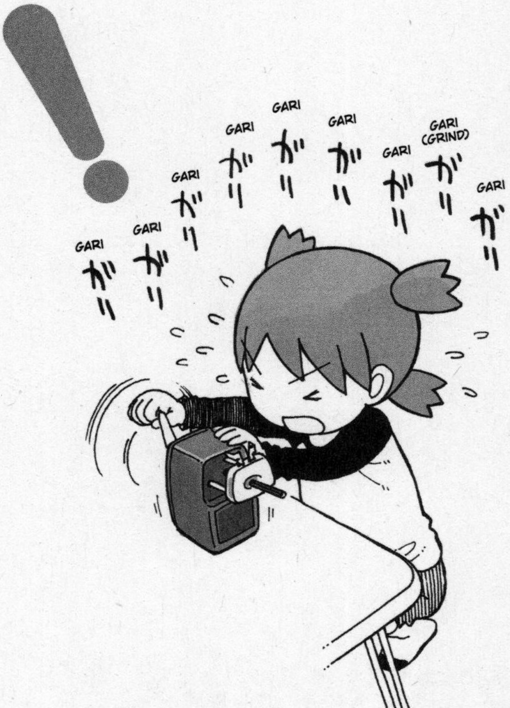
GARI
がり
GARI
(GRIND)
がり
GARI
がり
GARI
がり
GARI
がり
GARI
がり
GARI
がり
GARI
がり
GARI
がり
!

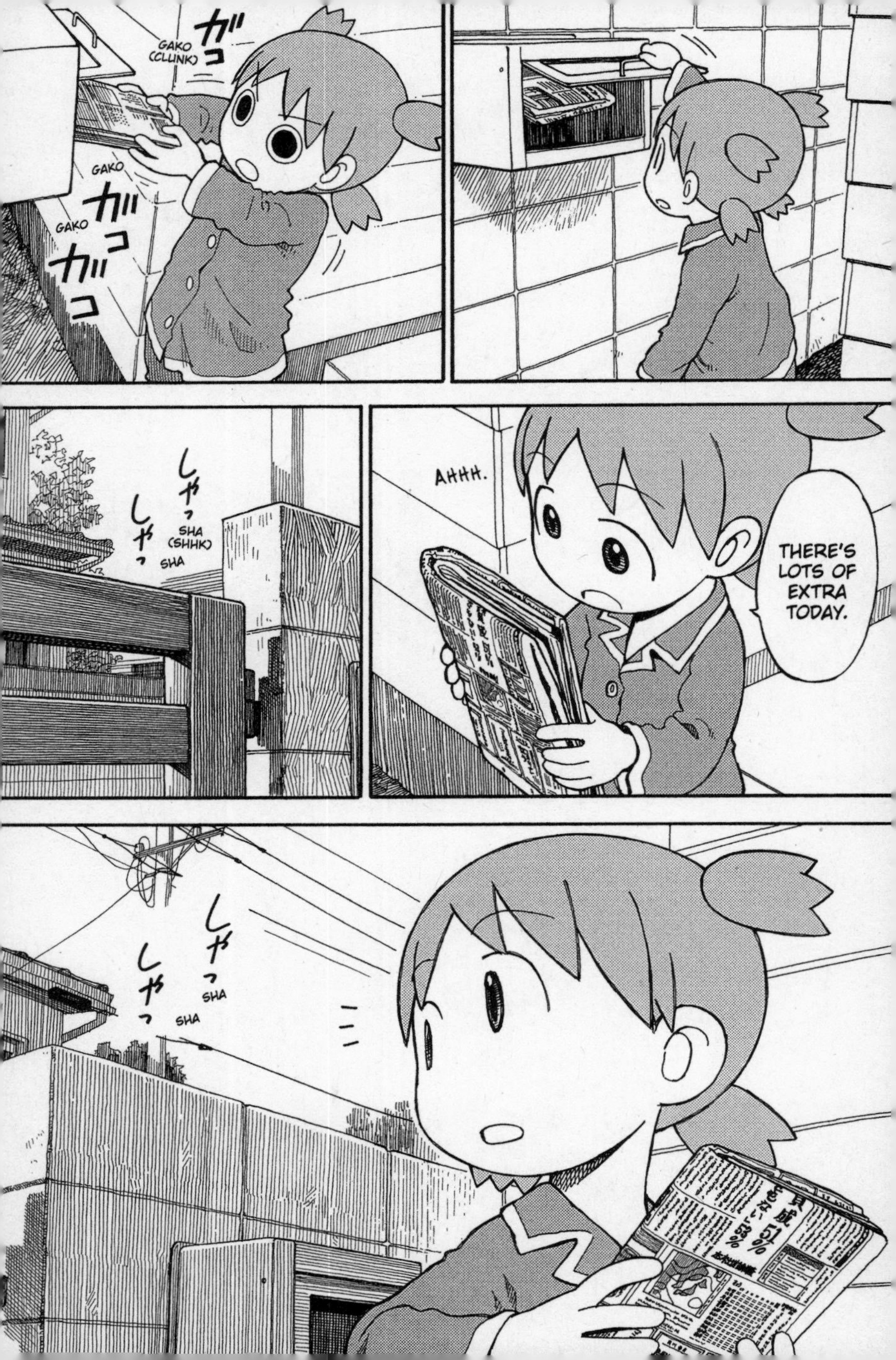
ガコ
GAKO (CLUNK)
ガコ
GAKO
ガコ
GAKO
AHHH.
THERE'S LOTS OF EXTRA TODAY.
しゃっ
SHA (SHHK)
しゃっ
SHA
しゃっ
SHA
しゃっ
SHA

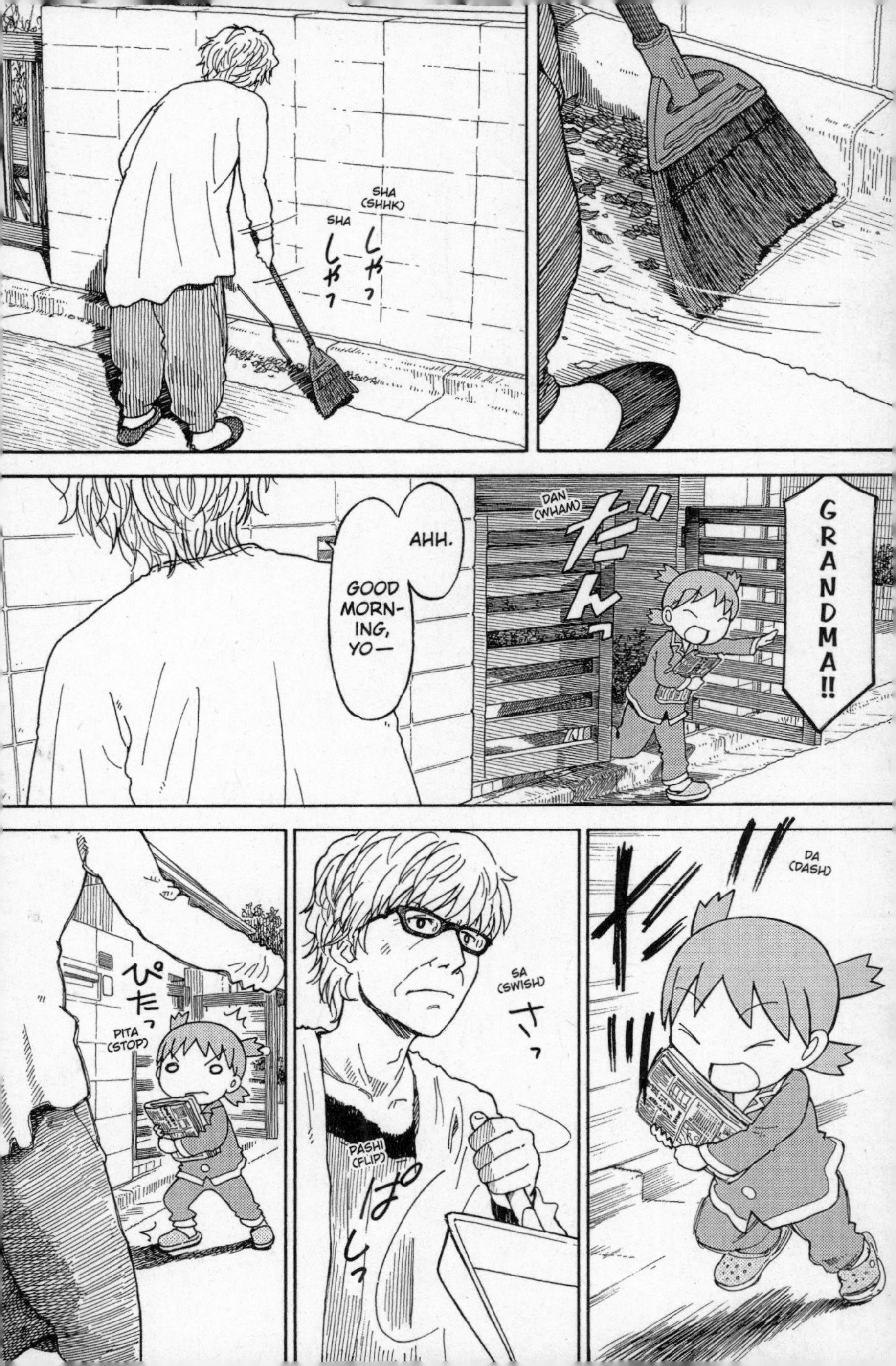
SHA (SHHK)
SHA
しゃっ
しゃっ
DAN (WHAM)
だんっ
GRANDMA!!
AHH.
GOOD MORNING, YO—
DA (DASH)
ダッ
SA (SWISH)
さっ
PASHI (FLIP)
ぱしっ
ぴたっ
PITA (STOP)

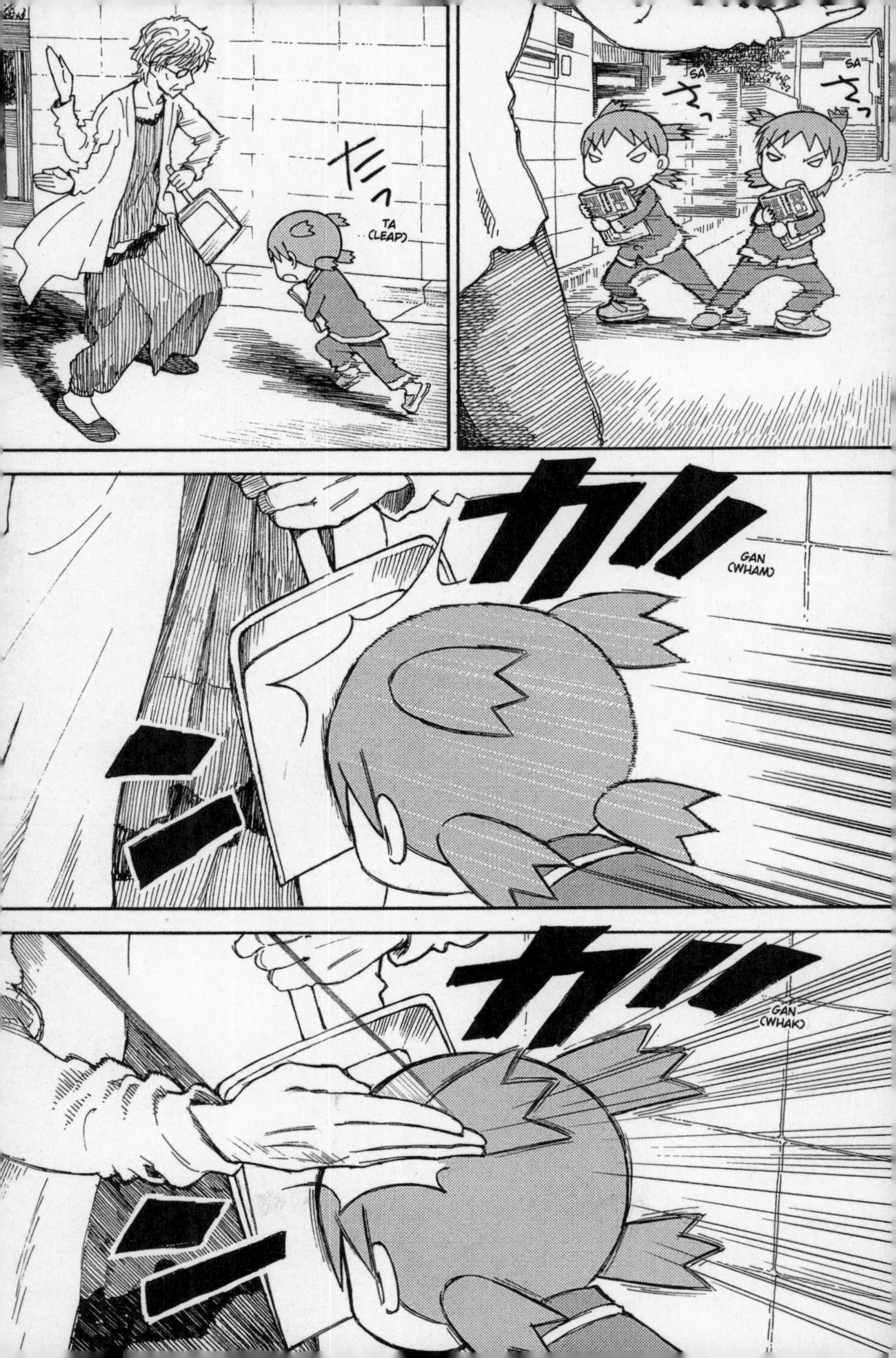
SA
さっ
SA
さっ
たっ
TA (LEAP)
ガン
GAN (WHAM)
ガン
GAN (WHAK)

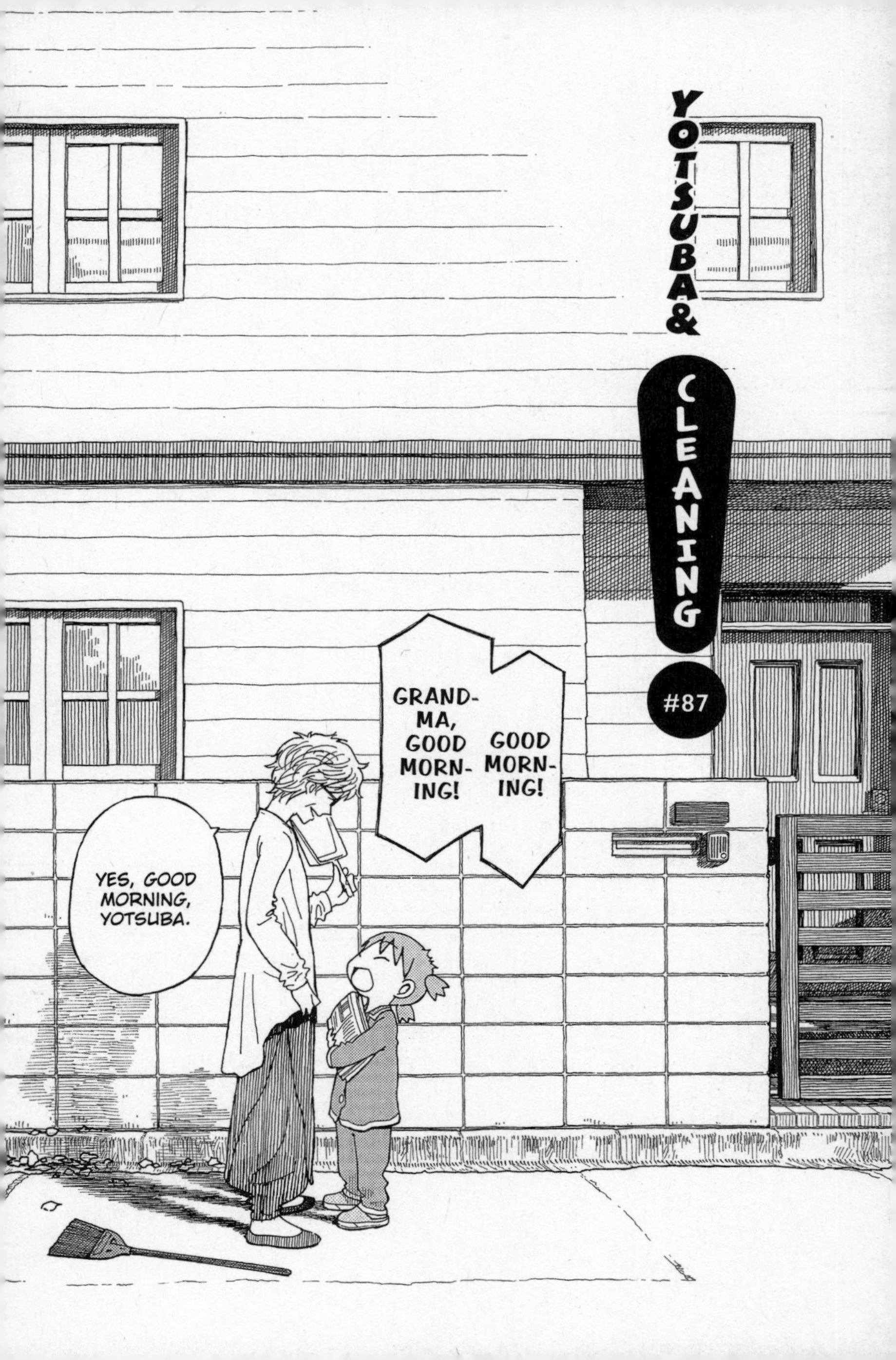
YOTSUBA&
CLEANING!
#87
GOOD MORNING!
GRANDMA, GOOD MORNING!
YES, GOOD MORNING, YOTSUBA.

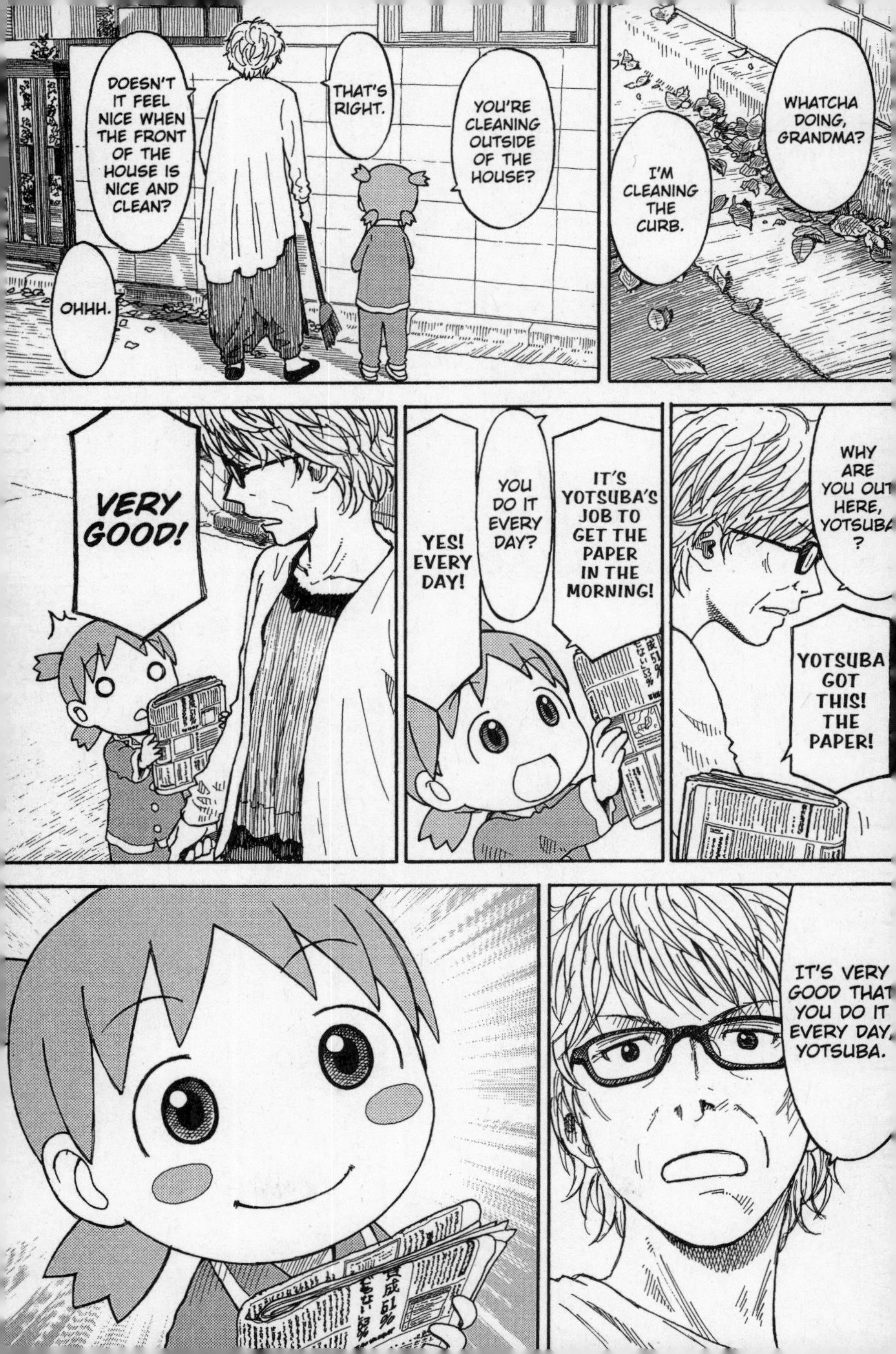
WHATCHA DOING, GRANDMA?
I'M CLEANING THE CURB.
YOU'RE CLEANING OUTSIDE OF THE HOUSE?
THAT'S RIGHT.
DOESN'T IT FEEL NICE WHEN THE FRONT OF THE HOUSE IS NICE AND CLEAN?
OHHH.
WHY ARE YOU OUT HERE, YOTSUBA?
YOTSUBA GOT THIS! THE PAPER!
IT'S YOTSUBA'S JOB TO GET THE PAPER IN THE MORNING!
YOU DO IT EVERY DAY?
YES! EVERY DAY!
VERY GOOD!
IT'S VERY GOOD THAT YOU DO IT EVERY DAY, YOTSUBA.

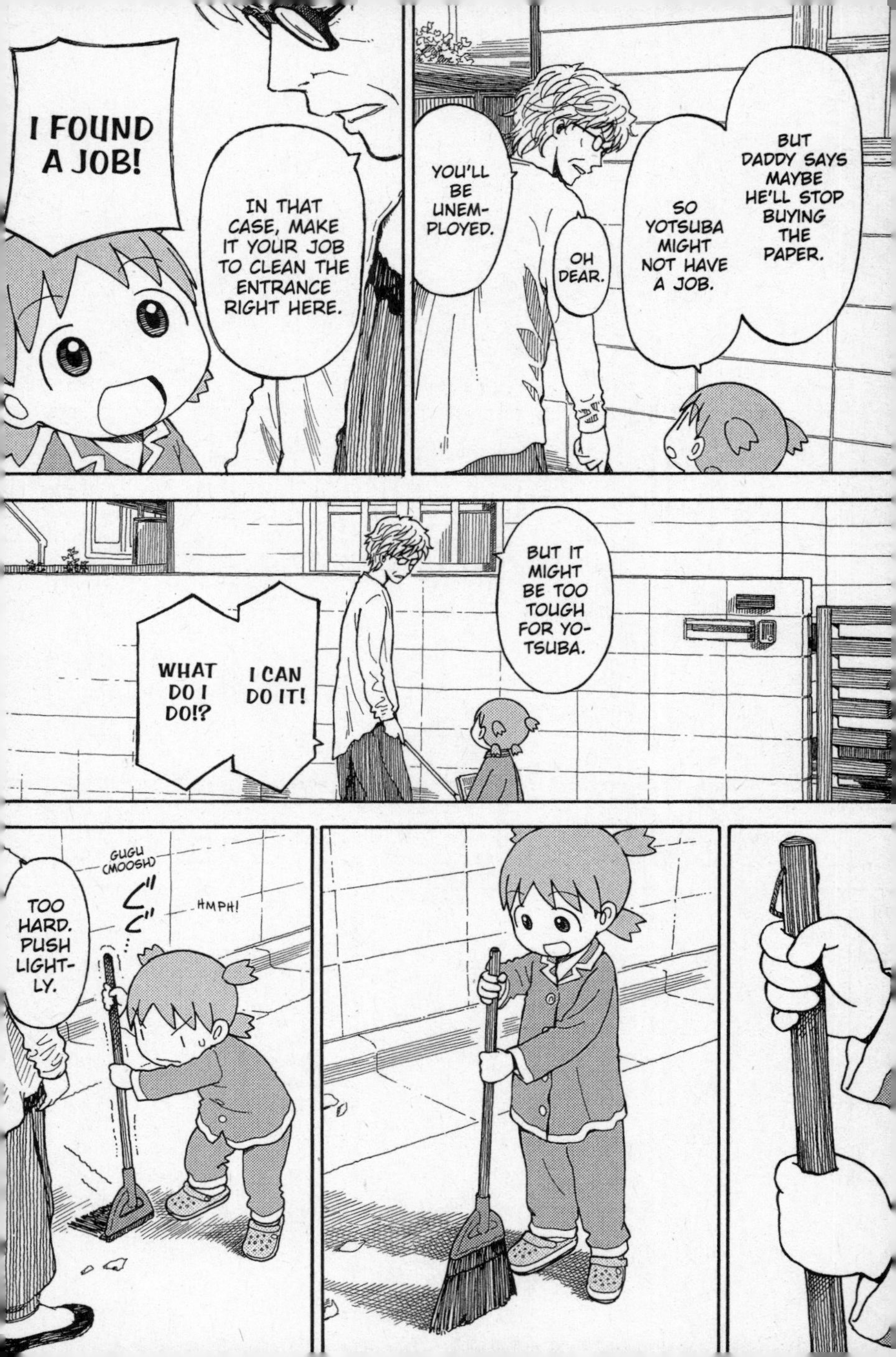

BUT DADDY SAYS MAYBE HE'LL STOP BUYING THE PAPER.
SO YOTSUBA MIGHT NOT HAVE A JOB.
OH DEAR.
YOU'LL BE UNEM-PLOYED.
IN THAT CASE, MAKE IT YOUR JOB TO CLEAN THE ENTRANCE RIGHT HERE.
I FOUND A JOB!
BUT IT MIGHT BE TOO TOUGH FOR YO-TSUBA.
I CAN DO IT!
WHAT DO I DO!?
HMPH!
GUGU (MOOSH)
TOO HARD. PUSH LIGHT-LY.

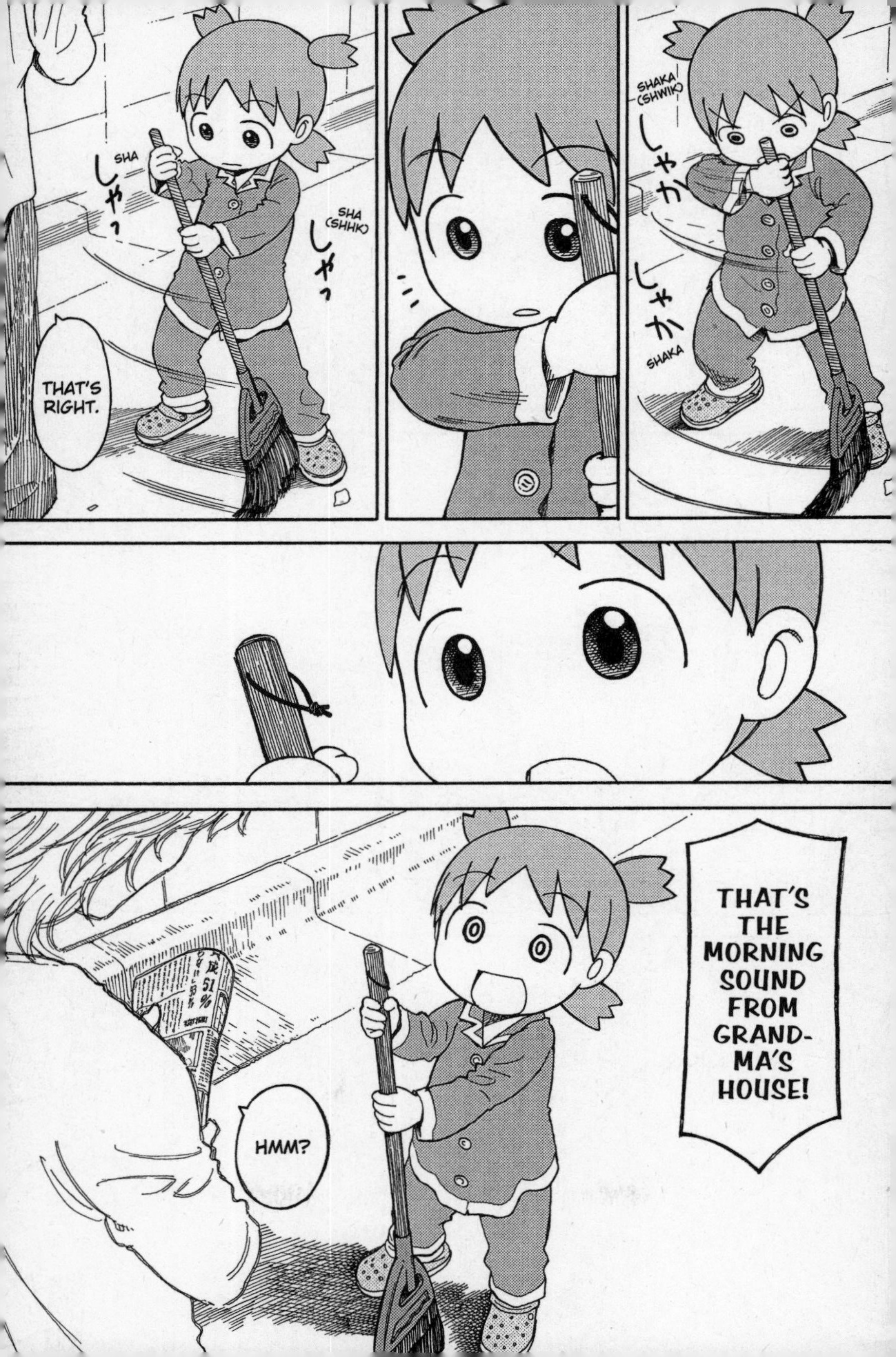
SHAKA (SHWIK)
しゃか
しゃか
SHAKA
SHA
しゃっ
SHA (SHHK)
しゃっ
THAT'S RIGHT.
THAT'S THE MORNING SOUND FROM GRAND-MA'S HOUSE!
HMM?

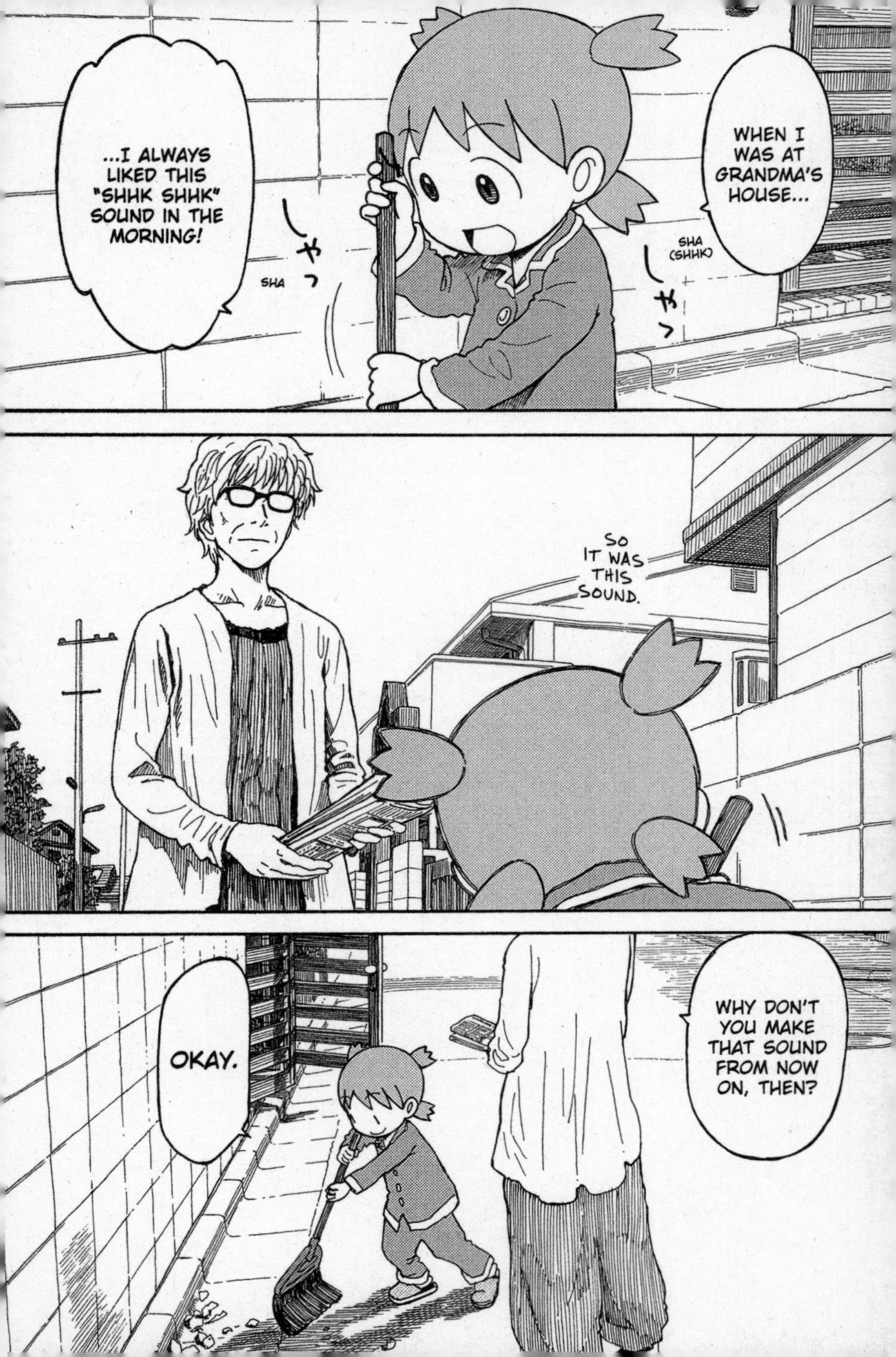

WHEN I WAS AT GRANDMA'S HOUSE...
SHA (SHHK)
...I ALWAYS LIKED THIS "SHHK SHHK" SOUND IN THE MORNING!
SHA
SO IT WAS THIS SOUND.
WHY DON'T YOU MAKE THAT SOUND FROM NOW ON, THEN?
OKAY.

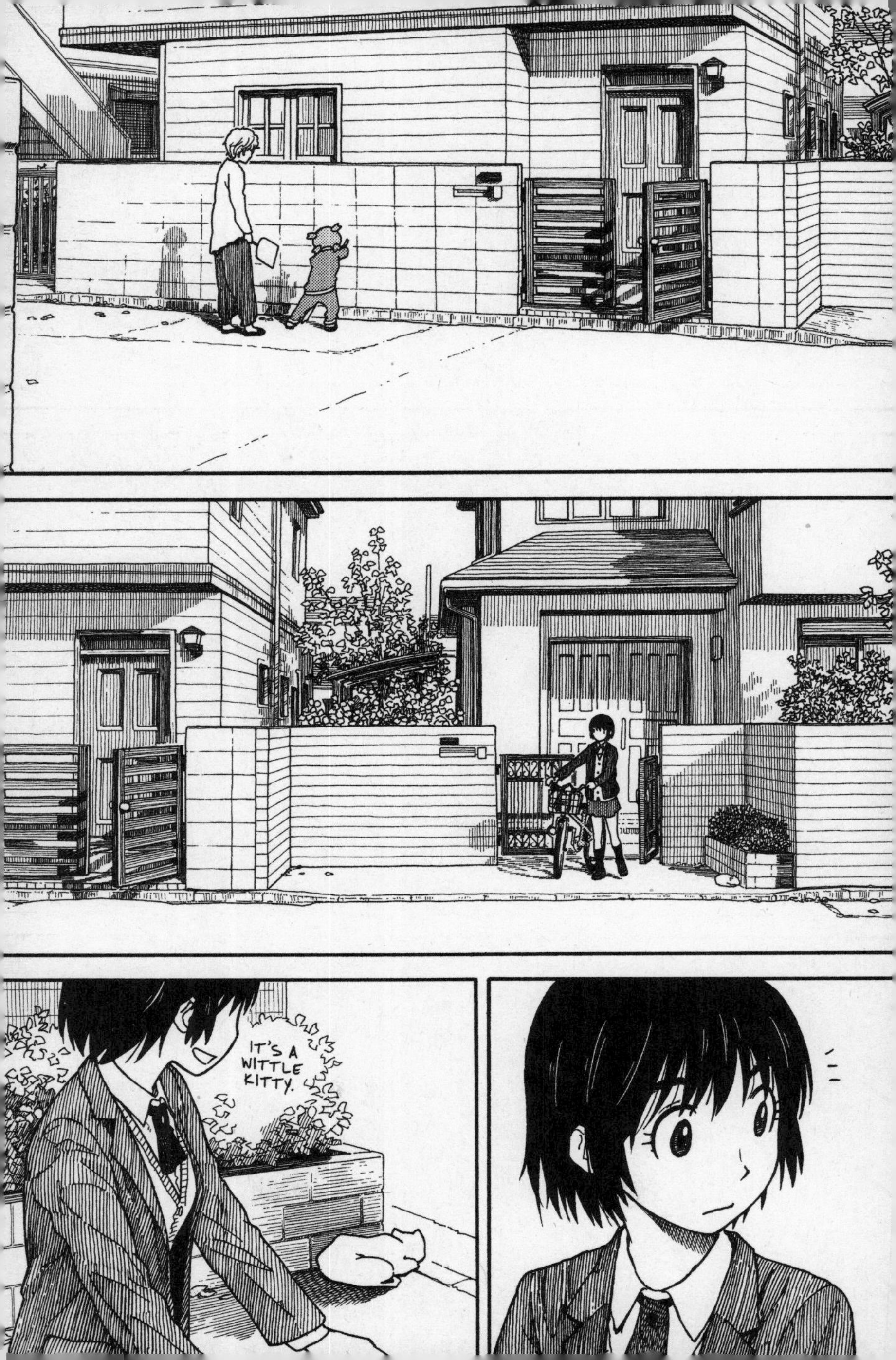
IT'S A WITTLE KITTY.

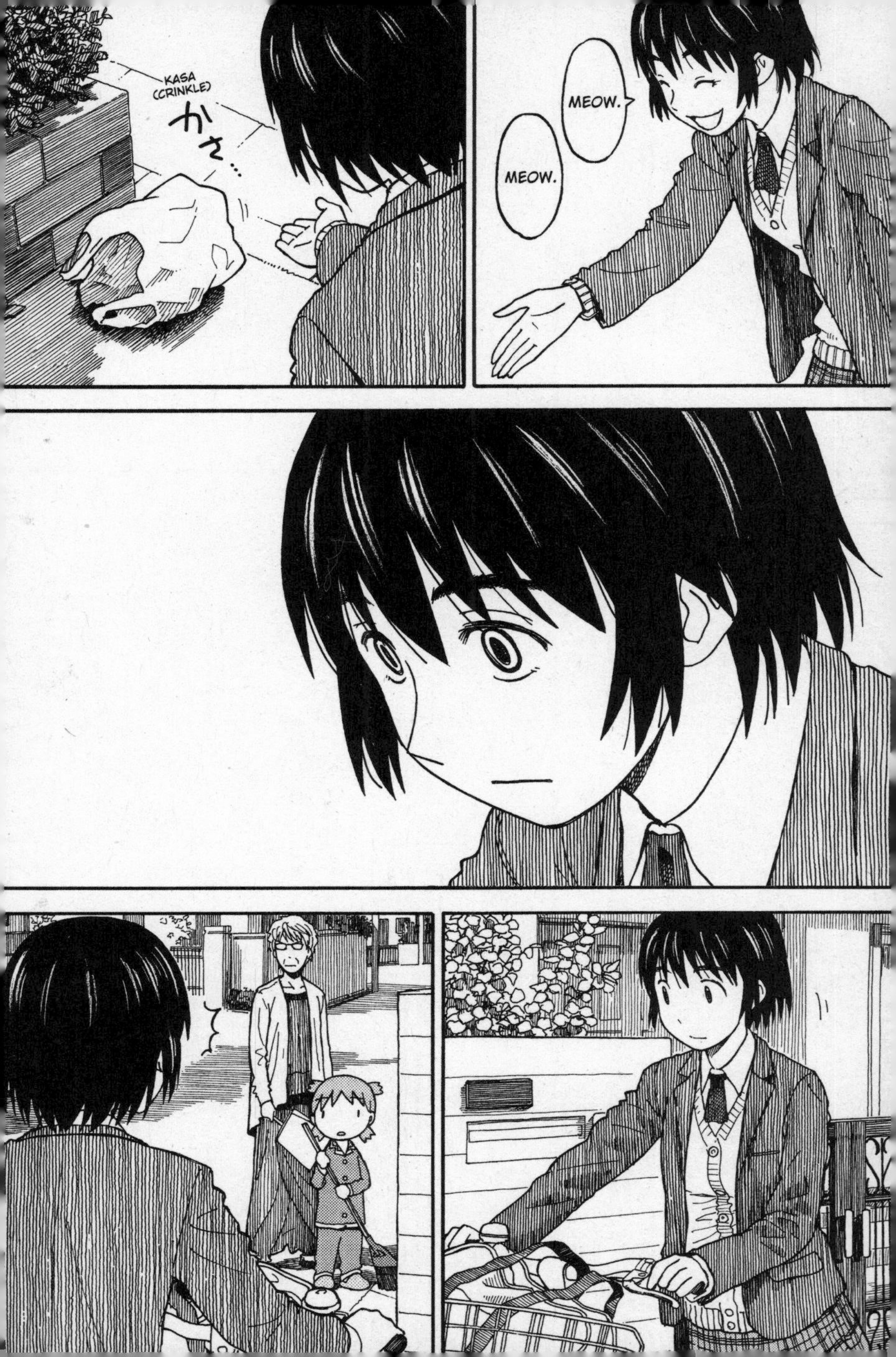
MEOW.
MEOW.
KASA (CRINKLE)
かさ…

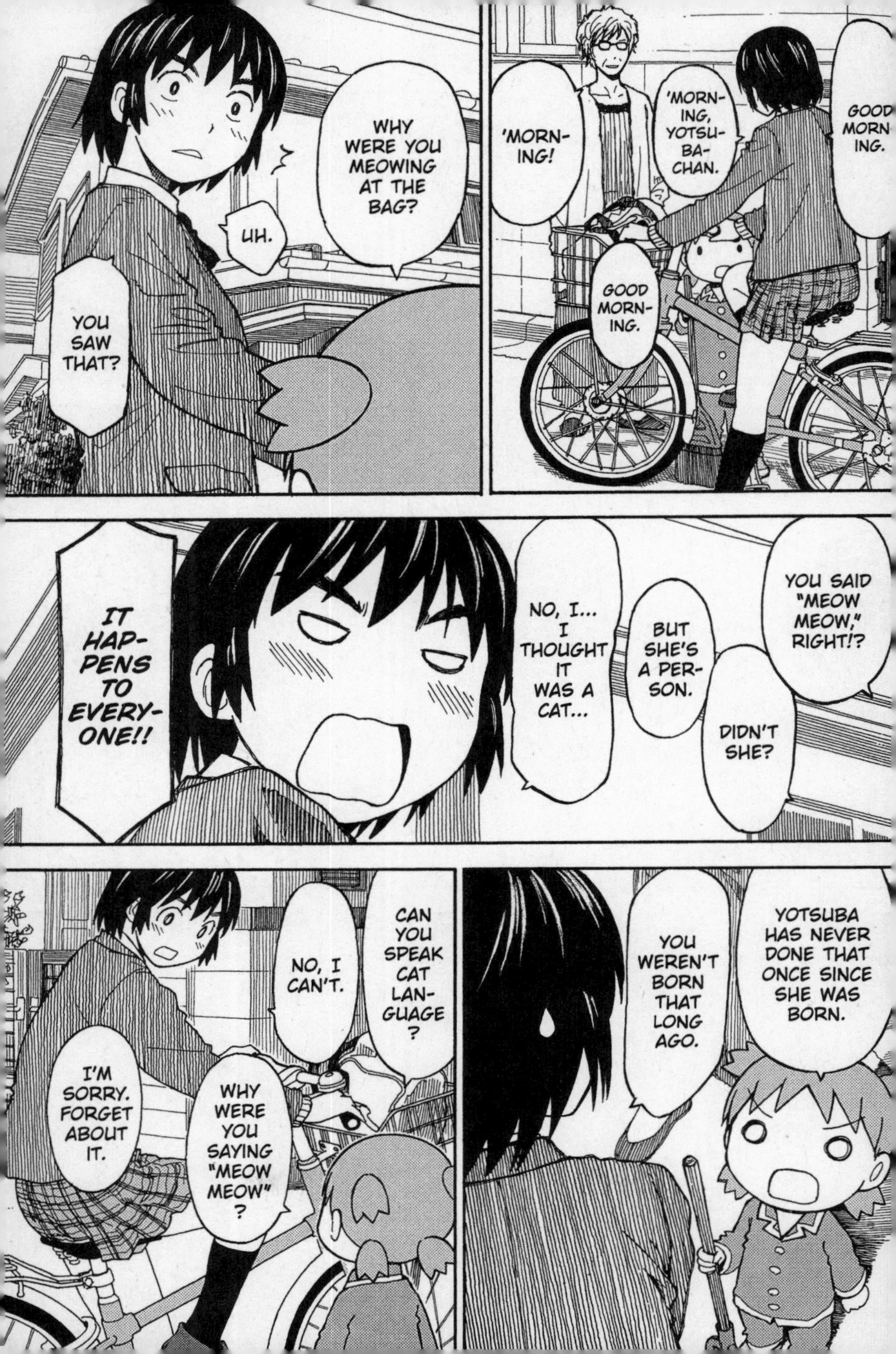
GOOD MORNING.
'MORNING, YOTSUBA-CHAN.
'MORNING!
GOOD MORNING.
WHY WERE YOU MEOWING AT THE BAG?
UH.
YOU SAW THAT?
YOU SAID "MEOW MEOW," RIGHT!?
DIDN'T SHE?
BUT SHE'S A PERSON.
NO, I... I THOUGHT IT WAS A CAT...
IT HAPPENS TO EVERYONE!!
YOTSUBA HAS NEVER DONE THAT ONCE SINCE SHE WAS BORN.
YOU WEREN'T BORN THAT LONG AGO.
CAN YOU SPEAK CAT LANGUAGE?
NO, I CAN'T.
WHY WERE YOU SAYING "MEOW MEOW"?
I'M SORRY. FORGET ABOUT IT.

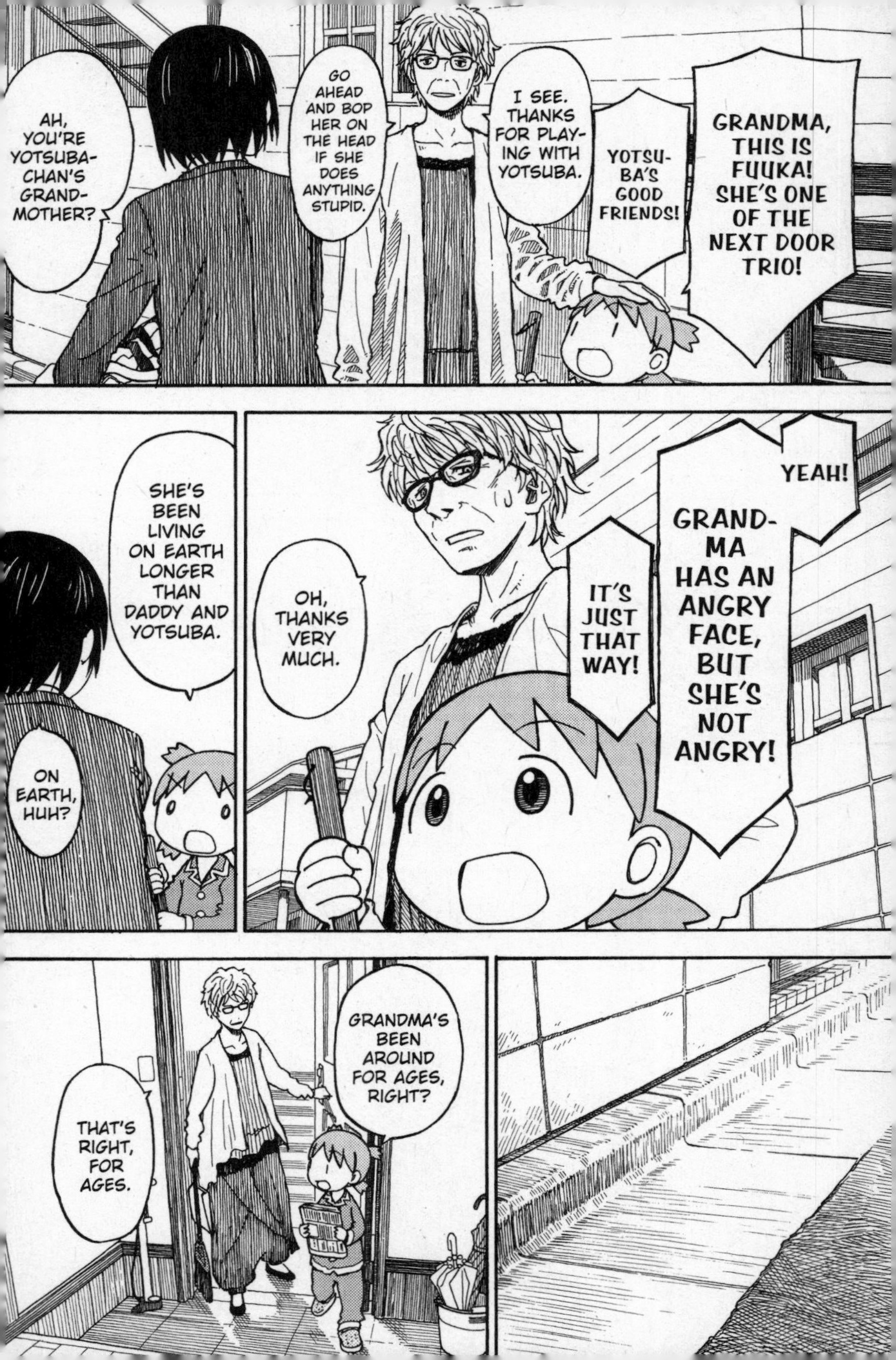
GRANDMA, THIS IS FUUKA! SHE'S ONE OF THE NEXT DOOR TRIO!
YOTSUBA'S GOOD FRIENDS!
I SEE. THANKS FOR PLAYING WITH YOTSUBA.
GO AHEAD AND BOP HER ON THE HEAD IF SHE DOES ANYTHING STUPID.
AH, YOU'RE YOTSUBA-CHAN'S GRANDMOTHER?
YEAH!
GRANDMA HAS AN ANGRY FACE, BUT SHE'S NOT ANGRY!
IT'S JUST THAT WAY!
OH, THANKS VERY MUCH.
SHE'S BEEN LIVING ON EARTH LONGER THAN DADDY AND YOTSUBA.
ON EARTH, HUH?
GRANDMA'S BEEN AROUND FOR AGES, RIGHT?
THAT'S RIGHT, FOR AGES.

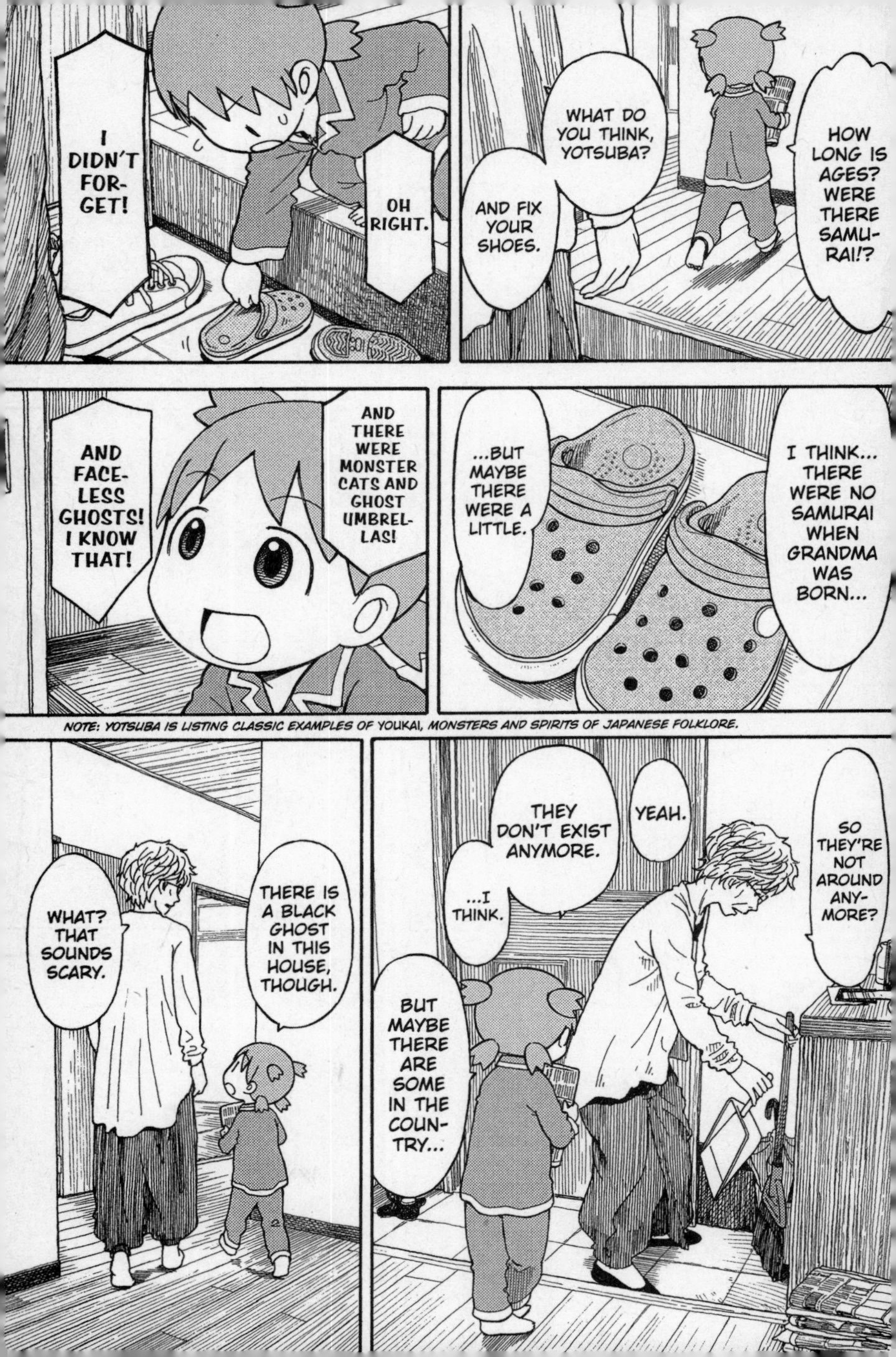
HOW LONG IS AGES? WERE THERE SAMURAI!?
WHAT DO YOU THINK, YOTSUBA?
AND FIX YOUR SHOES.
OH RIGHT.
I DIDN'T FORGET!
I THINK... THERE WERE NO SAMURAI WHEN GRANDMA WAS BORN...
...BUT MAYBE THERE WERE A LITTLE.
AND THERE WERE MONSTER CATS AND GHOST UMBRELLAS!
AND FACELESS GHOSTS! I KNOW THAT!
NOTE: YOTSUBA IS LISTING CLASSIC EXAMPLES OF YOUKAI, MONSTERS AND SPIRITS OF JAPANESE FOLKLORE.
SO THEY'RE NOT AROUND ANYMORE?
YEAH.
THEY DON'T EXIST ANYMORE.
...I THINK.
BUT MAYBE THERE ARE SOME IN THE COUNTRY...
THERE IS A BLACK GHOST IN THIS HOUSE, THOUGH.
WHAT? THAT SOUNDS SCARY.

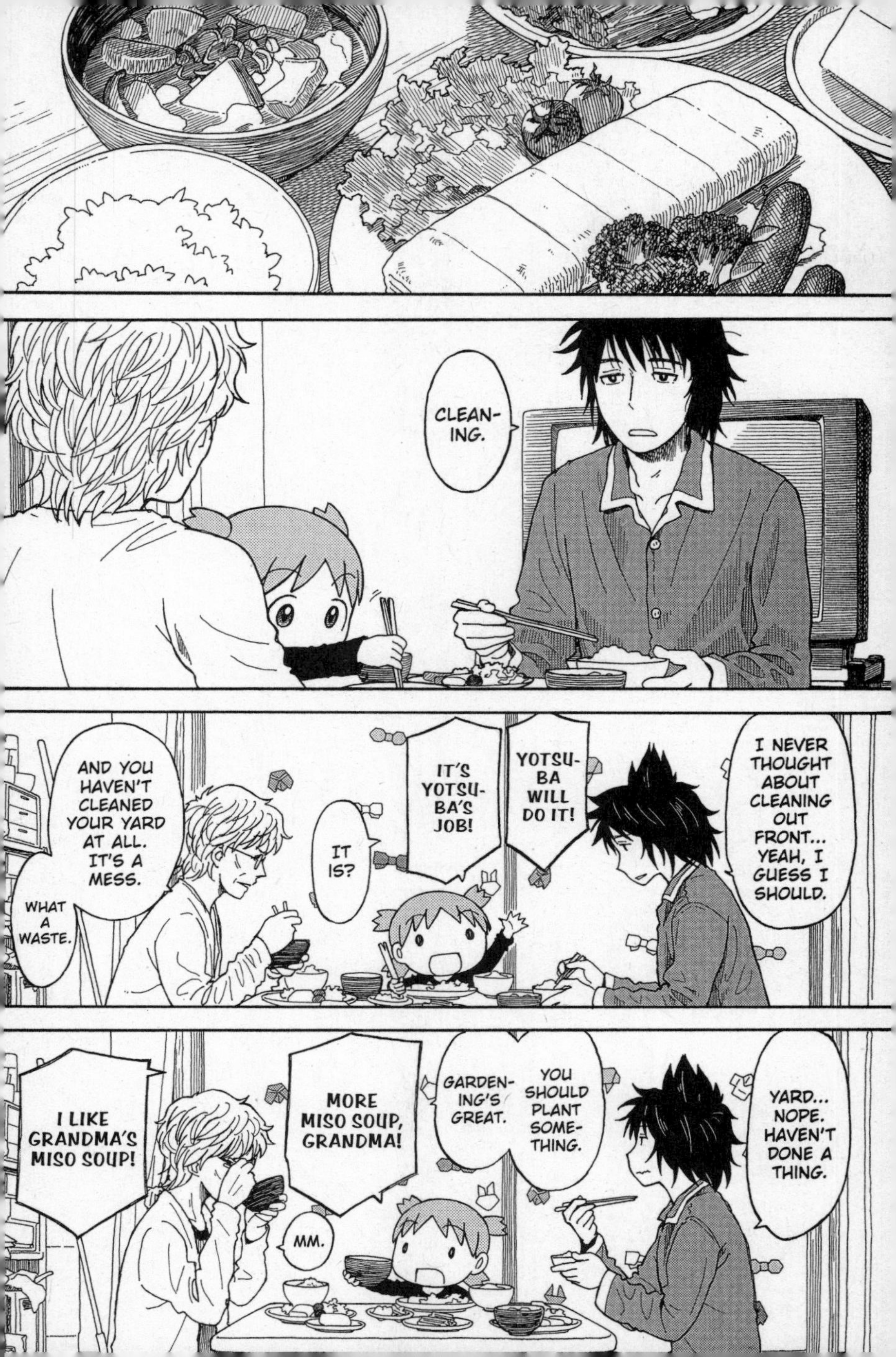
CLEAN-ING.
I NEVER THOUGHT ABOUT CLEANING OUT FRONT... YEAH, I GUESS I SHOULD.
YOTSU-BA WILL DO IT!
IT'S YOTSU-BA'S JOB!
IT IS?
AND YOU HAVEN'T CLEANED YOUR YARD AT ALL. IT'S A MESS.
WHAT A WASTE.
YARD... NOPE. HAVEN'T DONE A THING.
YOU SHOULD PLANT SOME-THING.
GARDEN-ING'S GREAT.
MORE MISO SOUP, GRANDMA!
MM.
I LIKE GRANDMA'S MISO SOUP!

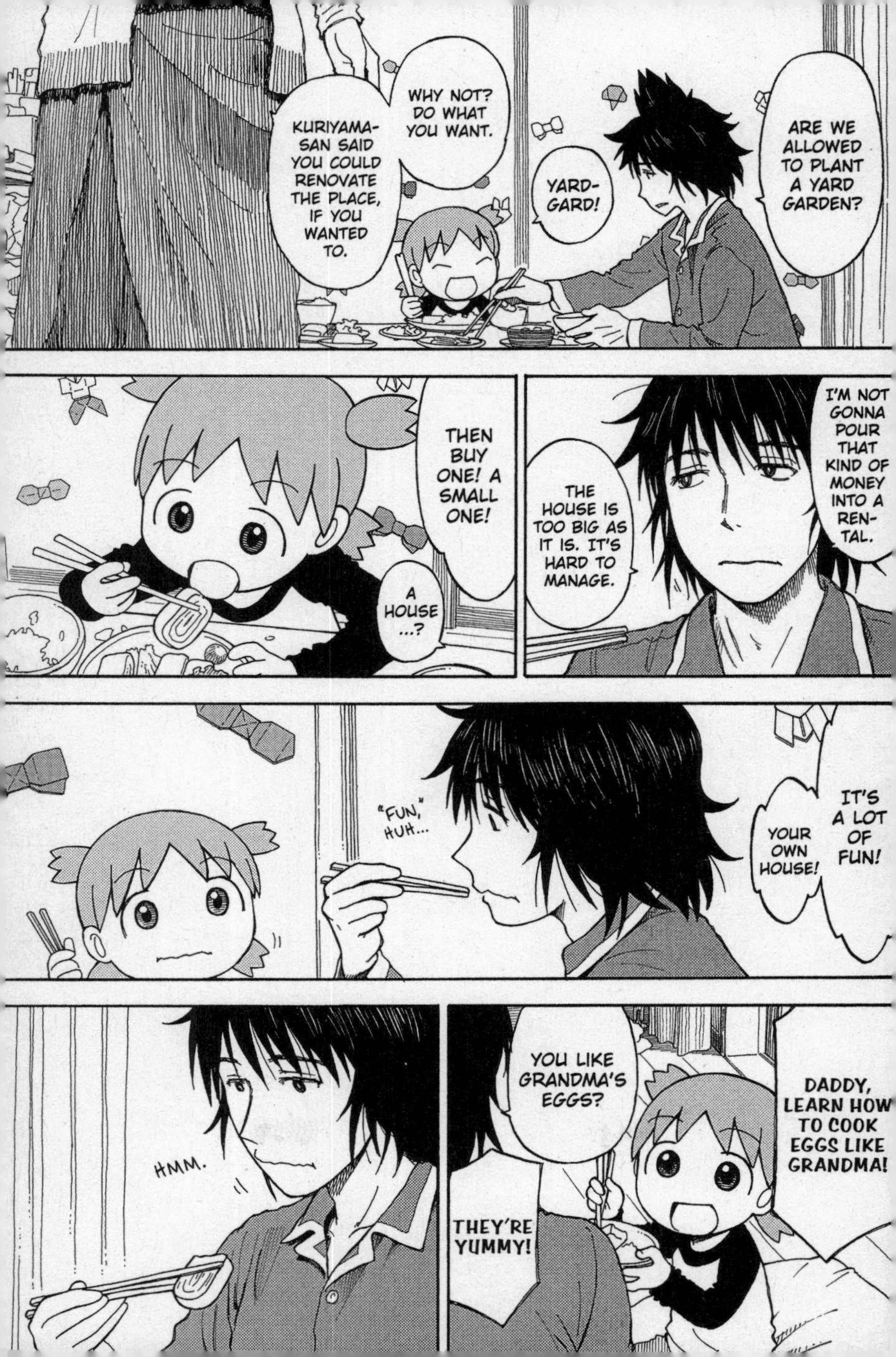
ARE WE ALLOWED TO PLANT A YARD GARDEN?
YARD-GARD!
WHY NOT? DO WHAT YOU WANT.
KURIYAMA-SAN SAID YOU COULD RENOVATE THE PLACE, IF YOU WANTED TO.
I'M NOT GONNA POUR THAT KIND OF MONEY INTO A RENTAL.
THE HOUSE IS TOO BIG AS IT IS. IT'S HARD TO MANAGE.
THEN BUY ONE! A SMALL ONE!
A HOUSE ...?
IT'S A LOT OF FUN!
YOUR OWN HOUSE!
"FUN," HUH...
DADDY, LEARN HOW TO COOK EGGS LIKE GRANDMA!
YOU LIKE GRANDMA'S EGGS?
THEY'RE YUMMY!
HMM.

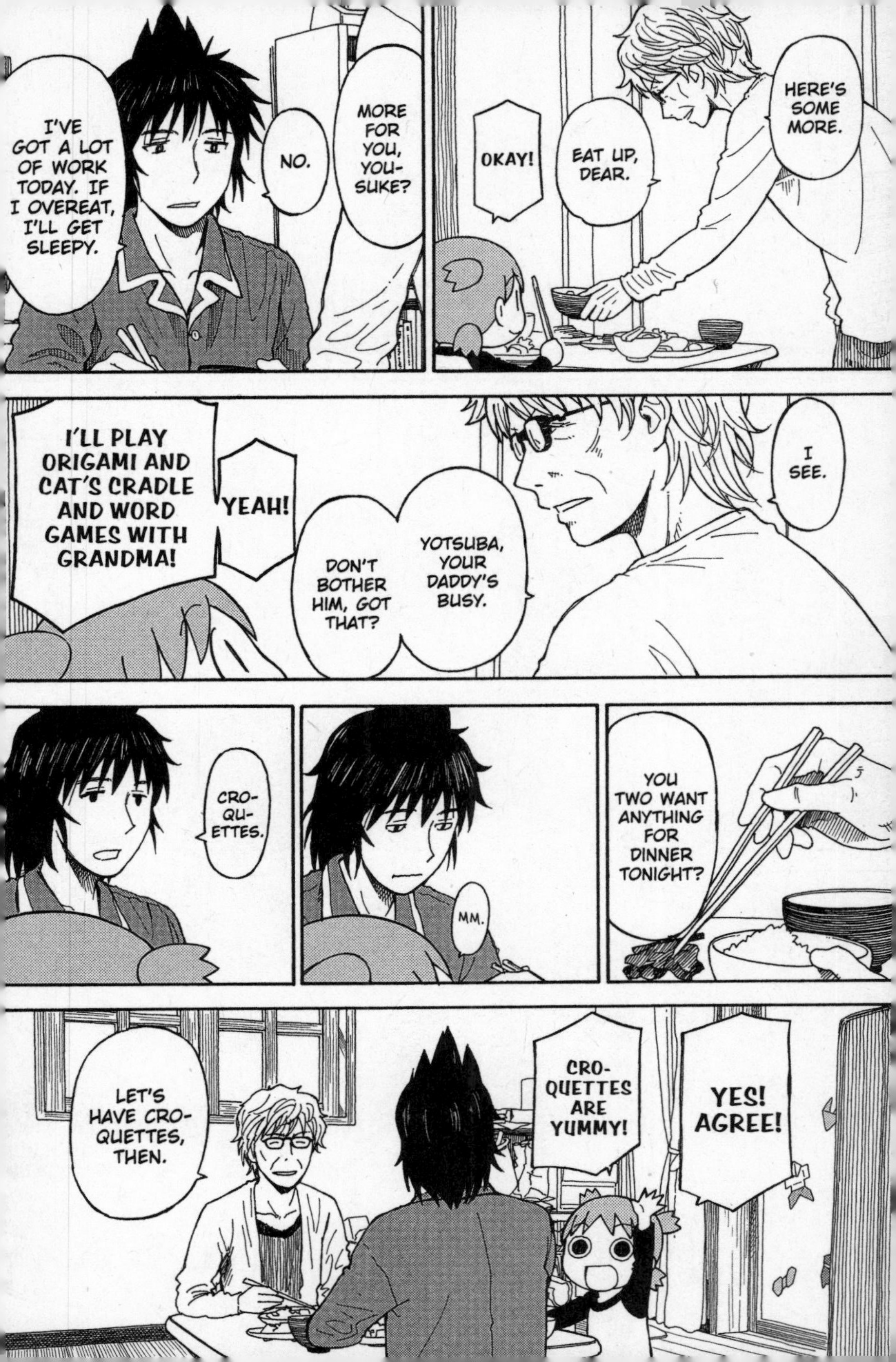
HERE'S SOME MORE.
EAT UP, DEAR.
OKAY!
MORE FOR YOU, YOUSUKE?
NO.
I'VE GOT A LOT OF WORK TODAY. IF I OVEREAT, I'LL GET SLEEPY.
I SEE.
YOTSUBA, YOUR DADDY'S BUSY.
DON'T BOTHER HIM, GOT THAT?
YEAH!
I'LL PLAY ORIGAMI AND CAT'S CRADLE AND WORD GAMES WITH GRANDMA!
YOU TWO WANT ANYTHING FOR DINNER TONIGHT?
MM.
CROQUETTES.
YES! AGREE!
CROQUETTES ARE YUMMY!
LET'S HAVE CROQUETTES, THEN.

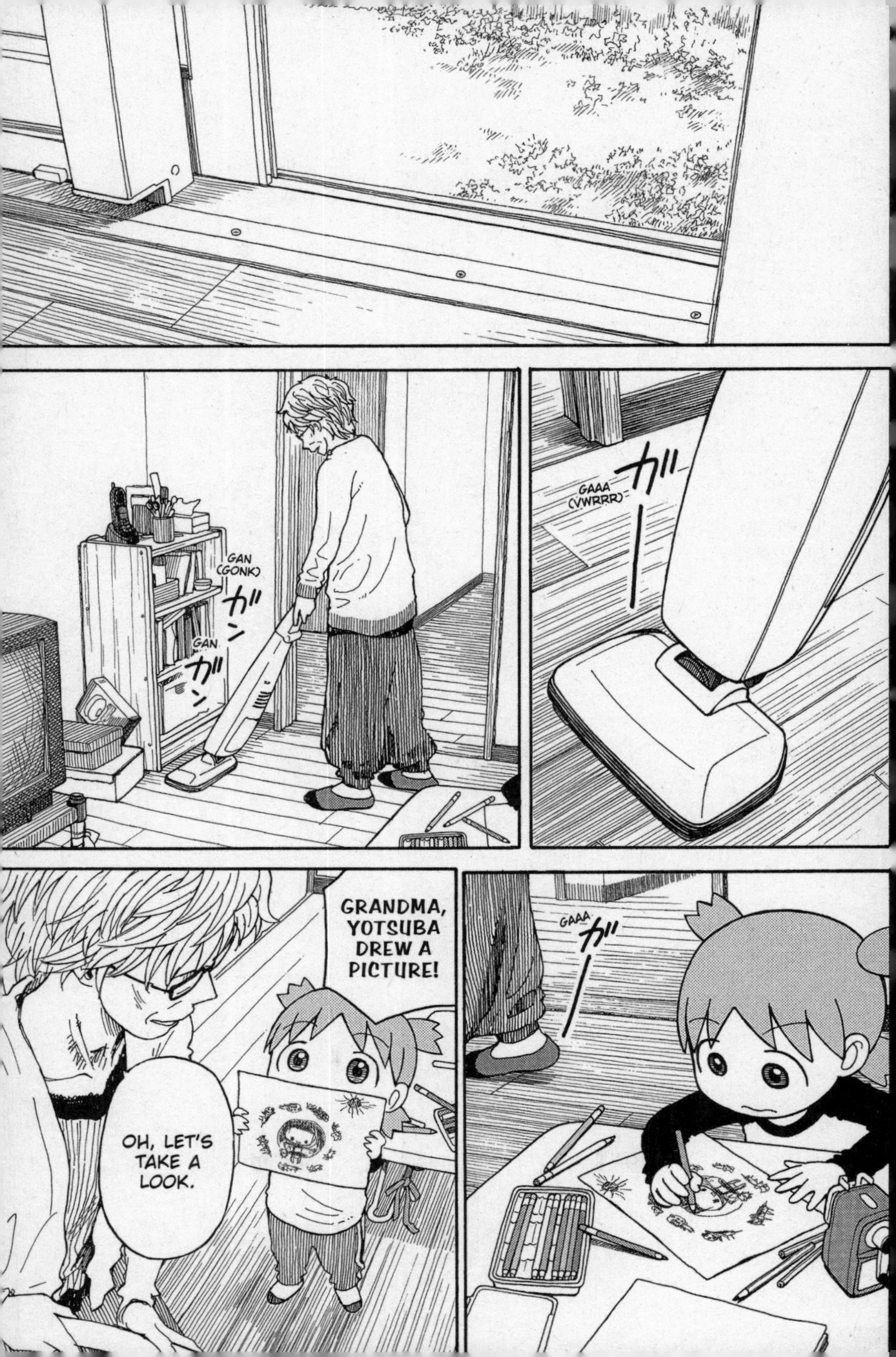
GAAA (VWRRR)
ガー
GAN (GONK)
ガン
GAN
ガン
GAAA
ガー
GRANDMA, YOTSUBA DREW A PICTURE!
OH, LET'S TAKE A LOOK.

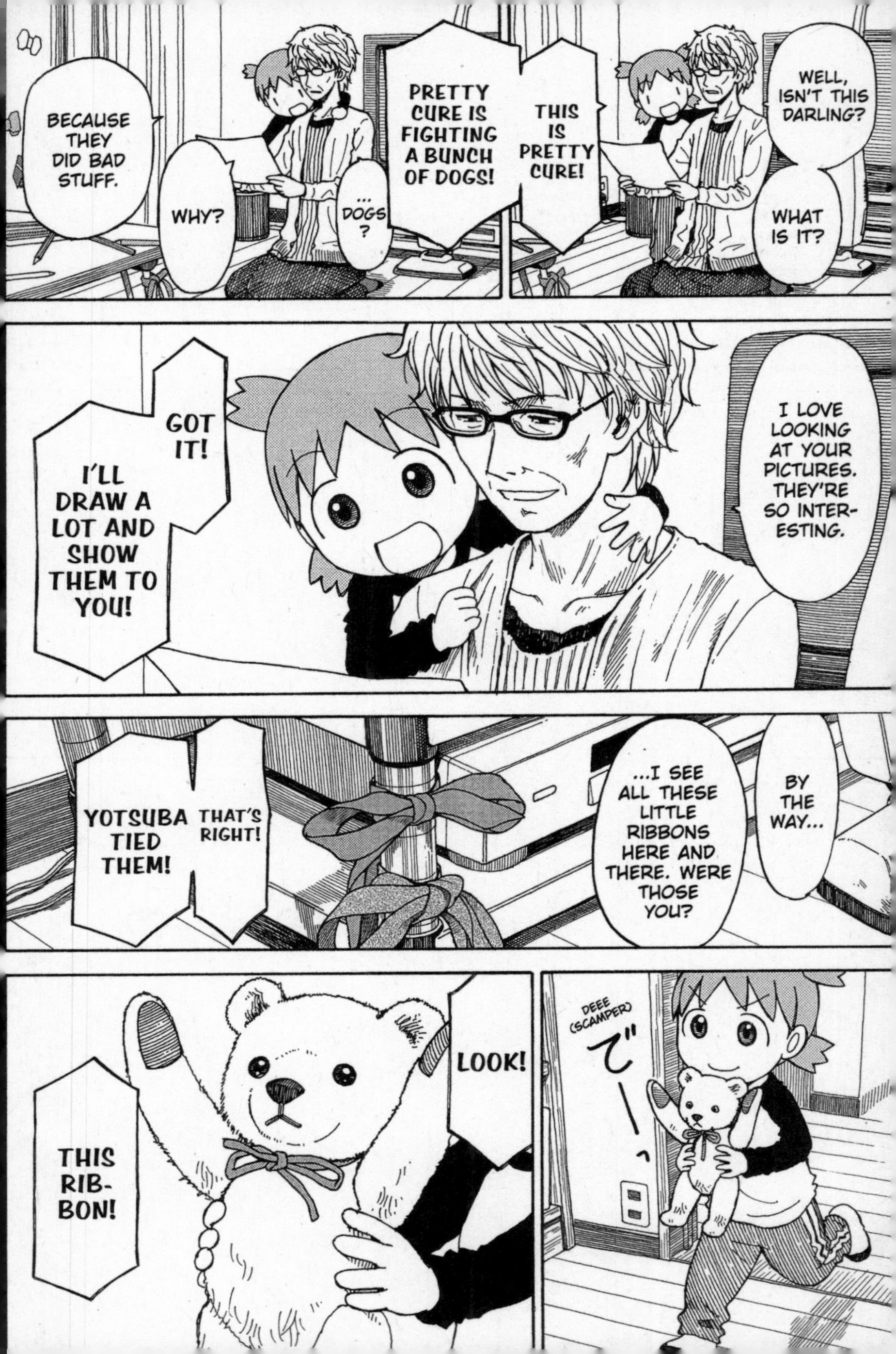
WELL, ISN'T THIS DARLING?
WHAT IS IT?
THIS IS PRETTY CURE!
PRETTY CURE IS FIGHTING A BUNCH OF DOGS!
...DOGS?
WHY?
BECAUSE THEY DID BAD STUFF.
I LOVE LOOKING AT YOUR PICTURES. THEY'RE SO INTER-ESTING.
GOT IT!
I'LL DRAW A LOT AND SHOW THEM TO YOU!
BY THE WAY...
...I SEE ALL THESE LITTLE RIBBONS HERE AND THERE. WERE THOSE YOU?
THAT'S RIGHT!
YOTSUBA TIED THEM!
DEEE (SCAMPER)
でー
LOOK!
THIS RIB-BON!

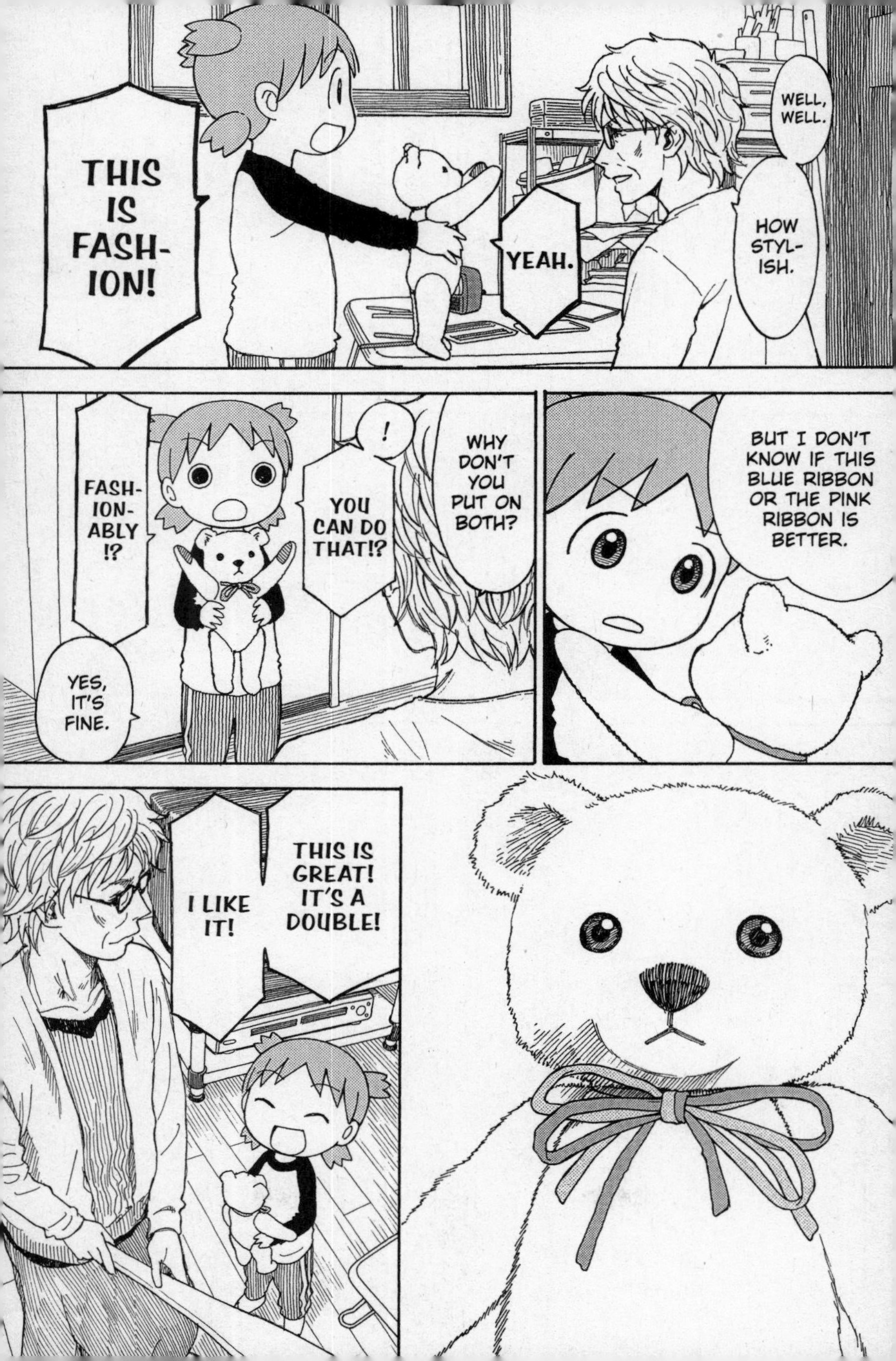
WELL, WELL.
HOW STYLISH.
YEAH.
THIS IS FASHION!
BUT I DON'T KNOW IF THIS BLUE RIBBON OR THE PINK RIBBON IS BETTER.
WHY DON'T YOU PUT ON BOTH?
!
YOU CAN DO THAT!?
FASHIONABLY!?
YES, IT'S FINE.
THIS IS GREAT! IT'S A DOUBLE!
I LIKE IT!

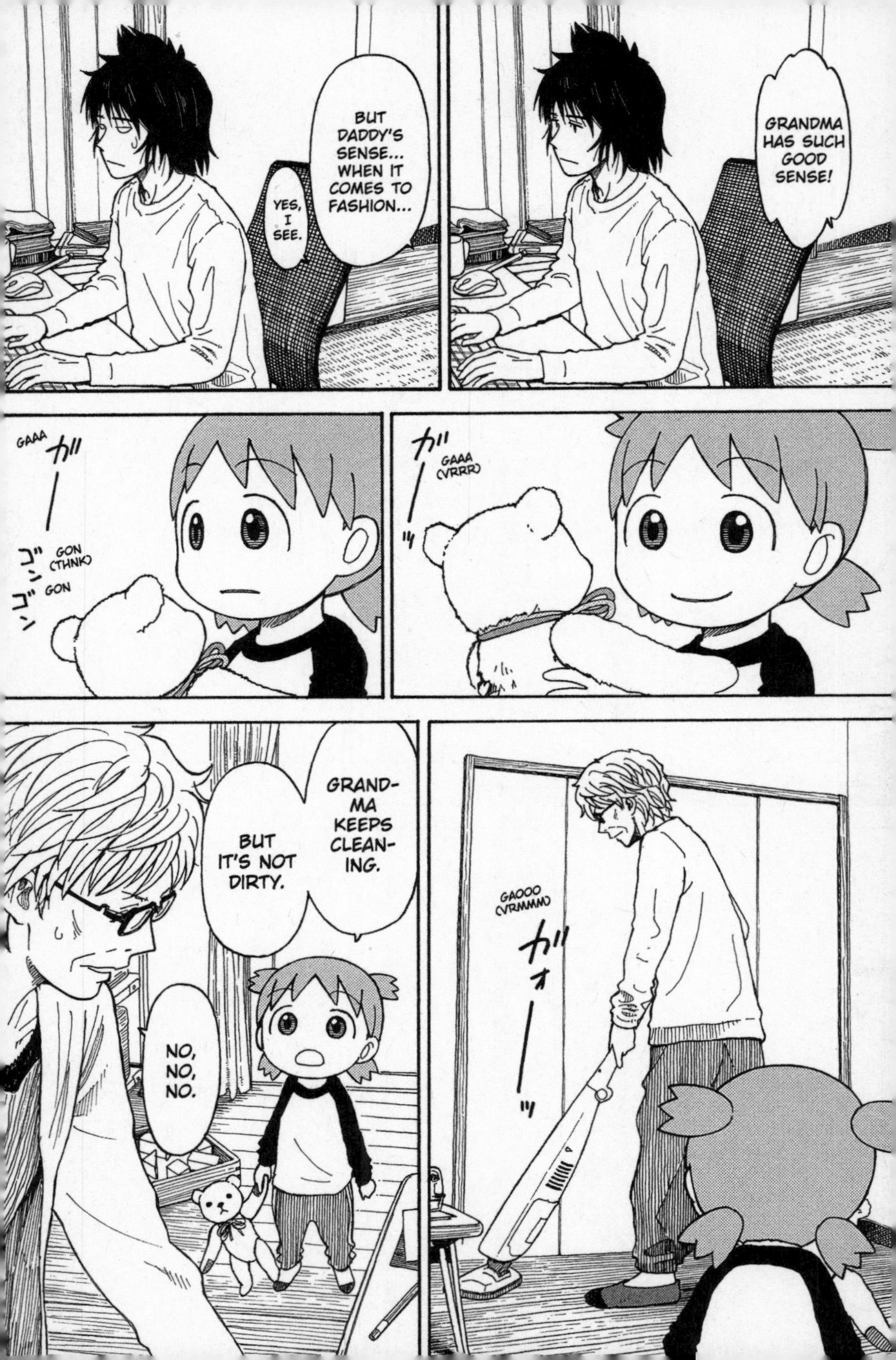

GRANDMA HAS SUCH GOOD SENSE!
BUT DADDY'S SENSE... WHEN IT COMES TO FASHION...
YES, I SEE.
ガーッ
GAAA (VRRR)
GAAA
ガー
ゴン
GON (THNK)
ゴン
GON
GAOOO (VRMMM)
ガオーーッ
GRAND-MA KEEPS CLEAN-ING.
BUT IT'S NOT DIRTY.
NO, NO, NO.

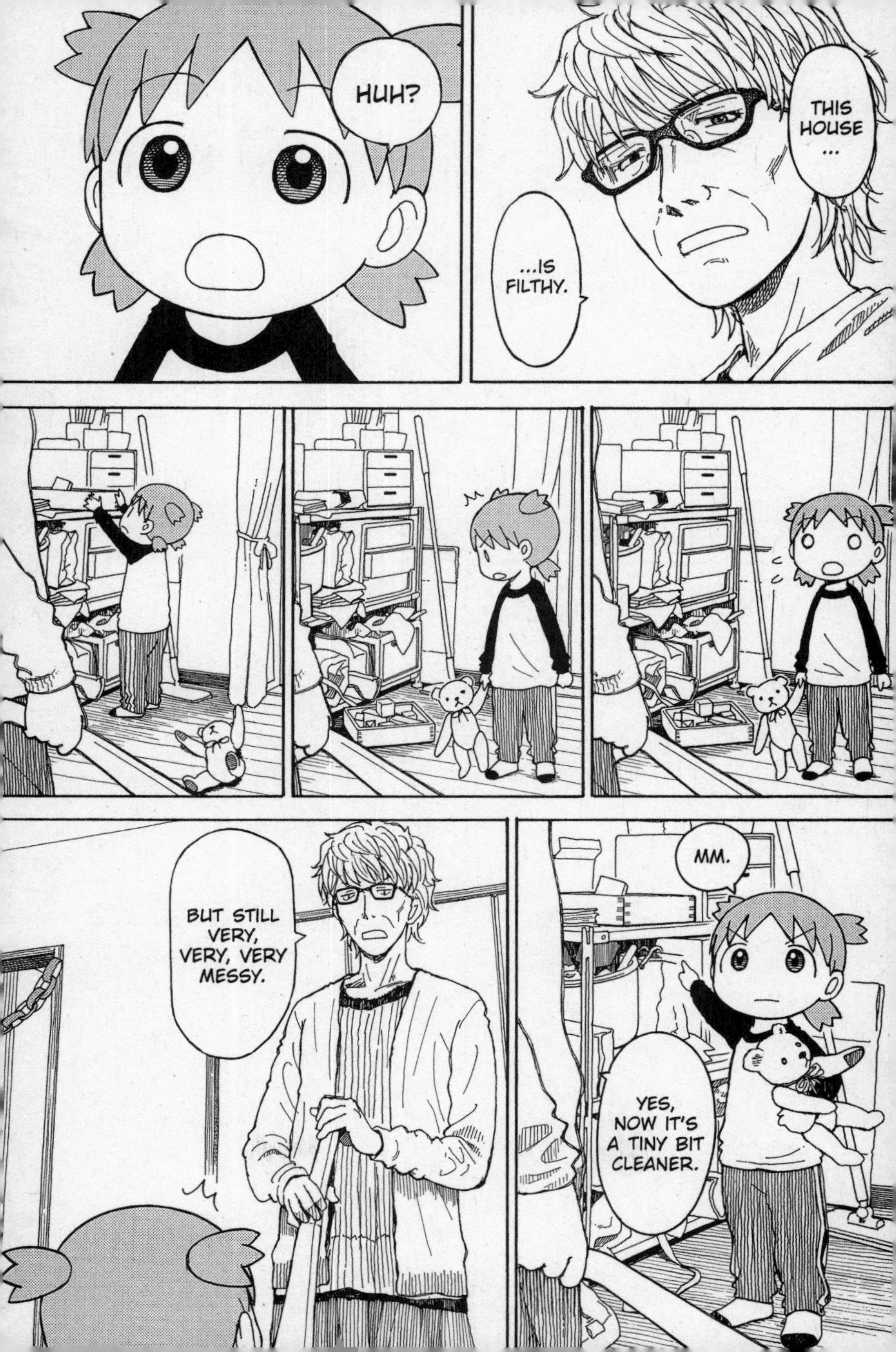
THIS HOUSE ...
...IS FILTHY.
HUH?
MM.
YES, NOW IT'S A TINY BIT CLEANER.
BUT STILL VERY, VERY, VERY MESSY.

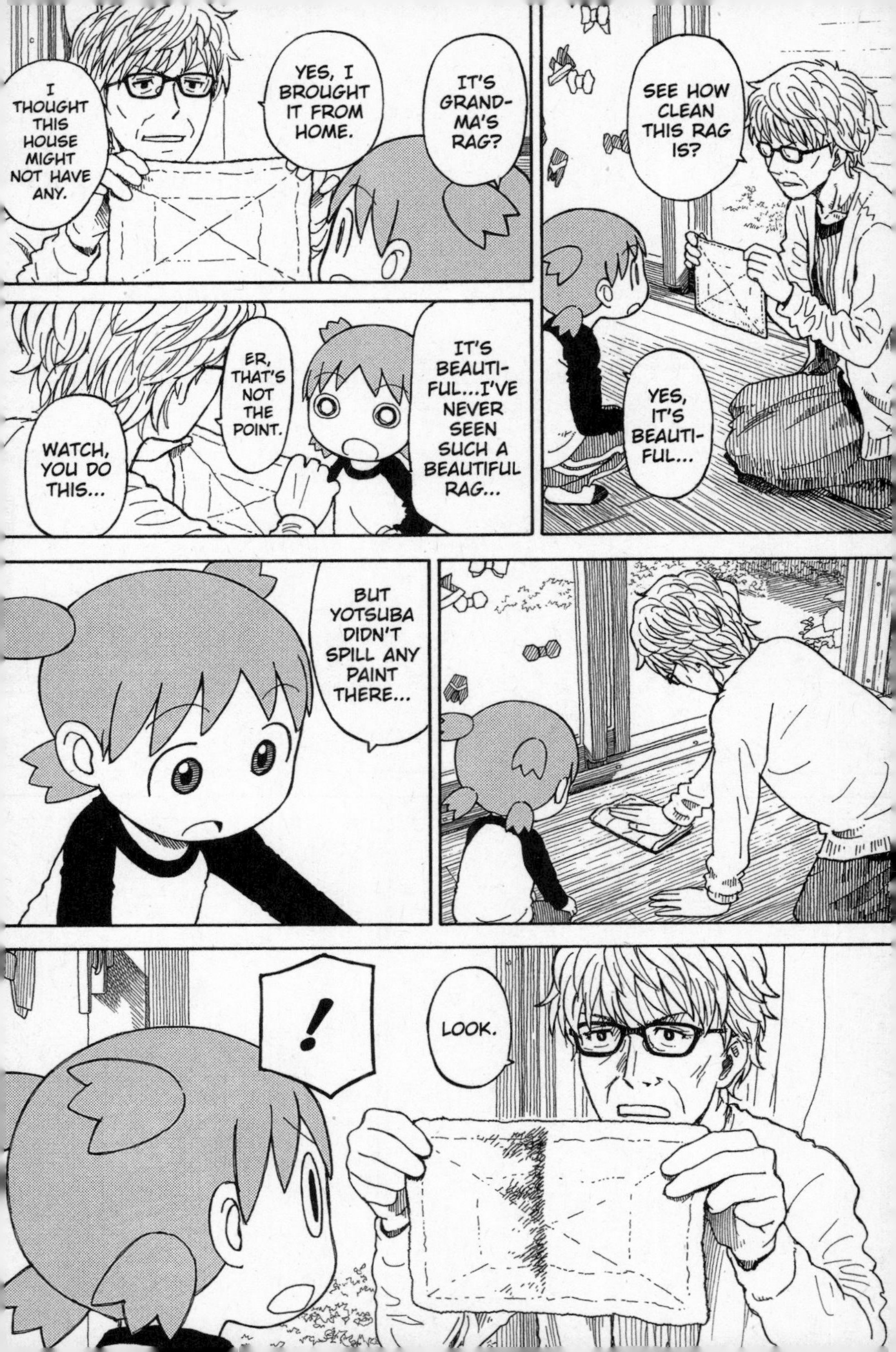
SEE HOW CLEAN THIS RAG IS?
YES, IT'S BEAUTIFUL...
IT'S GRANDMA'S RAG?
YES, I BROUGHT IT FROM HOME.
I THOUGHT THIS HOUSE MIGHT NOT HAVE ANY.
IT'S BEAUTIFUL...I'VE NEVER SEEN SUCH A BEAUTIFUL RAG...
ER, THAT'S NOT THE POINT.
WATCH, YOU DO THIS...
BUT YOTSUBA DIDN'T SPILL ANY PAINT THERE...
LOOK.
!

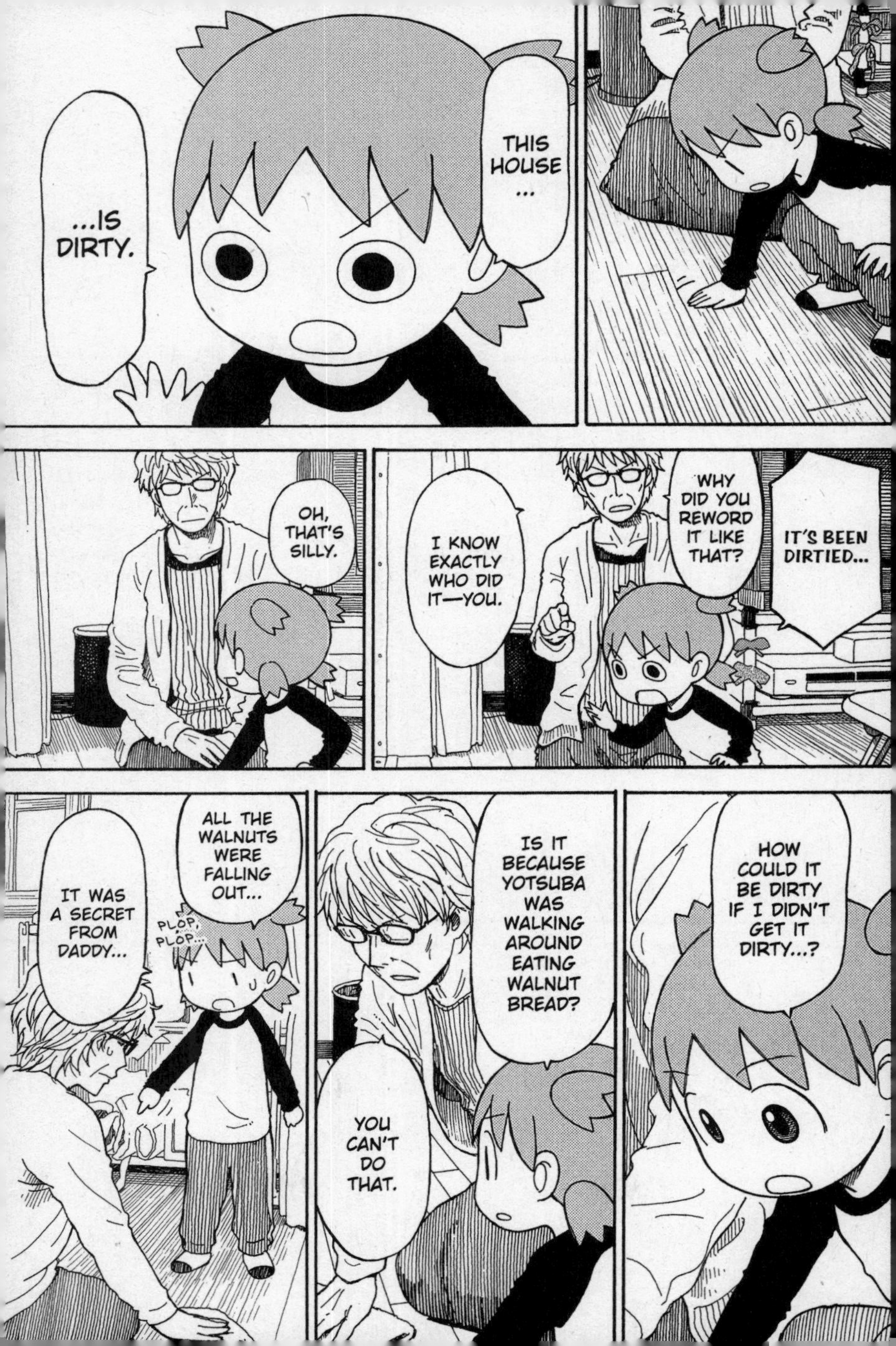
THIS HOUSE ...
...IS DIRTY.
IT'S BEEN DIRTIED...
WHY DID YOU REWORD IT LIKE THAT?
I KNOW EXACTLY WHO DID IT—YOU.
OH, THAT'S SILLY.
HOW COULD IT BE DIRTY IF I DIDN'T GET IT DIRTY...?
IS IT BECAUSE YOTSUBA WAS WALKING AROUND EATING WALNUT BREAD?
YOU CAN'T DO THAT.
ALL THE WALNUTS WERE FALLING OUT...
PLOP, PLOP...
IT WAS A SECRET FROM DADDY...

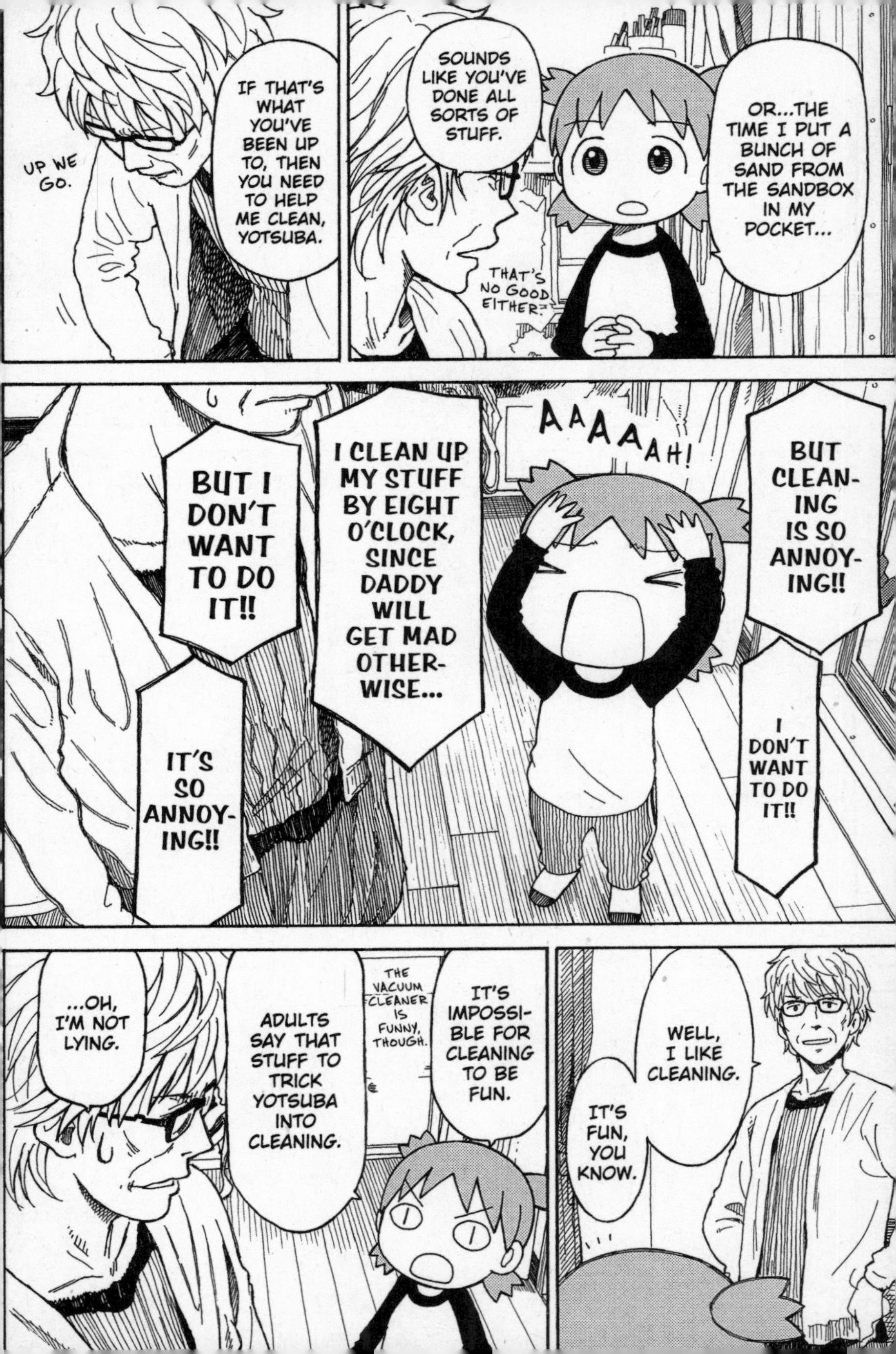
OR...THE TIME I PUT A BUNCH OF SAND FROM THE SANDBOX IN MY POCKET...
SOUNDS LIKE YOU'VE DONE ALL SORTS OF STUFF.
THAT'S NO GOOD EITHER.
IF THAT'S WHAT YOU'VE BEEN UP TO, THEN YOU NEED TO HELP ME CLEAN, YOTSUBA.
UP WE GO.
BUT CLEAN-ING IS SO ANNOY-ING!!
AAAAAH!
I DON'T WANT TO DO IT!!
I CLEAN UP MY STUFF BY EIGHT O'CLOCK, SINCE DADDY WILL GET MAD OTHER-WISE...
BUT I DON'T WANT TO DO IT!!
IT'S SO ANNOY-ING!!
WELL, I LIKE CLEANING.
IT'S FUN, YOU KNOW.
IT'S IMPOSSI-BLE FOR CLEANING TO BE FUN.
THE VACUUM CLEANER IS FUNNY, THOUGH.
ADULTS SAY THAT STUFF TO TRICK YOTSUBA INTO CLEANING.
...OH, I'M NOT LYING.

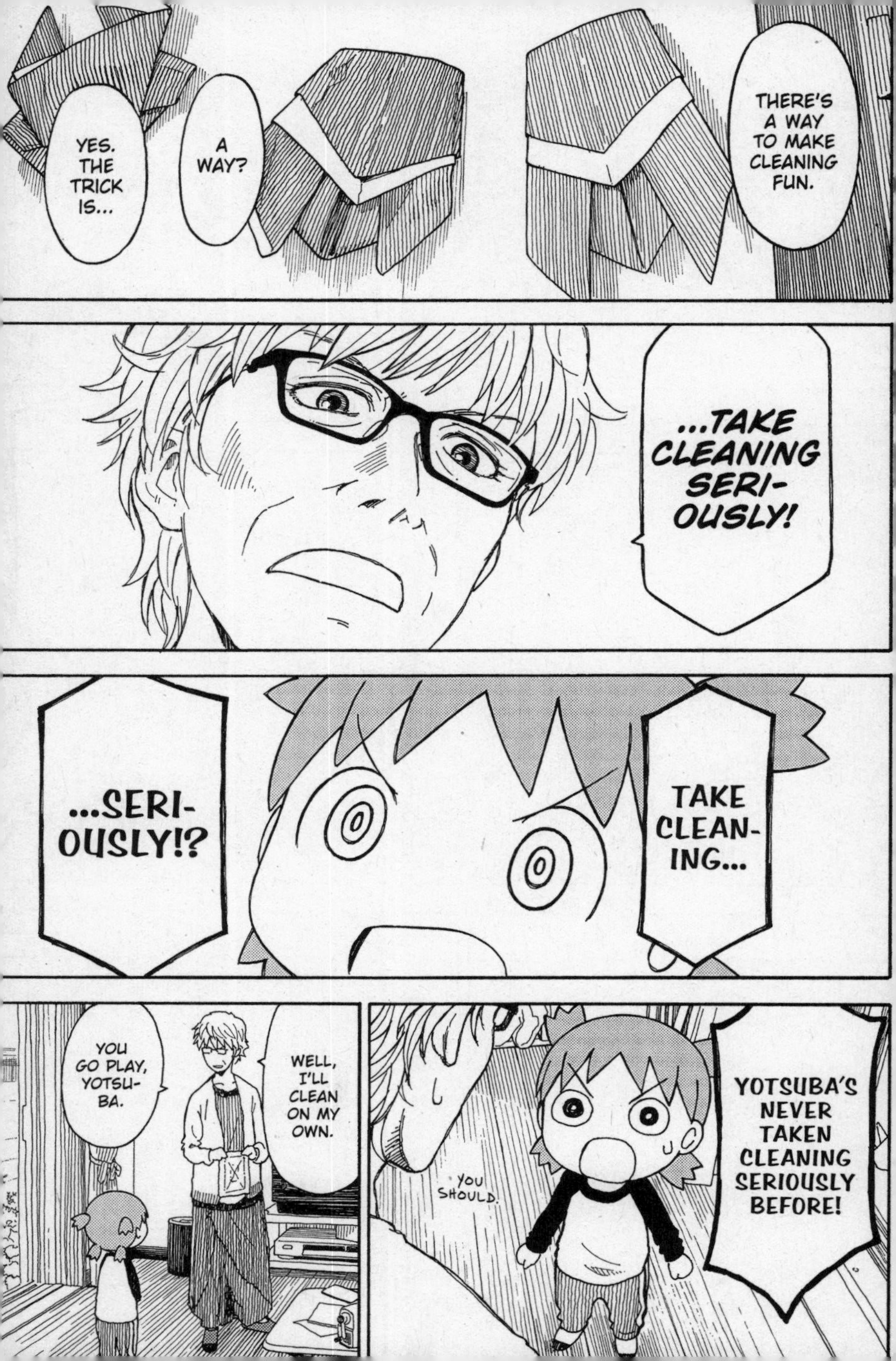
THERE'S A WAY TO MAKE CLEANING FUN.
A WAY?
YES. THE TRICK IS...
...TAKE CLEANING SERI-OUSLY!
TAKE CLEAN-ING...
...SERI-OUSLY!?
YOTSUBA'S NEVER TAKEN CLEANING SERIOUSLY BEFORE!
YOU SHOULD.
WELL, I'LL CLEAN ON MY OWN.
YOU GO PLAY, YOTSU-BA.

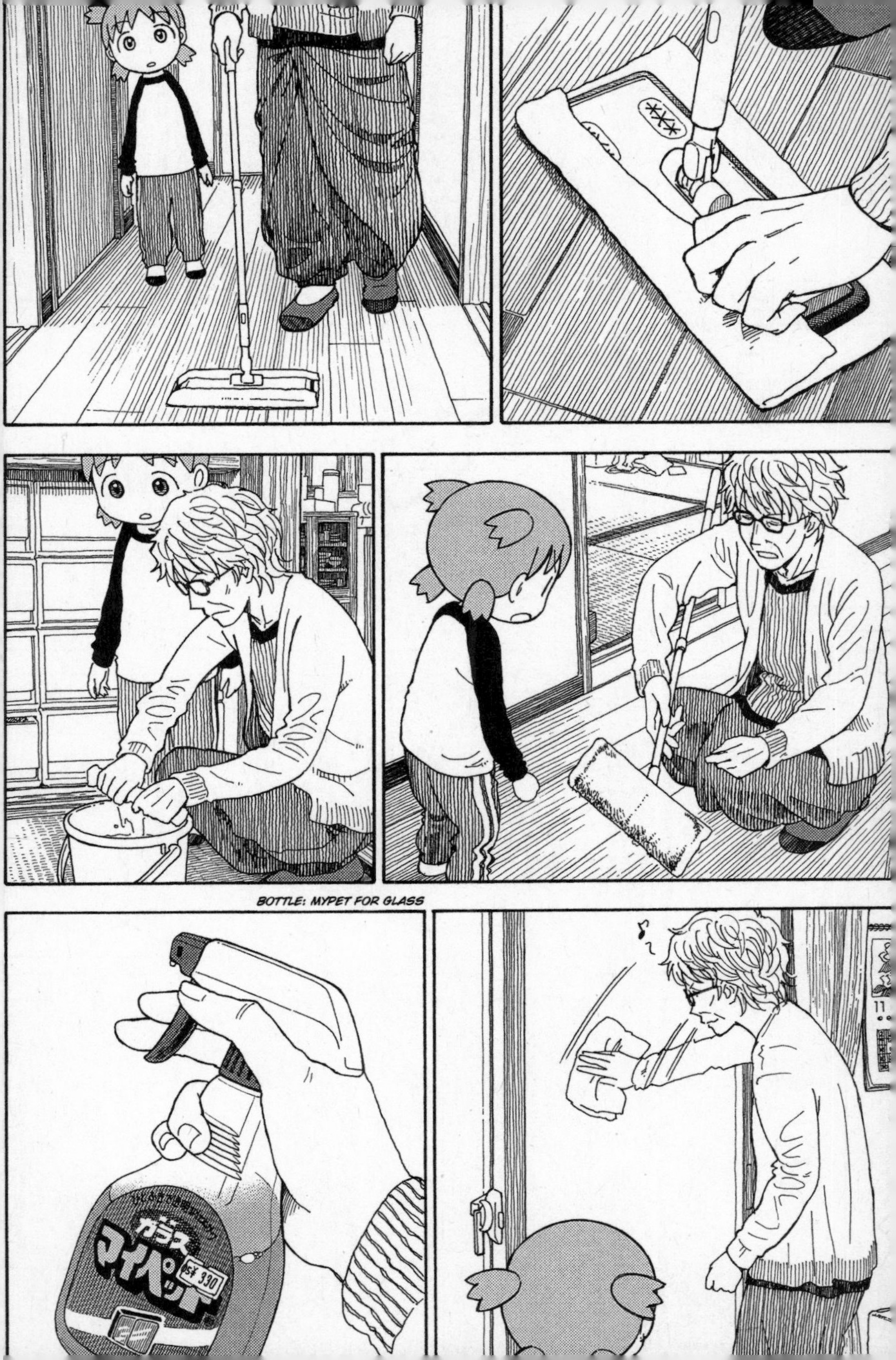
BOTTLE: MYPET FOR GLASS
ガラス
マイペット

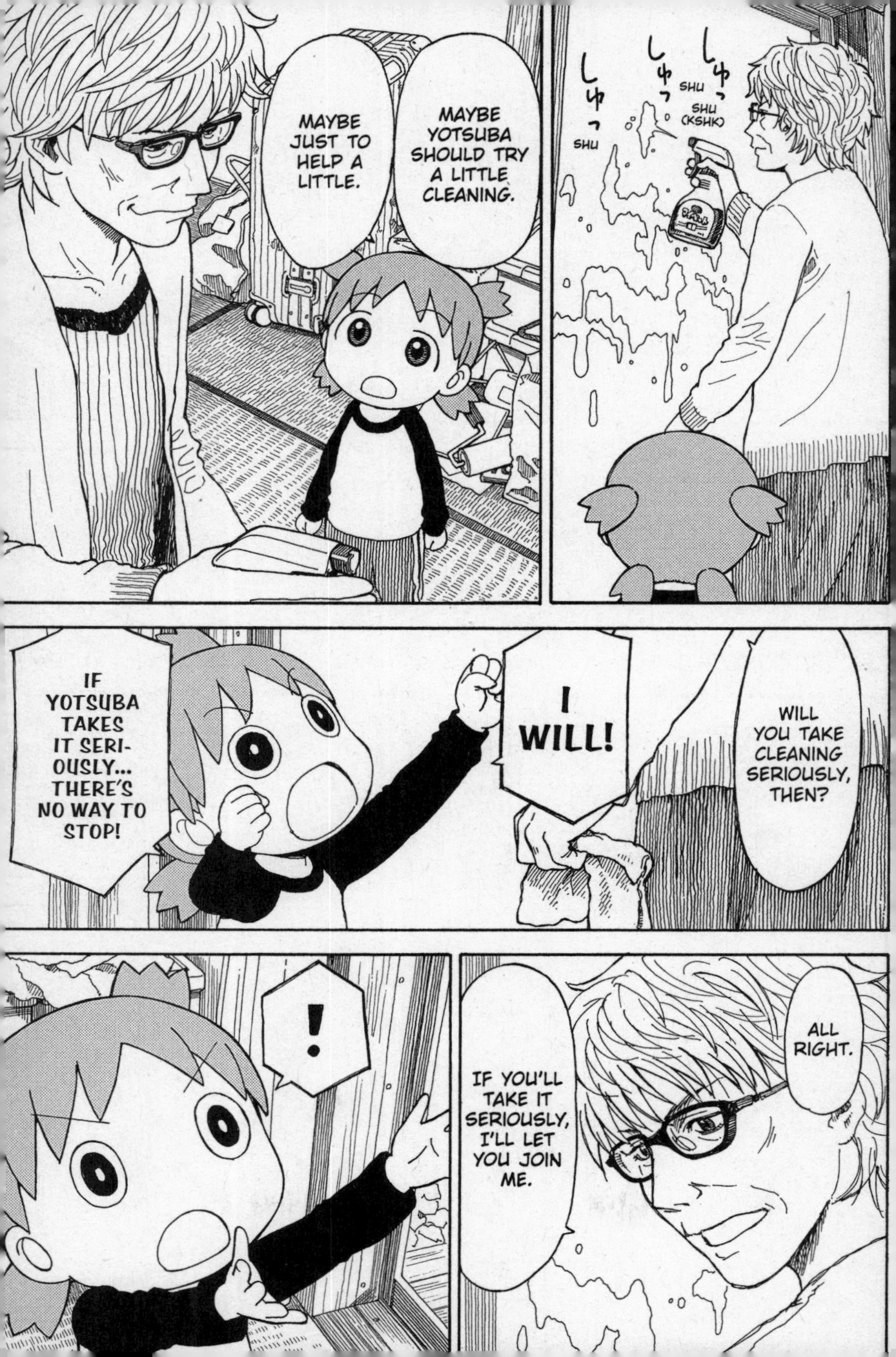
しゅっ
SHU
しゅっ
SHU (KSHK)
しゅっ
SHU
MAYBE YOTSUBA SHOULD TRY A LITTLE CLEANING.
MAYBE JUST TO HELP A LITTLE.
WILL YOU TAKE CLEANING SERIOUSLY, THEN?
I WILL!
IF YOTSUBA TAKES IT SERI-OUSLY... THERE'S NO WAY TO STOP!
ALL RIGHT.
IF YOU'LL TAKE IT SERIOUSLY, I'LL LET YOU JOIN ME.
!

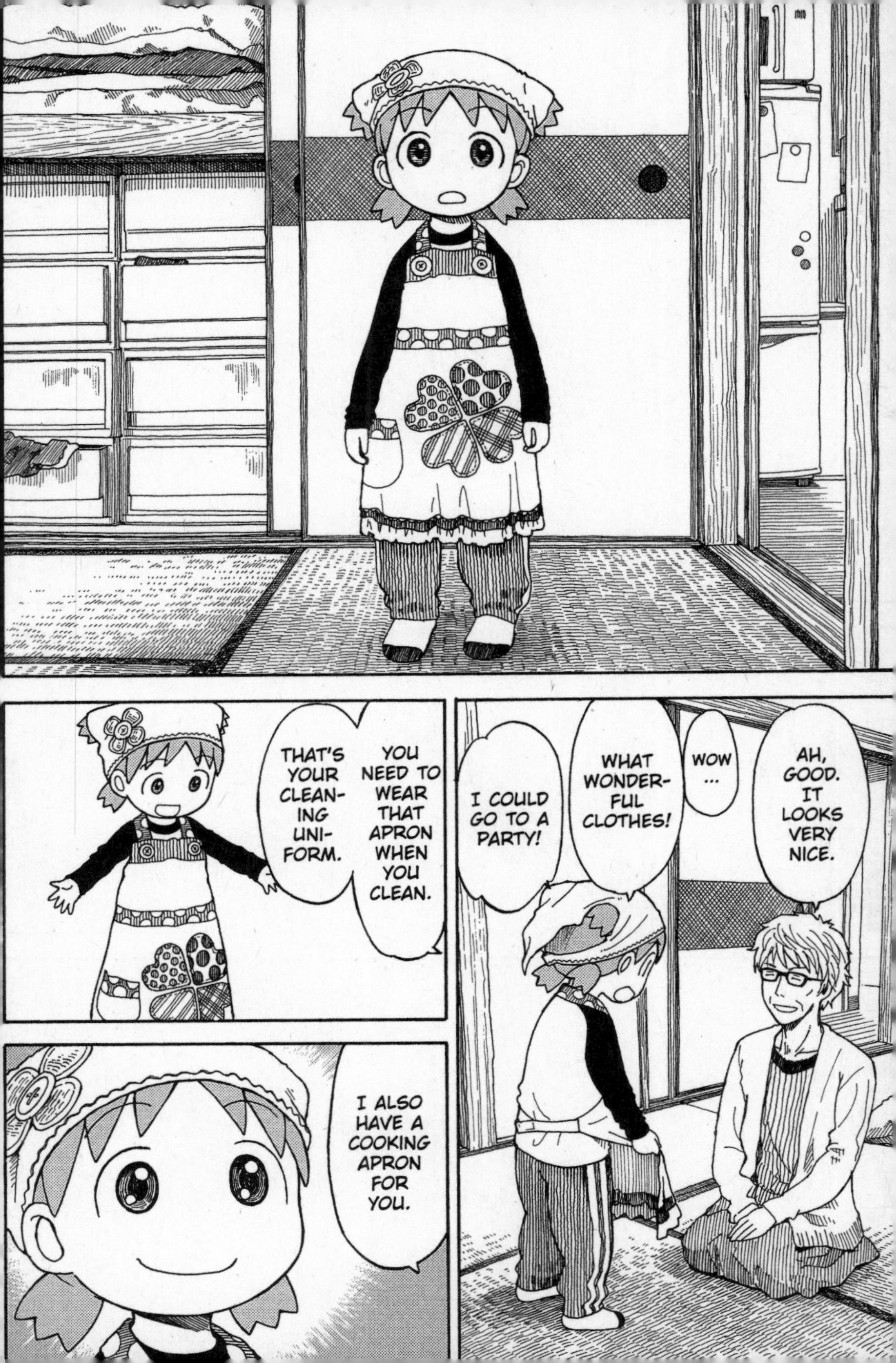
AH, GOOD. IT LOOKS VERY NICE.
WOW ...
WHAT WONDERFUL CLOTHES!
I COULD GO TO A PARTY!
YOU NEED TO WEAR THAT APRON WHEN YOU CLEAN.
THAT'S YOUR CLEANING UNIFORM.
I ALSO HAVE A COOKING APRON FOR YOU.

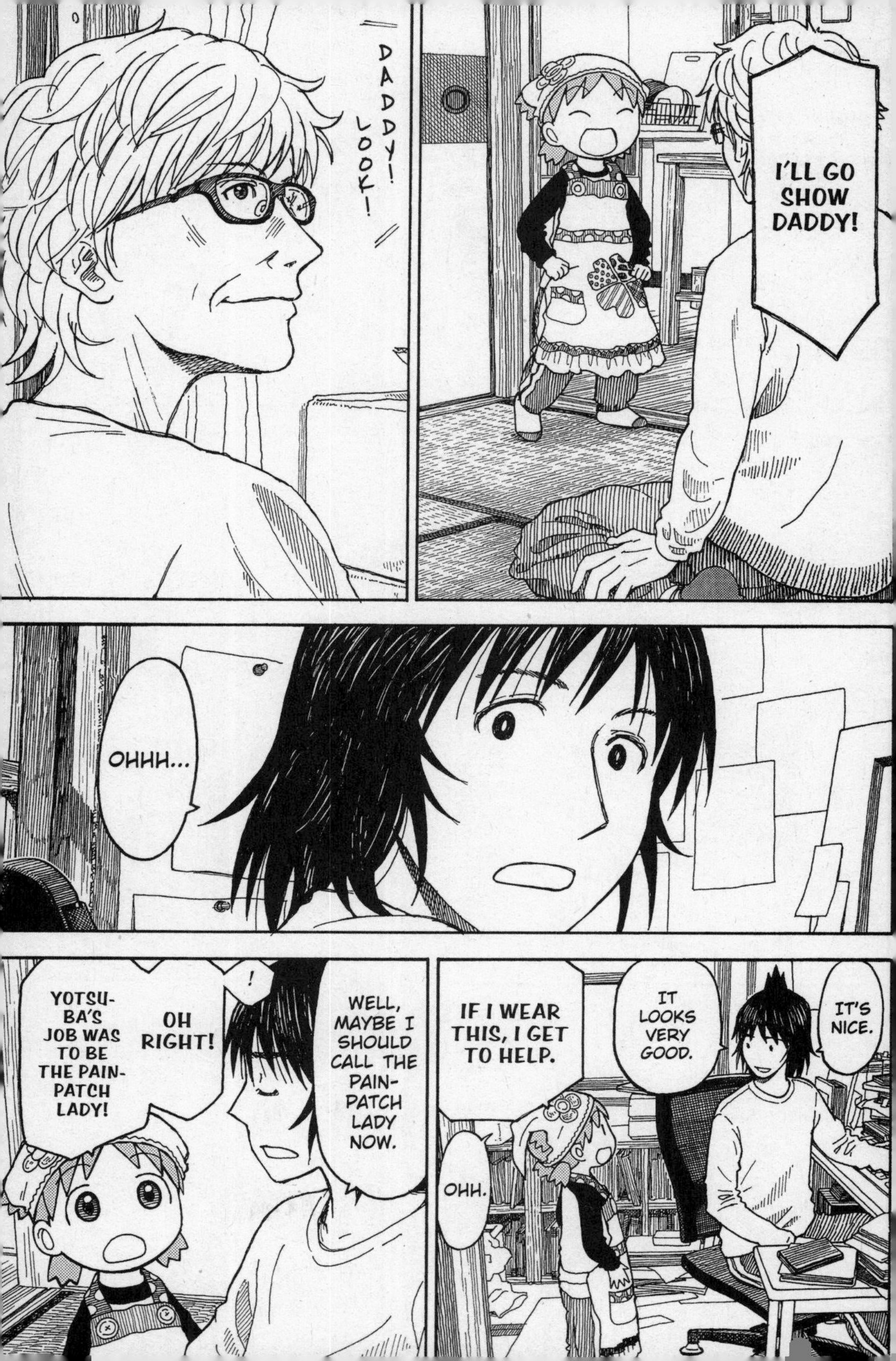
I'LL GO SHOW DADDY!
DADDY! LOOK!
OHHH...
IT'S NICE.
IT LOOKS VERY GOOD.
IF I WEAR THIS, I GET TO HELP.
OHH.
WELL, MAYBE I SHOULD CALL THE PAIN-PATCH LADY NOW.
!
OH RIGHT!
YOTSUBA'S JOB WAS TO BE THE PAIN-PATCH LADY!

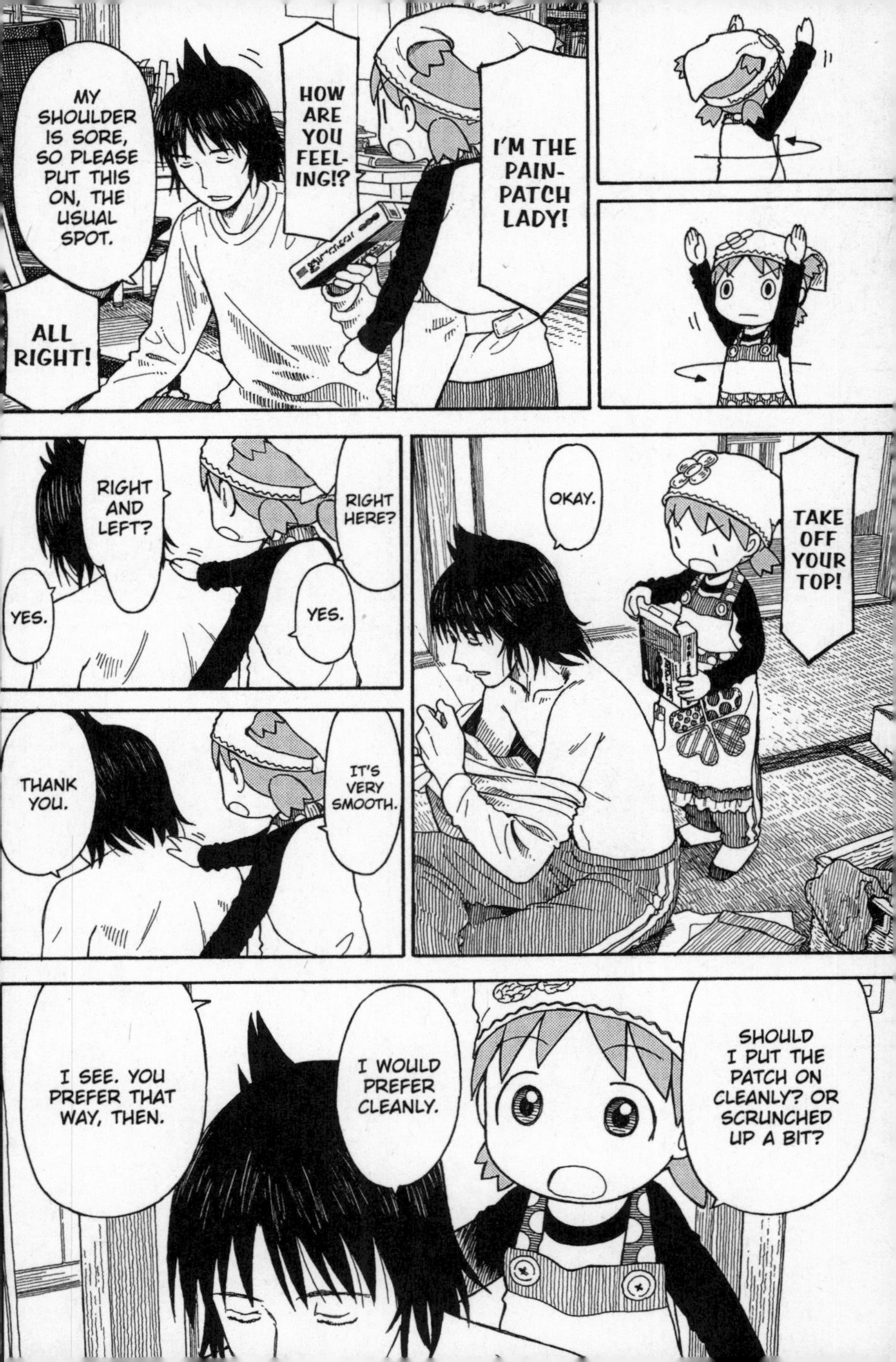
I'M THE PAIN-PATCH LADY!
HOW ARE YOU FEELING!?
MY SHOULDER IS SORE, SO PLEASE PUT THIS ON, THE USUAL SPOT.
ALL RIGHT!
TAKE OFF YOUR TOP!
OKAY.
RIGHT HERE?
RIGHT AND LEFT?
YES.
YES.
IT'S VERY SMOOTH.
THANK YOU.
SHOULD I PUT THE PATCH ON CLEANLY? OR SCRUNCHED UP A BIT?
I WOULD PREFER CLEANLY.
I SEE. YOU PREFER THAT WAY, THEN.

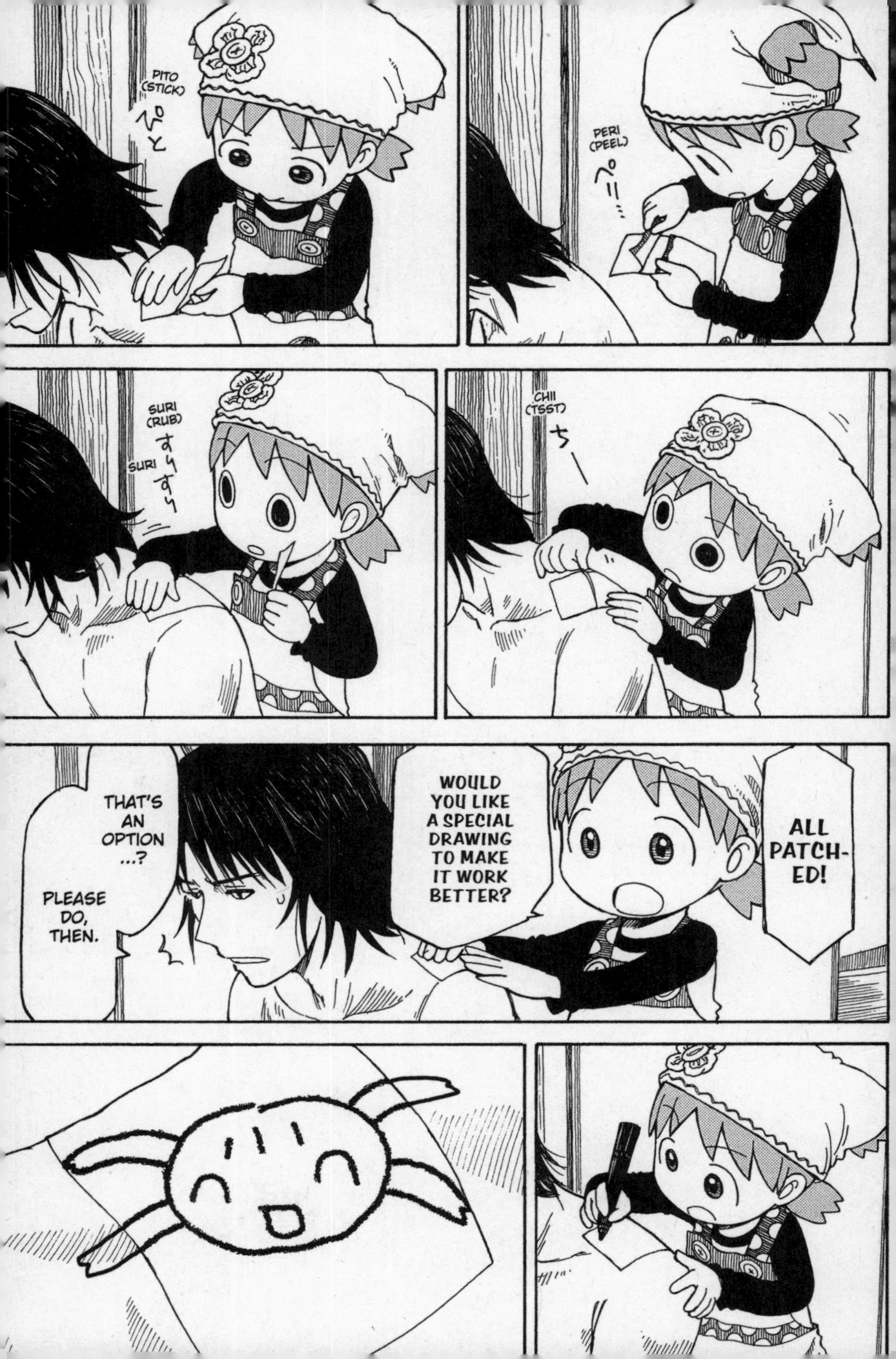
PERI (PEEL)
ぺりっ…
PITO (STICK)
ぴと
CHII (TSST)
ちー
SURI (RUB)
すりすり
SURI
ALL PATCHED!
WOULD YOU LIKE A SPECIAL DRAWING TO MAKE IT WORK BETTER?
THAT'S AN OPTION ...?
PLEASE DO, THEN.

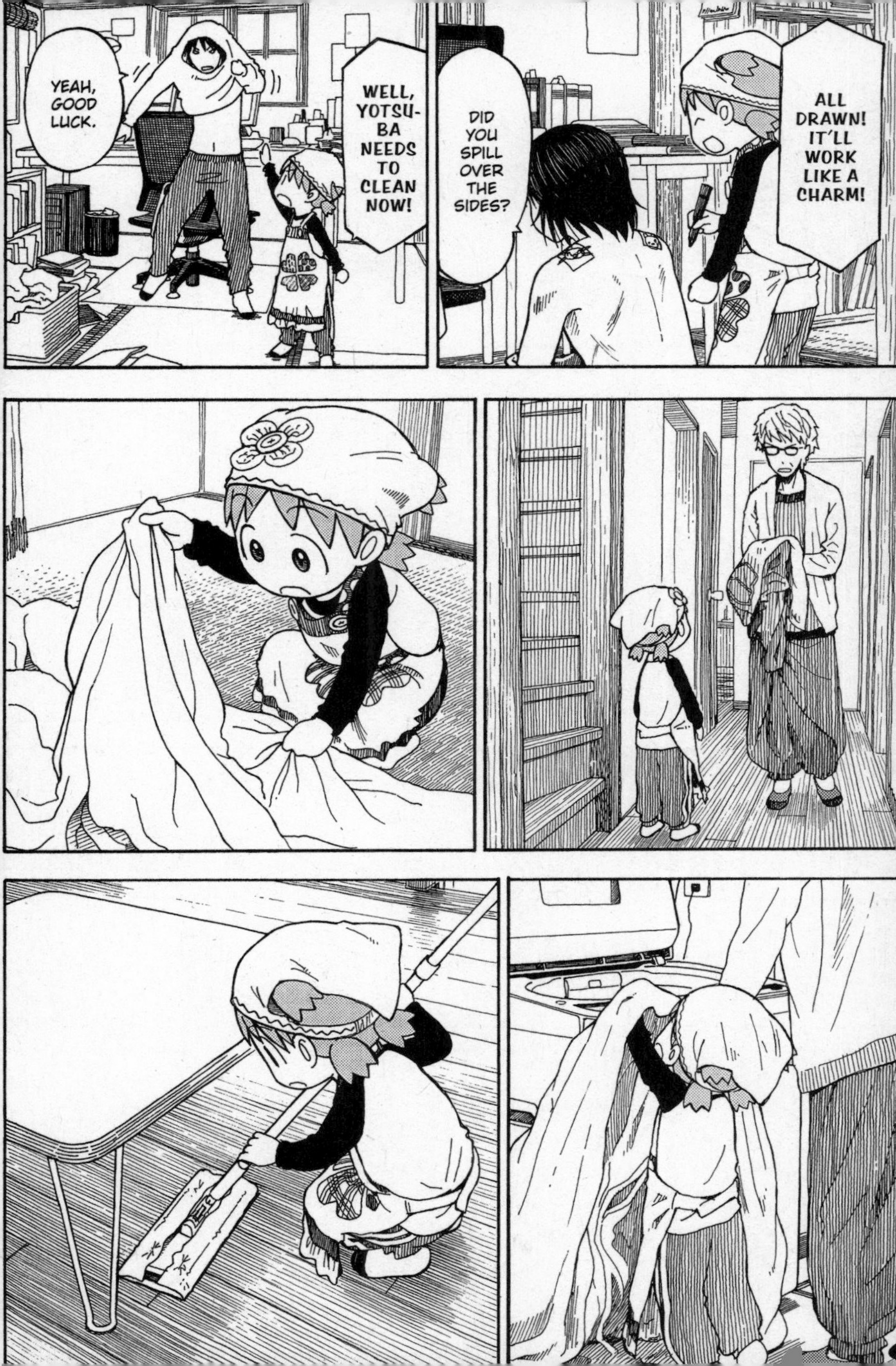
ALL DRAWN! IT'LL WORK LIKE A CHARM!
DID YOU SPILL OVER THE SIDES?
WELL, YOTSUBA NEEDS TO CLEAN NOW!
YEAH, GOOD LUCK.

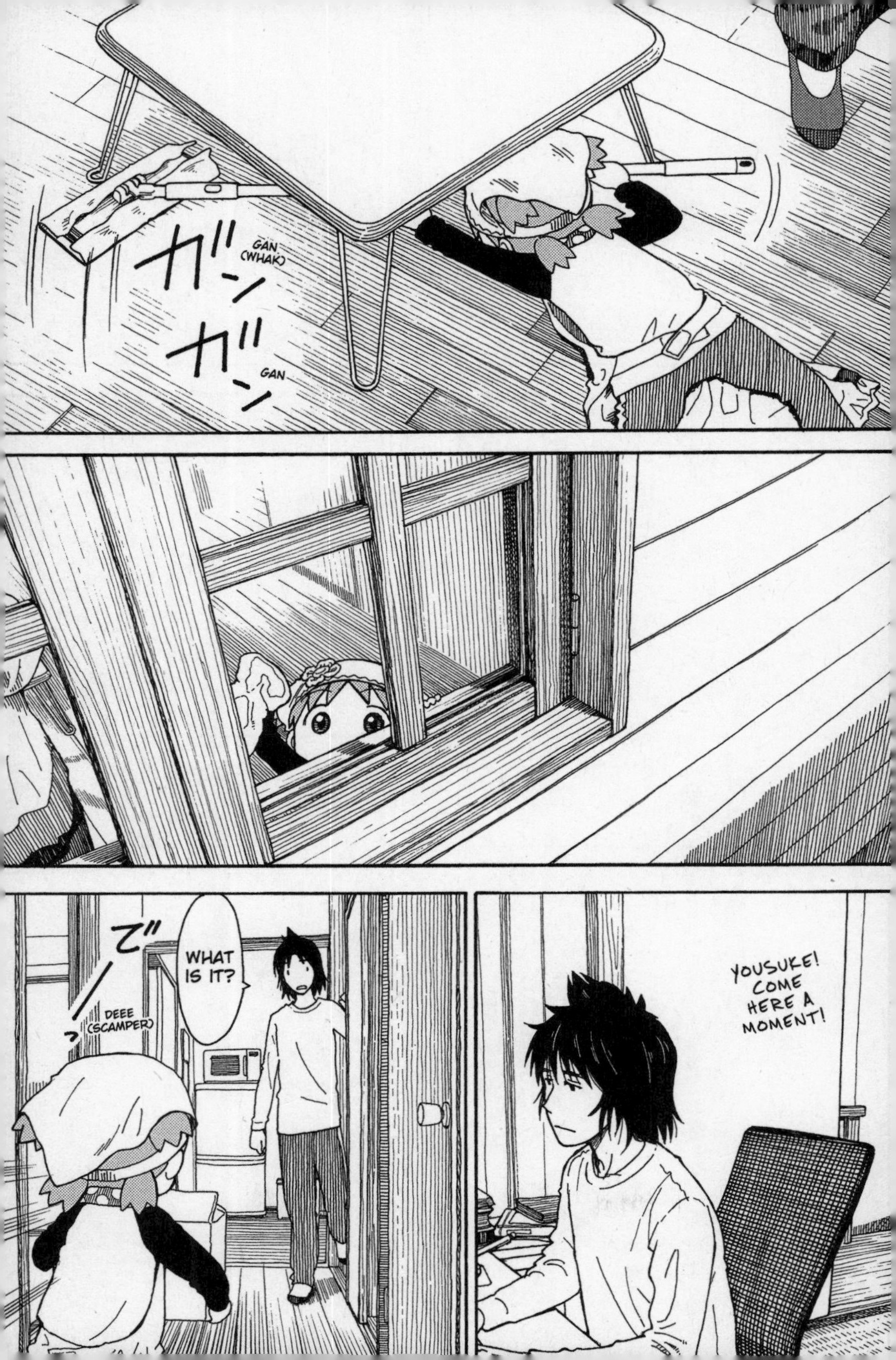
ガン
GAN (WHAK)
ガン
GAN
YOUSUKE! COME HERE A MOMENT!
WHAT IS IT?
で
DEEE (SCAMPER)

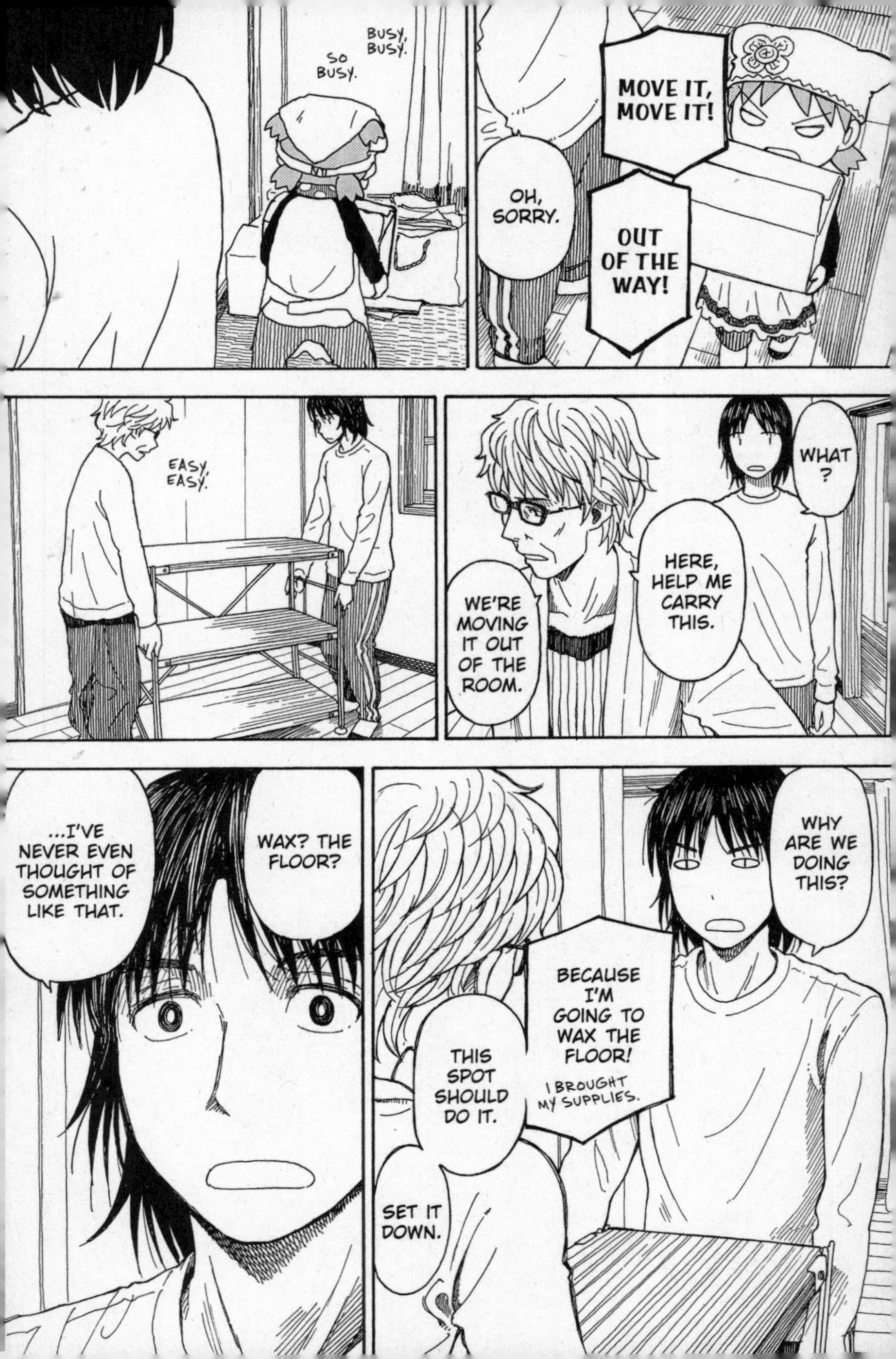
MOVE IT, MOVE IT!
OUT OF THE WAY!
OH, SORRY.
BUSY, BUSY.
SO BUSY.
WHAT?
HERE, HELP ME CARRY THIS.
WE'RE MOVING IT OUT OF THE ROOM.
EASY, EASY.
WHY ARE WE DOING THIS?
BECAUSE I'M GOING TO WAX THE FLOOR!
I BROUGHT MY SUPPLIES.
THIS SPOT SHOULD DO IT.
SET IT DOWN.
WAX? THE FLOOR?
...I'VE NEVER EVEN THOUGHT OF SOMETHING LIKE THAT.

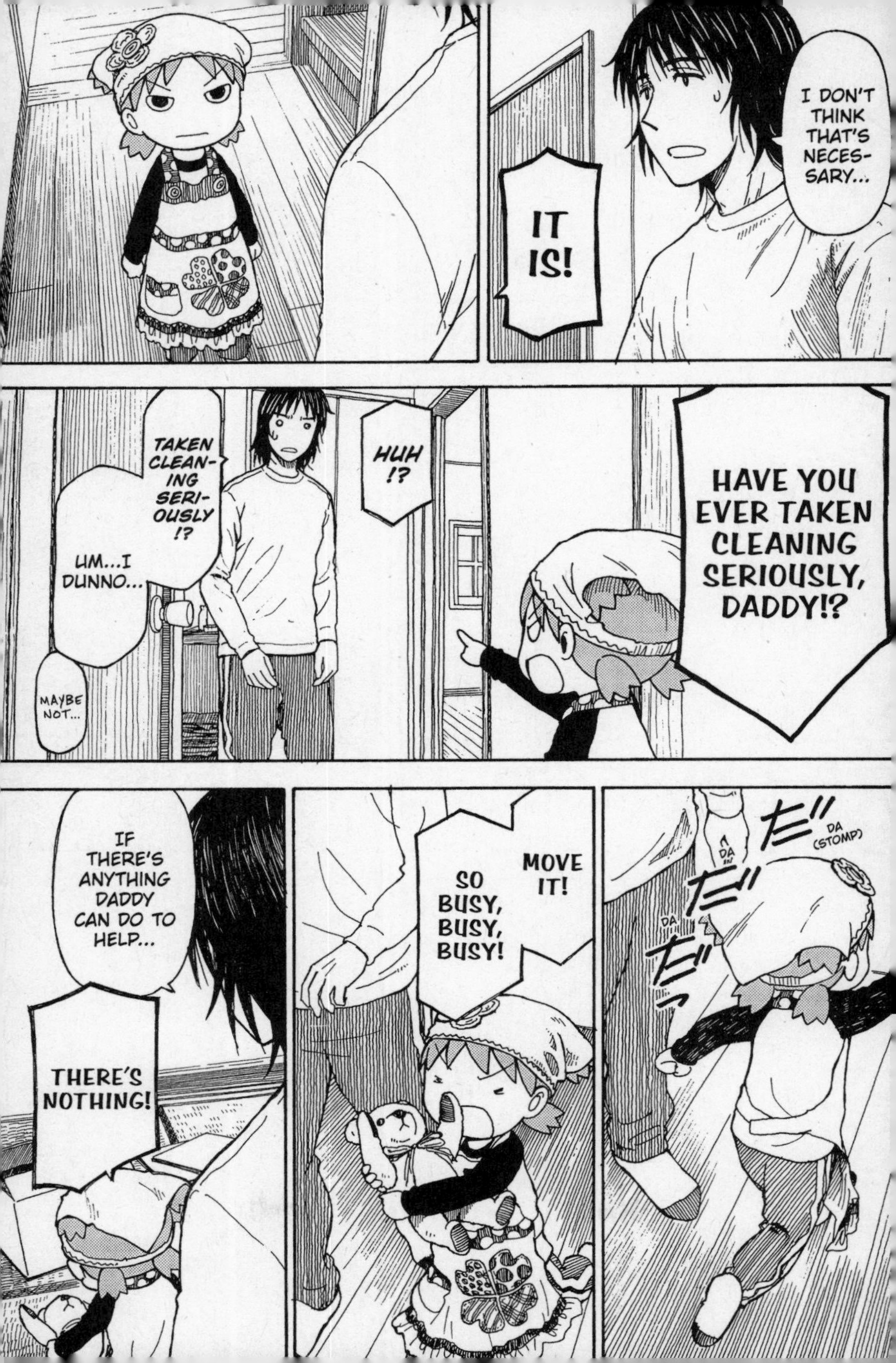
I DON'T THINK THAT'S NECES-SARY...
IT IS!
HAVE YOU EVER TAKEN CLEANING SERIOUSLY, DADDY!?
HUH !?
TAKEN CLEANING SERIOUSLY !?
UM...I DUNNO...
MAYBE NOT...
DA (STOMP)
DA
DA
MOVE IT!
SO BUSY, BUSY, BUSY!
IF THERE'S ANYTHING DADDY CAN DO TO HELP...
THERE'S NOTHING!

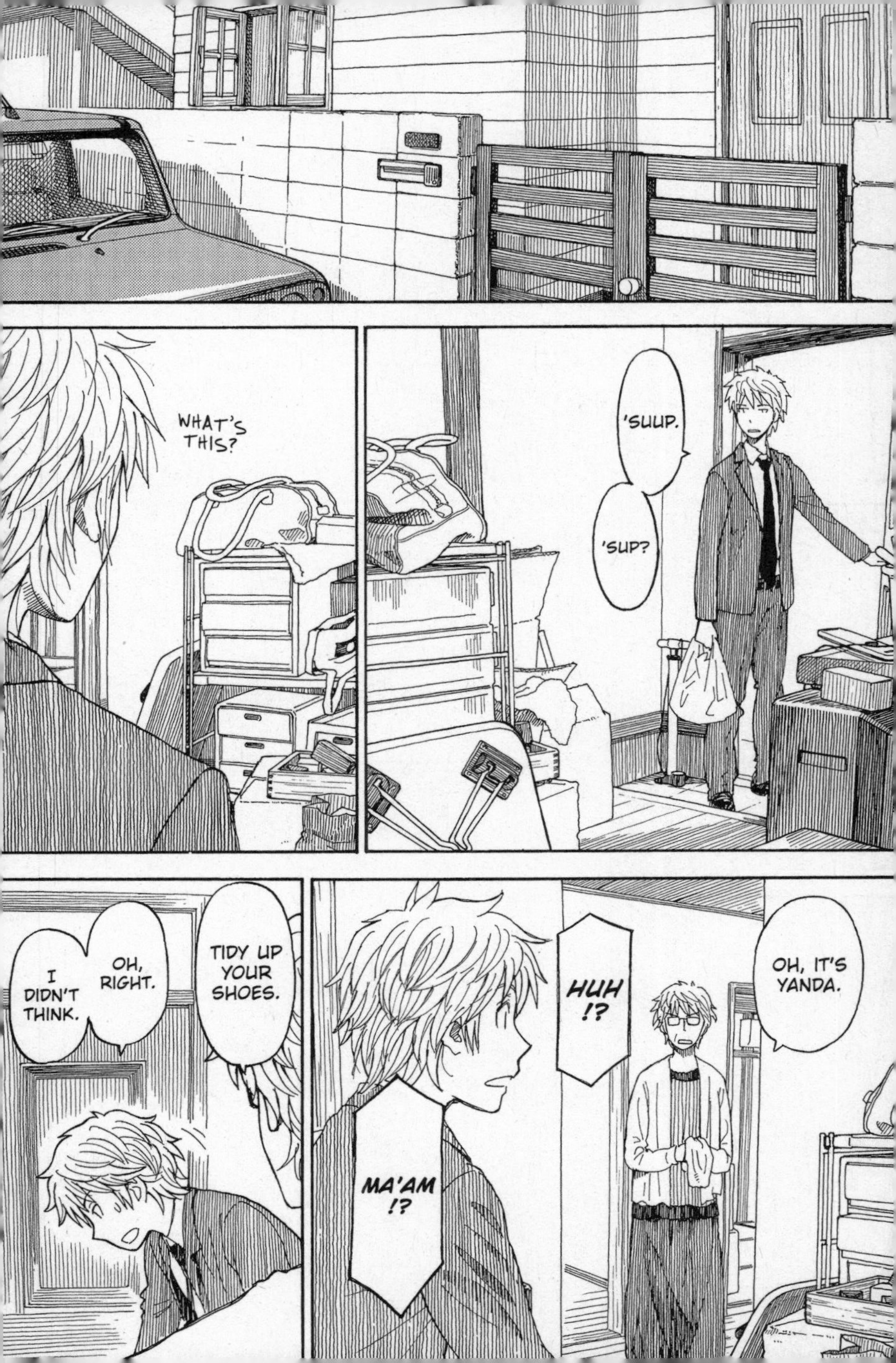
'SUUP.
'SUP?
WHAT'S THIS?
OH, IT'S YANDA.
HUH!?
MA'AM!?
TIDY UP YOUR SHOES.
OH, RIGHT.
I DIDN'T THINK.

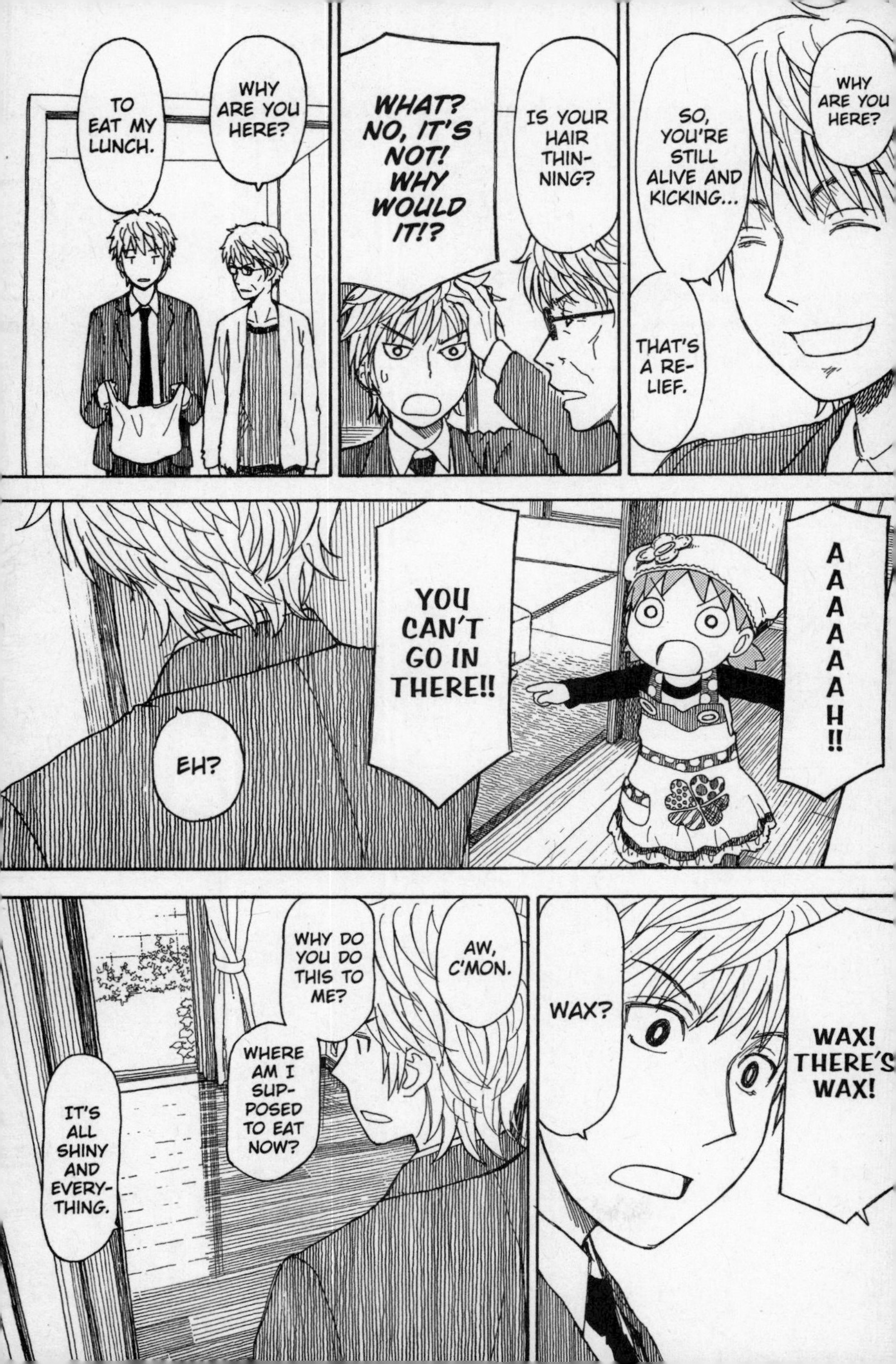

WHY ARE YOU HERE?
SO, YOU'RE STILL ALIVE AND KICKING...
THAT'S A RE-LIEF.
IS YOUR HAIR THIN-NING?
WHAT? NO, IT'S NOT! WHY WOULD IT!?
WHY ARE YOU HERE?
TO EAT MY LUNCH.
AAAAAAAH!!
YOU CAN'T GO IN THERE!!
EH?
WAX! THERE'S WAX!
WAX?
AW, C'MON.
WHY DO YOU DO THIS TO ME?
WHERE AM I SUP-POSED TO EAT NOW?
IT'S ALL SHINY AND EVERY-THING.

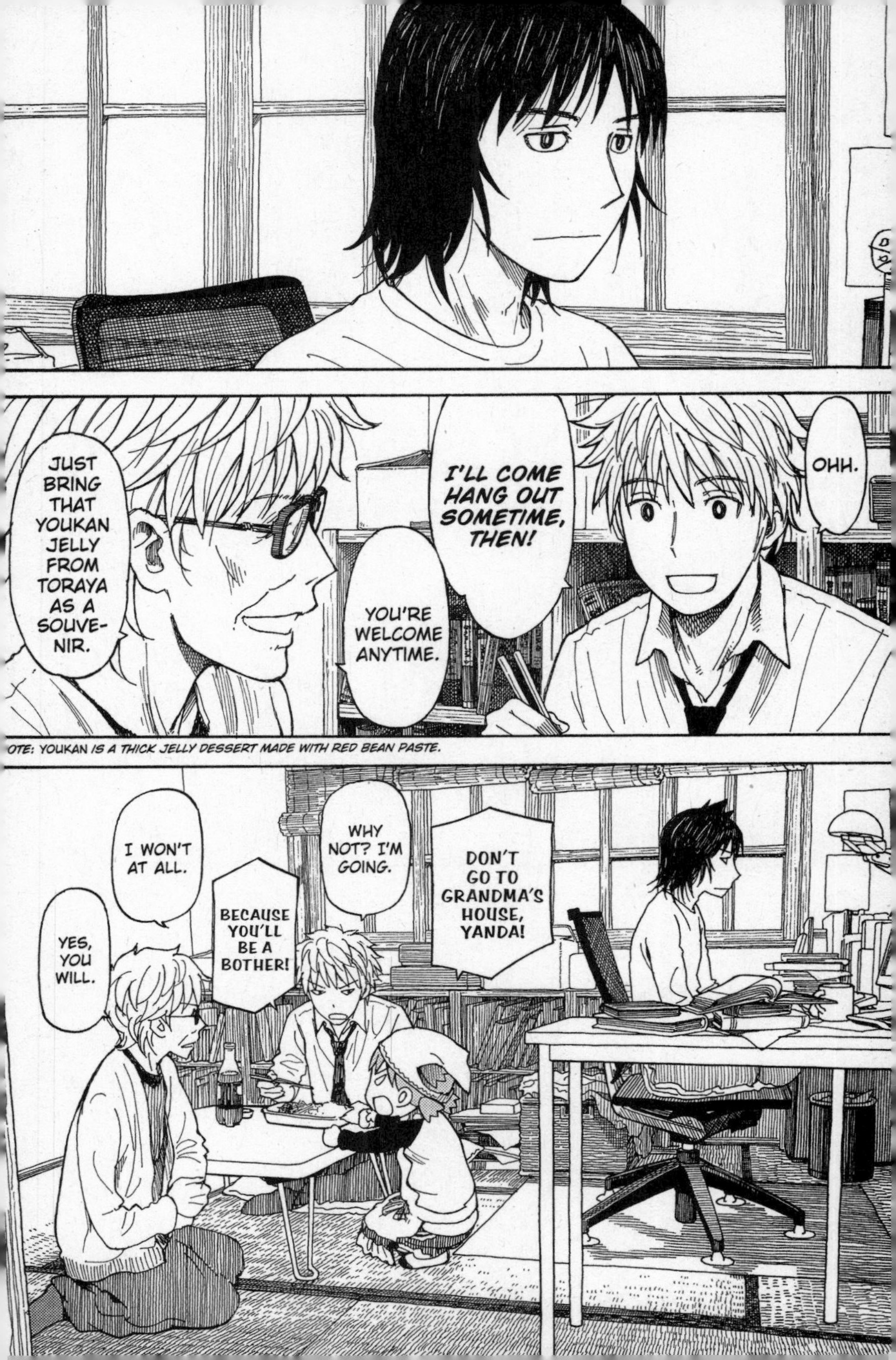
OHH.
I'LL COME HANG OUT SOMETIME, THEN!
YOU'RE WELCOME ANYTIME.
JUST BRING THAT YOUKAN JELLY FROM TORAYA AS A SOUVENIR.
OTE: YOUKAN IS A THICK JELLY DESSERT MADE WITH RED BEAN PASTE.
DON'T GO TO GRANDMA'S HOUSE, YANDA!
WHY NOT? I'M GOING.
BECAUSE YOU'LL BE A BOTHER!
I WON'T AT ALL.
YES, YOU WILL.

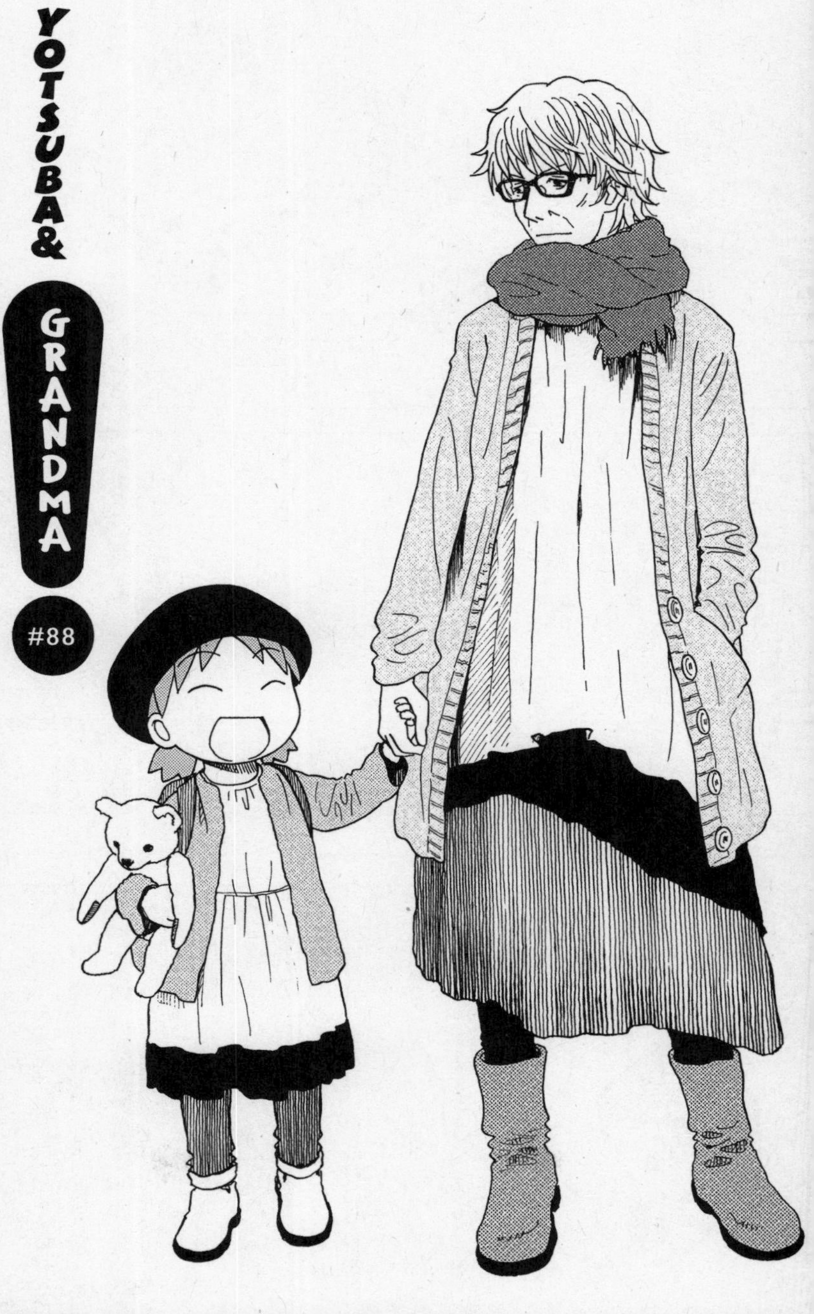
YOTSUBA&
GRANDMA
#88

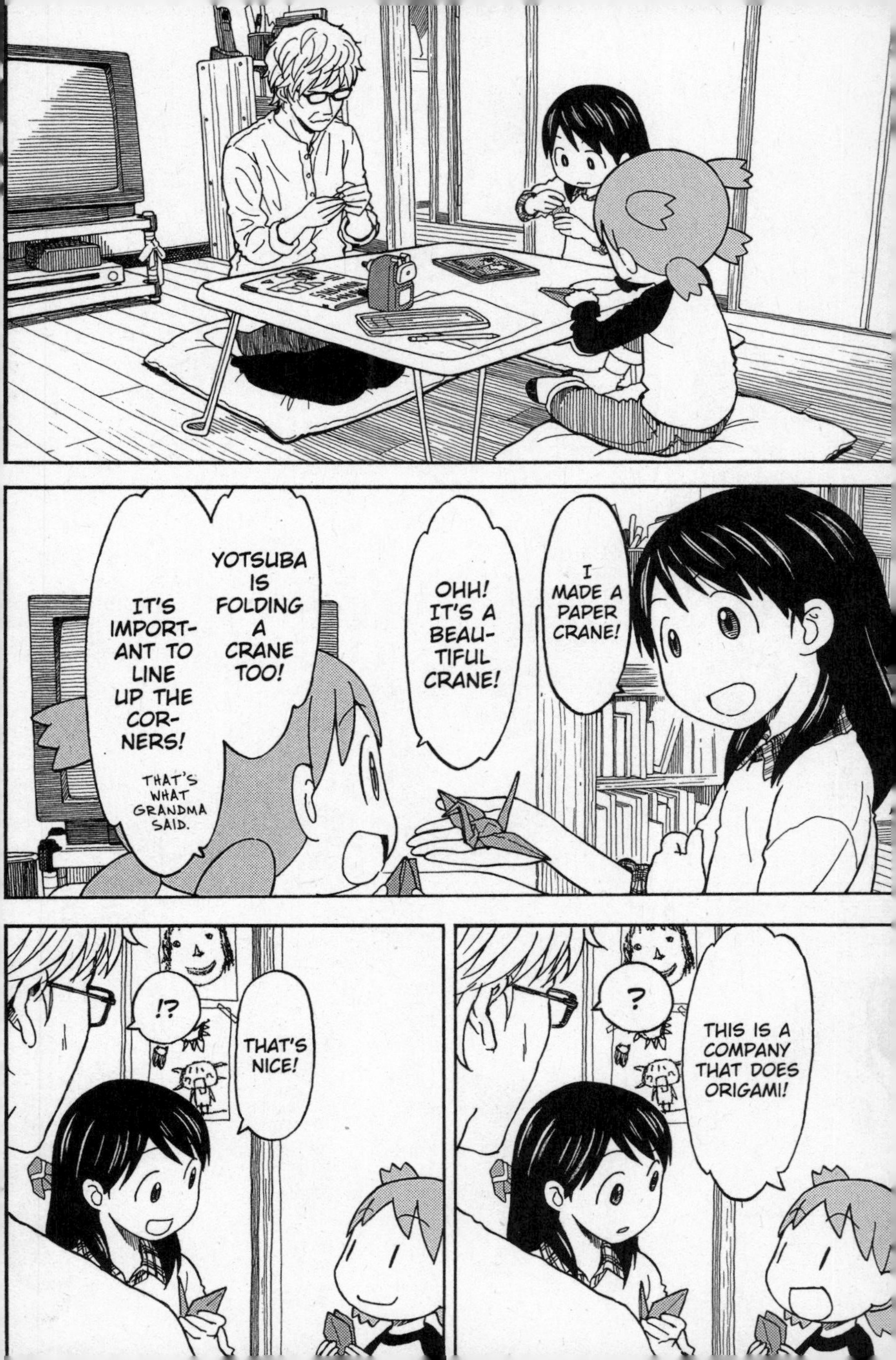
I MADE A PAPER CRANE!
OHH! IT'S A BEAUTIFUL CRANE!
YOTSUBA IS FOLDING A CRANE TOO!
IT'S IMPORTANT TO LINE UP THE CORNERS!
THAT'S WHAT GRANDMA SAID.
THIS IS A COMPANY THAT DOES ORIGAMI!
?
THAT'S NICE!
!?

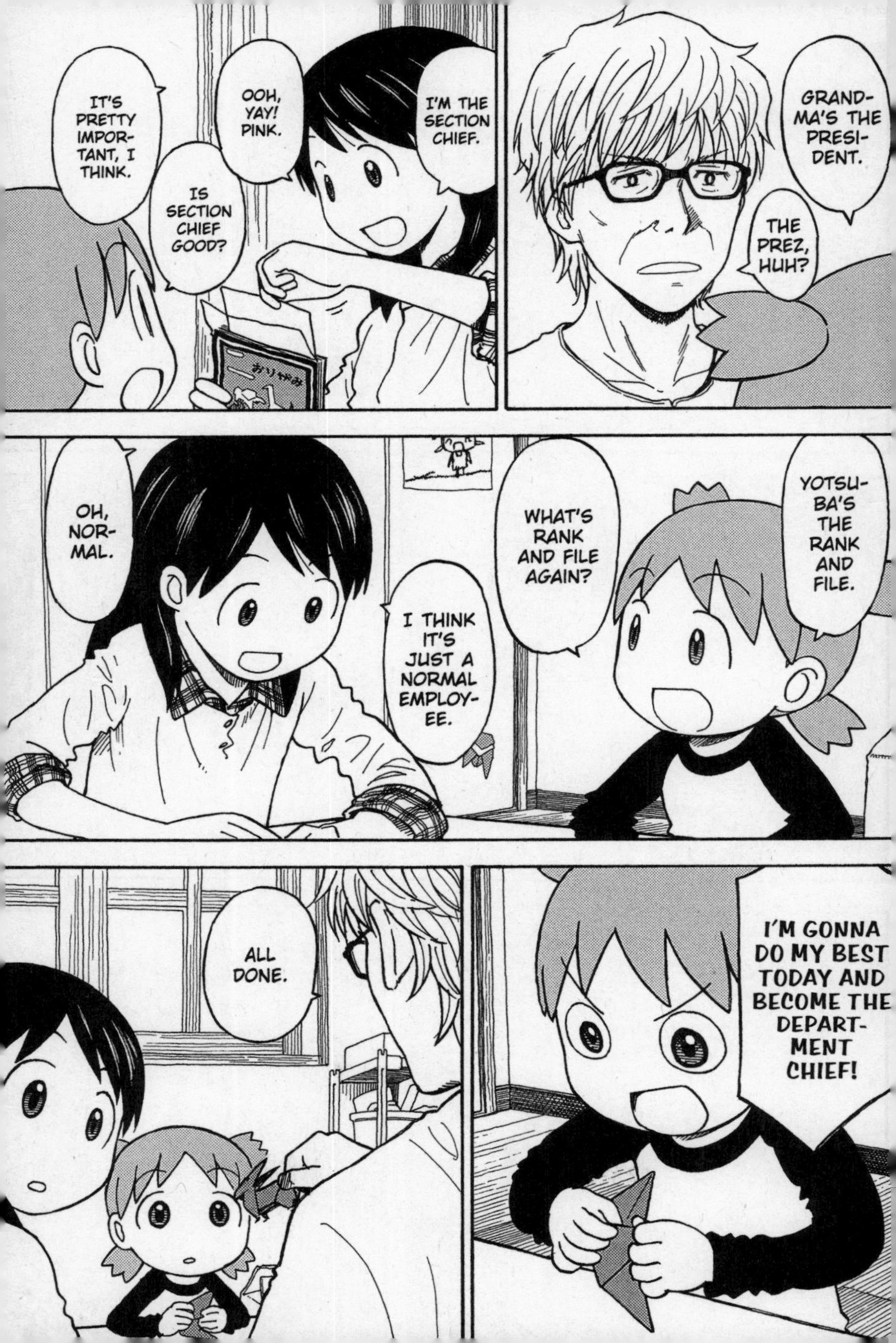

GRANDMA'S THE PRESIDENT.
THE PREZ, HUH?
I'M THE SECTION CHIEF.
OOH, YAY! PINK.
おりがみ
IS SECTION CHIEF GOOD?
IT'S PRETTY IMPORTANT, I THINK.
YOTSUBA'S THE RANK AND FILE.
WHAT'S RANK AND FILE AGAIN?
I THINK IT'S JUST A NORMAL EMPLOYEE.
OH, NORMAL.
I'M GONNA DO MY BEST TODAY AND BECOME THE DEPARTMENT CHIEF!
ALL DONE.

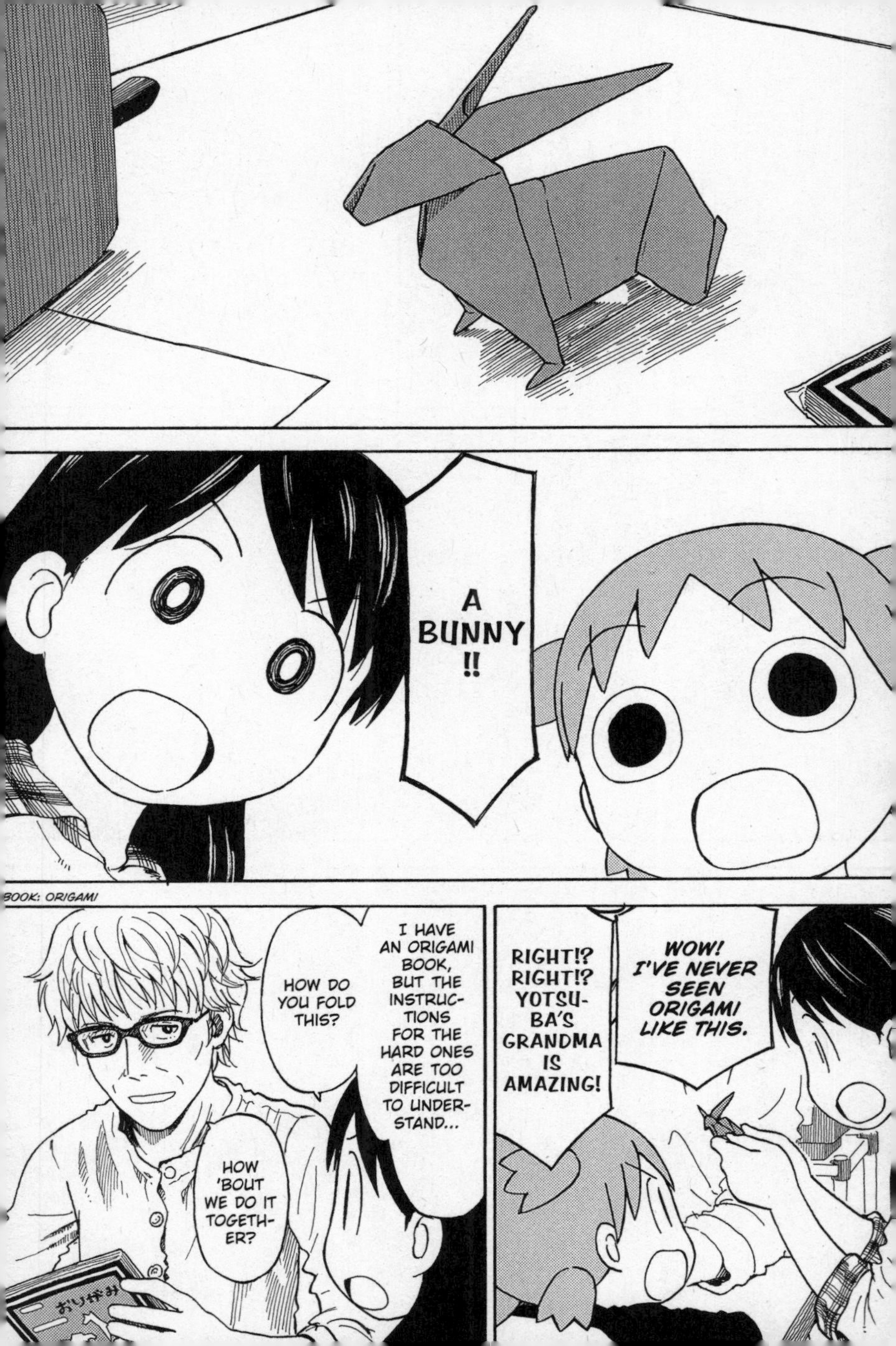
A BUNNY!!
BOOK: ORIGAMI
WOW! I'VE NEVER SEEN ORIGAMI LIKE THIS.
RIGHT!? RIGHT!? YOTSUBA'S GRANDMA IS AMAZING!
I HAVE AN ORIGAMI BOOK, BUT THE INSTRUCTIONS FOR THE HARD ONES ARE TOO DIFFICULT TO UNDERSTAND...
HOW DO YOU FOLD THIS?
HOW 'BOUT WE DO IT TOGETHER?
おりがみ

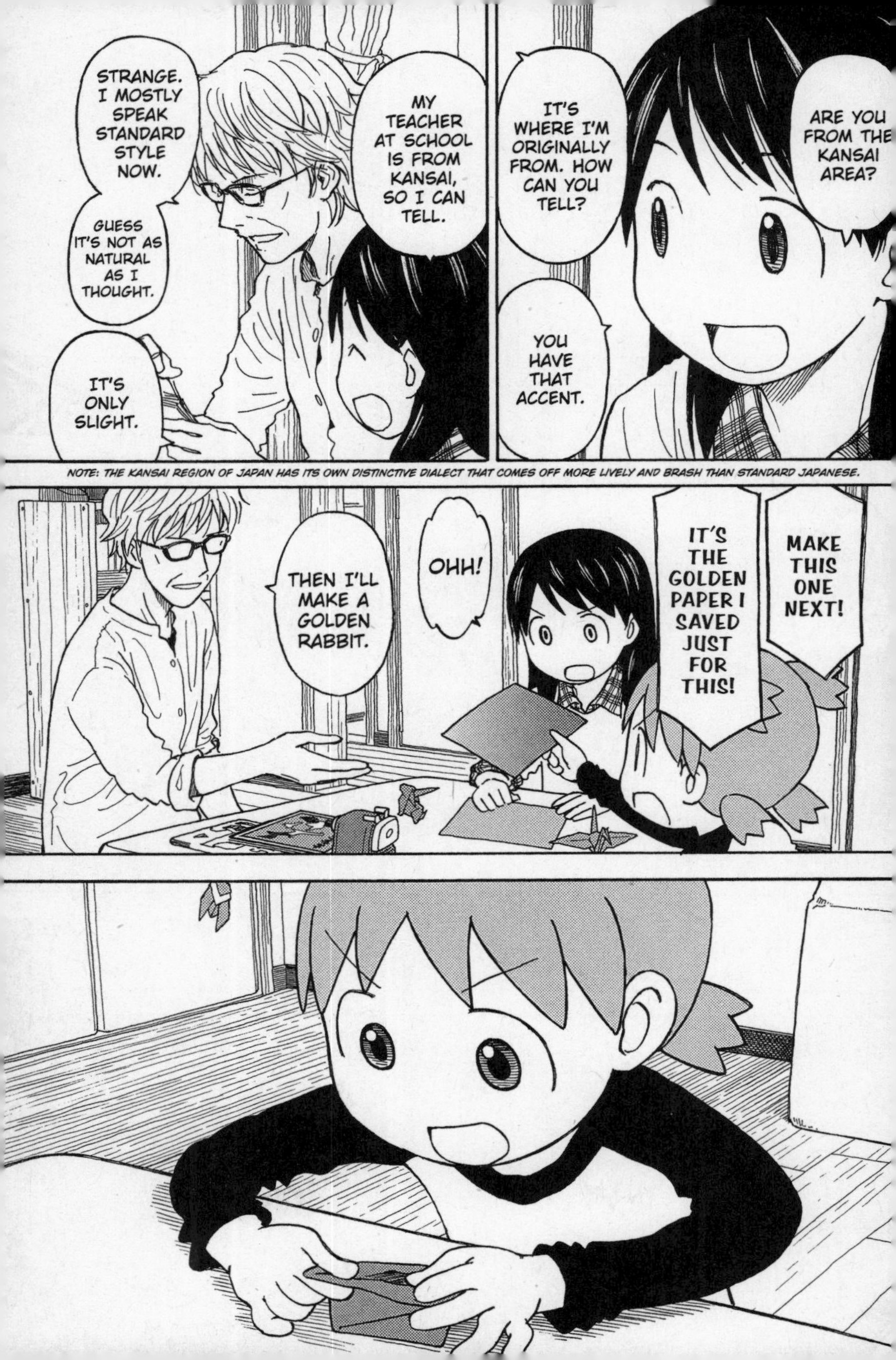
ARE YOU FROM THE KANSAI AREA?
IT'S WHERE I'M ORIGINALLY FROM. HOW CAN YOU TELL?
YOU HAVE THAT ACCENT.
MY TEACHER AT SCHOOL IS FROM KANSAI, SO I CAN TELL.
STRANGE. I MOSTLY SPEAK STANDARD STYLE NOW.
GUESS IT'S NOT AS NATURAL AS I THOUGHT.
IT'S ONLY SLIGHT.
NOTE: THE KANSAI REGION OF JAPAN HAS ITS OWN DISTINCTIVE DIALECT THAT COMES OFF MORE LIVELY AND BRASH THAN STANDARD JAPANESE.
MAKE THIS ONE NEXT!
IT'S THE GOLDEN PAPER I SAVED JUST FOR THIS!
OHH!
THEN I'LL MAKE A GOLDEN RABBIT.

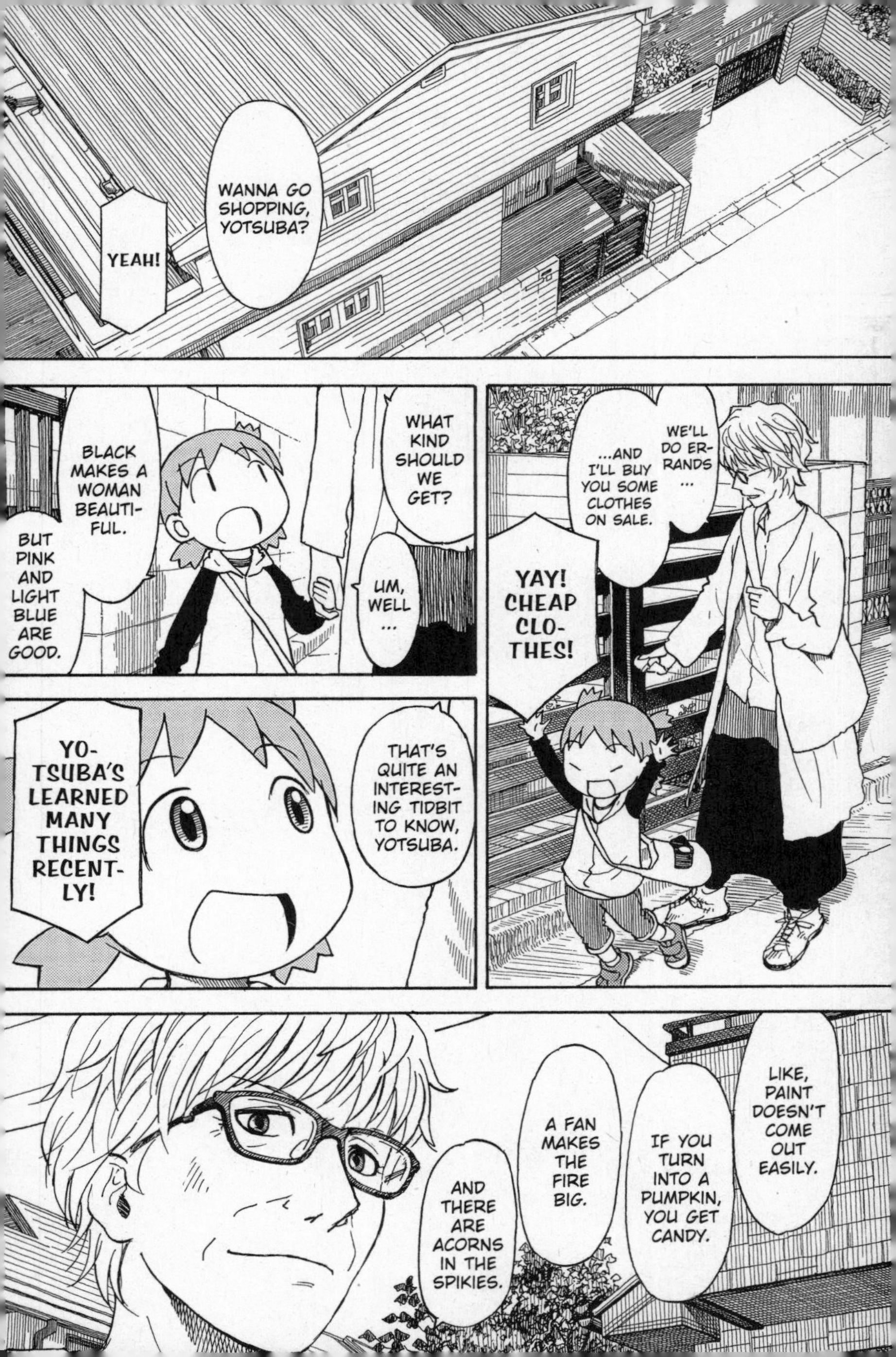
WANNA GO SHOPPING, YOTSUBA?
YEAH!
WE'LL DO ERRANDS...
...AND I'LL BUY YOU SOME CLOTHES ON SALE.
YAY! CHEAP CLOTHES!
WHAT KIND SHOULD WE GET?
UM, WELL ...
BLACK MAKES A WOMAN BEAUTIFUL.
BUT PINK AND LIGHT BLUE ARE GOOD.
THAT'S QUITE AN INTERESTING TIDBIT TO KNOW, YOTSUBA.
YOTSUBA'S LEARNED MANY THINGS RECENTLY!
LIKE, PAINT DOESN'T COME OUT EASILY.
IF YOU TURN INTO A PUMPKIN, YOU GET CANDY.
A FAN MAKES THE FIRE BIG.
AND THERE ARE ACORNS IN THE SPIKIES.

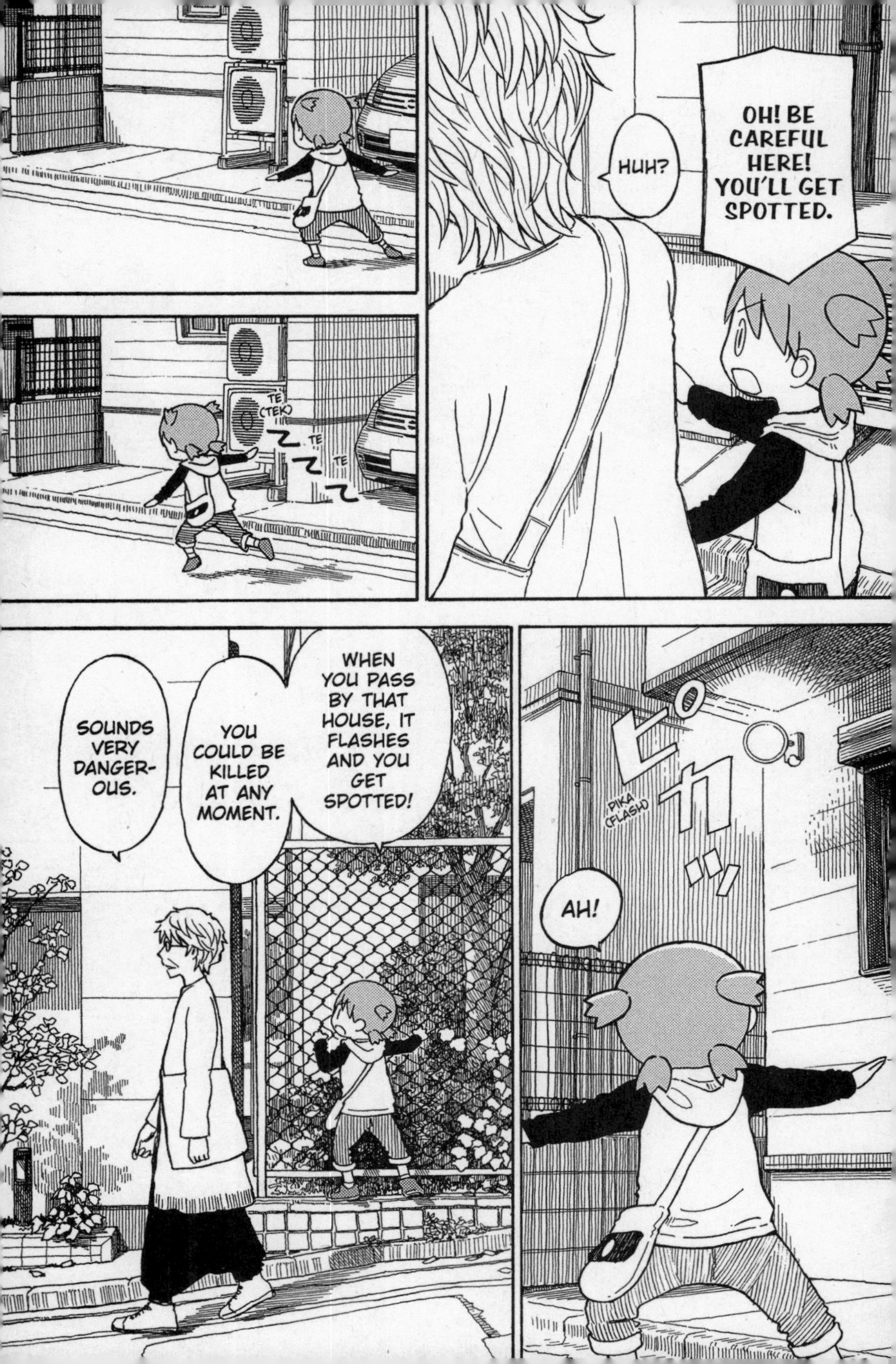
OH! BE CAREFUL HERE! YOU'LL GET SPOTTED.
HUH?
TE (TEK)
TE
TE
ピカッ
PIKA (FLASH)
AH!
WHEN YOU PASS BY THAT HOUSE, IT FLASHES AND YOU GET SPOTTED!
YOU COULD BE KILLED AT ANY MOMENT.
SOUNDS VERY DANGER-OUS.

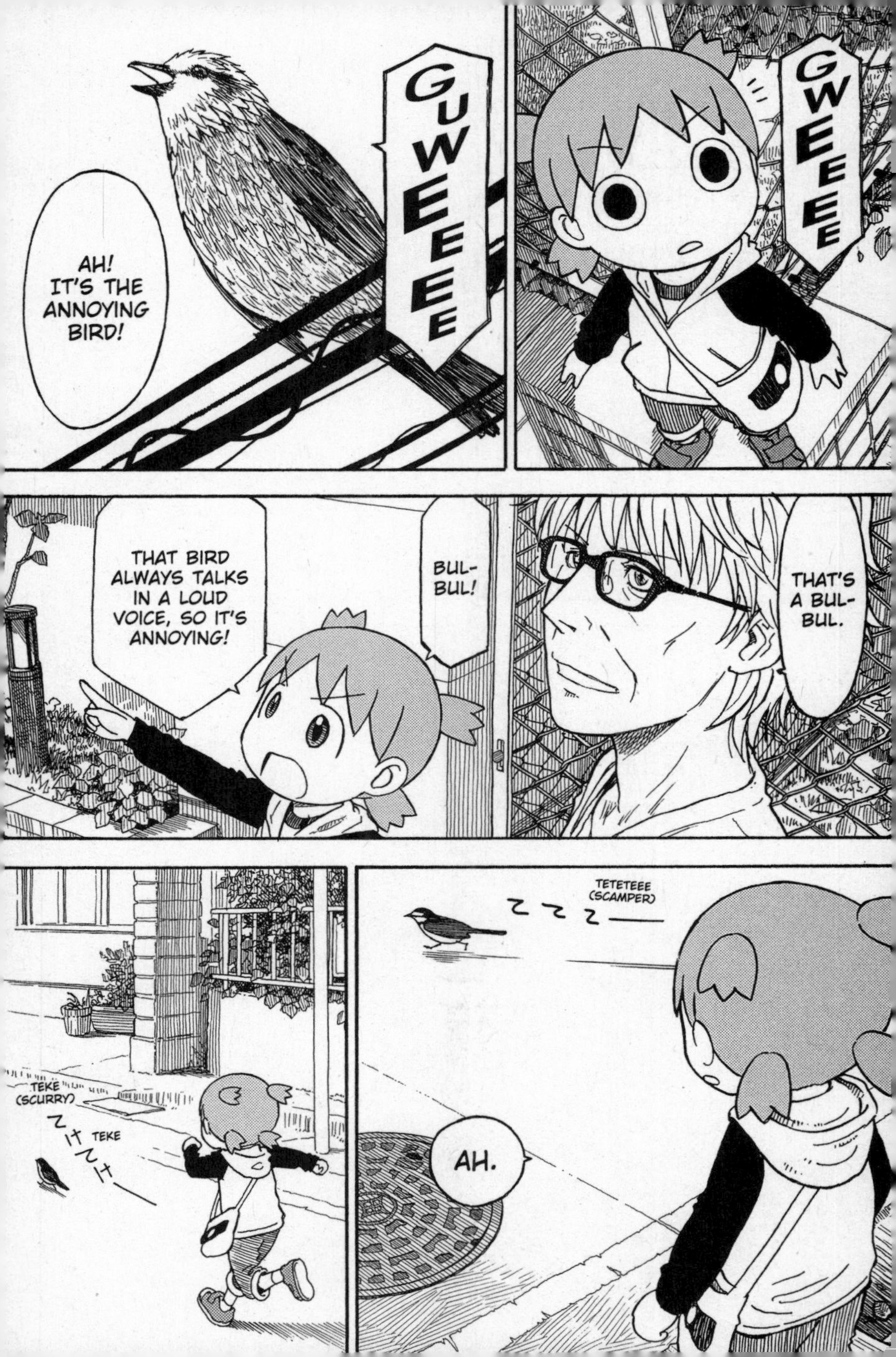
GWEEEE
GUWEEEE
AH! IT'S THE ANNOYING BIRD!
THAT'S A BUL-BUL.
BUL-BUL!
THAT BIRD ALWAYS TALKS IN A LOUD VOICE, SO IT'S ANNOYING!
TETETEEE (SCAMPER)
AH.
TEKE (SCURRY)
TEKE

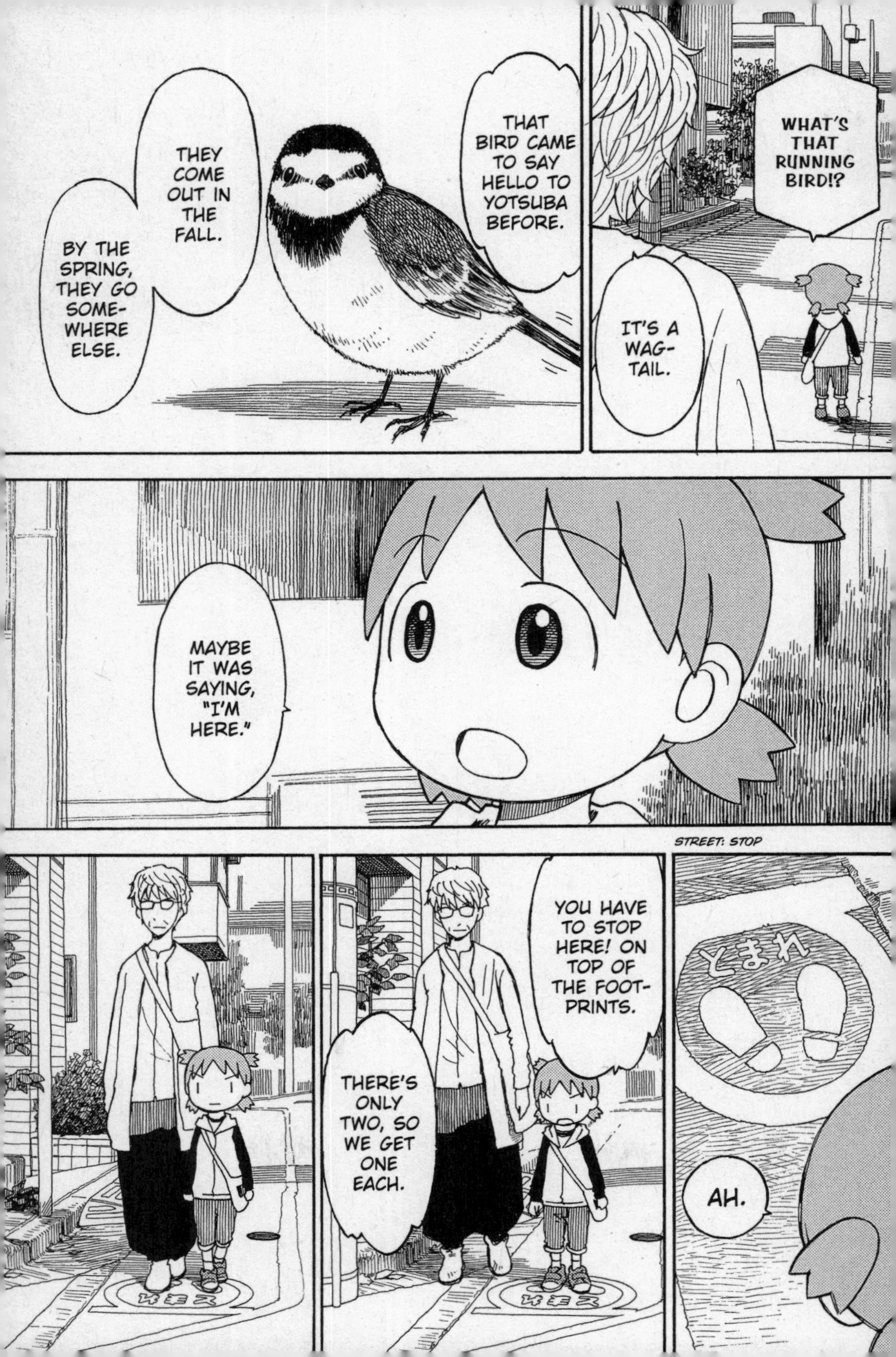
WHAT'S THAT RUNNING BIRD!?
IT'S A WAG-TAIL.
THAT BIRD CAME TO SAY HELLO TO YOTSUBA BEFORE.
THEY COME OUT IN THE FALL.
BY THE SPRING, THEY GO SOME-WHERE ELSE.
MAYBE IT WAS SAYING, "I'M HERE."
STREET: STOP
とまれ
AH.
YOU HAVE TO STOP HERE! ON TOP OF THE FOOT-PRINTS.
THERE'S ONLY TWO, SO WE GET ONE EACH.

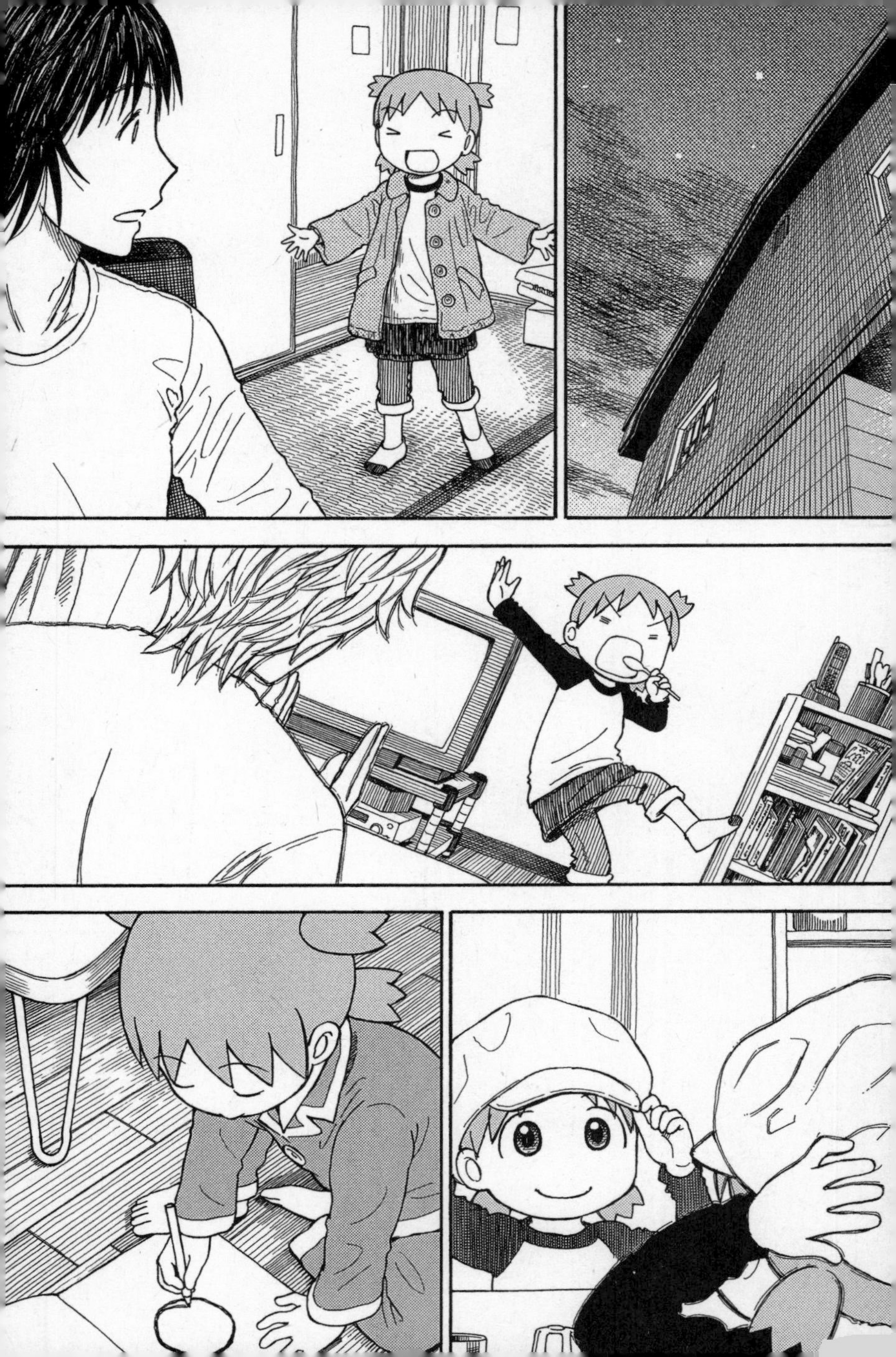

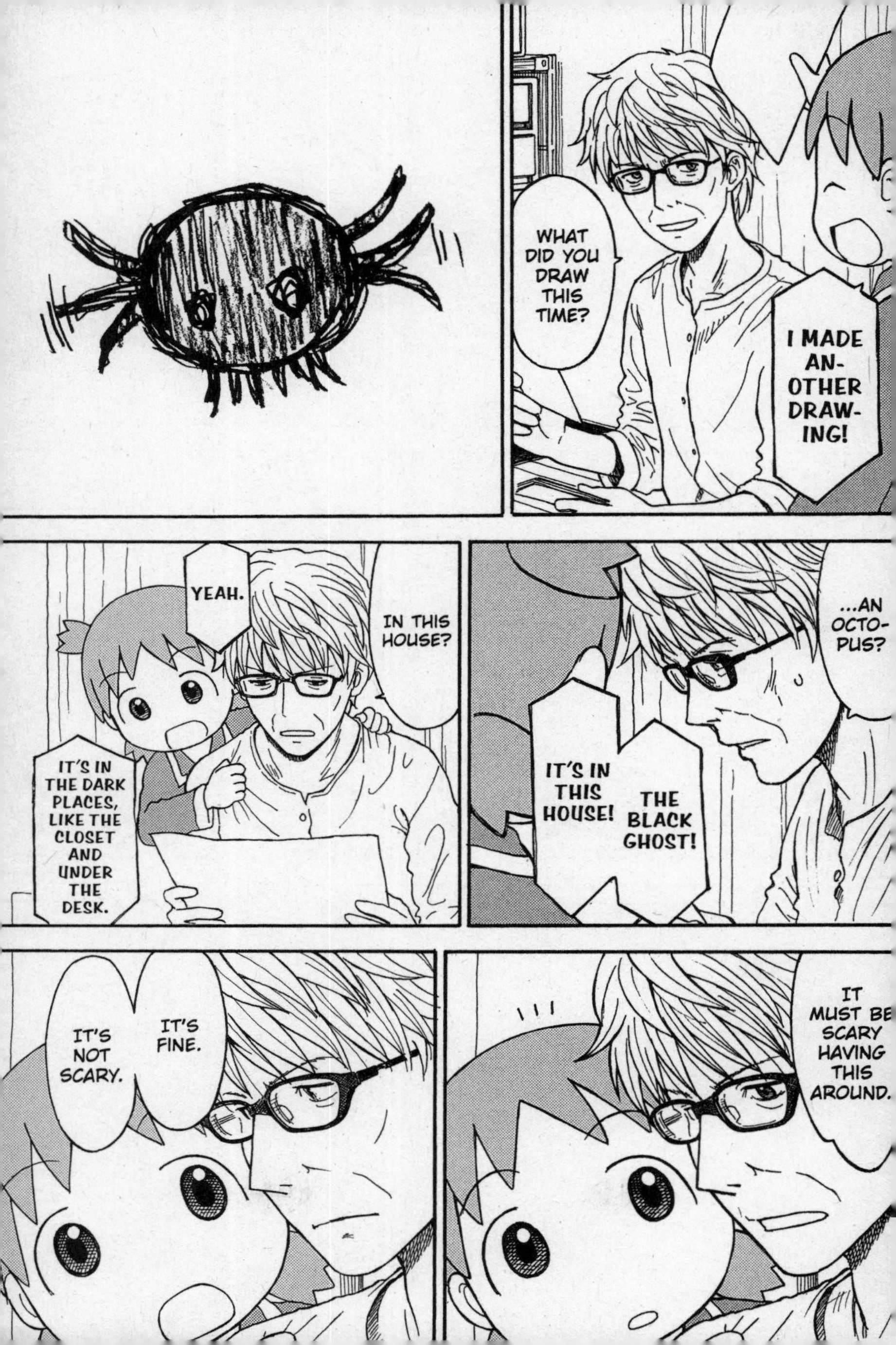
WHAT DID YOU DRAW THIS TIME?
I MADE AN-OTHER DRAW-ING!
...AN OCTO-PUS?
IT'S IN THIS HOUSE!
THE BLACK GHOST!
IN THIS HOUSE?
YEAH.
IT'S IN THE DARK PLACES, LIKE THE CLOSET AND UNDER THE DESK.
IT MUST BE SCARY HAVING THIS AROUND.
IT'S FINE.
IT'S NOT SCARY.

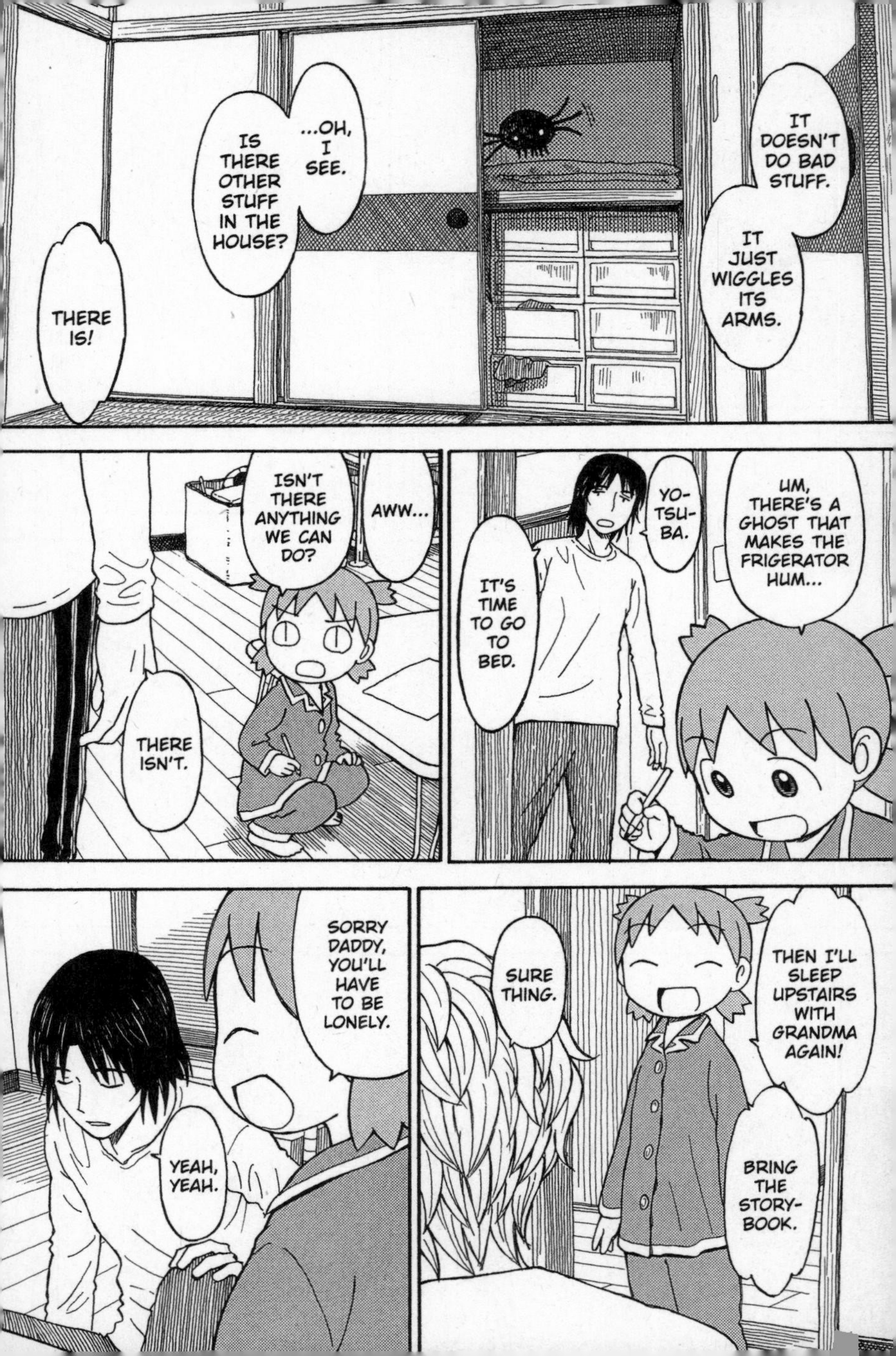
IT DOESN'T DO BAD STUFF.
IT JUST WIGGLES ITS ARMS.
...OH, I SEE.
IS THERE OTHER STUFF IN THE HOUSE?
THERE IS!
UM, THERE'S A GHOST THAT MAKES THE FRIGERATOR HUM...
YO-TSU-BA.
IT'S TIME TO GO TO BED.
AWW...
ISN'T THERE ANYTHING WE CAN DO?
THERE ISN'T.
THEN I'LL SLEEP UPSTAIRS WITH GRANDMA AGAIN!
SURE THING.
BRING THE STORY-BOOK.
SORRY DADDY, YOU'LL HAVE TO BE LONELY.
YEAH, YEAH.

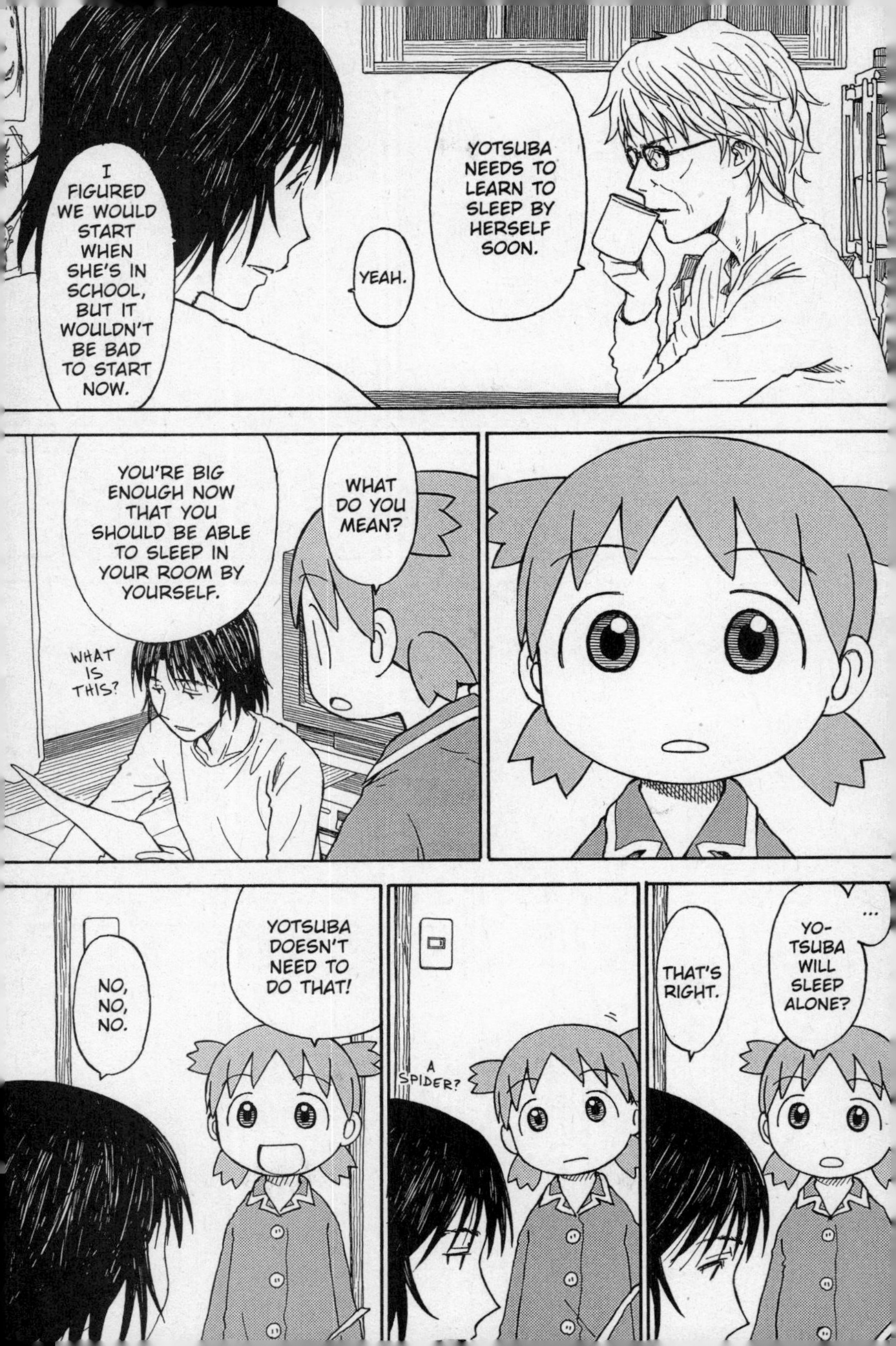
YOTSUBA NEEDS TO LEARN TO SLEEP BY HERSELF SOON.
YEAH.
I FIGURED WE WOULD START WHEN SHE'S IN SCHOOL, BUT IT WOULDN'T BE BAD TO START NOW.
WHAT DO YOU MEAN?
YOU'RE BIG ENOUGH NOW THAT YOU SHOULD BE ABLE TO SLEEP IN YOUR ROOM BY YOURSELF.
WHAT IS THIS?
...
YO-TSUBA WILL SLEEP ALONE?
THAT'S RIGHT.
A SPIDER?
YOTSUBA DOESN'T NEED TO DO THAT!
NO, NO, NO.

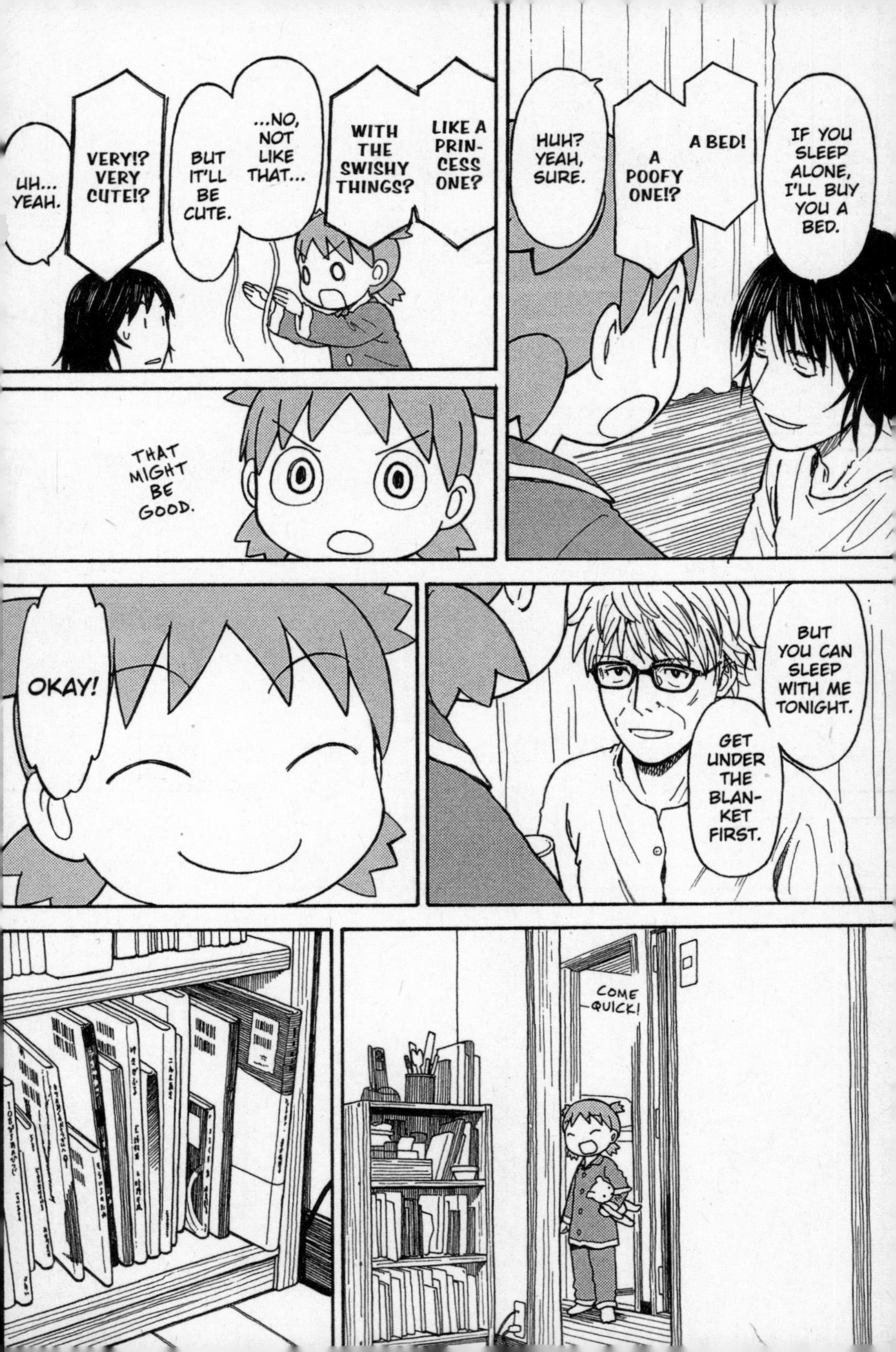
IF YOU SLEEP ALONE, I'LL BUY YOU A BED.
A BED!
A POOFY ONE!?
HUH? YEAH, SURE.
LIKE A PRINCESS ONE?
WITH THE SWISHY THINGS?
...NO, NOT LIKE THAT...
BUT IT'LL BE CUTE.
VERY!? VERY CUTE!?
UH... YEAH.
THAT MIGHT BE GOOD.
BUT YOU CAN SLEEP WITH ME TONIGHT.
GET UNDER THE BLANKET FIRST.
OKAY!
COME QUICK!

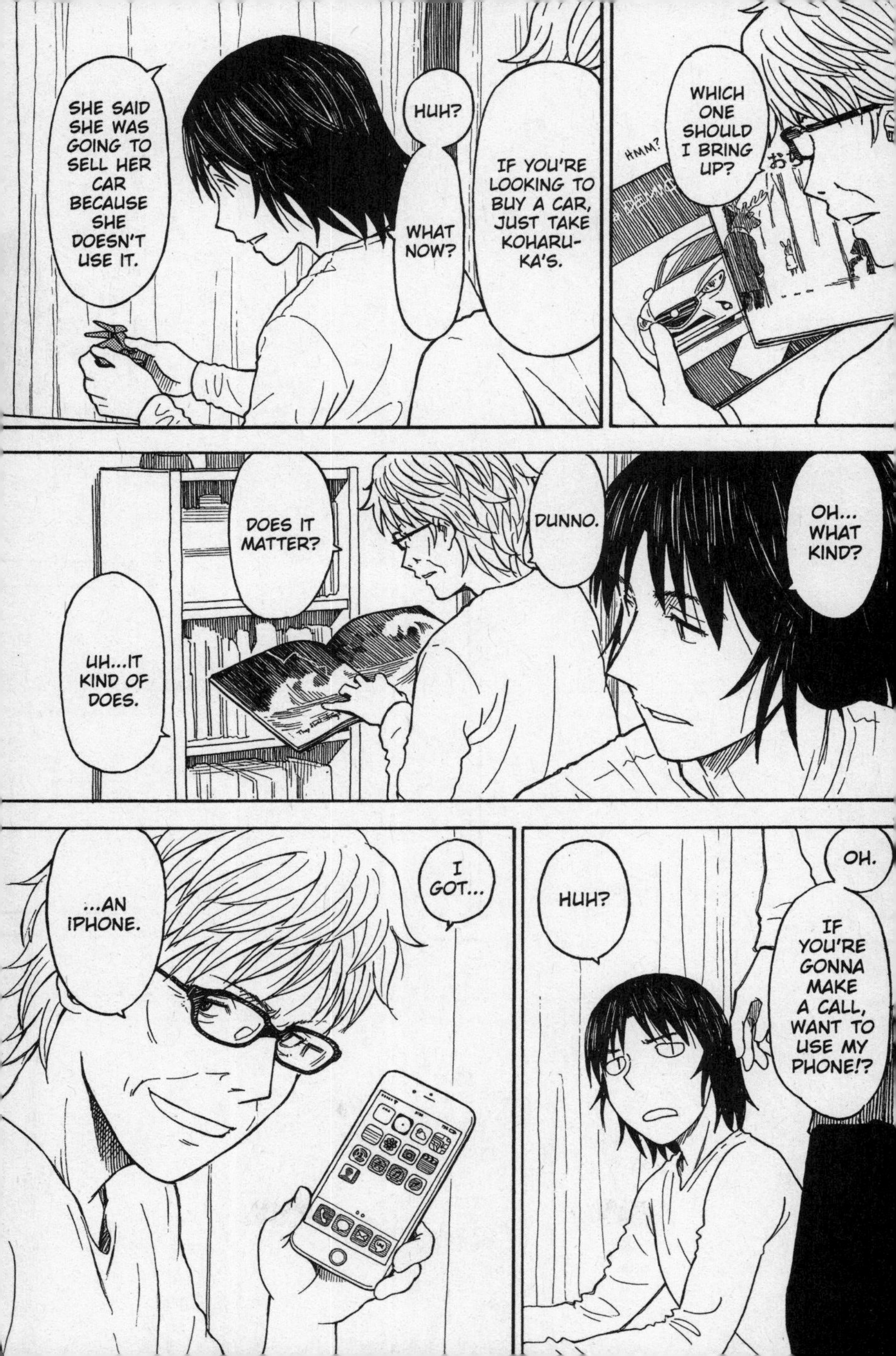

WHICH ONE SHOULD I BRING UP?
HMM?
IF YOU'RE LOOKING TO BUY A CAR, JUST TAKE KOHARU-KA'S.
HUH?
WHAT NOW?
SHE SAID SHE WAS GOING TO SELL HER CAR BECAUSE SHE DOESN'T USE IT.
OH... WHAT KIND?
DUNNO.
DOES IT MATTER?
UH...IT KIND OF DOES.
OH.
IF YOU'RE GONNA MAKE A CALL, WANT TO USE MY PHONE!?
HUH?
I GOT...
...AN iPHONE.

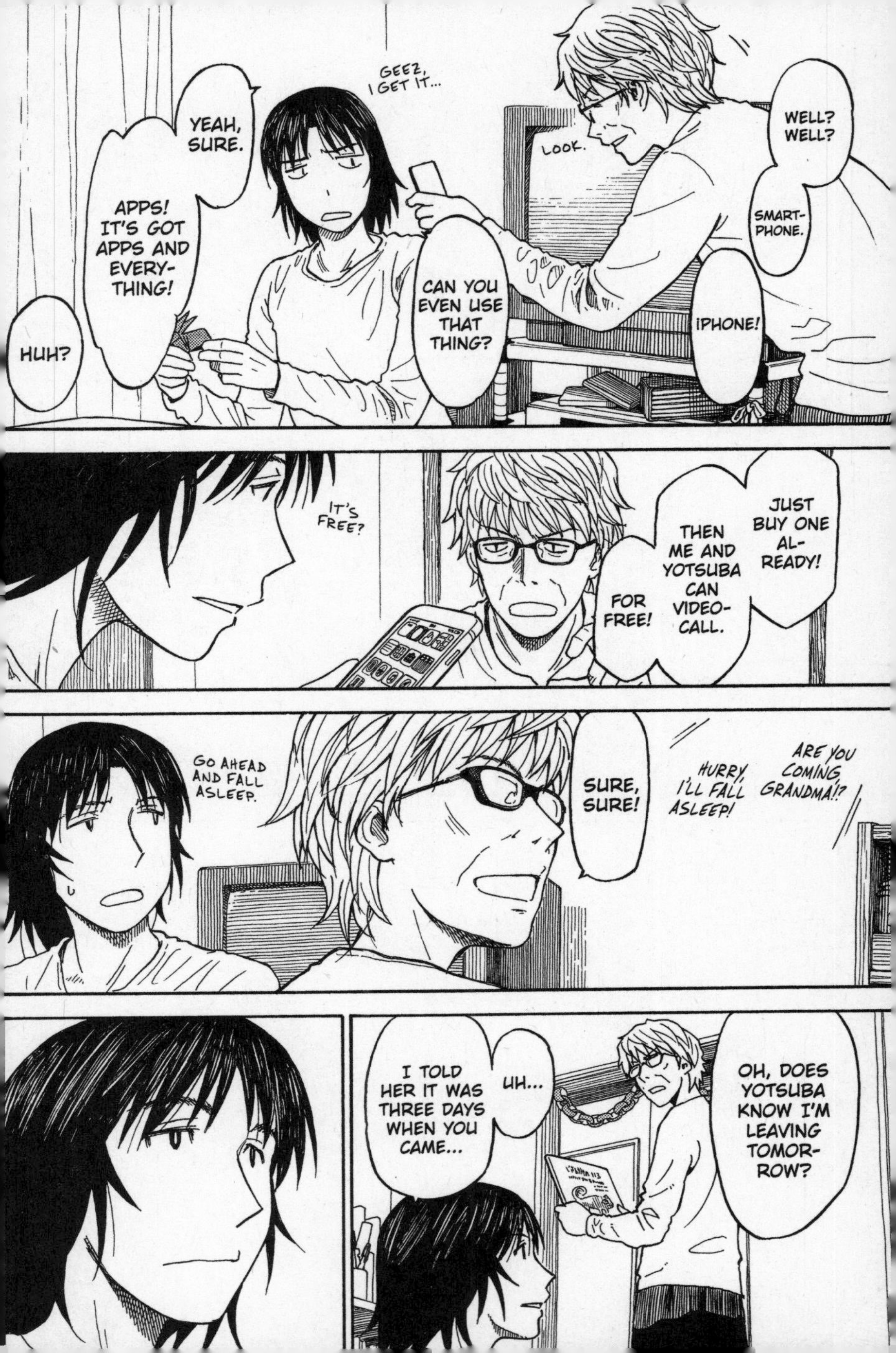
WELL? WELL?
SMART-PHONE.
IPHONE!
LOOK.
CAN YOU EVEN USE THAT THING?
GEEZ, I GET IT...
YEAH, SURE.
APPS! IT'S GOT APPS AND EVERY-THING!
HUH?
JUST BUY ONE AL-READY!
THEN ME AND YOTSUBA CAN VIDEO-CALL.
FOR FREE!
IT'S FREE?
ARE YOU COMING, GRANDMA!?
HURRY, I'LL FALL ASLEEP!
SURE, SURE!
GO AHEAD AND FALL ASLEEP.
OH, DOES YOTSUBA KNOW I'M LEAVING TOMOR-ROW?
UH...
I TOLD HER IT WAS THREE DAYS WHEN YOU CAME...

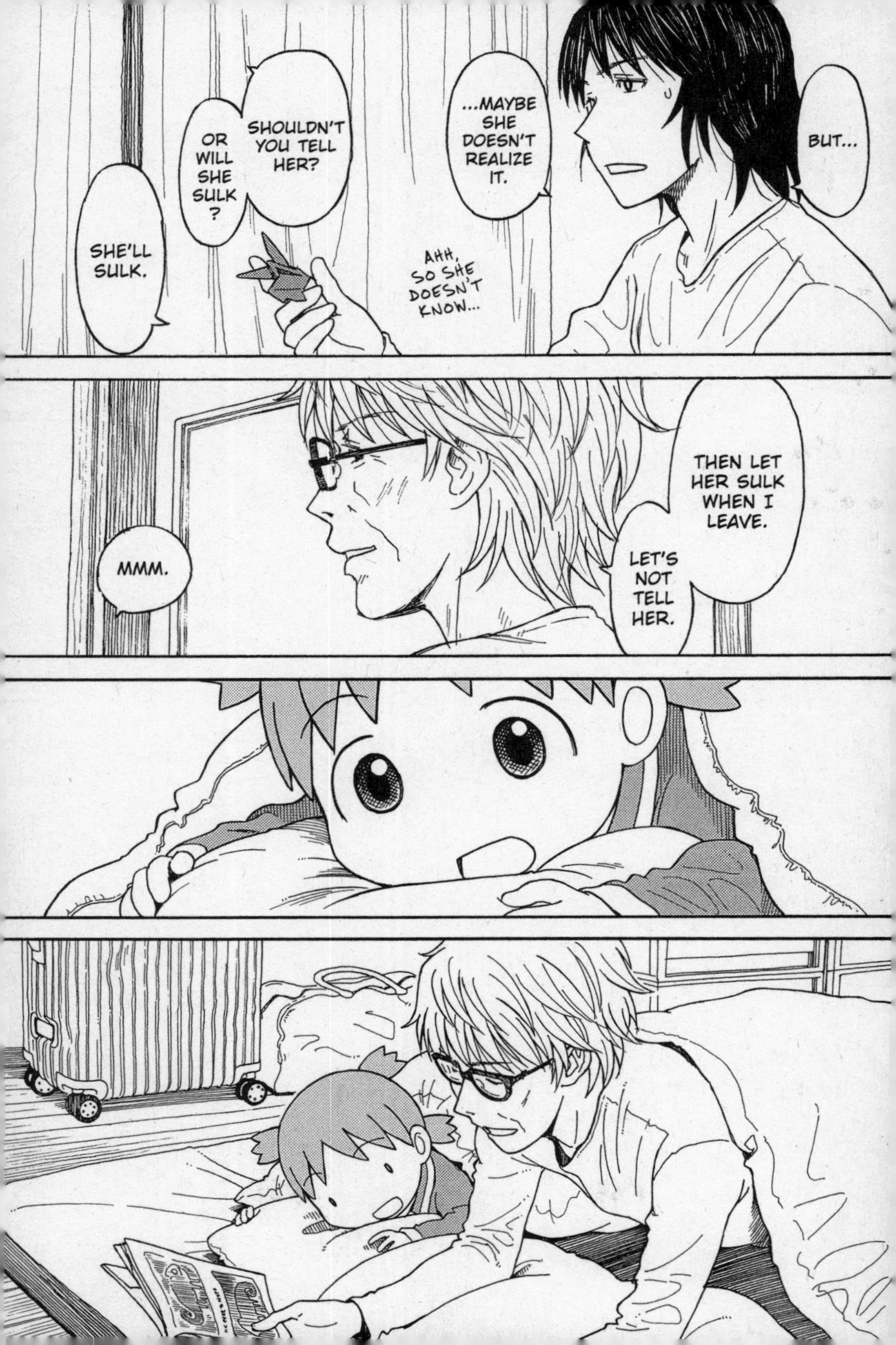
BUT...
...MAYBE SHE DOESN'T REALIZE IT.
AHH, SO SHE DOESN'T KNOW...
SHOULDN'T YOU TELL HER?
OR WILL SHE SULK?
SHE'LL SULK.
THEN LET HER SULK WHEN I LEAVE.
LET'S NOT TELL HER.
MMM.

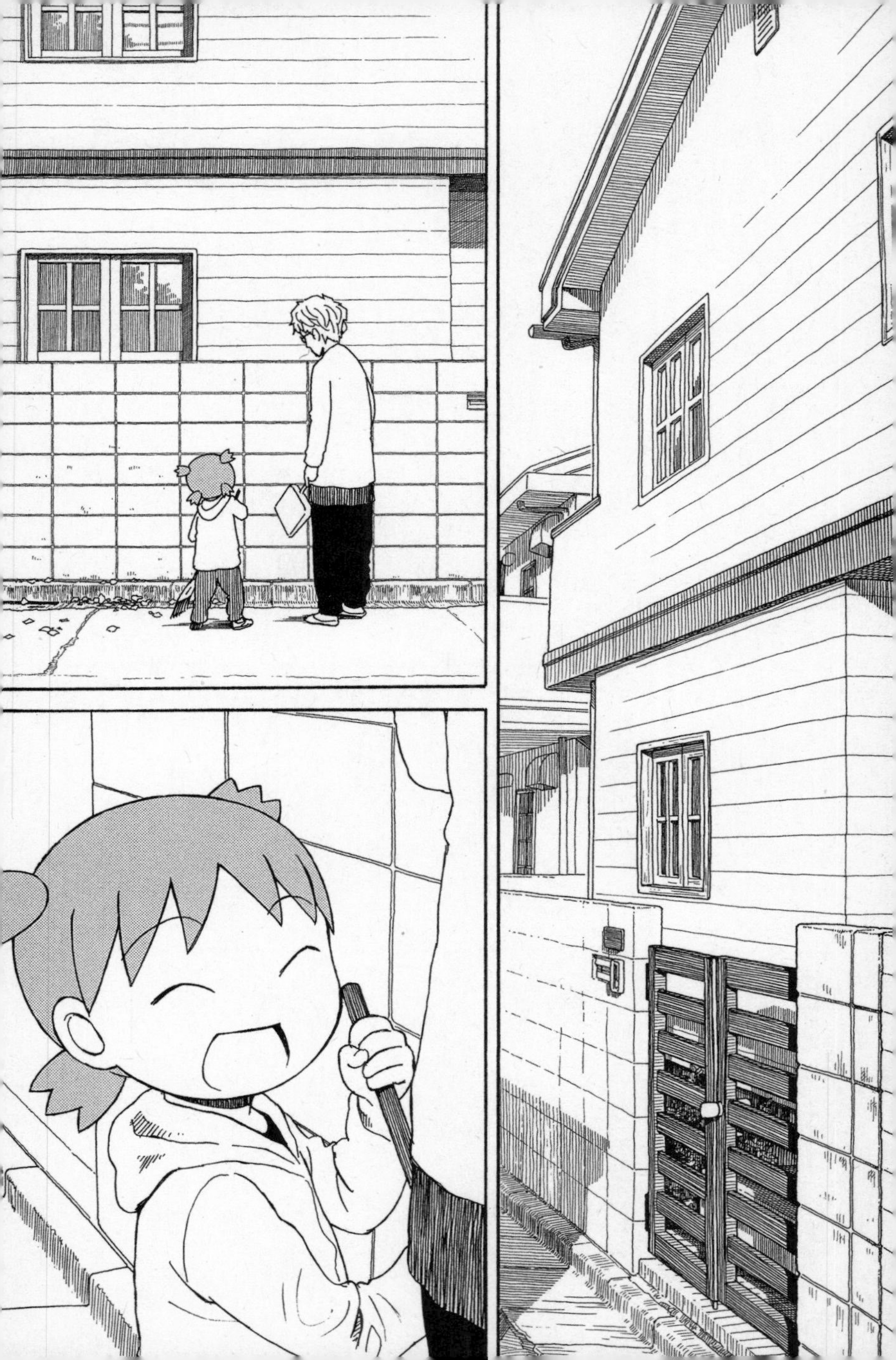

YOTSUBA&!

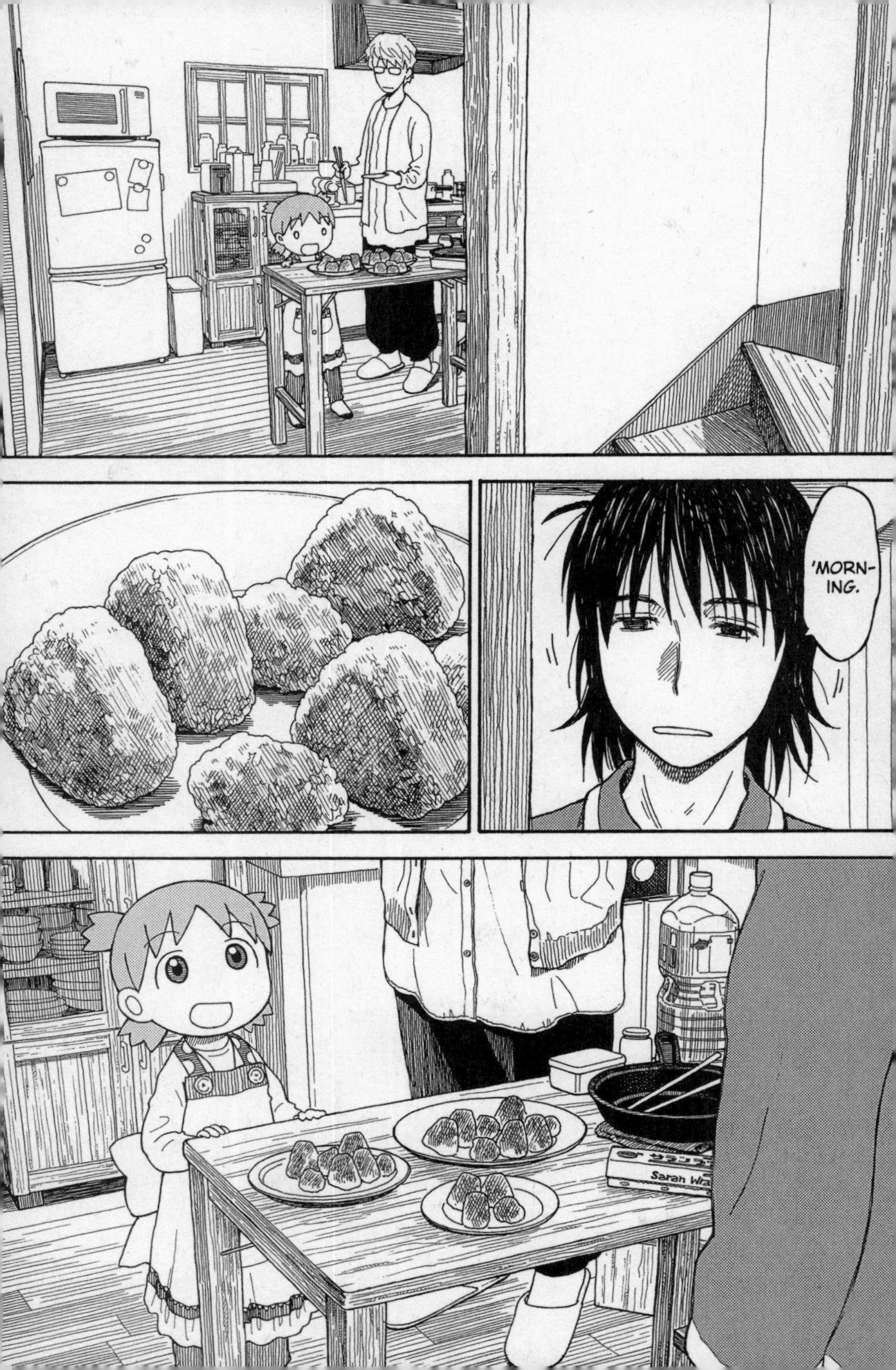
'MORN-
ING.

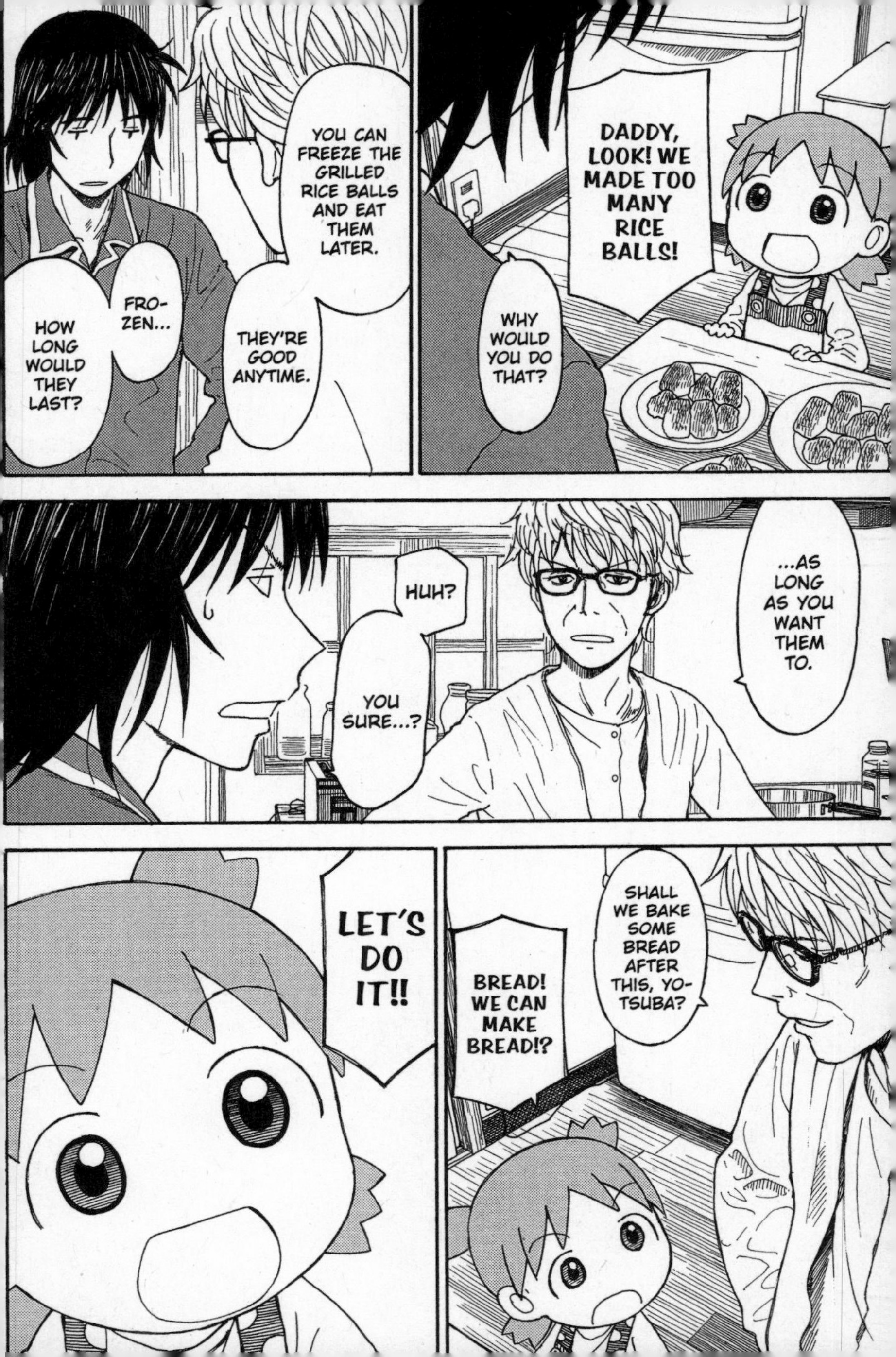
DADDY, LOOK! WE MADE TOO MANY RICE BALLS!
WHY WOULD YOU DO THAT?
YOU CAN FREEZE THE GRILLED RICE BALLS AND EAT THEM LATER.
THEY'RE GOOD ANYTIME.
FRO-ZEN...
HOW LONG WOULD THEY LAST?
...AS LONG AS YOU WANT THEM TO.
HUH?
YOU SURE...?
SHALL WE BAKE SOME BREAD AFTER THIS, YO-TSUBA?
BREAD! WE CAN MAKE BREAD!?
LET'S DO IT!!

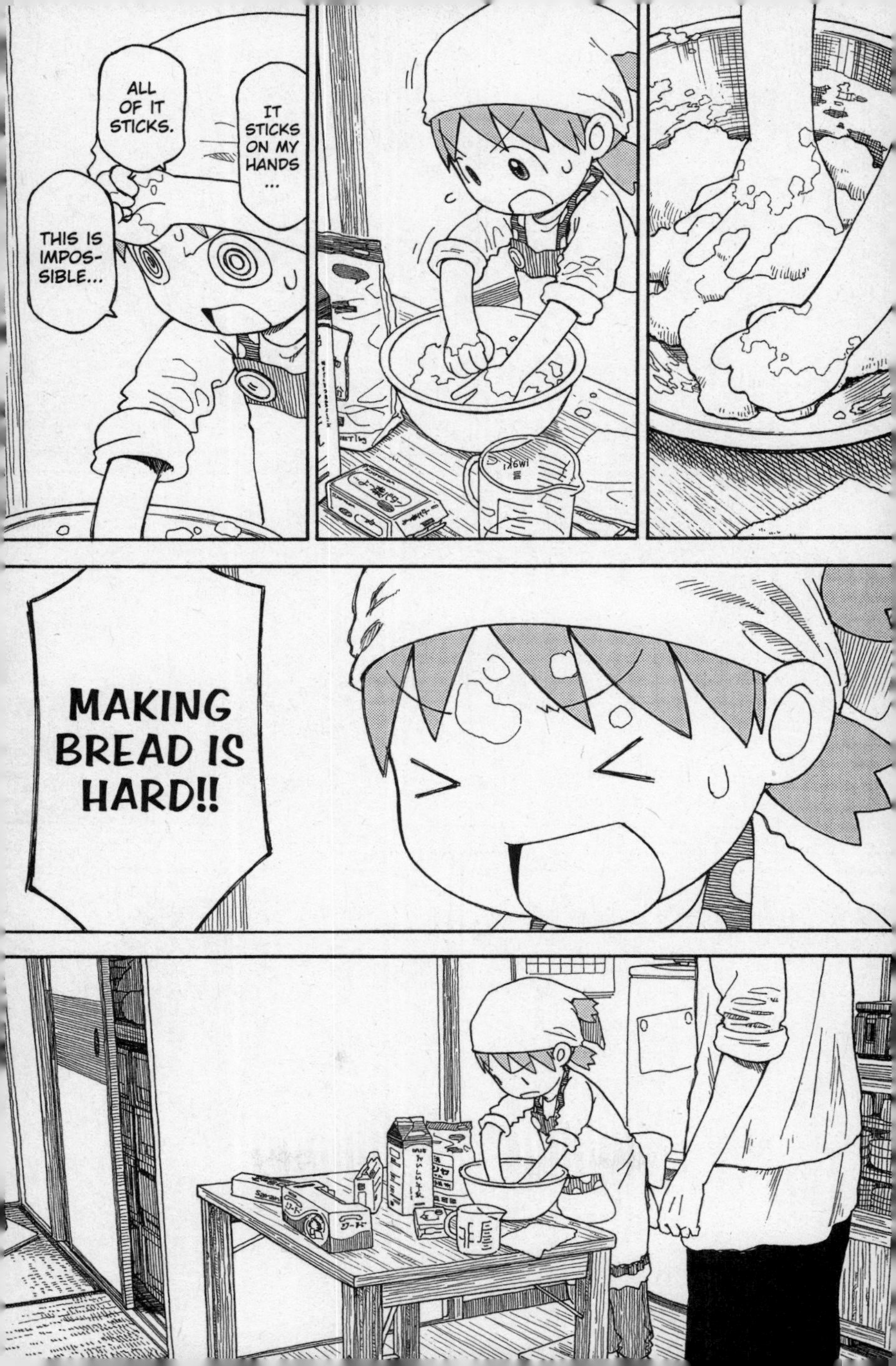
IT STICKS ON MY HANDS...
ALL OF IT STICKS.
THIS IS IMPOSSIBLE...
MAKING BREAD IS HARD!!

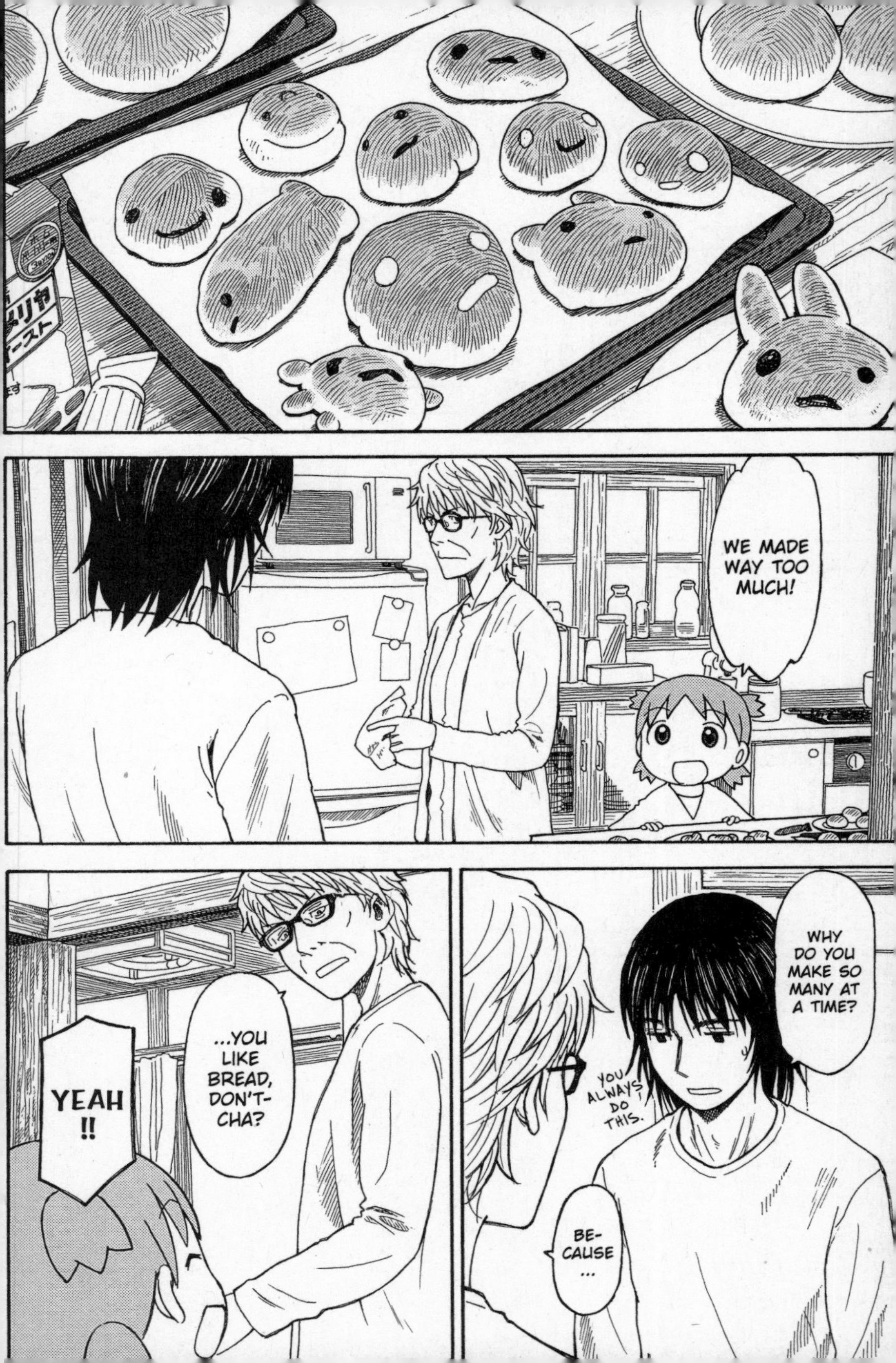
WE MADE WAY TOO MUCH!
WHY DO YOU MAKE SO MANY AT A TIME?
YOU ALWAYS DO THIS.
BE-CAUSE ...
...YOU LIKE BREAD, DON'T-CHA?
YEAH !!

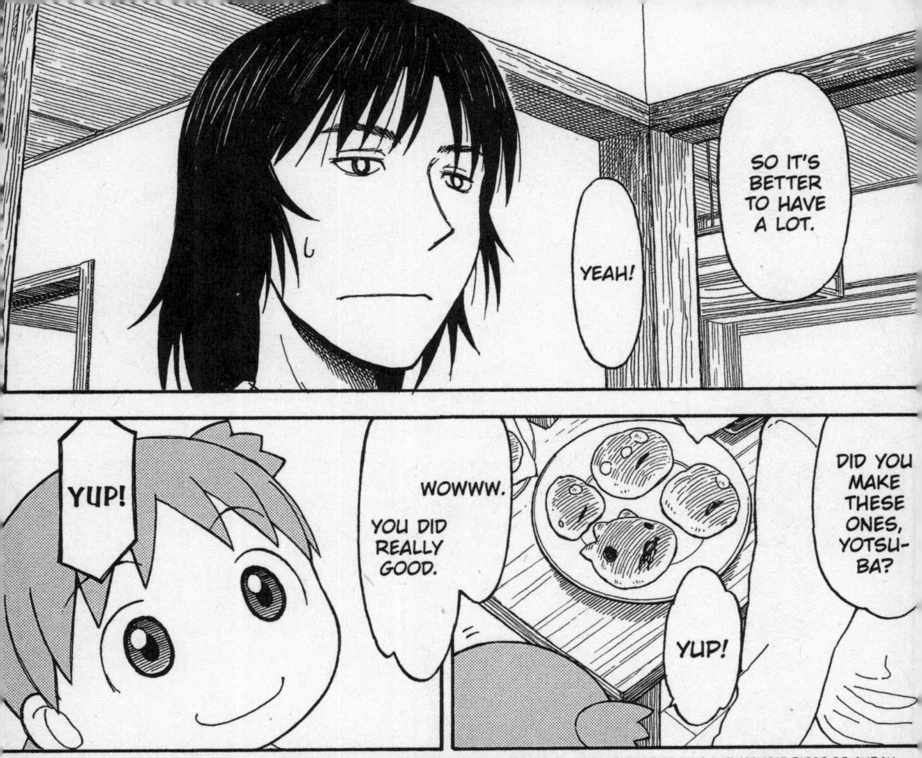
SO IT'S BETTER TO HAVE A LOT.
YEAH!
DID YOU MAKE THESE ONES, YOTSUBA?
YUP!
WOWWW.
YOU DID REALLY GOOD.
YUP!

NORMAL-PAN-MAN: A REFERENCE TO THE CLASSIC CHILDREN'S HERO, ANPANMAN, WHO IS ESSENTIALLY A HUMANOID PIECE OF ANPAN.

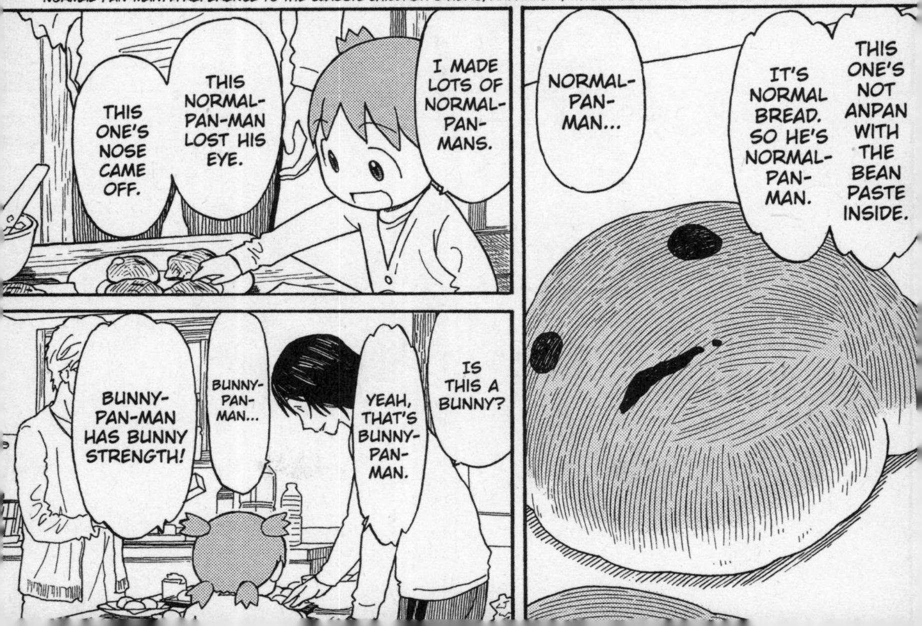
THIS ONE'S NOT ANPAN WITH THE BEAN PASTE INSIDE.
IT'S NORMAL BREAD. SO HE'S NORMAL-PAN-MAN.
NORMAL-PAN-MAN...
I MADE LOTS OF NORMAL-PAN-MANS.
THIS NORMAL-PAN-MAN LOST HIS EYE.
THIS ONE'S NOSE CAME OFF.
IS THIS A BUNNY?
YEAH, THAT'S BUNNY-PAN-MAN.
BUNNY-PAN-MAN...
BUNNY-PAN-MAN HAS BUNNY STRENGTH!

YOTSUBA&

THE BLACK GHOST!

#89

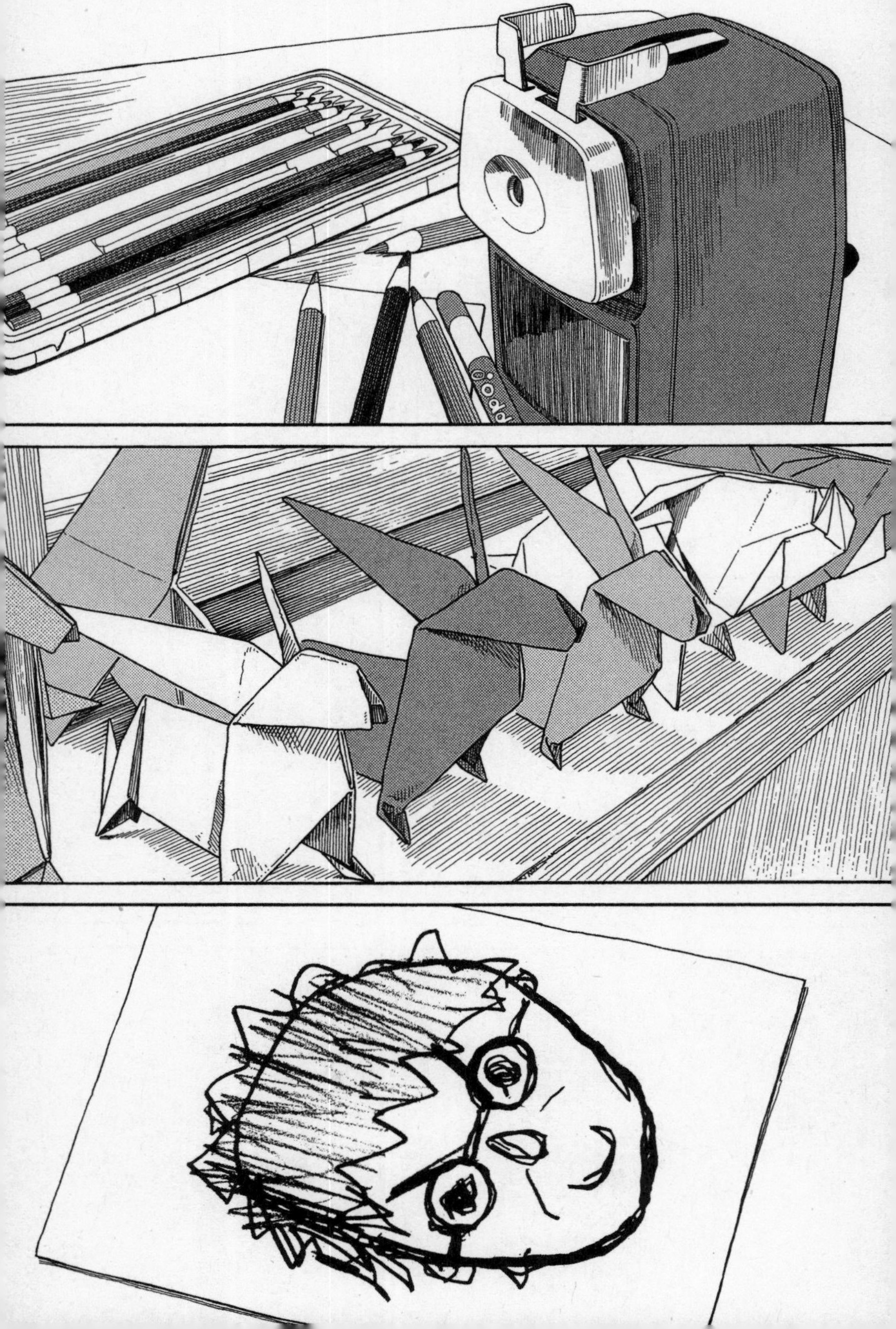

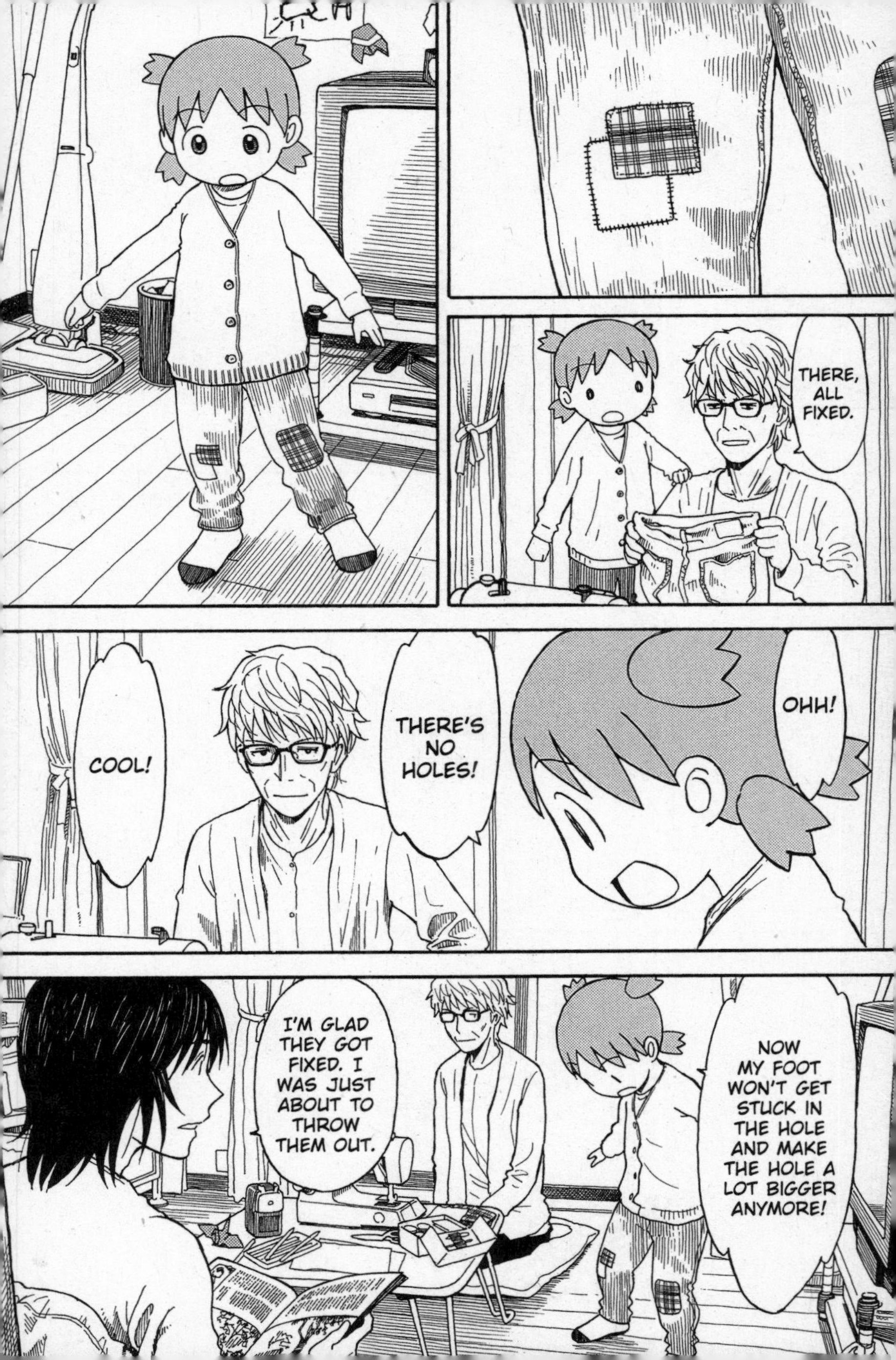
THERE, ALL FIXED.
OHH!
THERE'S NO HOLES!
COOL!
NOW MY FOOT WON'T GET STUCK IN THE HOLE AND MAKE THE HOLE A LOT BIGGER ANYMORE!
I'M GLAD THEY GOT FIXED. I WAS JUST ABOUT TO THROW THEM OUT.

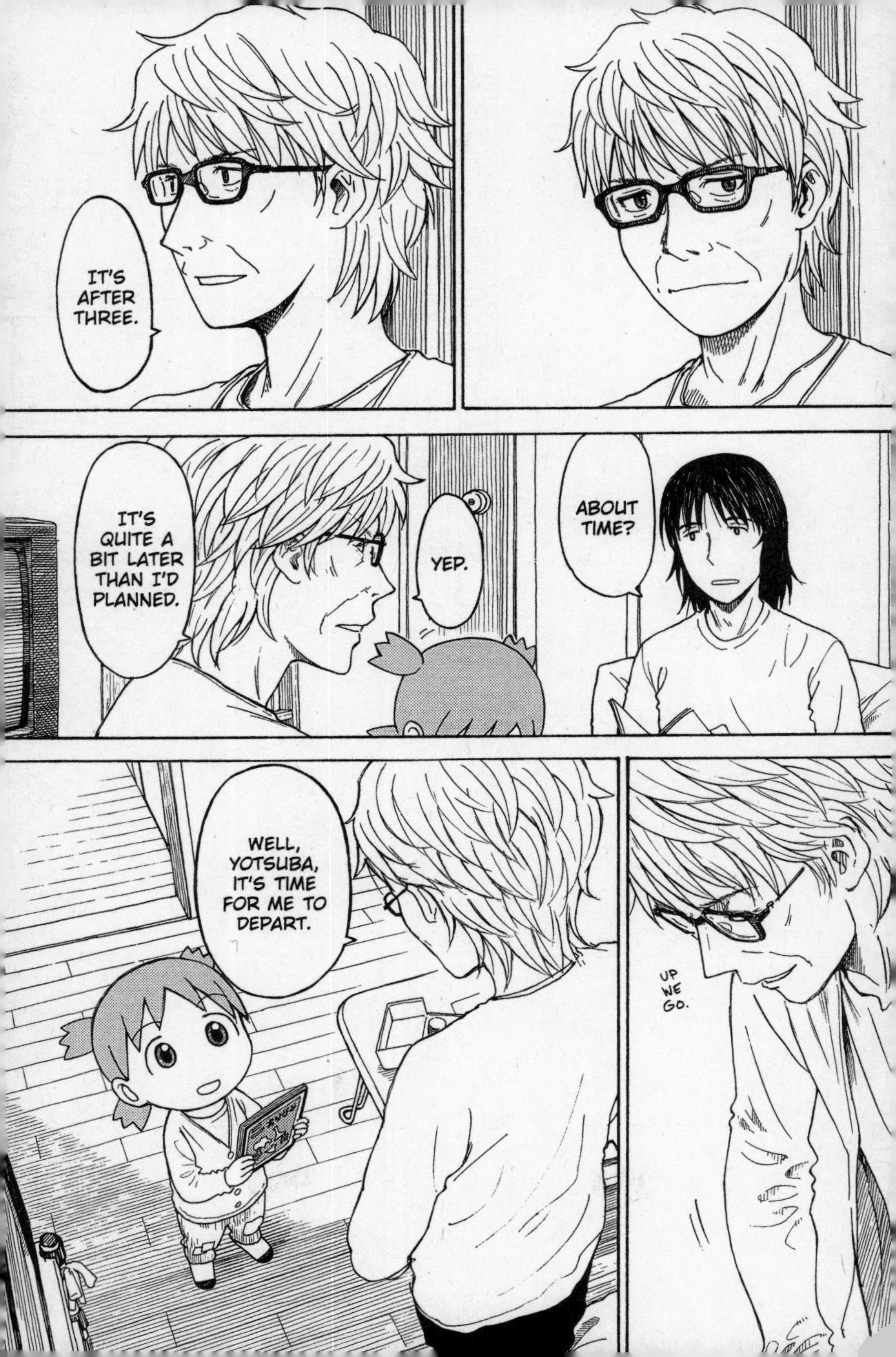
IT'S AFTER THREE.
ABOUT TIME?
YEP.
IT'S QUITE A BIT LATER THAN I'D PLANNED.
UP WE GO.
WELL, YOTSUBA, IT'S TIME FOR ME TO DEPART.

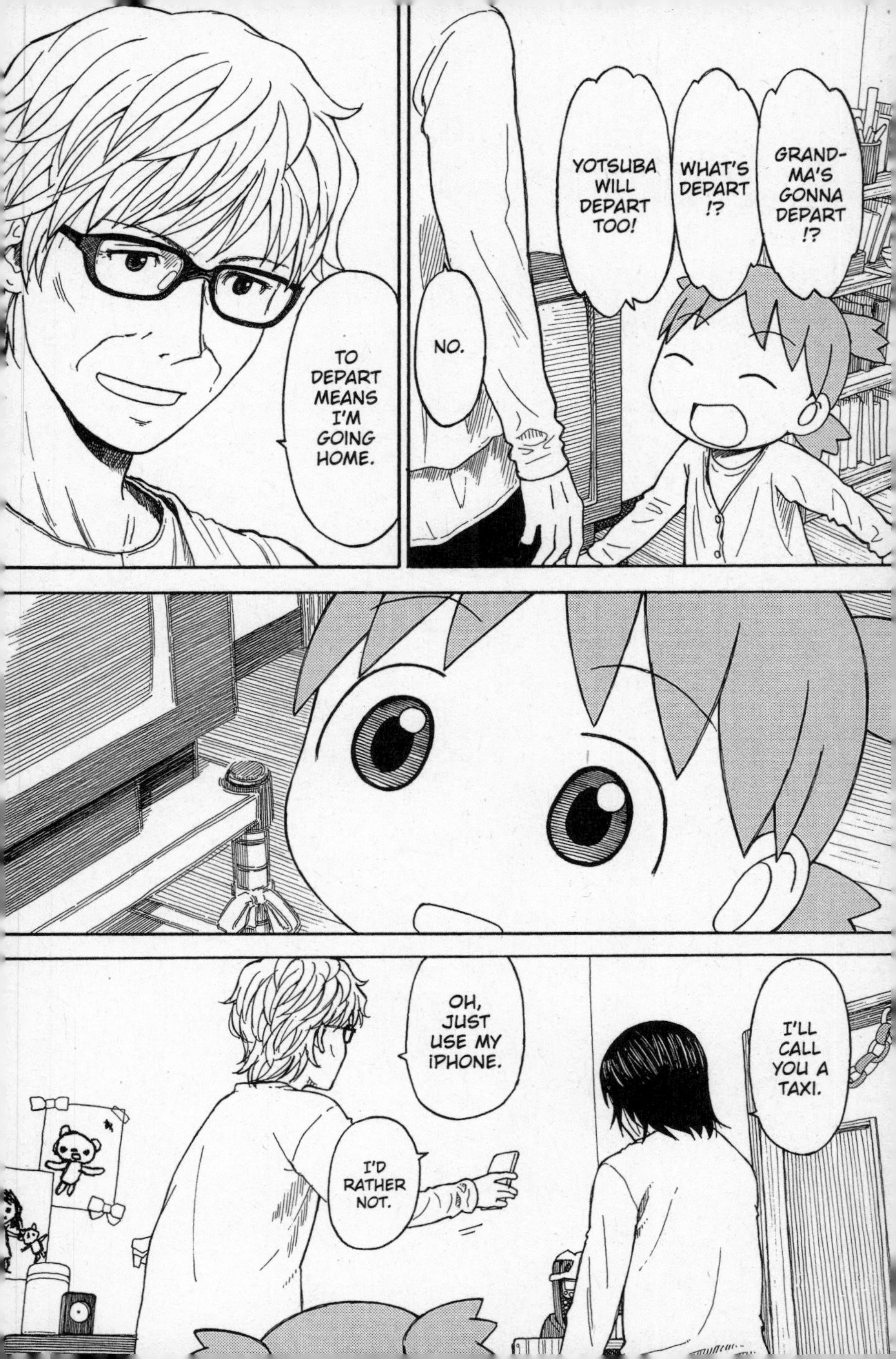
GRAND-MA'S GONNA DEPART !?
WHAT'S DEPART !?
YOTSUBA WILL DEPART TOO!
NO.
TO DEPART MEANS I'M GOING HOME.
I'LL CALL YOU A TAXI.
OH, JUST USE MY iPHONE.
I'D RATHER NOT.

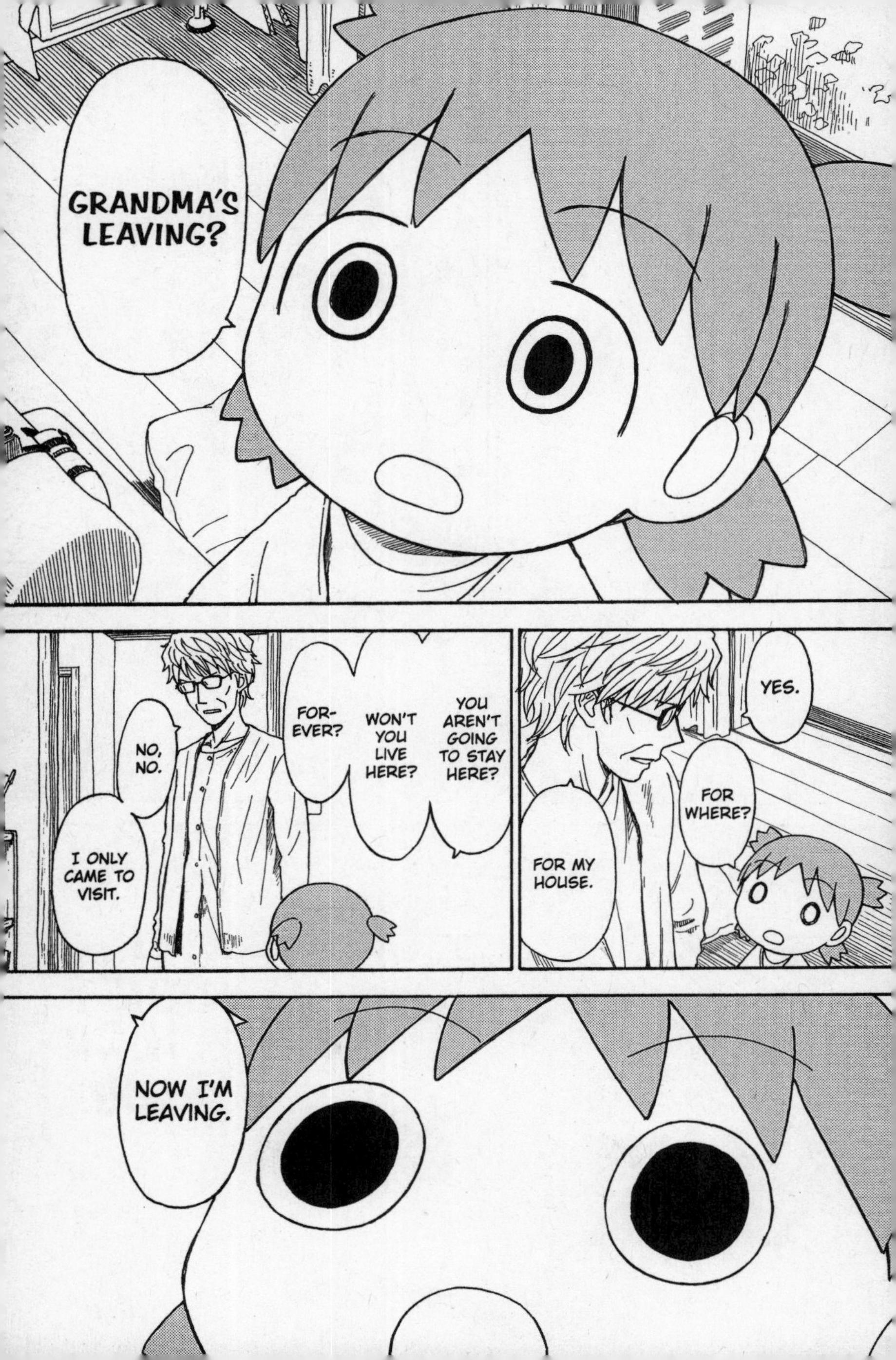
GRANDMA'S LEAVING?
YES.
FOR WHERE?
FOR MY HOUSE.
YOU AREN'T GOING TO STAY HERE?
WON'T YOU LIVE HERE?
FOR-EVER?
NO, NO.
I ONLY CAME TO VISIT.
NOW I'M LEAVING.

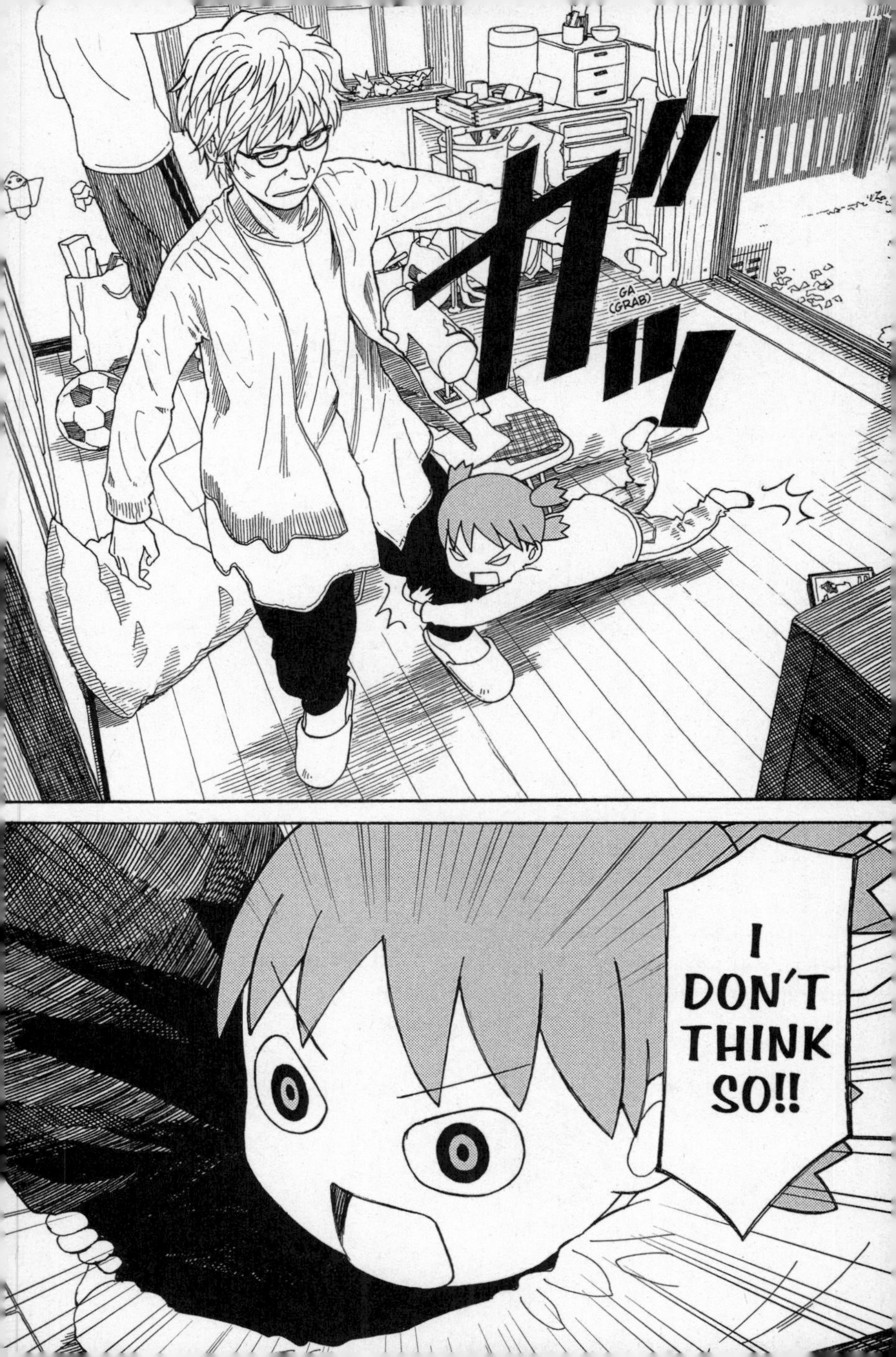
GA
(GRAB)
I DON'T THINK SO!!

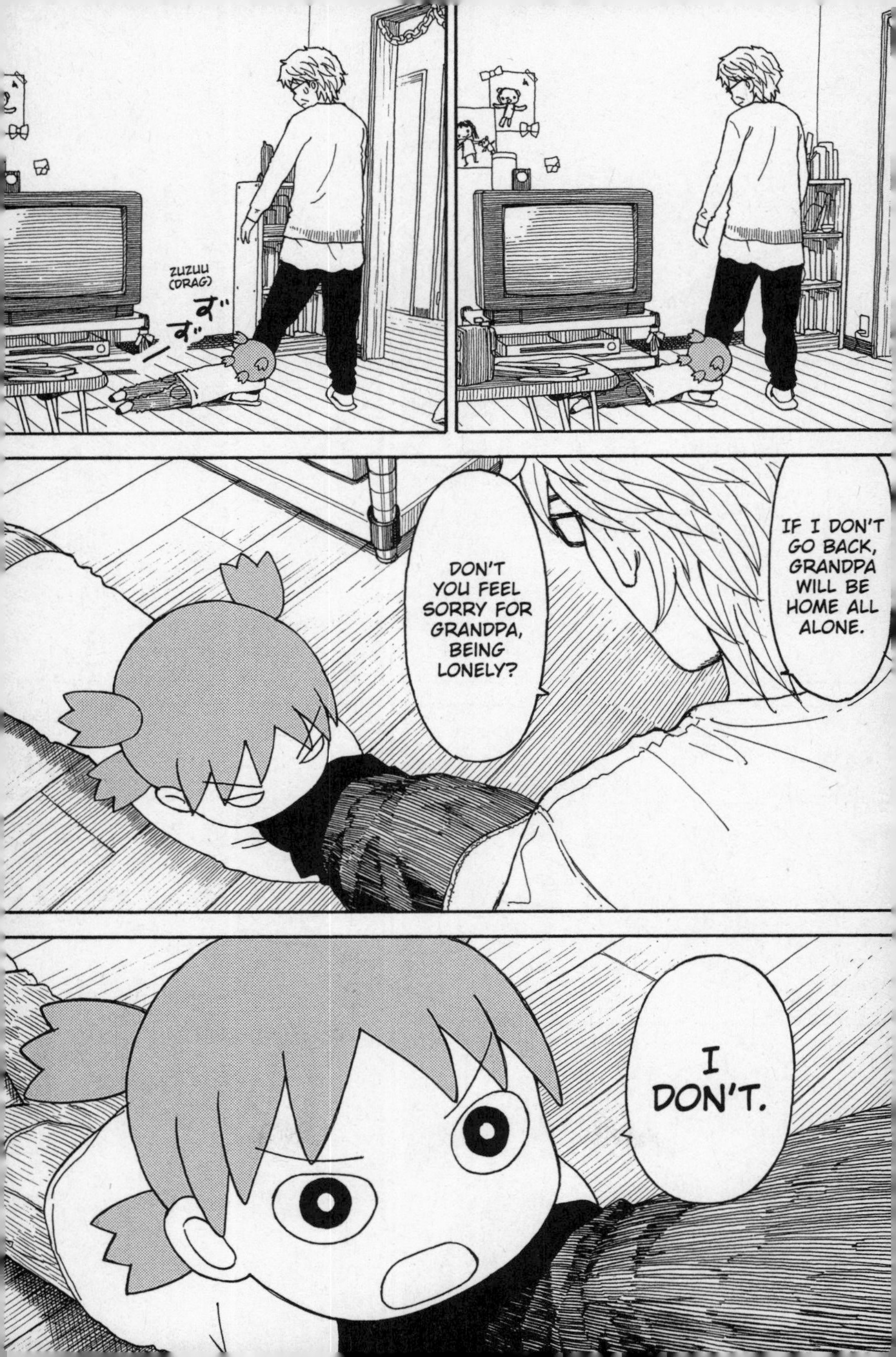
ZUZUU (DRAG)
ずず
IF I DON'T GO BACK, GRANDPA WILL BE HOME ALL ALONE.
DON'T YOU FEEL SORRY FOR GRANDPA, BEING LONELY?
I DON'T.

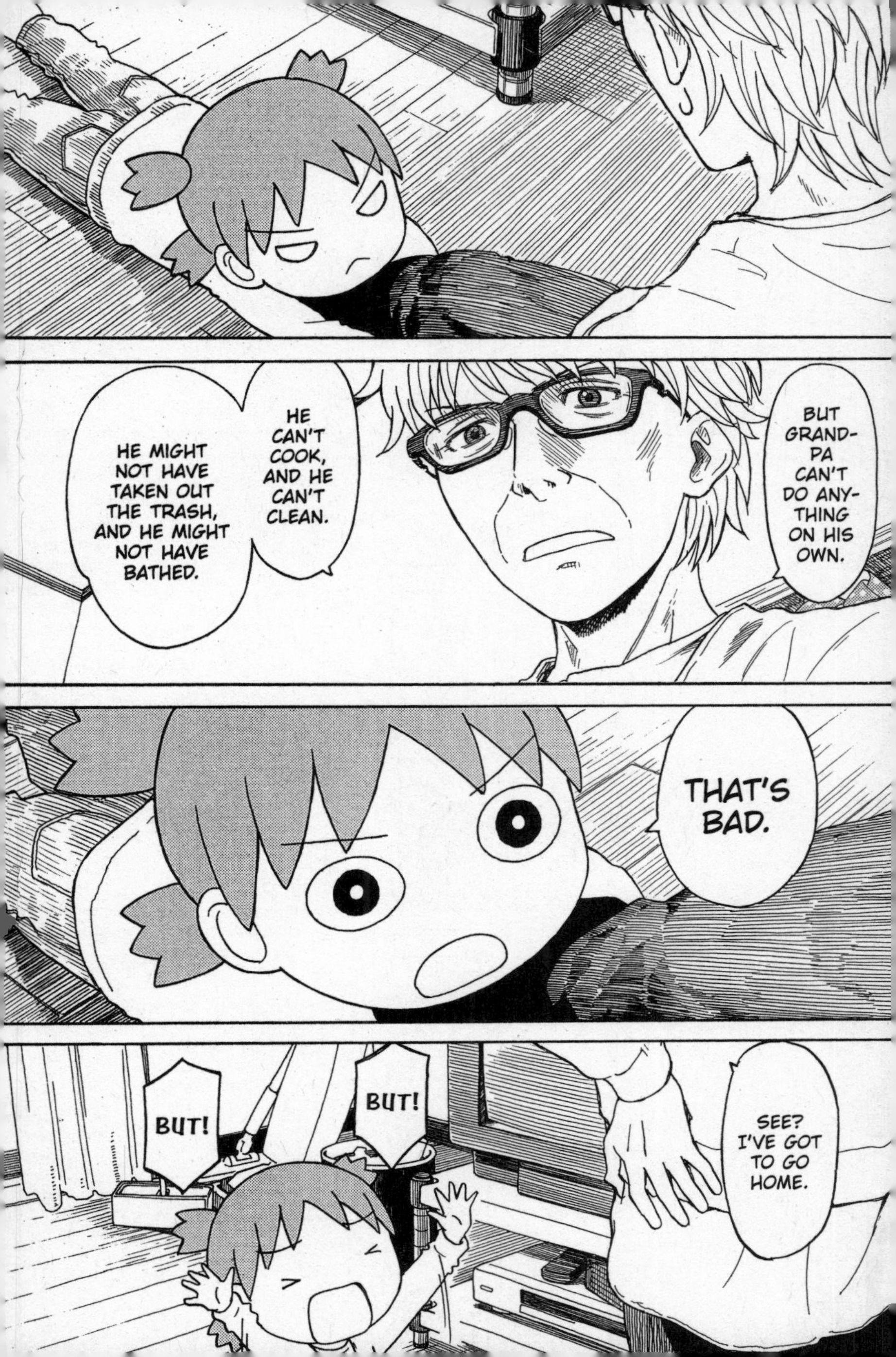
BUT GRANDPA CAN'T DO ANYTHING ON HIS OWN.
HE CAN'T COOK, AND HE CAN'T CLEAN.
HE MIGHT NOT HAVE TAKEN OUT THE TRASH, AND HE MIGHT NOT HAVE BATHED.
THAT'S BAD.
SEE? I'VE GOT TO GO HOME.
BUT!
BUT!

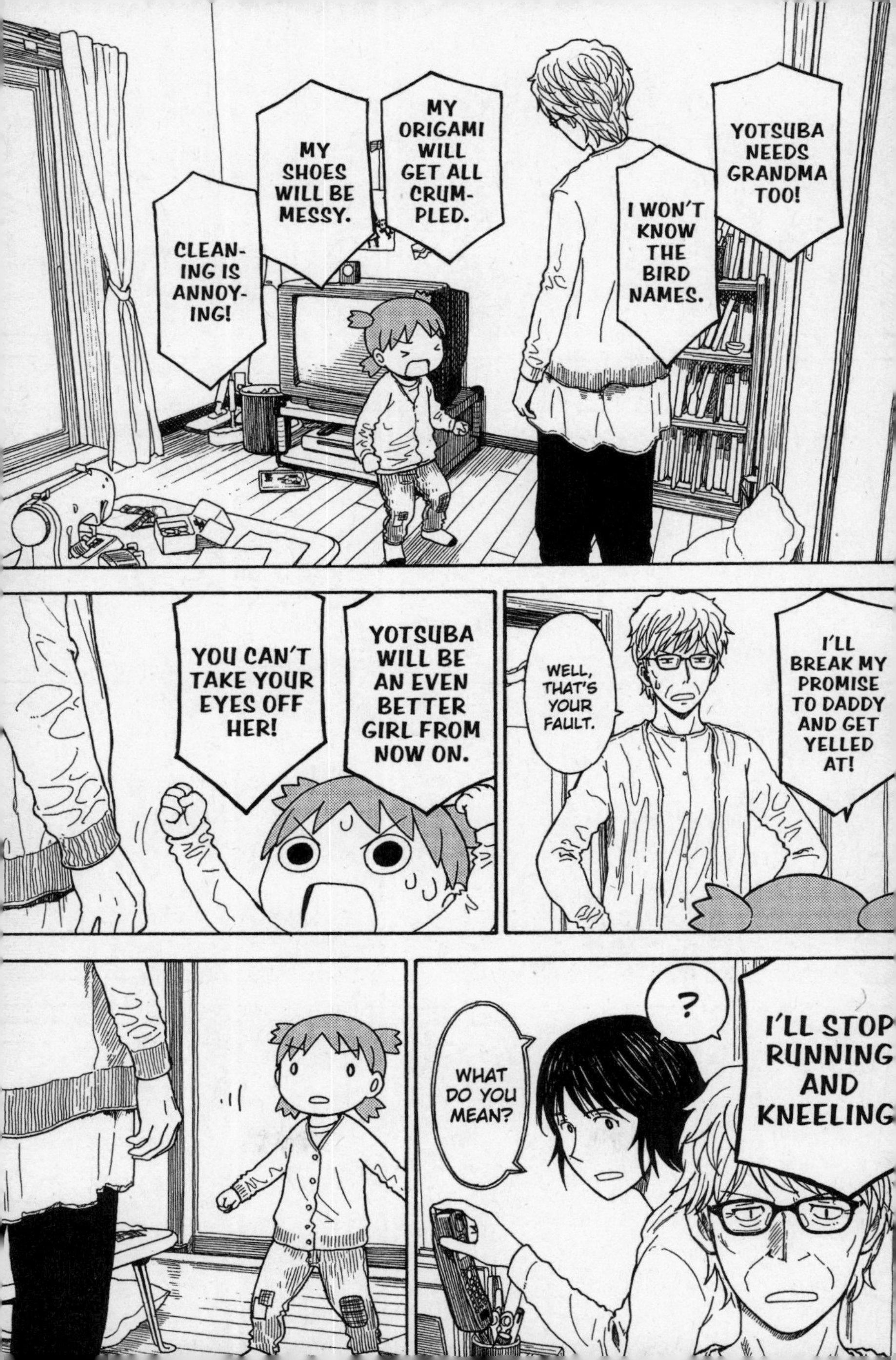
YOTSUBA NEEDS GRANDMA TOO!
I WON'T KNOW THE BIRD NAMES.
MY ORIGAMI WILL GET ALL CRUMPLED.
MY SHOES WILL BE MESSY.
CLEANING IS ANNOYING!
I'LL BREAK MY PROMISE TO DADDY AND GET YELLED AT!
WELL, THAT'S YOUR FAULT.
YOTSUBA WILL BE AN EVEN BETTER GIRL FROM NOW ON.
YOU CAN'T TAKE YOUR EYES OFF HER!
I'LL STOP RUNNING AND KNEELING
?
WHAT DO YOU MEAN?

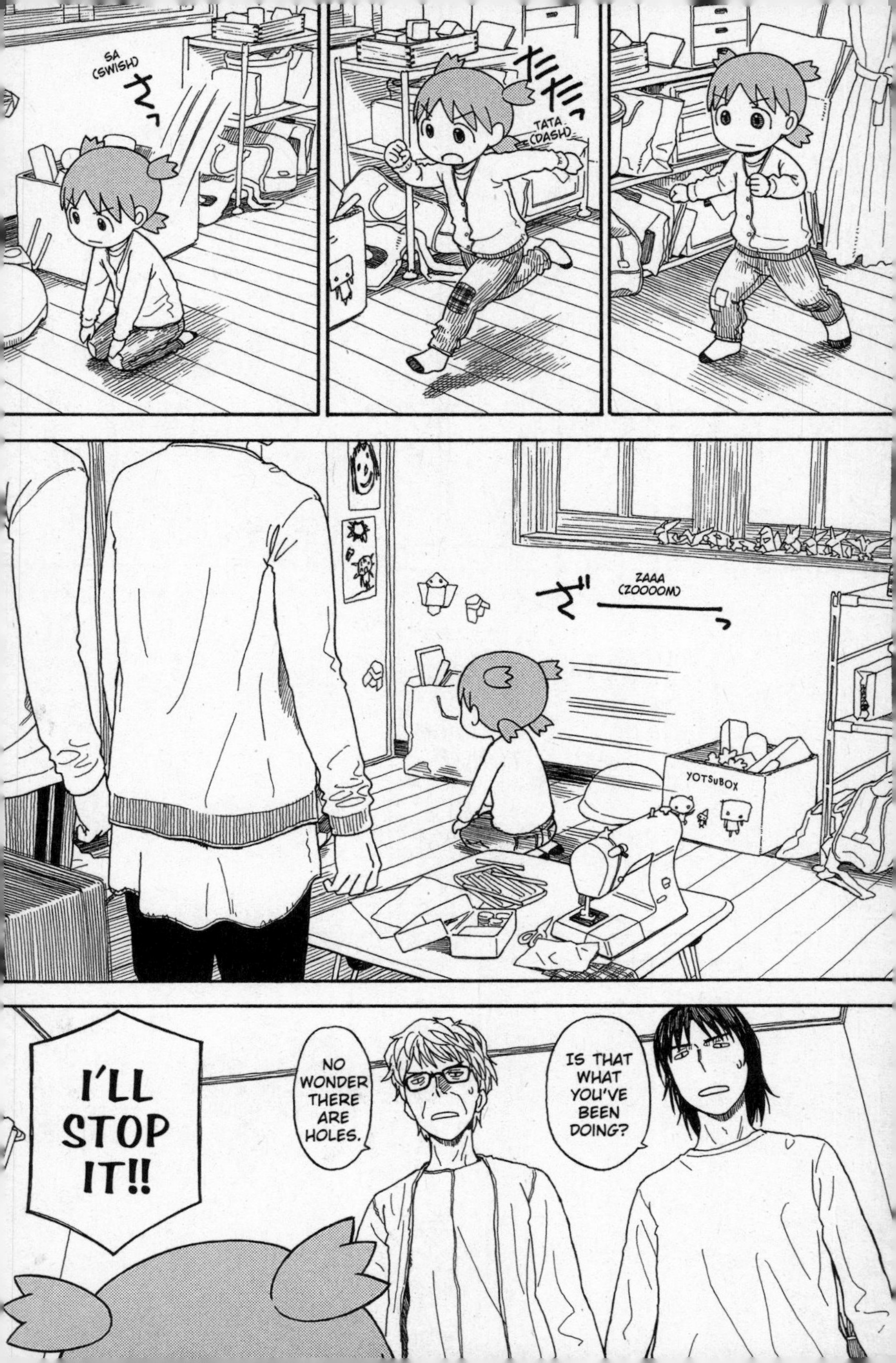
たたっ
TATA (DASH)
さっ
SA (SWISH)
ざーっ
ZAAA (ZOOOOM)
YOTSUBOX
IS THAT WHAT YOU'VE BEEN DOING?
NO WONDER THERE ARE HOLES.
I'LL STOP IT!!

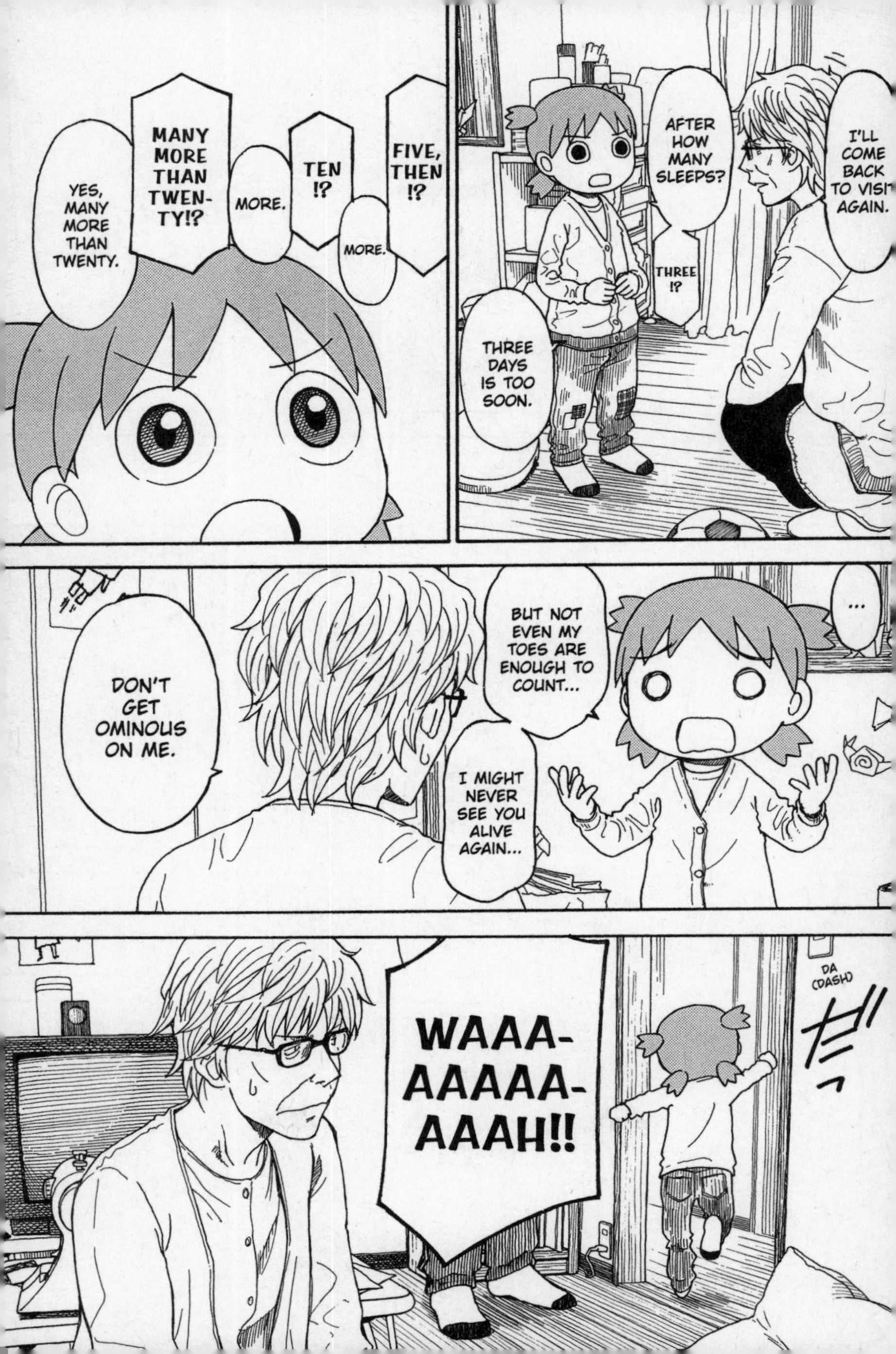
I'LL COME BACK TO VISIT AGAIN.
AFTER HOW MANY SLEEPS?
THREE!?
THREE DAYS IS TOO SOON.
FIVE, THEN!?
MORE.
TEN!?
MORE.
MANY MORE THAN TWENTY!?
YES, MANY MORE THAN TWENTY.
...
BUT NOT EVEN MY TOES ARE ENOUGH TO COUNT...
I MIGHT NEVER SEE YOU ALIVE AGAIN...
DON'T GET OMINOUS ON ME.
DA (DASH)
WAAAAAAAAAAH!!

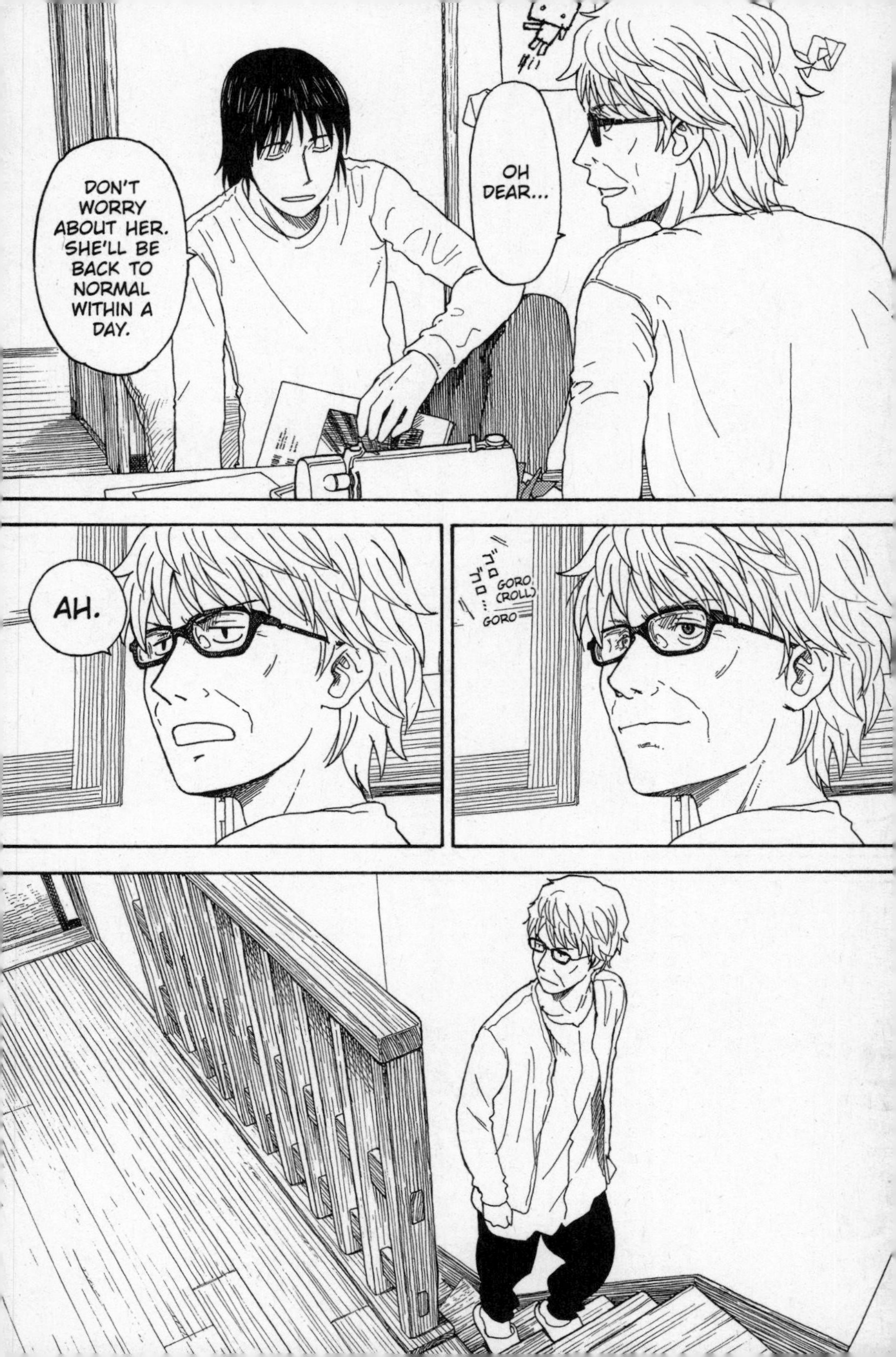
OH DEAR...
DON'T WORRY ABOUT HER. SHE'LL BE BACK TO NORMAL WITHIN A DAY.
ゴロゴロ…
GORO (ROLL) GORO
AH.

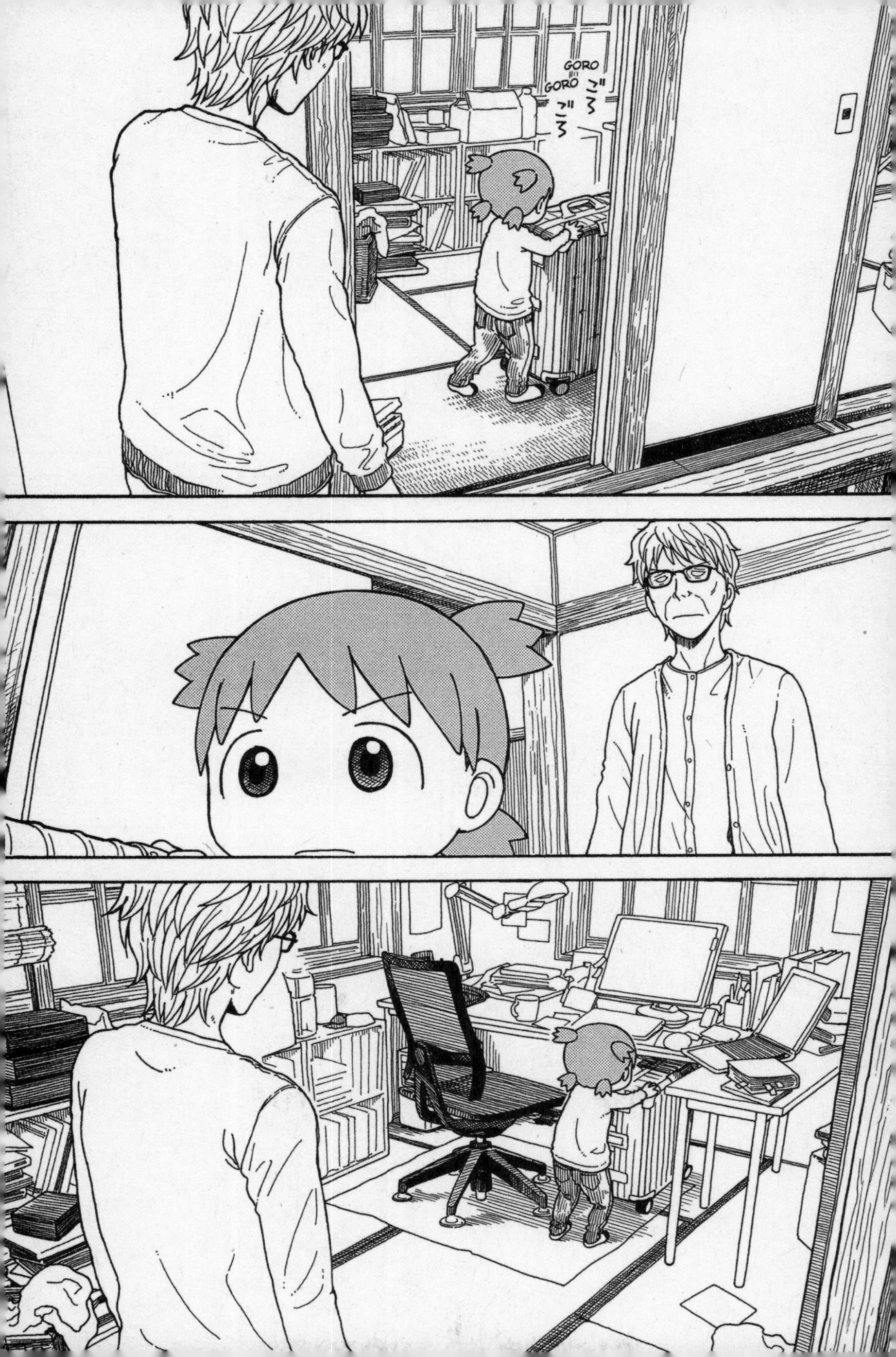
GORO GORO
ごろ ごろ

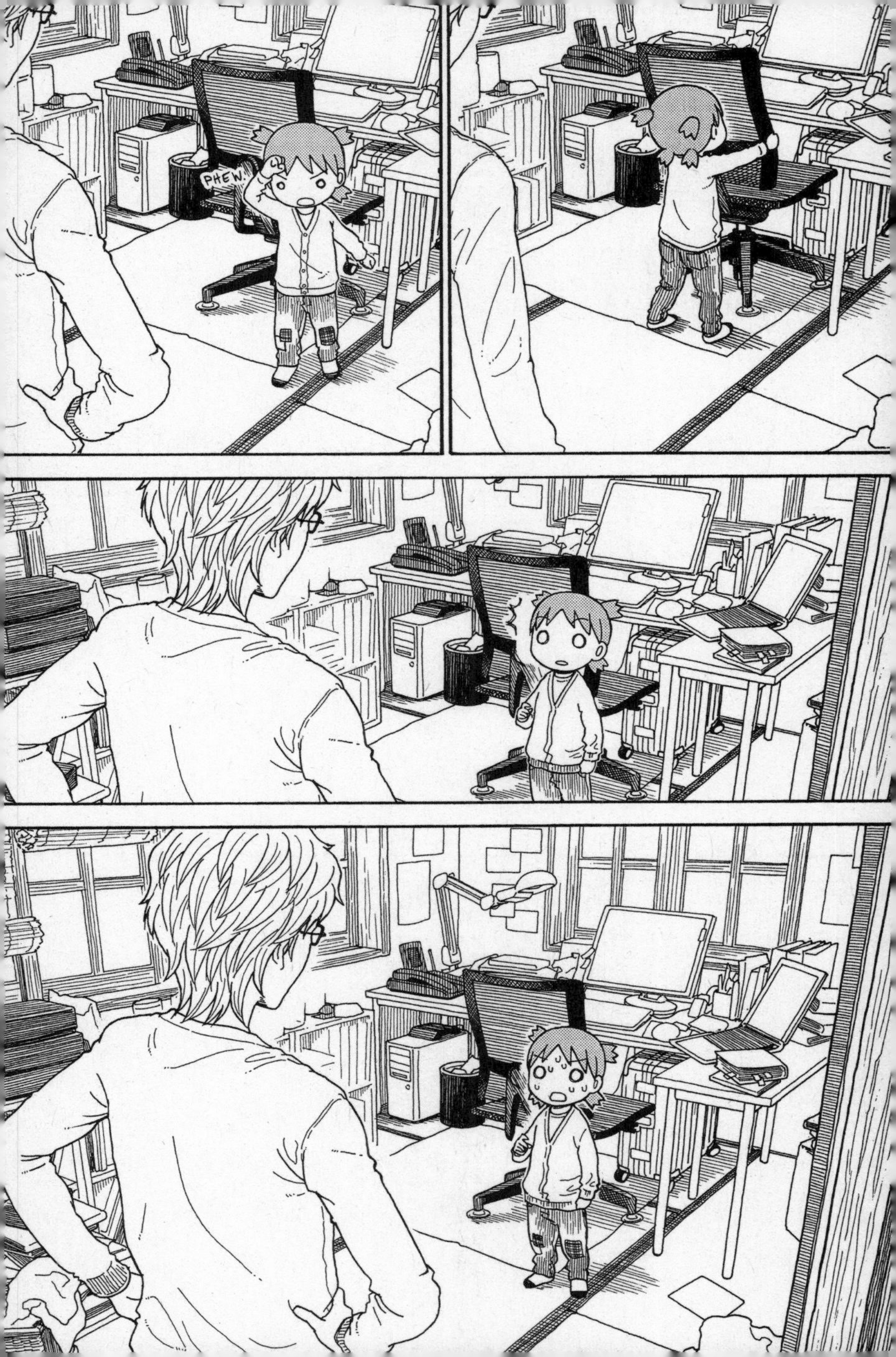
PHEW.

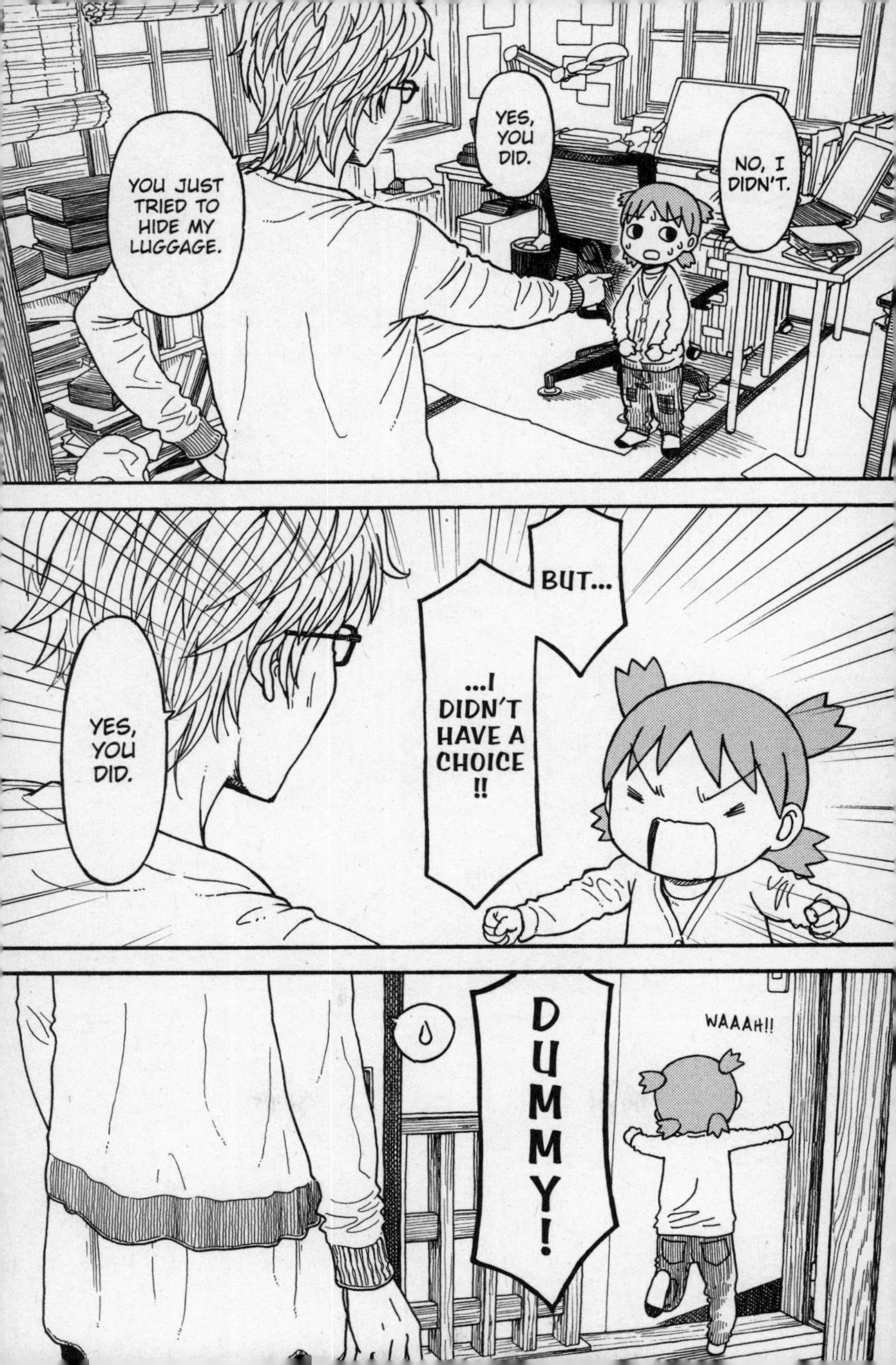
NO, I DIDN'T.
YES, YOU DID.
YOU JUST TRIED TO HIDE MY LUGGAGE.
BUT...
...I DIDN'T HAVE A CHOICE !!
YES, YOU DID.
WAAAH!!
DUMMY!

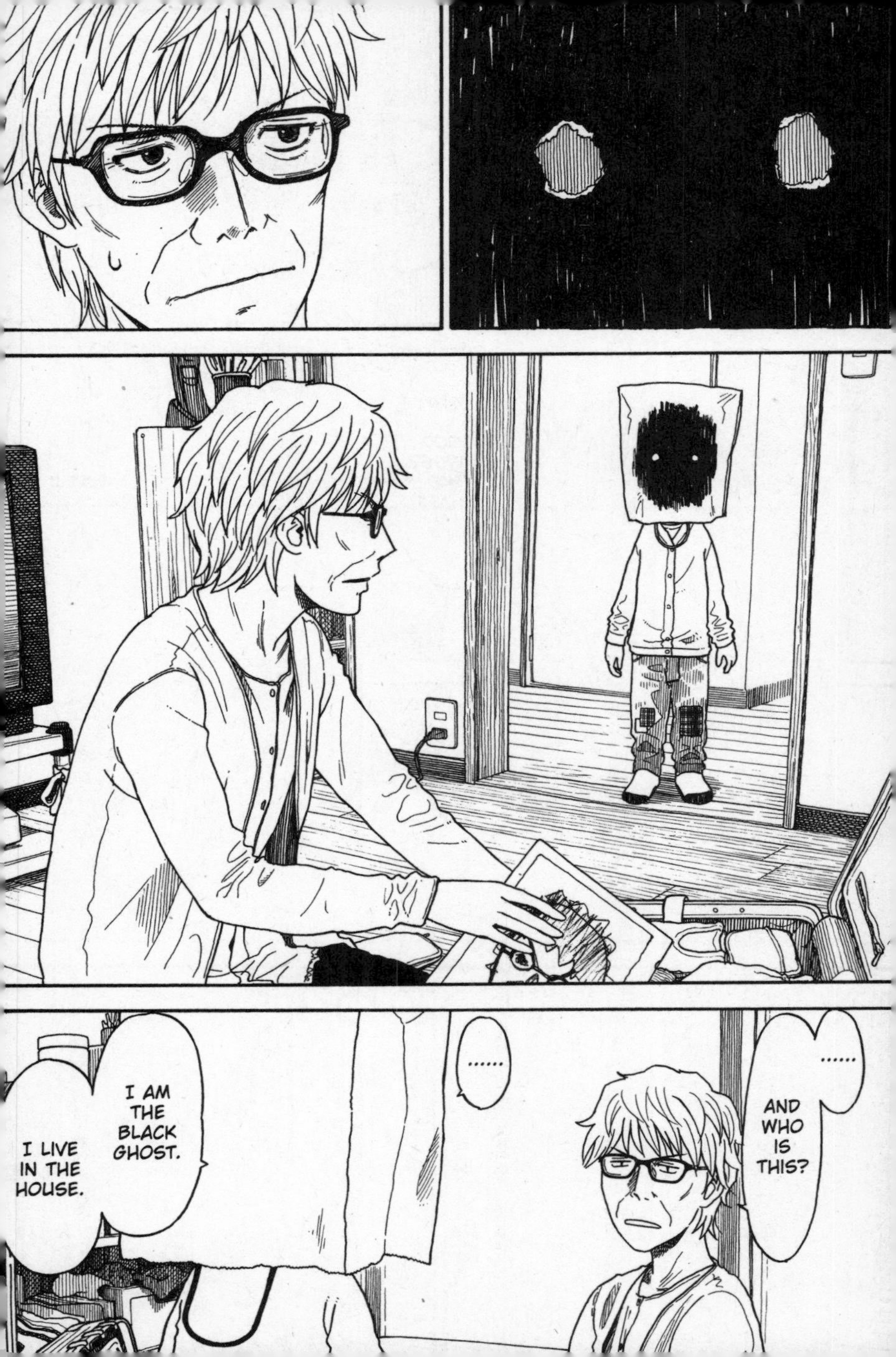
......
AND WHO IS THIS?
......
I AM THE BLACK GHOST.
I LIVE IN THE HOUSE.

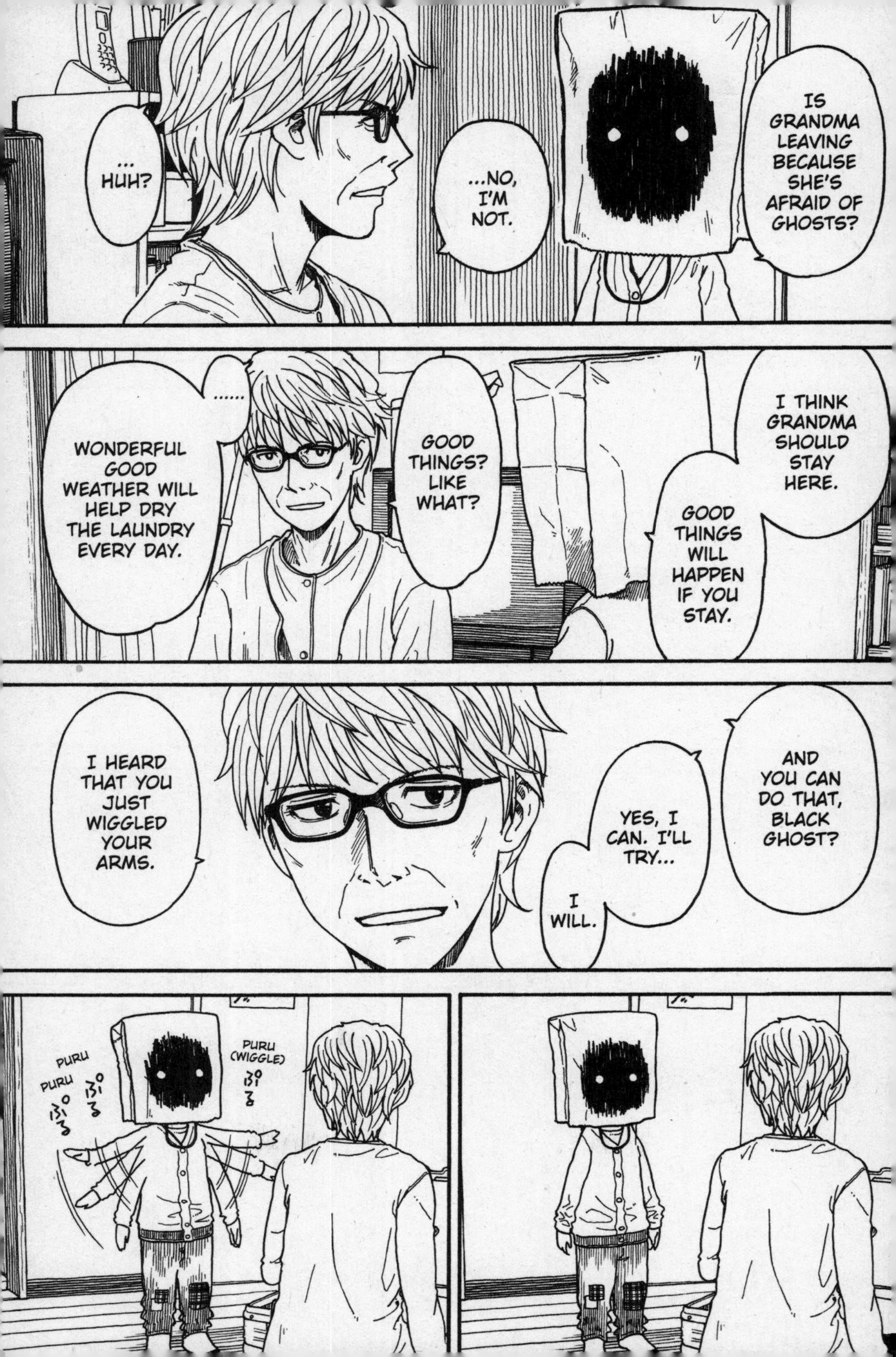
IS GRANDMA LEAVING BECAUSE SHE'S AFRAID OF GHOSTS?
...NO, I'M NOT.
... HUH?
I THINK GRANDMA SHOULD STAY HERE.
GOOD THINGS WILL HAPPEN IF YOU STAY.
GOOD THINGS? LIKE WHAT?
......
WONDERFUL GOOD WEATHER WILL HELP DRY THE LAUNDRY EVERY DAY.
AND YOU CAN DO THAT, BLACK GHOST?
YES, I CAN. I'LL TRY...
I WILL.
I HEARD THAT YOU JUST WIGGLED YOUR ARMS.
PURU (WIGGLE)
ぷる
PURU PURU
ぷる ぷる

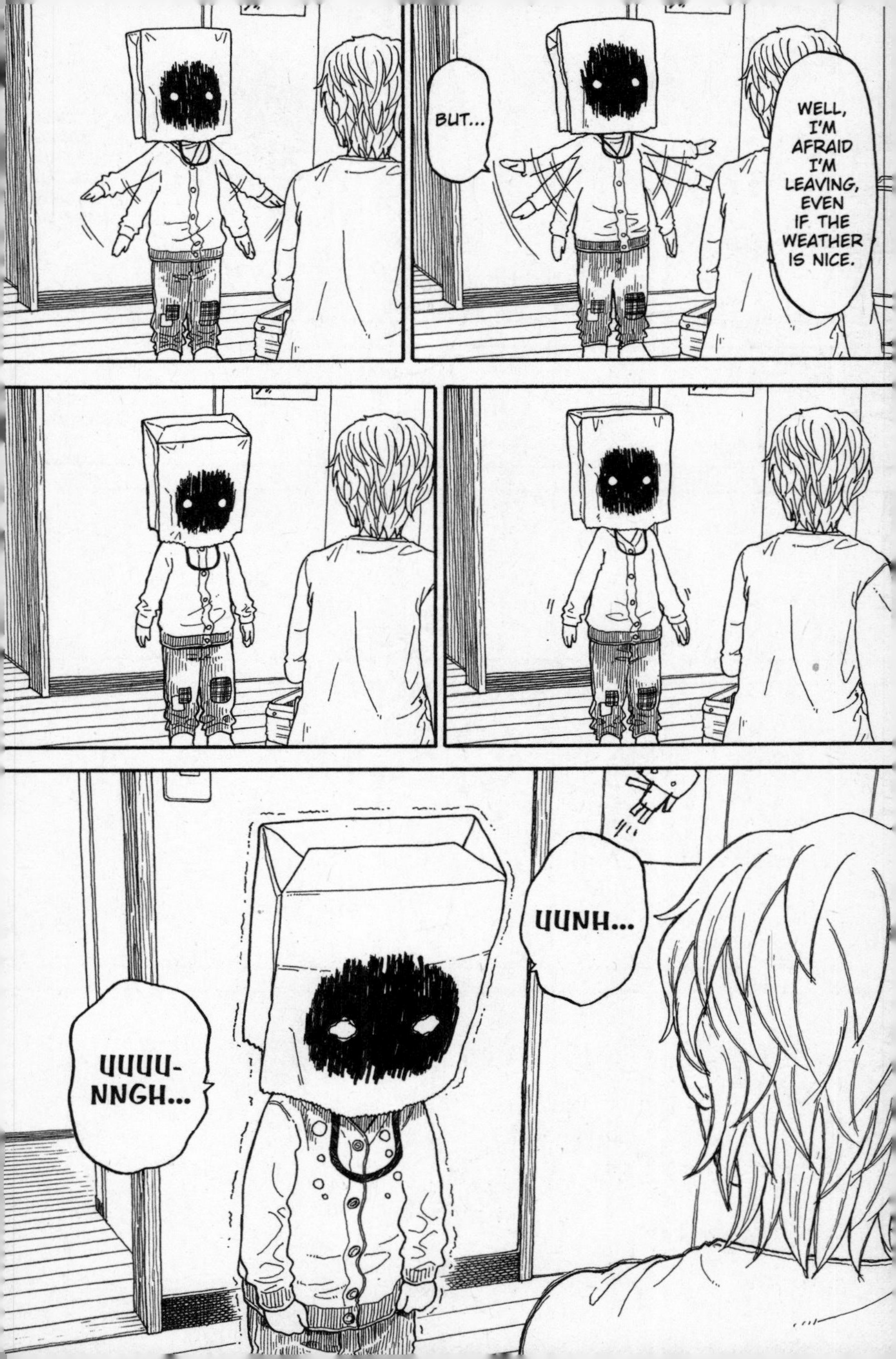
WELL, I'M AFRAID I'M LEAVING, EVEN IF THE WEATHER IS NICE.
BUT...
UUNH...
UUUU-NNGH...

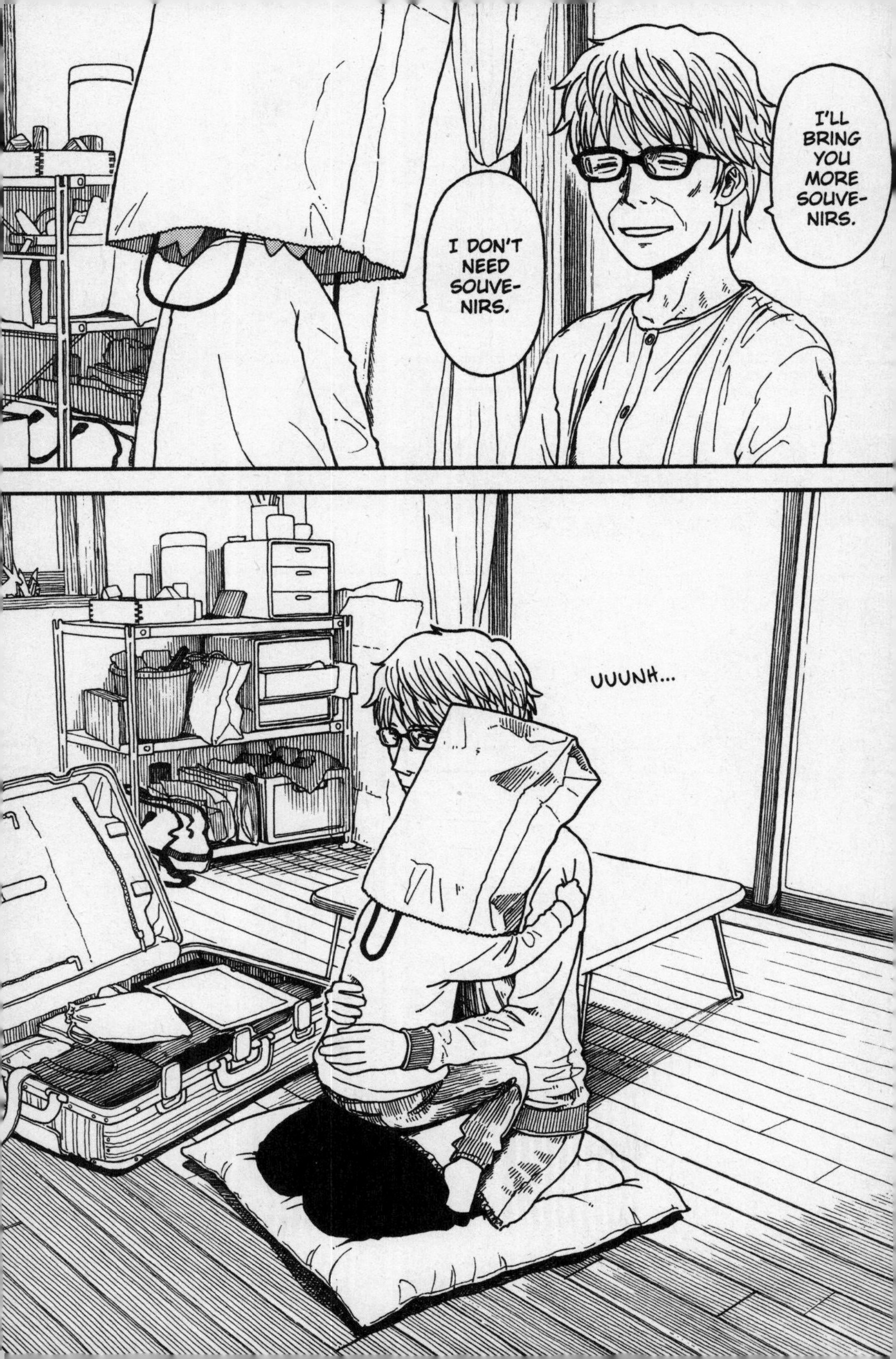
I'LL BRING YOU MORE SOUVE-NIRS.
I DON'T NEED SOUVE-NIRS.
UUUNH...

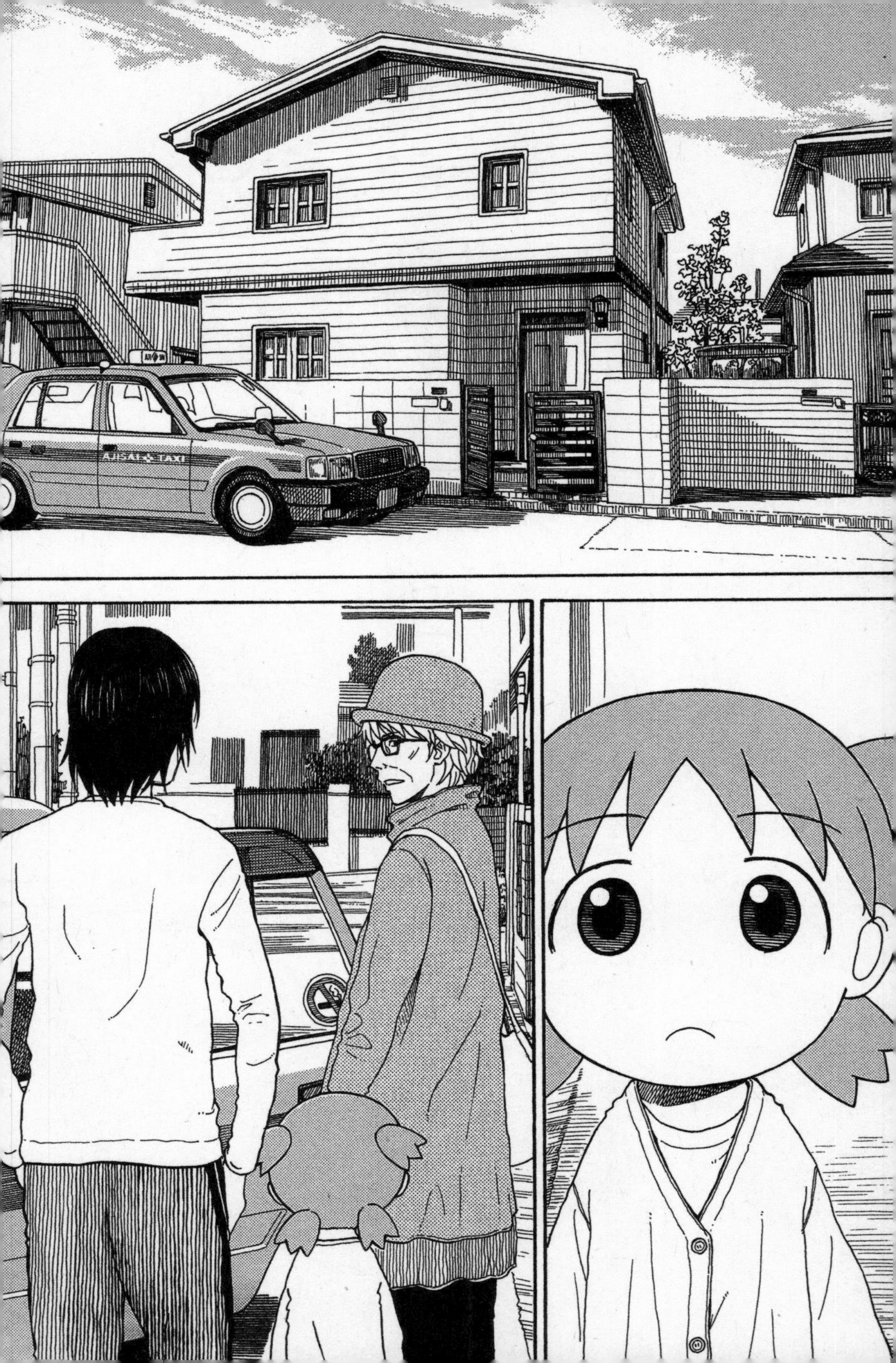
AJISAI TAXI

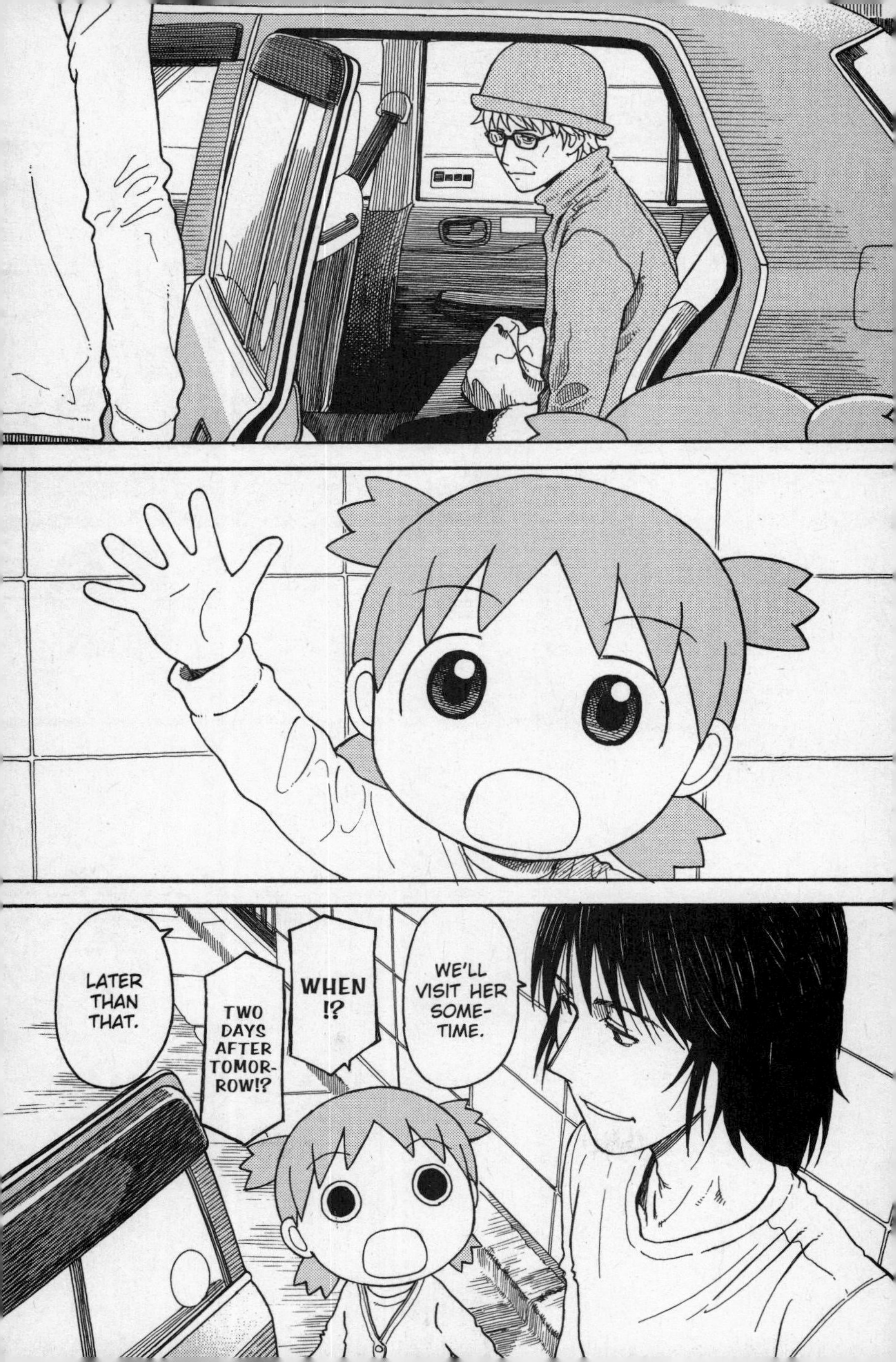
WE'LL VISIT HER SOME-TIME.
WHEN!?
TWO DAYS AFTER TOMOR-ROW!?
LATER THAN THAT.

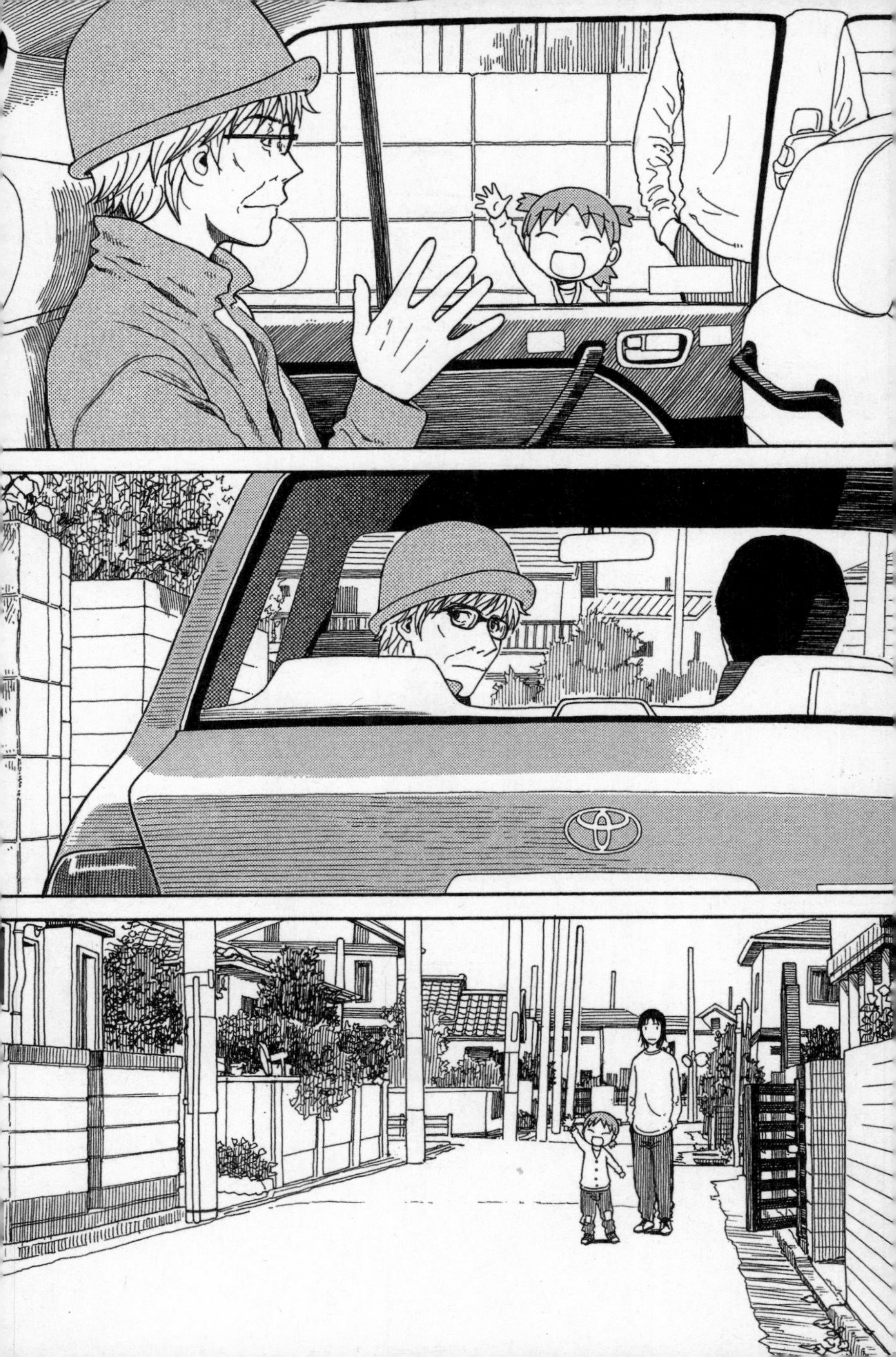

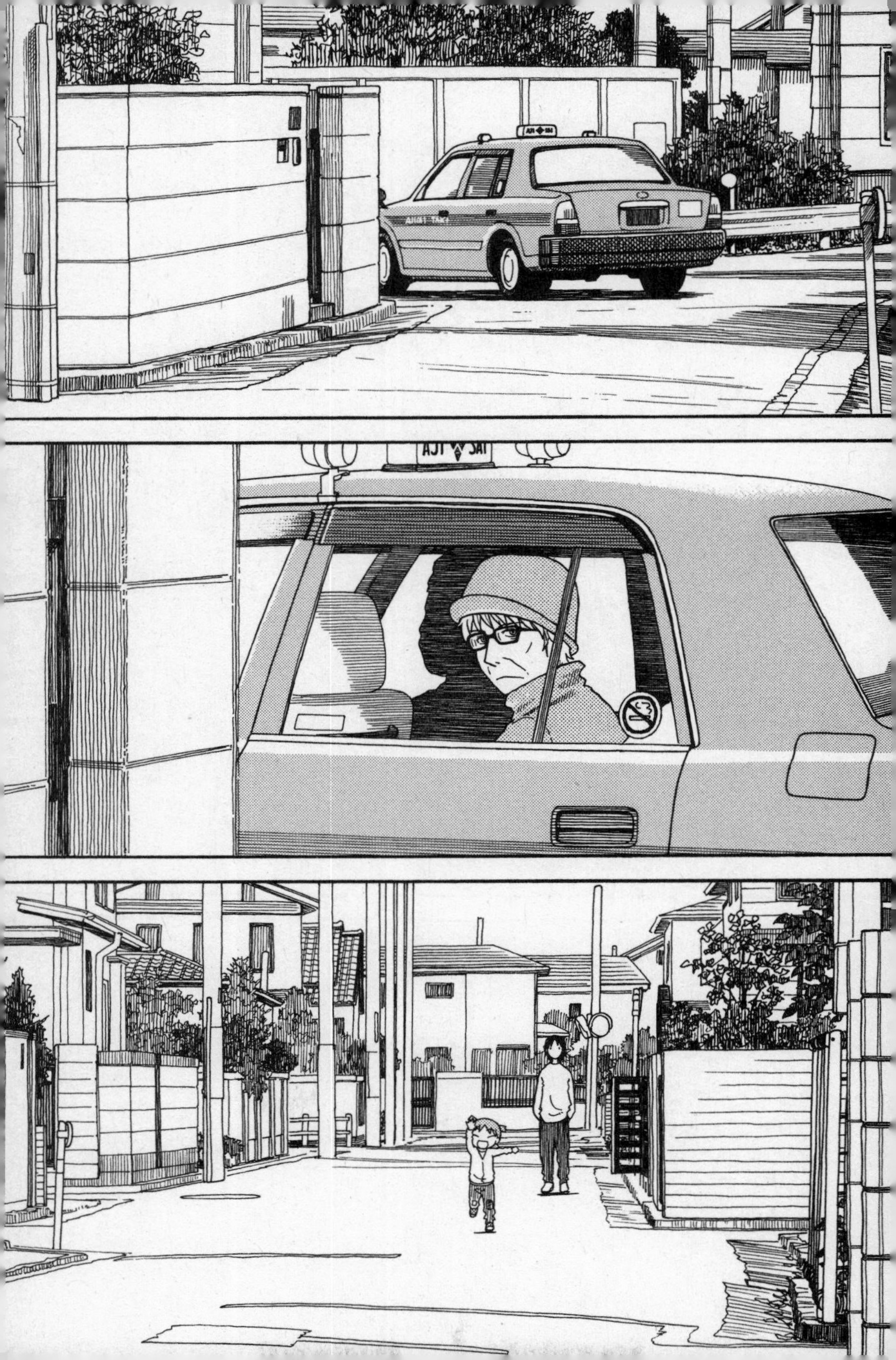

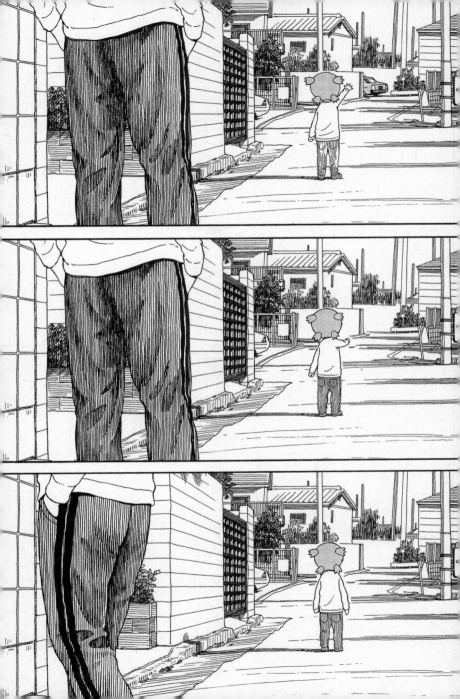

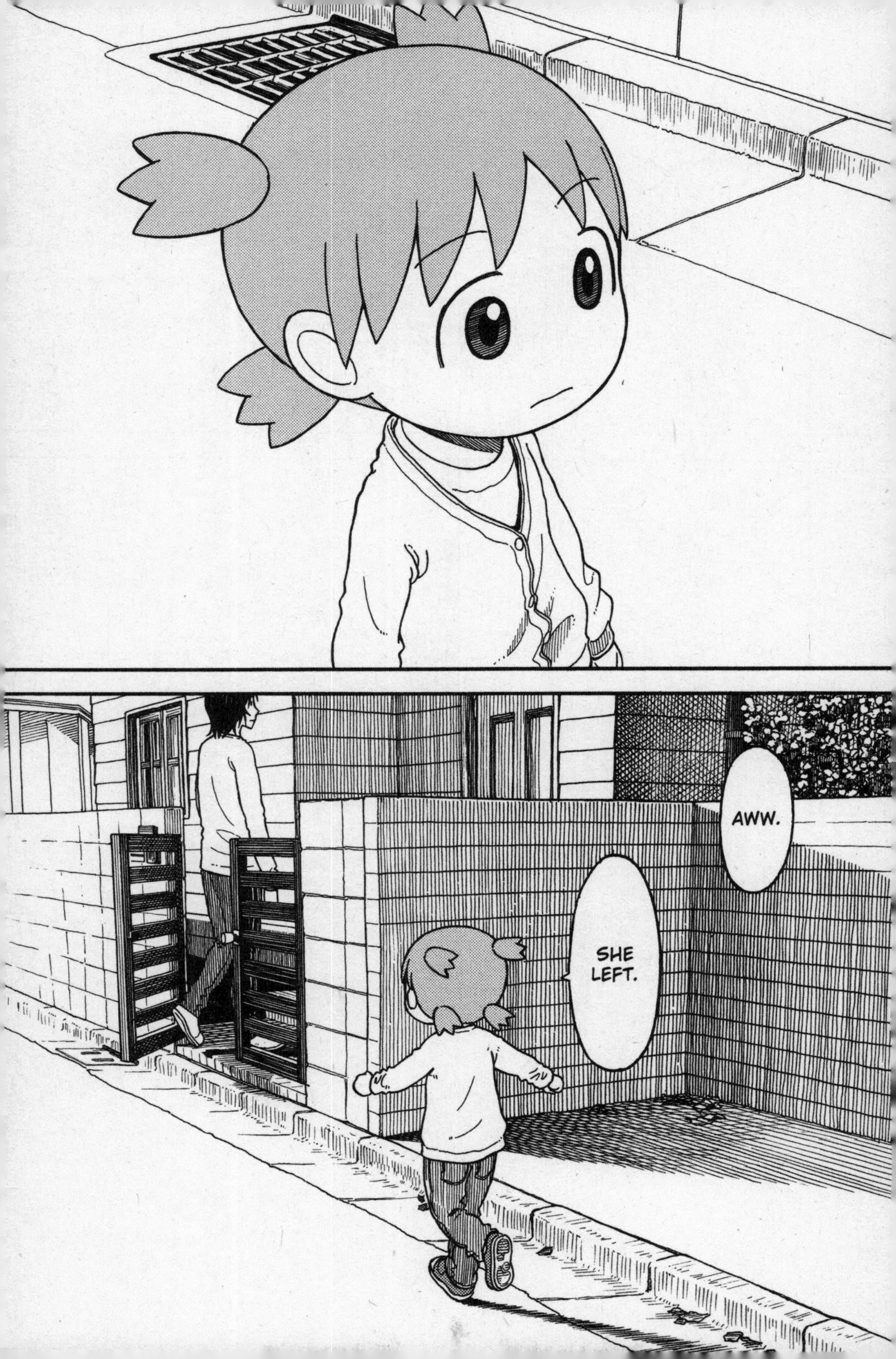
AWW.
SHE LEFT.

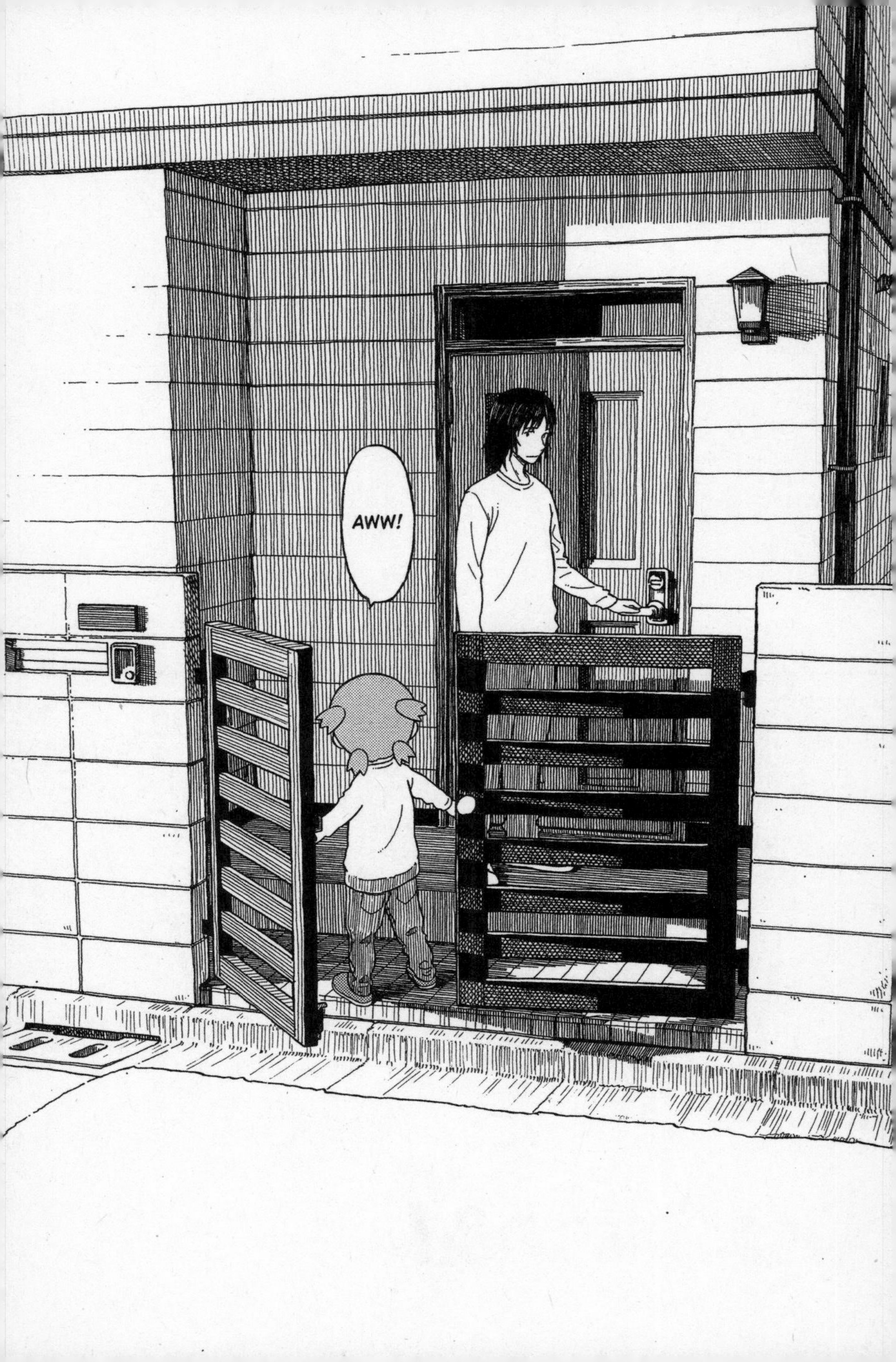
AWW!

YOTSUBA&!

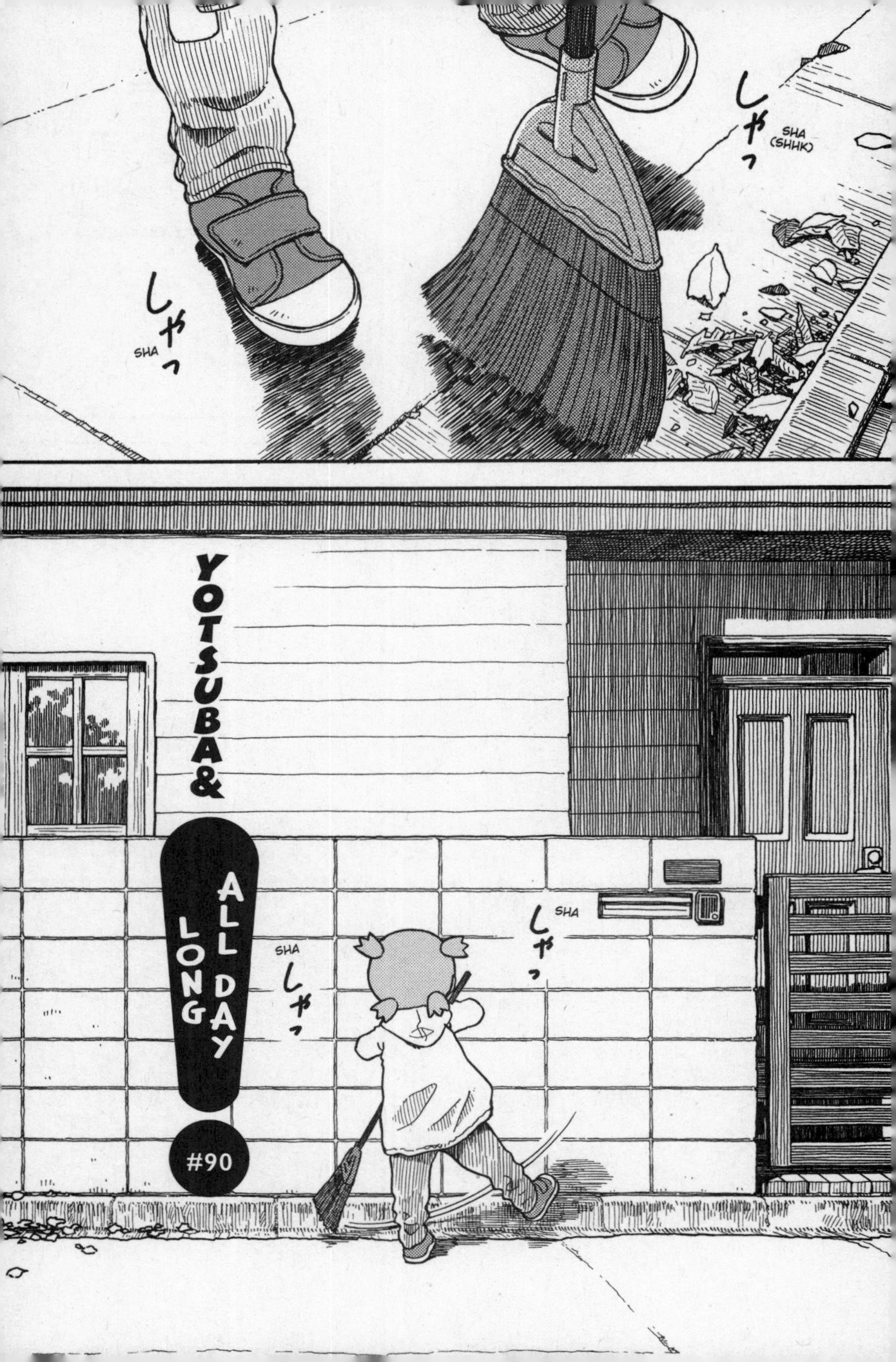

しゃっ
SHA (SHHK)
しゃっ
SHA
YOTSUBA&
ALL DAY LONG!
#90
しゃっ
SHA
しゃっ
SHA

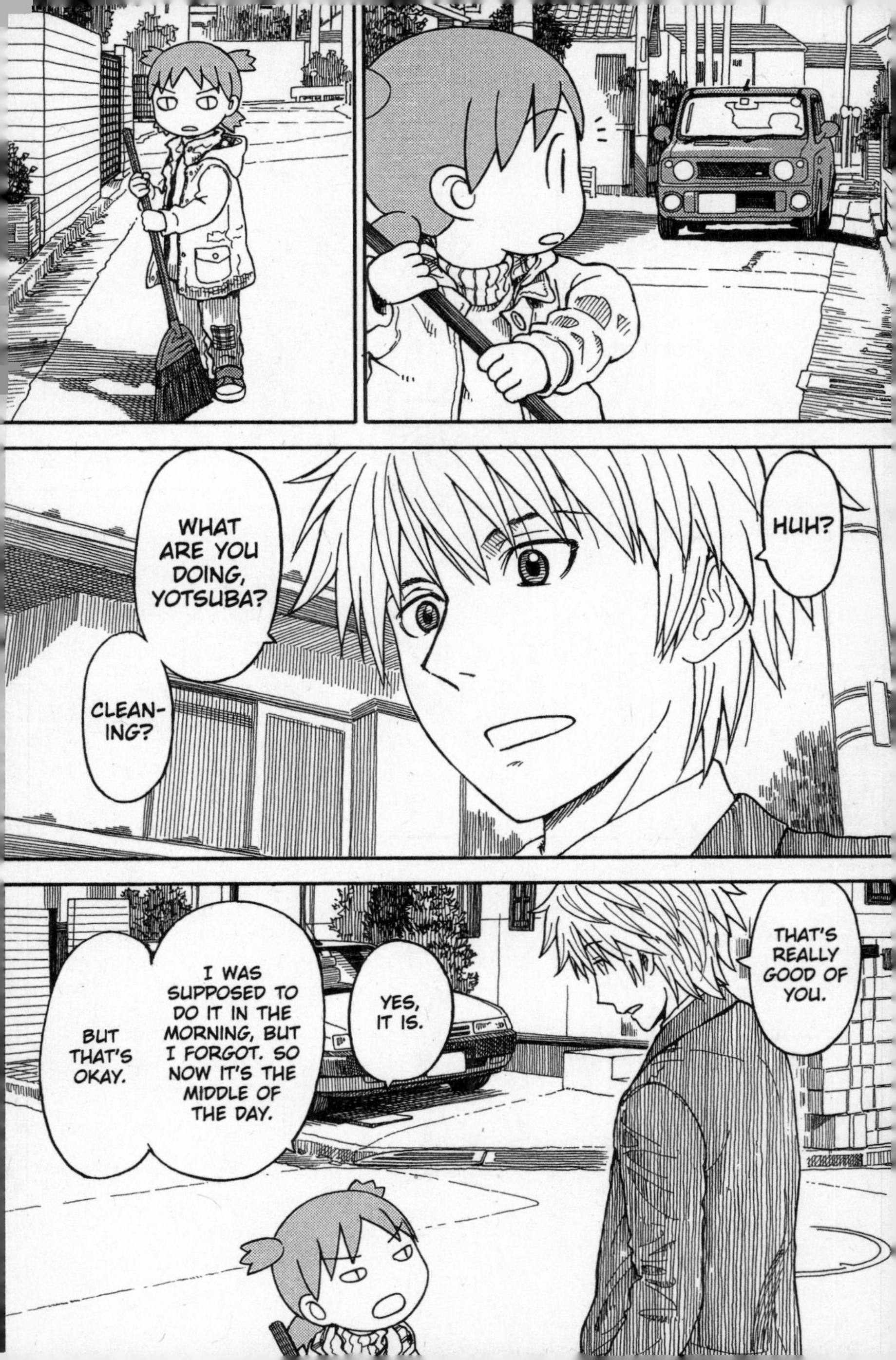
HUH?
WHAT ARE YOU DOING, YOTSUBA?
CLEAN-ING?
THAT'S REALLY GOOD OF YOU.
YES, IT IS.
I WAS SUPPOSED TO DO IT IN THE MORNING, BUT I FORGOT. SO NOW IT'S THE MIDDLE OF THE DAY.
BUT THAT'S OKAY.

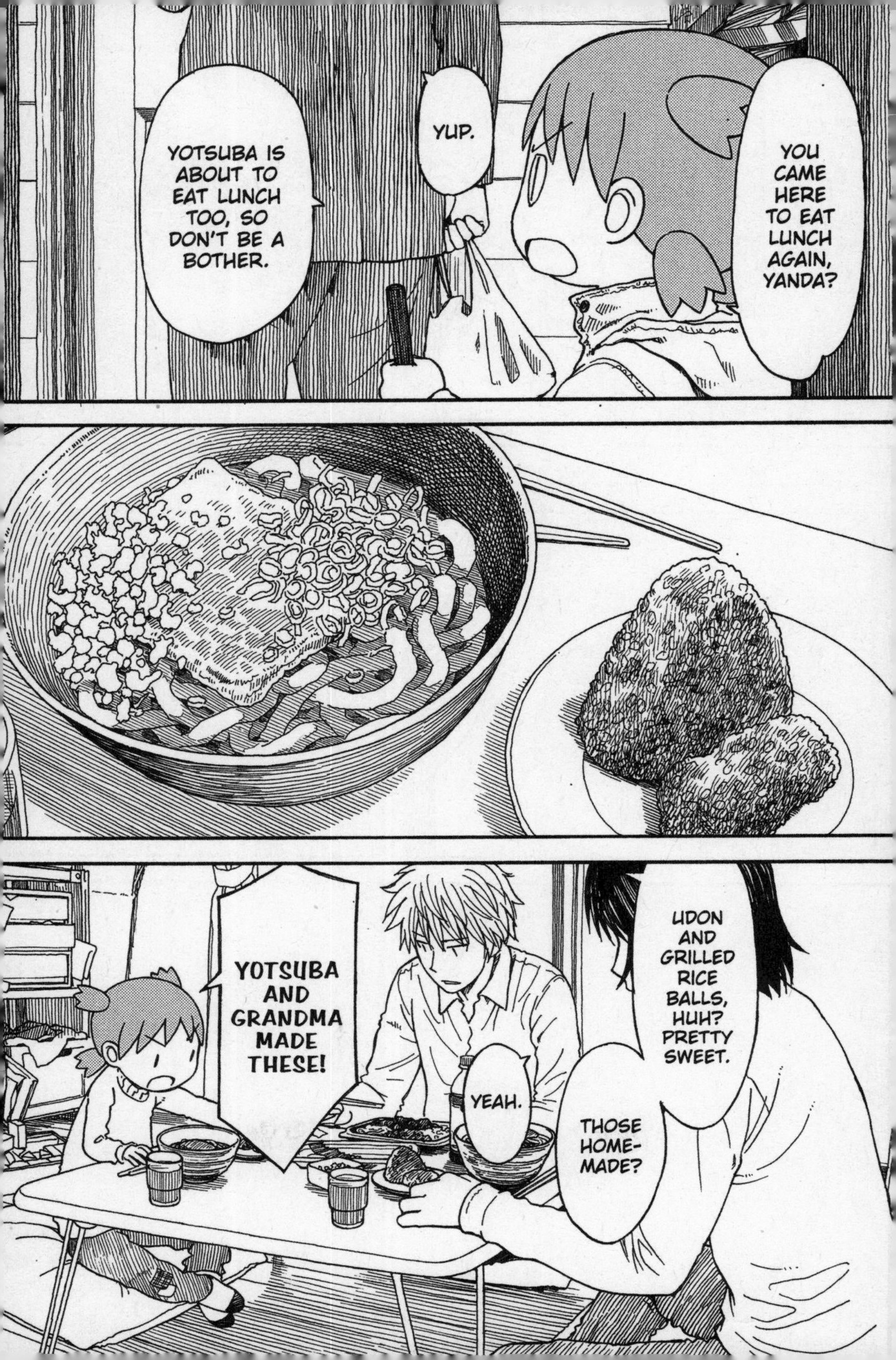
YOU CAME HERE TO EAT LUNCH AGAIN, YANDA?
YUP.
YOTSUBA IS ABOUT TO EAT LUNCH TOO, SO DON'T BE A BOTHER.
UDON AND GRILLED RICE BALLS, HUH? PRETTY SWEET.
THOSE HOME-MADE?
YEAH.
YOTSUBA AND GRANDMA MADE THESE!

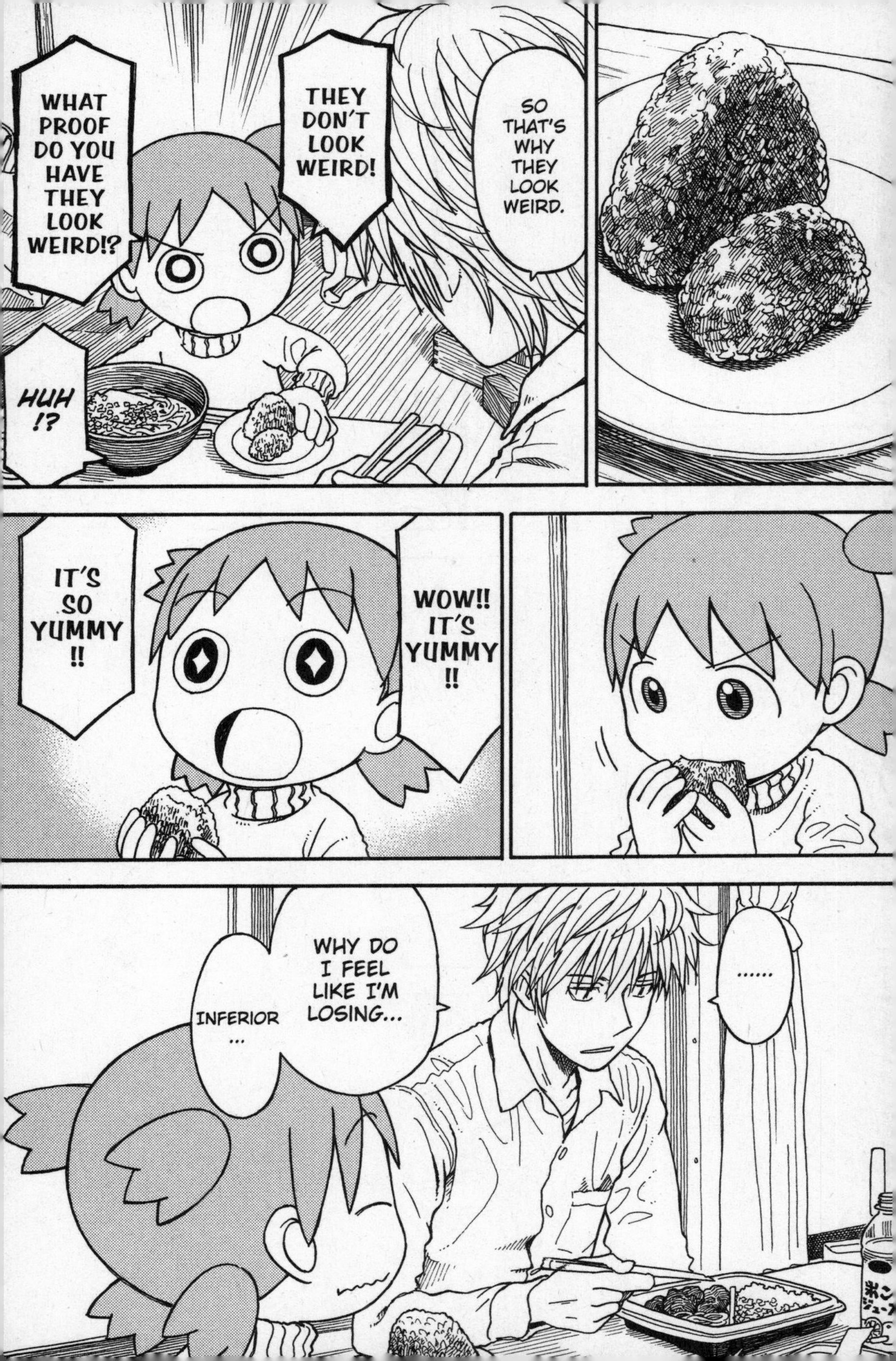
SO THAT'S WHY THEY LOOK WEIRD.
THEY DON'T LOOK WEIRD!
WHAT PROOF DO YOU HAVE THEY LOOK WEIRD!?
HUH!?
WOW!! IT'S YUMMY!!
IT'S SO YUMMY!!
......
WHY DO I FEEL LIKE I'M LOSING...
INFERIOR...

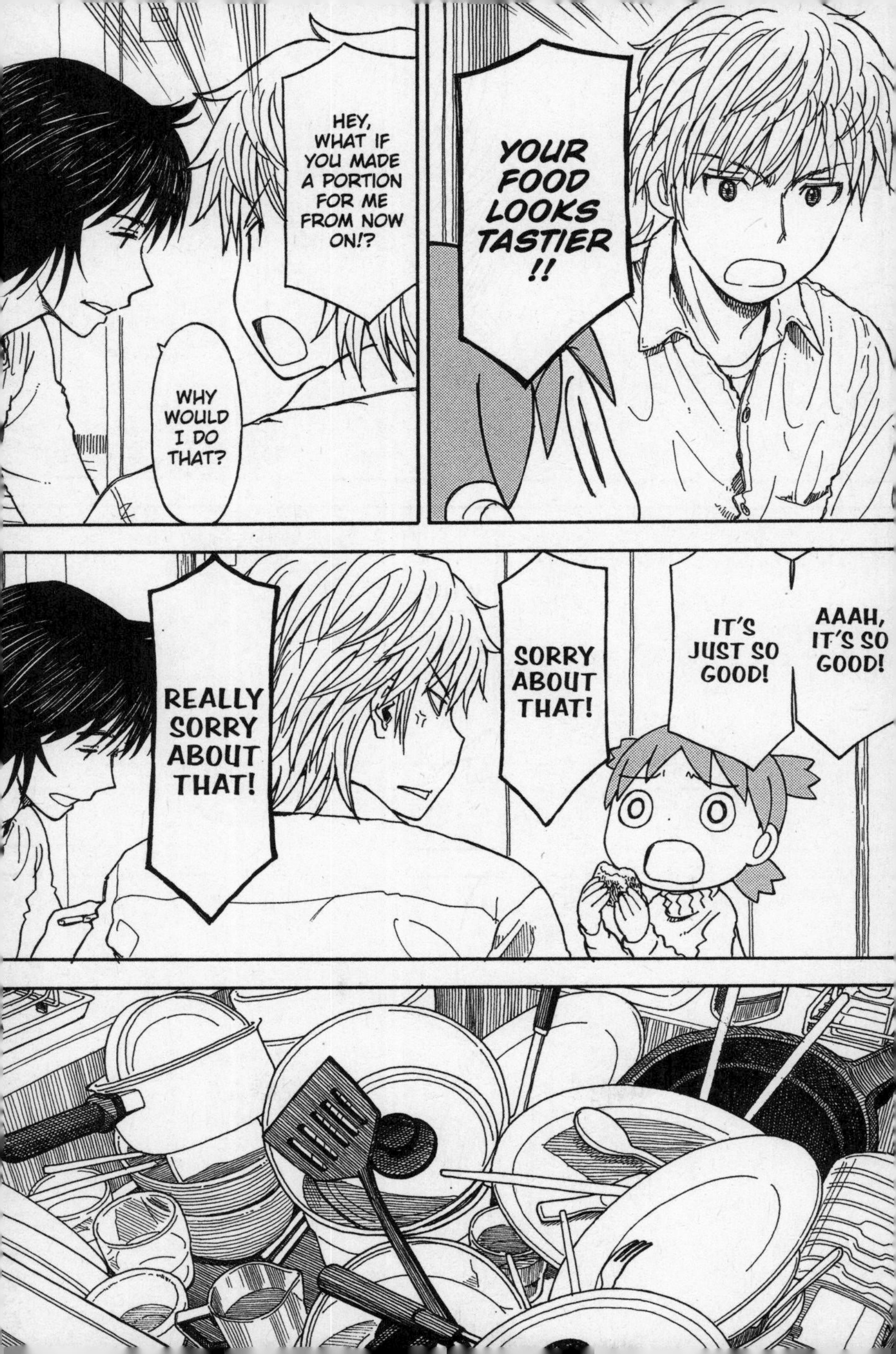
YOUR FOOD LOOKS TASTIER!!
HEY, WHAT IF YOU MADE A PORTION FOR ME FROM NOW ON!?
WHY WOULD I DO THAT?
AAAH, IT'S SO GOOD!
IT'S JUST SO GOOD!
SORRY ABOUT THAT!
REALLY SORRY ABOUT THAT!

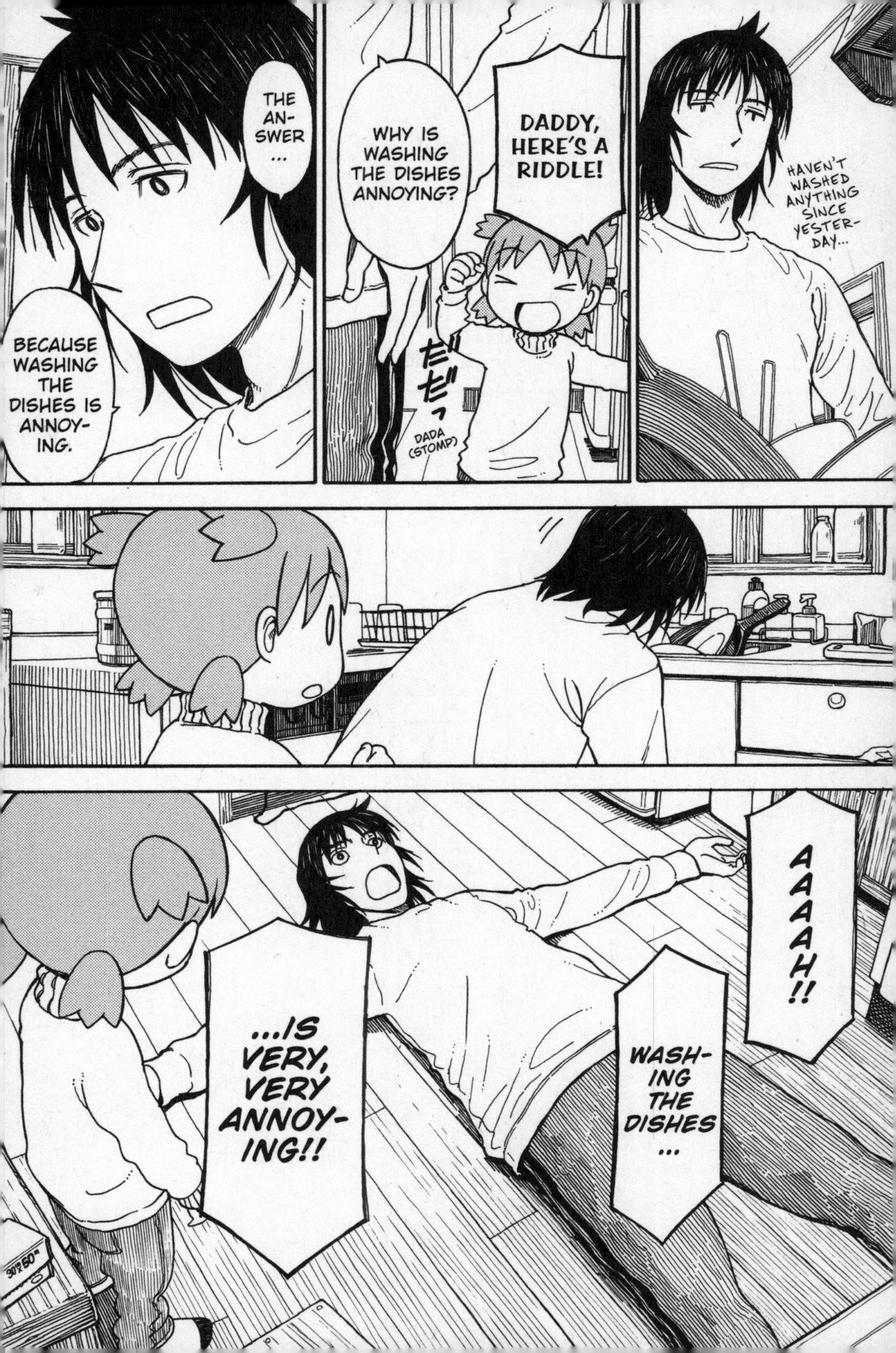
HAVEN'T WASHED ANYTHING SINCE YESTER-DAY...
DADDY, HERE'S A RIDDLE!
WHY IS WASHING THE DISHES ANNOYING?
だだっ
DADA (STOMP)
THE AN-SWER ...
BECAUSE WASHING THE DISHES IS ANNOY-ING.
AAAAH!!
WASH-ING THE DISHES ...
...IS VERY, VERY ANNOY-ING!!

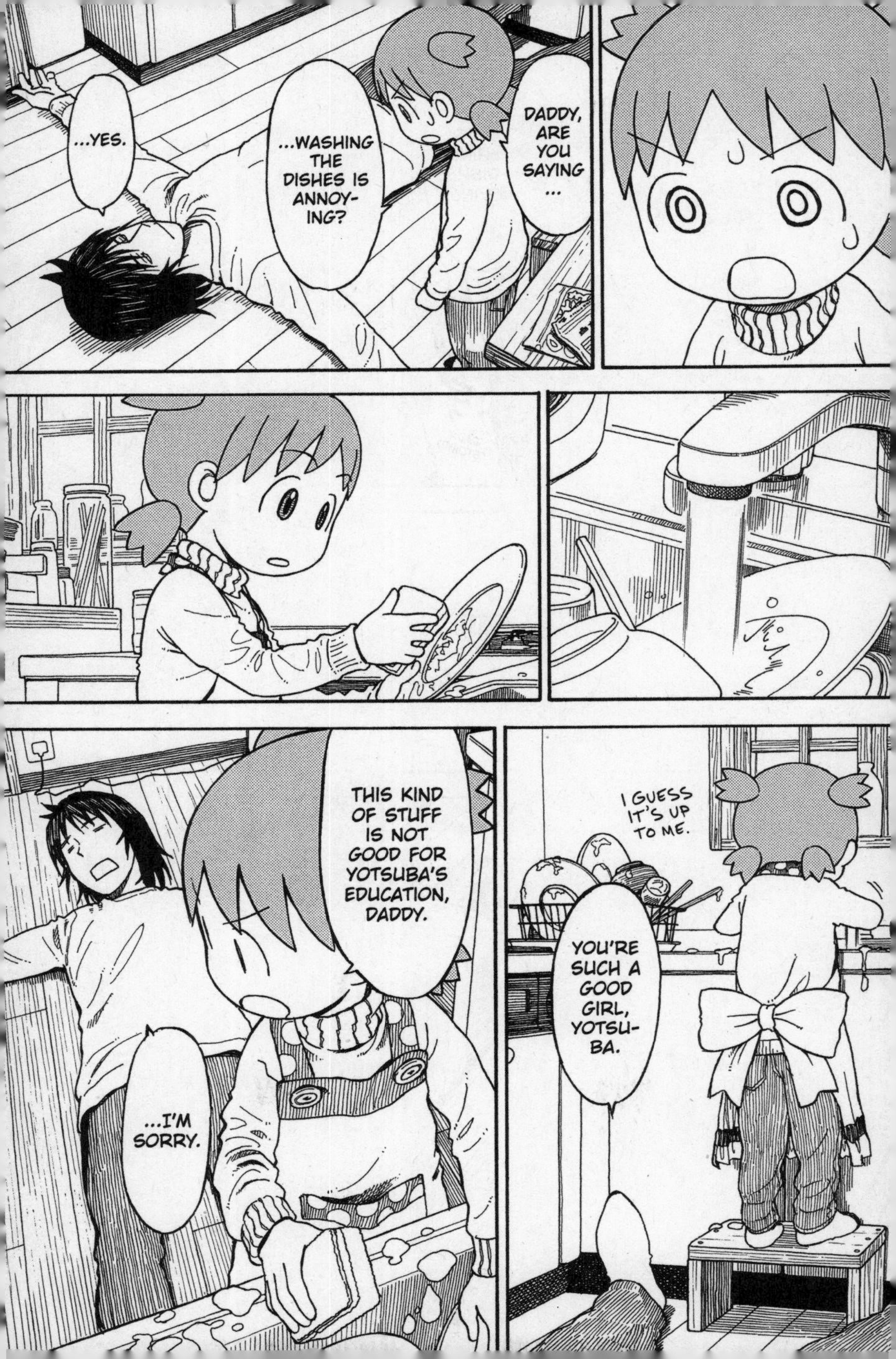
DADDY, ARE YOU SAYING...
...WASHING THE DISHES IS ANNOYING?
...YES.
I GUESS IT'S UP TO ME.
YOU'RE SUCH A GOOD GIRL, YOTSUBA.
THIS KIND OF STUFF IS NOT GOOD FOR YOTSUBA'S EDUCATION, DADDY.
...I'M SORRY.

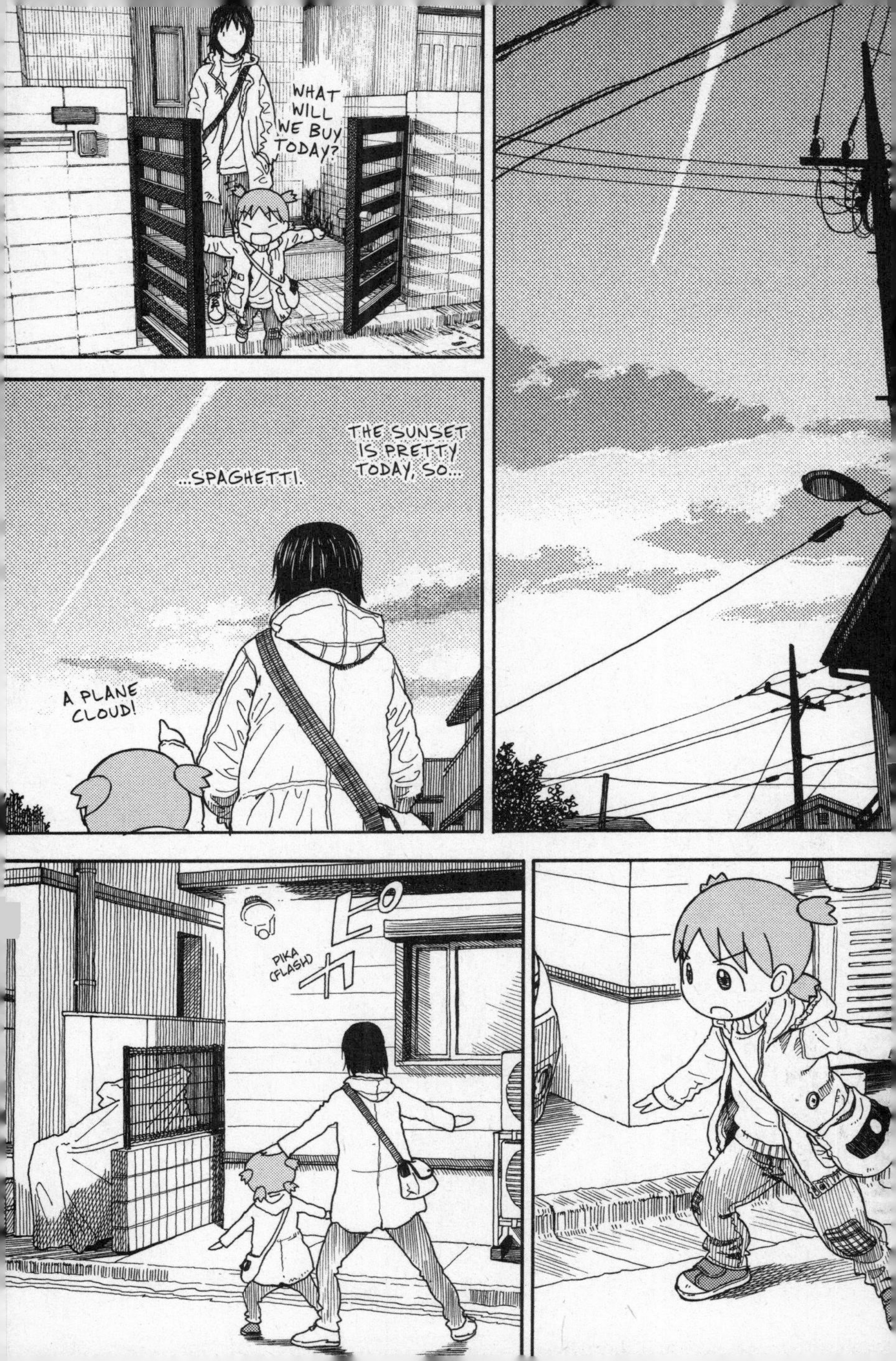
WHAT WILL WE BUY TODAY?
THE SUNSET IS PRETTY TODAY, SO...
...SPAGHETTI.
A PLANE CLOUD!
ピカ
PIKA (FLASH)

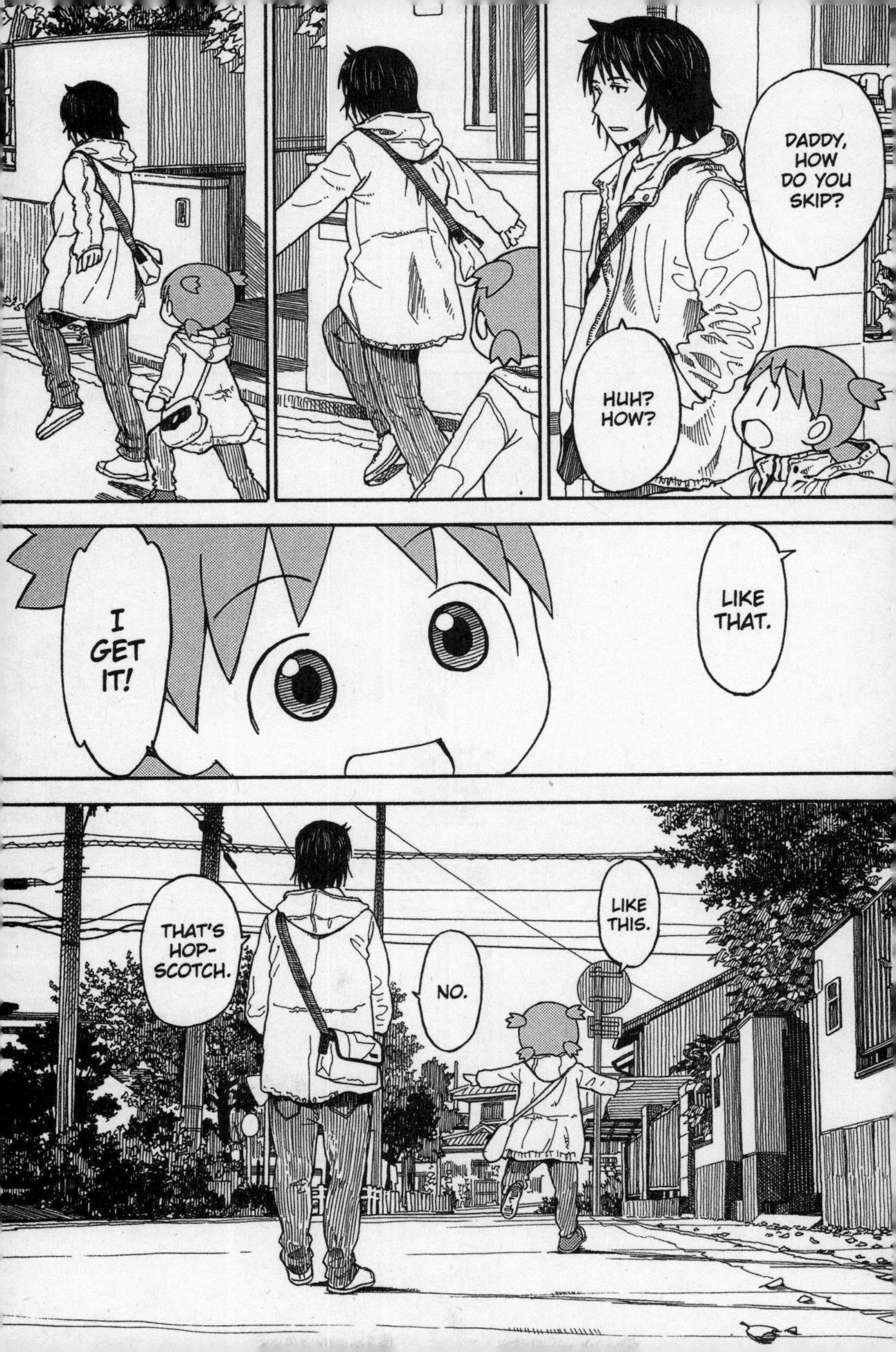
DADDY, HOW DO YOU SKIP?
HUH? HOW?
LIKE THAT.
I GET IT!
LIKE THIS.
NO.
THAT'S HOP-SCOTCH.

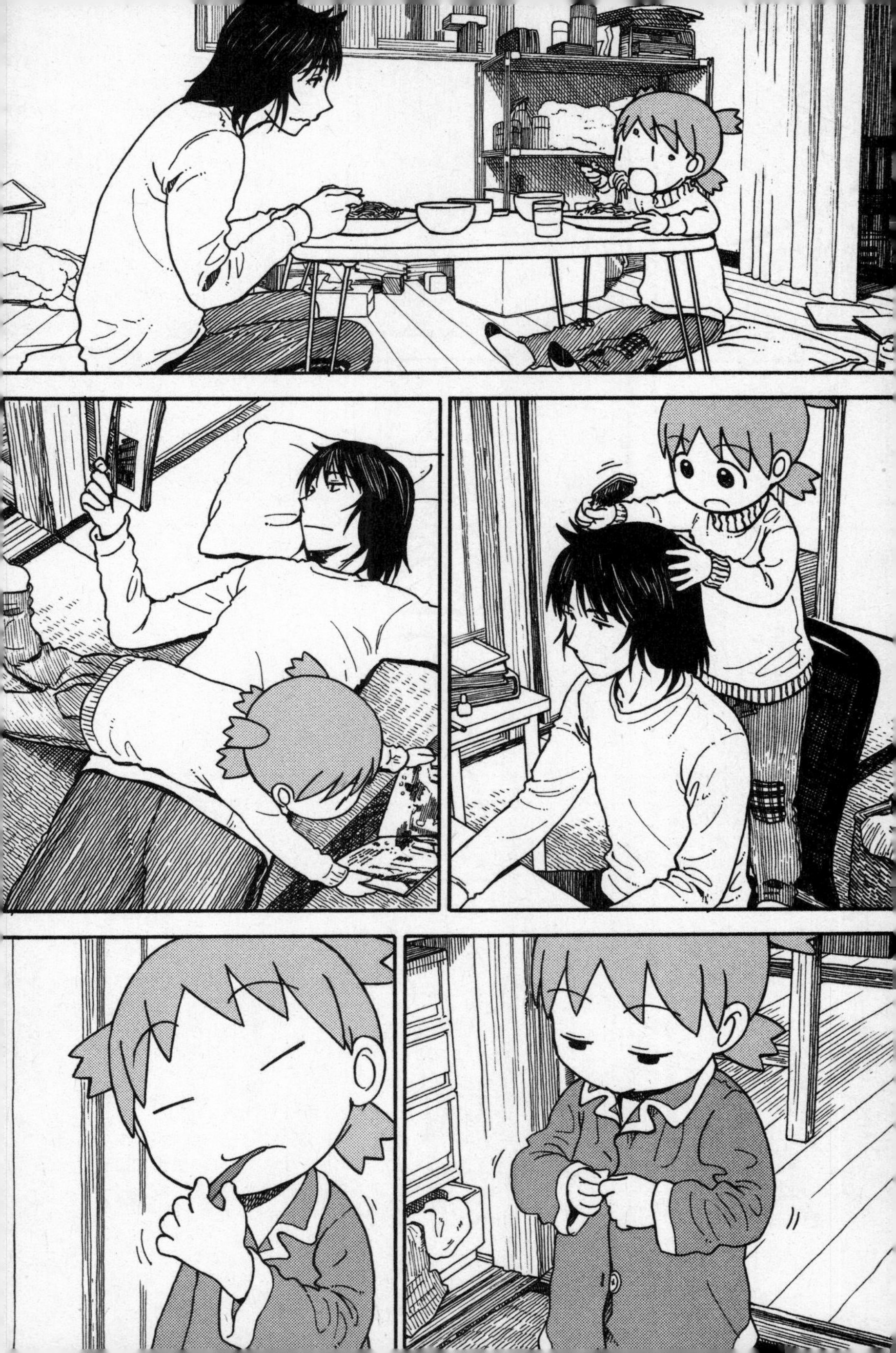

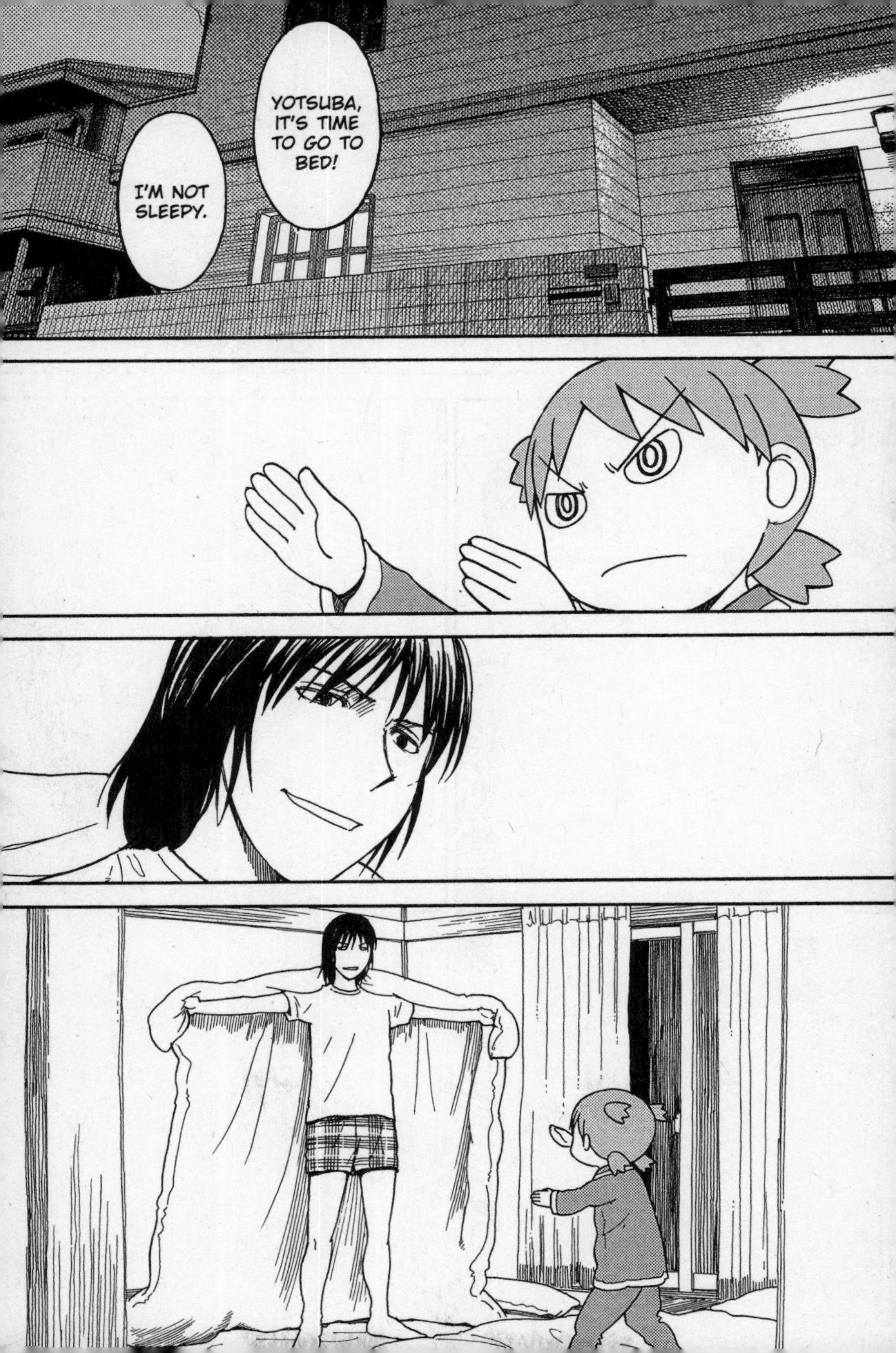
YOTSUBA, IT'S TIME TO GO TO BED!
I'M NOT SLEEPY.

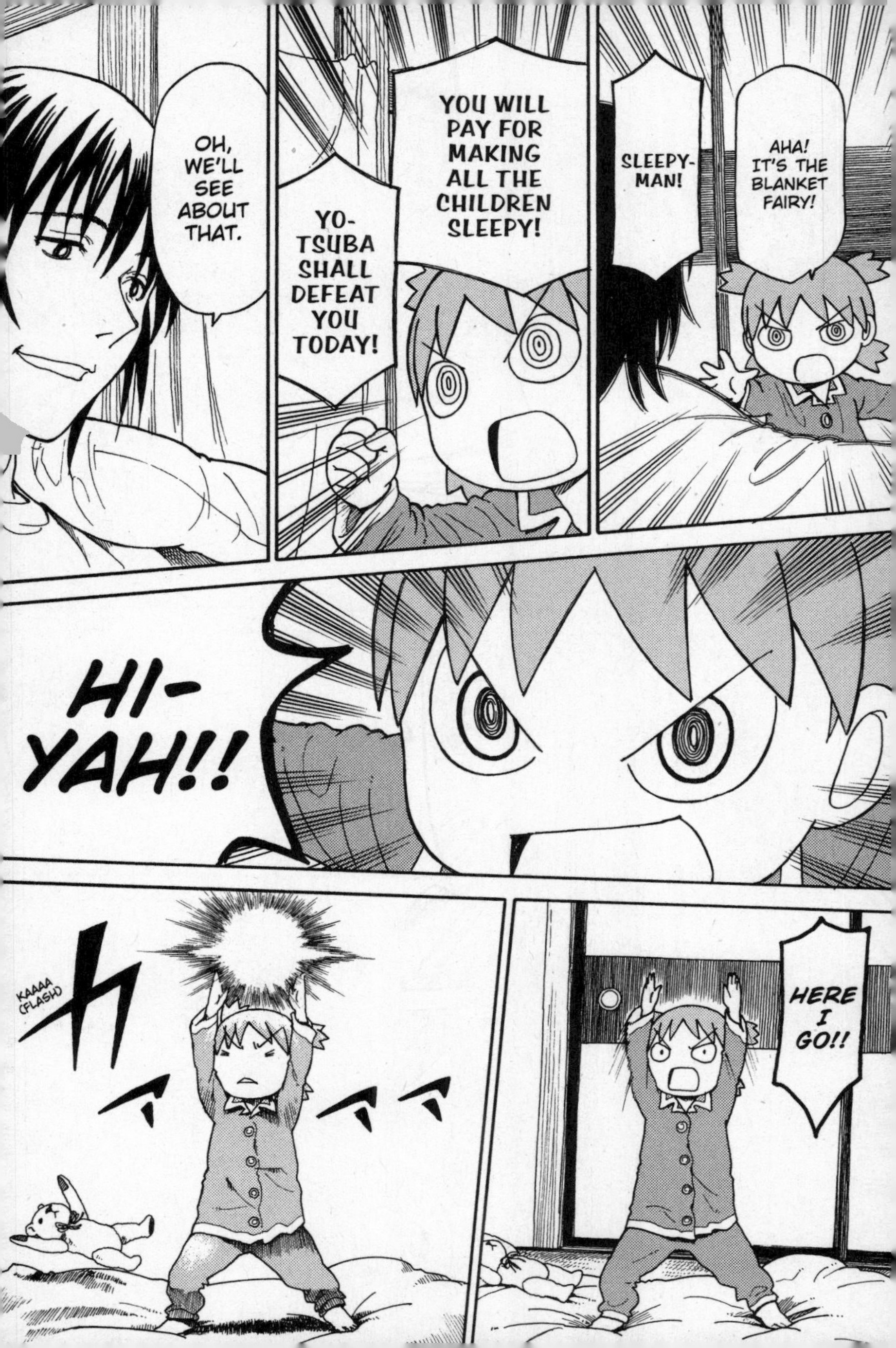
AHA! IT'S THE BLANKET FAIRY!
SLEEPY-MAN!
YOU WILL PAY FOR MAKING ALL THE CHILDREN SLEEPY!
YO-TSUBA SHALL DEFEAT YOU TODAY!
OH, WE'LL SEE ABOUT THAT.
HI-YAH!!
HERE I GO!!
KAAAA (FLASH)

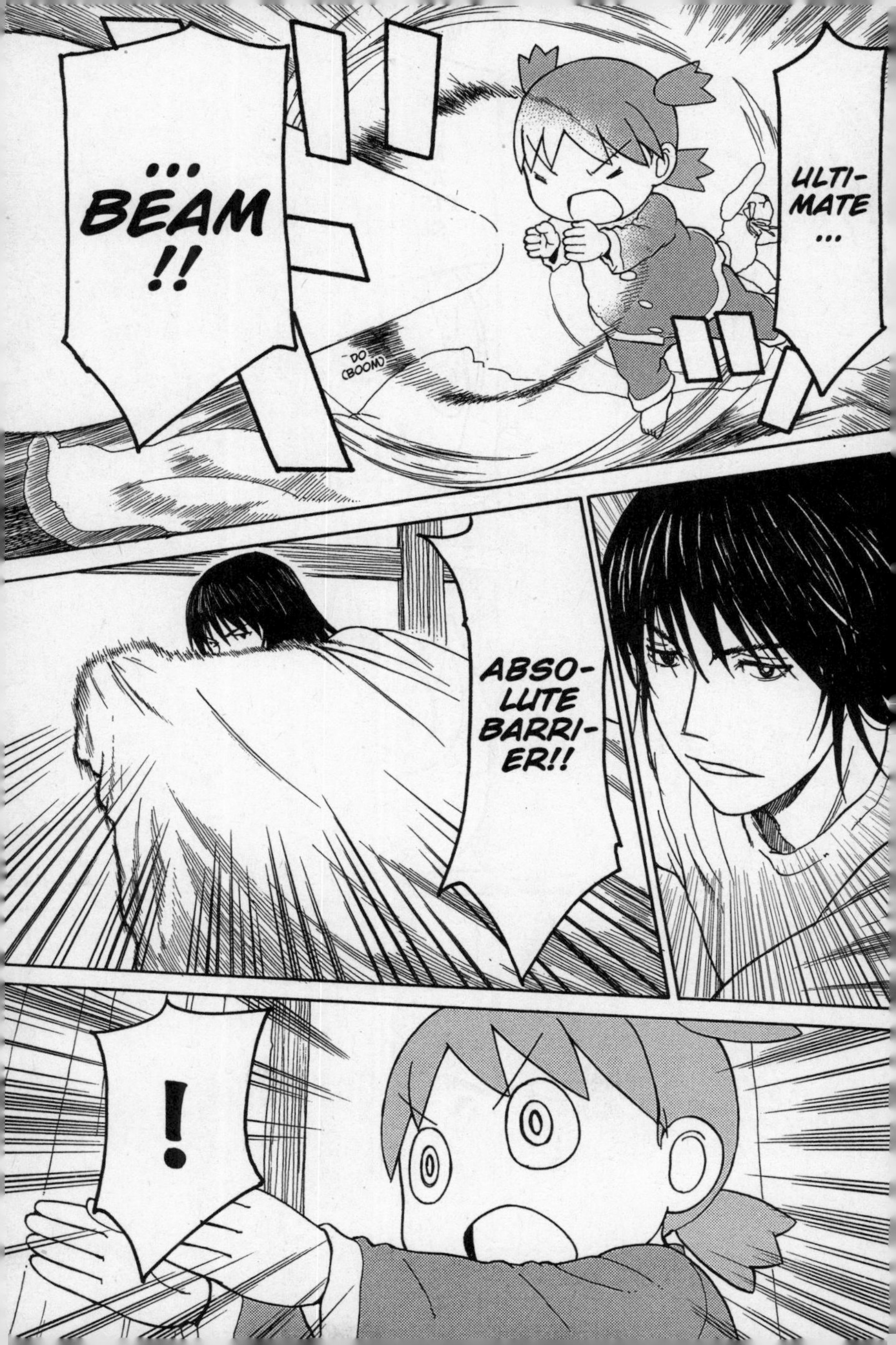
ULTI-MATE ...
DO (BOOM)
... BEAM !!
ABSO-LUTE BARRI-ER!!
!

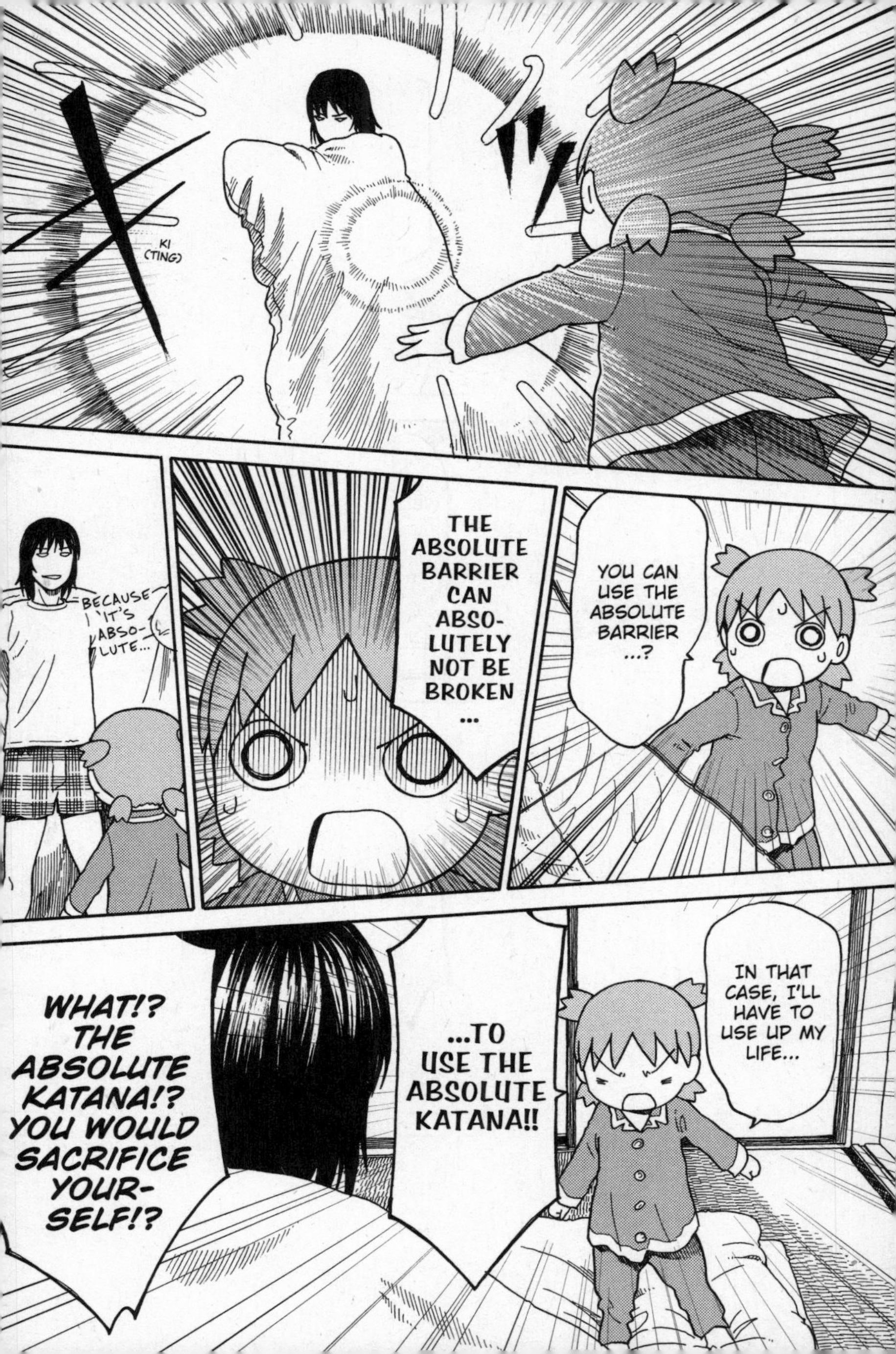
KI (TING)
YOU CAN USE THE ABSOLUTE BARRIER ...?
THE ABSOLUTE BARRIER CAN ABSOLUTELY NOT BE BROKEN ...
BECAUSE IT'S ABSOLUTE...
IN THAT CASE, I'LL HAVE TO USE UP MY LIFE...
...TO USE THE ABSOLUTE KATANA!!
WHAT!? THE ABSOLUTE KATANA!? YOU WOULD SACRIFICE YOURSELF!?

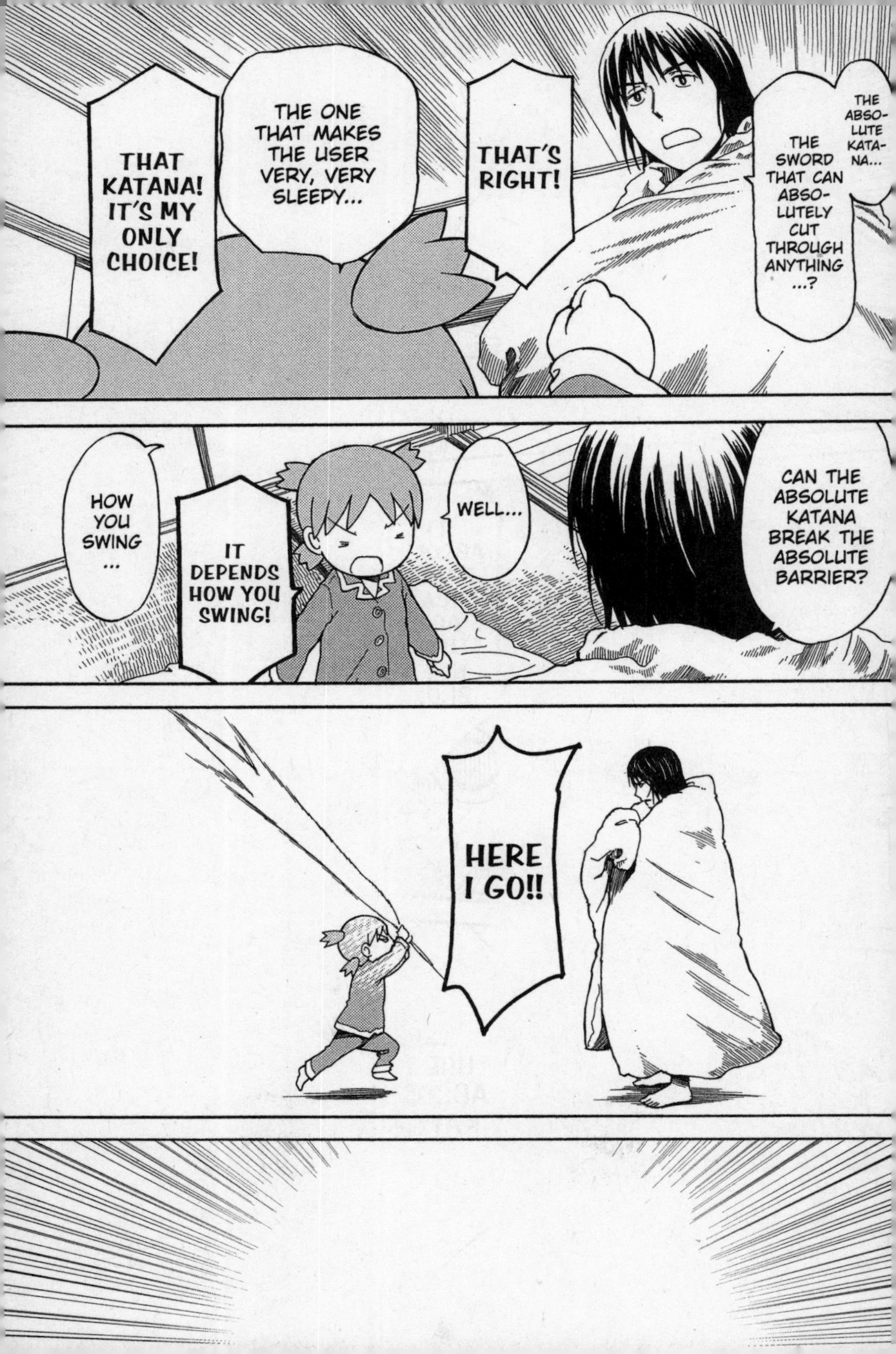
THE ABSO-LUTE KATA-NA...
THE SWORD THAT CAN ABSO-LUTELY CUT THROUGH ANYTHING ...?
THAT'S RIGHT!
THE ONE THAT MAKES THE USER VERY, VERY SLEEPY...
THAT KATANA! IT'S MY ONLY CHOICE!
CAN THE ABSOLUTE KATANA BREAK THE ABSOLUTE BARRIER?
WELL...
IT DEPENDS HOW YOU SWING!
HOW YOU SWING ...
HERE I GO!!

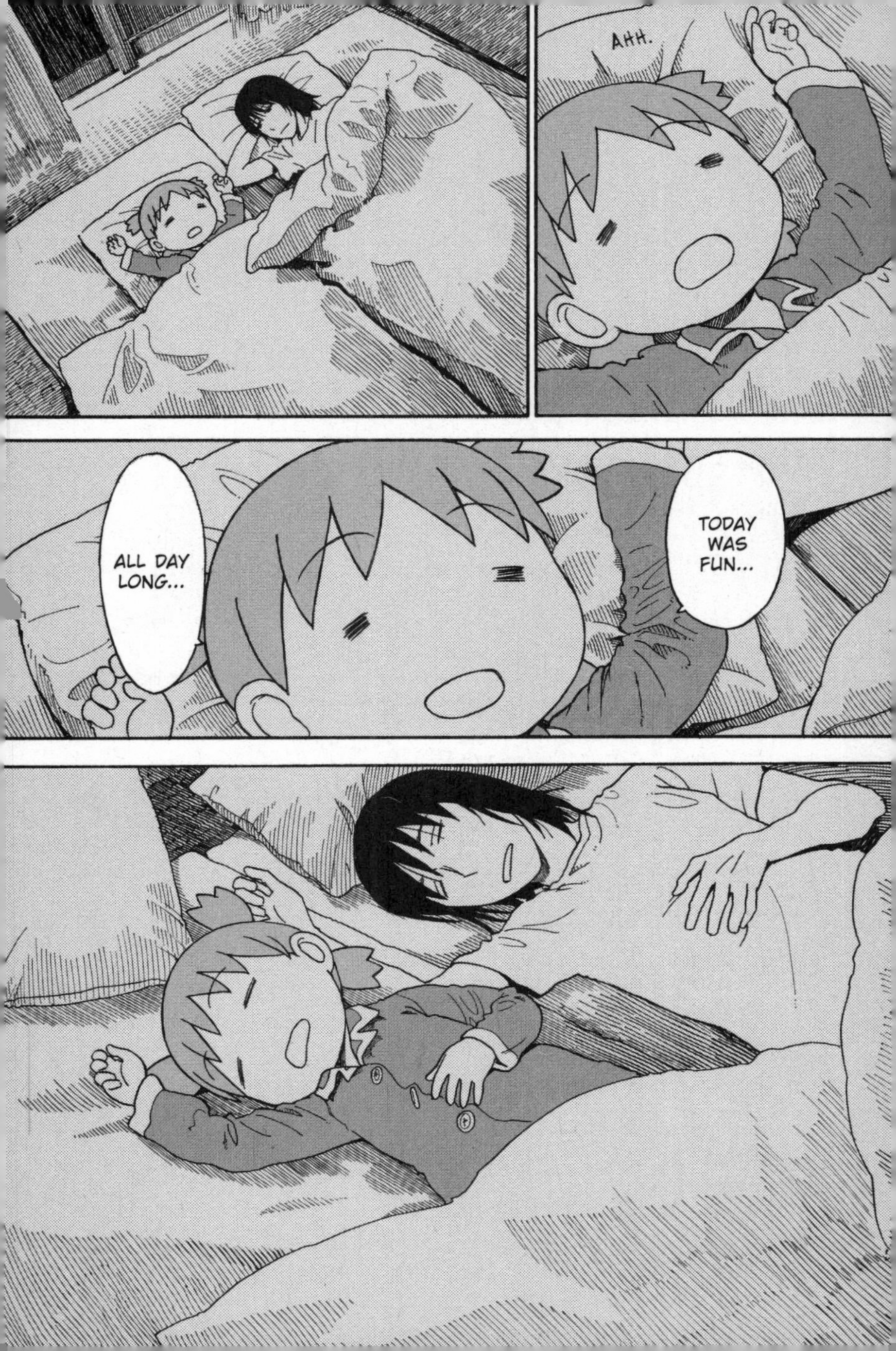
AHH.
TODAY WAS FUN...
ALL DAY LONG...

YOTSUBA&! 13
KIYOHIKO AZUMA

Translation: Stephen Paul
Lettering: Abigail Blackman

YOTSUBA&! Vol. 13 © KIYOHIKO AZUMA / YOTUBA SUTAZIO 2015. All rights reserved. First published in Japan in 2015 by ASCII MEDIA WORKS INC., Tokyo. English translation rights in USA, Canada, and UK arranged with ASCII MEDIA WORKS INC. through Tuttle-Mori Agency, Inc., Tokyo.

English translation © 2016 Yen Press, LLC

Yen Press
1290 Avenue of the Americas
New York, NY 10104

www.YenPress.com

Yen Press is an imprint of Yen Press, LLC. The Yen Press name and logo are trademarks of Yen Press, LLC.

The publisher is not responsible for websites (or their content) that are not owned by the publisher.

Library of Congress of Control Number: 2016932334

First Yen Press Edition: May 2016

ISBN: 978-0-316-31921-8

10 9 8 7 6 5 4 3

BVG

Printed in the United States of America

YOTSUBA&!

ENJOY EVERYTHING.

TO BE CONTINUED!